HOOK OF RORKE'S DRIFT

The Life of Henry Hook, V.C.:
1850-1905

Also by Bartletts Press:

*LOST IN THE ALPS: A Portrait of Robert Proctor, the "great bibliographer",
and of his Career in the British Musuem.* 52pp., 5 ill., paperbound.
ISBN 0-9517115-4-7.

*TEA AND ANARCHY!: The Bloomsbury Diary of Olive Garnett, 1890-
1893.* 264 pp., 12 ill., paperbound. ISBN 0-9517115-1-2.

*OLIVE AND STEPNIAK: The Bloomsbury Diary of Olive Garnett, 1893-
1895.* 310 pp., 11 ill. Cloth ed.: ISBN 0-9517115-2-0; Paperbound
ed.: ISBN 0-9517115-3-9.

The right of Barry C. Johnson to be identified as the author of this work has
been asserted by him in accordance with the Copyright, Designs and Patents
Act, 1998.

Hook was seldom photographed in plain clothes and, although details of this photograph are lacking, it was probably taken in London c. 1881. (Furness Collection.)

HOOK OF RORKE'S DRIFT

The Life of Henry Hook, V.C.:
1850-1905

by
Barry C. Johnson

BARTLETTS PRESS
2004

To my Mother
Mrs. GLADYS EDITH JOHNSON:
1900-1995
in grateful remembrance.

BARTLETTS PRESS
37, Larchmere Drive, Hall Green, Birmingham, B28 8JB

CONTENTS

ILLUSTRATIONS

Maps

A Note on Hook's copy of de Neuville's Engraving

It was reported in the Gloucester *Citizen* for 13 March 1905 that a copy of Alphonse de Neuville's "The Defence of Rorke's Drift" hung over Hook's bed at the time of his death. (The oil painting, in full colour, is often reproduced, and either the original, or a copy, is in the officers' mess at Brecon.) Hook's copy, on the death of his widow, descended to his eldest daughter by his second marriage (Mrs. V.C. Smith) and was, in turn, passed to her daughter, Mrs. Jean Furness, the present owner.

It is not, in fact, a literal copy of the painting but an engraving taken from it and reproduced on a heavy cartridge paper. The original frame, of dark wood, was broken during a house move. The engraving proper measures 35½" wide by 21½" deep, and there is a very wide border all round, making the whole thing, when framed, of unusual size. It is signed by the artist in the bottom right-hand corner and dated 1880. The name of the etcher is given outside the picture as Leopold Flameng. Also below the picture is the statement that the engraving was done by the Fine Art Society of 148, New Bond St., London, on the 15th of July 1881. The caption reads:

The Defence of Rorke's Drift

22-3 January 1879

To Her Majesty the Queen this plate is, by special

permission, dedicated by Her Majesty's Obedient

Servant the Fine Art Society.

Although the engraving carries no hint of the number of copies produced, the edition was almost certainly extremely small. The left-hand side has been used for the cover of the paperbound edition of this book, showing what is thought to be a representation of Hook carrying a man from the hospital.

Acknowledgements

Many people helped me with the first two versions of Hook's life and I have not repeated here the acknowledgements made at page 64 of *Rorke's Drift and the British Museum*. For this rewriting, my main debt has been to the four people named in the Introduction: Mrs. Patricia M. Davis, Mrs. Jean Furness, Mr. Norman R. Hook and Mrs. Pat Kitto.

It will be obvious that Chapters III, VIII and XII, and part of the Epilogue, owe much to material supplied by several descendants of Hook by his first marriage. They have provided the personal details, and the family photographs, to "bring alive" official information from certificates and Census returns. I want to thank particularly Mrs. June Dutton for reminiscences of her grandmother, Julia Ann Matthews, and of life at "The Bungalow", Kilcot; Mrs. Heather Warman-Johnston for recollections of Edith A. Wills (Birmingham's first woman M.P.) and for passing on to me a great deal of information from her own researches into the Wood family; Mrs. Kim Hamilton, a grand-daughter of Mrs. Wills, for family information; Mrs. Evelyn Hudson for many details of the Wood family's life in Birmingham during the first half of the twentieth century; and Messrs. Denis and Frank McCarthy for giving me their recollections of those days. I would have had very little but "official" information about the family of Hook's only son, Raymond, but for Mr. Cecil Berrington, whose sister married Raymond Powell Hook. I am most grateful to Mr. Berrington for his help, and for showing me the various buildings in Abergavenny associated with Hook's son and grandson.

Although they are not related to Hook's first family, I received considerable help from Mrs. L.R. James, and her daughter, Miss Lilian James, both of Culver St., Newent, concerning Julia Ann Matthews and her life at Kilcot.

I am also indebted to Mrs. Alison Arnold, of "The Crescent", Gorsley, for information about her house (described in Chapter III); and to Mrs. Phyllis Davis, of Abergavenny, for recollections and a photograph of Raymond Hook. I gratefully acknowledge my debt to Mr. F.W.D. Jackson for supplying materials, suggesting sources and for discussing with me many aspects of the Victorian Army. The citations will show that I have relied heavily on Norman Holme's *The Noble 24th* (as I had done with its predecessor, *The Silver Wreath*). My discussions with him were most valuable; and I was very saddened by his death in July 1999.

It would be impossible to do justice to Hook's life without access to the papers in the Regimental Museums at Brecon (24th Regt.) and Monmouth (Royal Monmouthshire Militia). I would like to thank particularly Major Martin Everett and Mrs. Celia Green, respectively Curator and Customer Services Manager at Brecon; and Mr. Keith Kissack, Hon. Curator at Monmouth, for their help and advice. I am extremely grateful to Col. M.C.E. Rixon, Bursar of The Royal School, Hampstead, for making available the records of the Royal Soldiers' Daughters' Home and for discussing with me the organisation's history. I would also like to thank Mr. Christopher Date and his colleagues at the British Museum Archives; and Mr. John Hopson, the British Library Archivist, for their friendly help over many years.

I also wish to thank Mr. Robert Gomme, for a critical reading of the proofs; and Mr. H.E.R. Bunting (Hook's surviving grandson); Commander Michael Hooke; and Mr. John Young (founder of The Anglo-Zulu War Research Society) for their help on various points.

Finally, as most of the writing was done at St. Deiniol's Library, Hawarden, I would like to thank all the staff for their many kindnesses, especially the Warden, the Revd. Peter Francis; the Administrator, Mr. Gregory Morris; and the Librarian, Miss Patsy Williams.

Introduction

Twenty years after Henry Hook was born, his grandfather died in the workhouse. Yet forty years after his own remains were borne through the streets of Gloucester on a gun carriage, his granddaughter entered the House of Commons as one of the first women M.P.s. This is a remarkable family story, which has never been told before.

Hook's own life has been told twice before and this is my third version. The first account was an article in *Colonnade*, the staff magazine of the British Museum (1967); and this was considerably expanded as *Rorke's Drift and the British Museum: The Life of Henry Hook, V.C.* (1986). Until recently, this booklet was kept in print but it had become badly in need both of revision and of further expansion. The new and more direct title of the present book reflects Hook's increasing fame.

Although his first marriage is mentioned in the *Colonnade* article, all details were then lacking and it was ignored in *Rorke's Drift and the British Museum*. Substantial articles in Gloucester newspapers failed to bring out any convincing evidence about this marriage, and it was not until it was discussed in a Radio Gloucestershire programme in January 1996 that there was a "break-through." A notebook which had been left in the Parish Church at Churcham fulfilled what was no doubt its purpose when part of its text was read out "over the air." Most of the information in the notebook was both precise and accurate but some essential facts were missing because they were not apparently known to the anonymous writer. Eventually, Norman R. Hook, of Stroud—not related to the V.C.-winner but a leading authority on the Hook family in general—"found" Henry Hook's first family in the 1881 Census returns. My debt to Mr. Hook is thus immense. I doubt very much whether I would ever have made the discovery for myself, as diligent researchers in Gloucestershire had been baffled by this "mystery" wife and family for over thirty years. The documentary research which I was able to do, based on Mr. Hook's discovery, led to contacts with descendants from the first marriage and to a mutual exchange of information and impressions. The whole of Chapter III, and parts of Chapters VIII, XII and the Epilogue, are entirely new and stem directly from this work. (I thank the members of the family individually in the Acknowledgements.)

While this account of the first marriage is the main justification for an enlarged and rewritten biography, there have been valuable additions to knowledge in other parts of Hook's life. Mrs. Jean Furness—grand-daughter from his second marriage—has made available the newspaper cuttings and papers which he collected during the latter half of his life and which form, in effect, his personal archive. Then Mrs. Pat Kitto supplied important biographical details about the Taylor family, into which Hook married in 1897. Taken together, these batches of material add very considerably to what was known about his life from 1880 onwards. Finally, Mrs. Patricia M. Davis, a great niece of the V.C.-winner, has provided much genealogical information about her family, and I have relied very largely on her work in Chapter I, which deals with Hook's ancestry and early life. His life up to 1869, when he enrolled in the Monmouth Militia, remains vague but most of his life is now revealed in remarkable detail for a working man who left no autobiography. Accounts of their lives by men in the ranks—such as *The Recollections of Rifleman Harris* and Timothy Gowing's *Voice from the Ranks*—tend to deal almost entirely with their years as soldiers. By contrast, Hook's life can now be seen "in the round"—his background, his friends, his family life and his work as a civilian, as well as his very varied military service.

Hook served in the last Kaffir War (now usually called the Ninth Cape Frontier War) and in the Zulu War; but this, of course, is a biography and not a history of those wars. An essential task of any biographer is to evoke the true atmosphere of the times in which his subject lived, and one of the most effective means of doing this is through a careful selection of words and phrases. For South African tribal names and geographical features I have therefore generally used the spellings which would have been familiar to Hook and his contemporaries, rather than those based on modern orthography. The modern spellings are given in the Glossary.

Lastly, the question of money values should be mentioned. This is sometimes dealt with by putting modern decimal values after Victorian sums: for instance, 24/- (Hook's weekly wage in his earlier London years) would be followed by: £1.20. As no-one could now live on £1.20 per week, while Hook quite evidently lived on 24/- (and without being in poverty), this sort of comparison seems pointless. The only meaningful comparison is reached by multiplying Victorian sums by a given factor, even though the choice of a factor is itself beset with difficulties. The late Lord Jenkins, in his life of Gladstone (1995), decided on a factor of fifty; and I feel more than willing to accept the opinion of a former Chancellor of the Exchequer who was also an expert on the Victorian age. By applying this factor to Hook's pay, we arrive at a modern equivalent of £60 per week; but Hook's 24/- no doubt "went further" than £60 would at present. How *much* further is a question which could be argued over endlessly; but one salient point is that Hook lived a much simpler life than a man doing equivalent work would today.

Birmingham
November 2003.   Barry C. Johnson

Chapter I

"A STURDY GLOUCESTERSHIRE WOODMAN":
TO 1869[1]

1.

The most famous private soldier in the annals of the British Army was born in Gloucestershire.

His family can safely be traced back to the end of the seventeenth century, when James Hook(e) was baptised at Taynton, a parish to the south of Newent. Beyond that time, there are misty figures and legendary events, including a possible link between the Battle of Agincourt and Rorke's Drift.[2] In 1718, James Hook married Mary Jenkins at Bulley, which is a couple of miles from Taynton and near the old Roman road between Gloucester and Ross-on-Wye. The couple had a son and three daughters and when the son was baptised at Churcham in 1723, he was given his father's name. The parish of Churcham lies to the south of the old road, and from the baptism of the second James Hook, a long association was established between Churcham and this branch of the family.

These James Hooks were yeoman farmers. The elder James described himself as a "Yeoman of Oxenhall"; and he left his son "all those my leasehold Messuages or Tenements with the Lands & Estates thereunto belonging called Greenaways & Stewards ... [and] all my Stock of Cattle Grain & Implements of Husbandry." Although this farming was probably on quite a modest scale, it no doubt underlies the story that the Hooks once "owned farms in Taynton, Tibberton and Newent."[3]

The second James Hook married Elizabeth Hulet, a Churcham woman considerably older than himself, and only one of their children survived into adulthood. This was the third James—baptised at Churcham in 1754—who became the V.C.-man's great grandfather.[4] This James held the tenure ("copyhold") of what was later called "Hook's Farm" from the Lords of the Manor of Churcham, which is probably the origin of the story that his great grandson spent his early life on a family farm.[5] Hook's Farm was in the hamlet of Oakle Street and after the time of the third James, the land was traversed by the Gloucester and Dean Forest Railway. All that now remains of the farm is a modern "barn conversion"; but the visitor can look across the fields and see—very prominent on the sky-line—the spire of St. Andrew's, Churcham.[6]

The third James married twice and had, in all, thirteen children (nine by the first marriage). His first wife is buried at Oxenhall, where five of her children were born; and her death in 1796 severed the family connection with the Newent area. In the following year, James married Mary Hodges at Churcham: he was then forty-three and she was thirty. Their four children were all baptised at Churcham.[7] James and Mary Hook lived on their "copyhold estate" for the next quarter-of-a-century, through the period of the French Revolutionary and Napoleonic Wars. Whether it was the collapse of the wartime agricultural boom, or bad luck, or bad management, which brought about their ruin is never likely to be known. The certain fact is that on the 10th of June 1822, James Hook surrendered his copyhold to the Lords of the Manor and the estate passed to a butcher at Bulley. For the Hooks, the status and independence of tenant farming gave way to the uncertainties of labouring for others; and the severity of the blow could hardly have been lessened by the knowledge that such descents were not uncommon. Early in 1829, James Hook died intestate, which might suggest that he had little to leave to his large family.[8]

Richard, the only son by James's second marriage, was born at Churcham on the 5th of February 1800. He lived to be seventy-one and was the soldier's grandfather. It was perhaps from him that the boy heard stories of the old life on Hook's Farm which he, in turn, passed down to his own children. Like his father, Richard Hook married twice and survived both his wives. His first wife, Mary Kear, came from Minsterworth, a village which straggles along the Severn, to the south of Churcham. She was a year older than her bridegroom and before her early death in 1831 (probably in childbirth) she bore him four sons and two daughters.[9] Richard and Mary Hook moved around in rural Gloucestershire: their first two children were baptised in Minsterworth; their fourth was born in the parish of Shurdington, to the east of Gloucester; their fifth was baptised at Churcham; and the last at Hartpury, a village about five miles to the north. But when Richard married again, in 1839, the four children of *that* marriage were all baptised at Churcham.[10]

The child born at Shurdington stands out from amongst all the other members of the family up to this point. His life is comparatively well recorded; he was a regular soldier and army pensioner; and he became the V.C.-winner's uncle. He was in the Army during his nephew's boyhood and youth, and even allowing for the slow communications of the mid-Victorian era, some news of him would probably have seeped through to Churcham.

Joseph Hook was born in 1826 and enlisted at Gloucester when he was nearly eighteen, giving his "trade" as "Labourer."[11] He joined the 85th of Foot, which was then stationed in the West Indies. His regiment served in Ireland during the Famine years (when its historian chronicles "great excitement" but no action) and was in Mauritius during "a terrible outbreak of Asiatic cholera." Yet by being in Mauritius, the 85th missed the Crimean War, which affected it only because it was posted to South Africa to take the place of other troops. When the regiment disembarked there in the summer of 1856, there were disturbances on the frontier but the 85th remained "passive spectators." Of its seven years at the Cape, it is recorded that officers and men enjoyed "the good looks of the Dutch girls"; "some good private theatricals"; and "very fair shooting"—but nothing more stirring.[12] When he arrived back in England in 1863, Joseph Hook was within two years of the twenty-one years' service which would earn him a pension. A regimental board at Aldershot found that "his conduct and character have been very good—in possession of 4 good conduct badges"; and he was discharged on the 16th of May 1865. Compared to what was to be his nephew's much shorter service, he had had an uneventful life in the Army—no campaigns and therefore no medals, nor any promotion. He settled in Minsterworth in apparent good health, married and, in a modest way, prospered.

His younger brother, Henry, had been born at Churcham on the 26th of May 1828. His mother died when he was three, and he was nine before his father married Fanny Maria Trigg.[13] In between mother and stepmother, he was probably brought up by aunts. By about the time of the second marriage, the family was living in a cottage near Birdwood Coppice, with a garden "20 Perches" (one-eighth of an acre).[14]

The parish of Churcham then consisted of two manors or divisions: Churcham itself, to the west, and Highnam, to the east. Birdwood was the hamlet on the western edge of Churcham manor and its substantial Coppice stretched for half-a-mile along the south side of the road from Gloucester to Ross-on-Wye. Up to 1803, Birdwood Common faced the Coppice, on the other side of the old road, but the common land was then "Enclosed." The heart of the hamlet lies a further half-mile towards Churcham proper, at a cross-roads where Birdwood House—an elegant, three-storey brick residence—faces an old Methodist chapel. The two historic and principal buildings in that part of the parish are nearly two miles beyond the cross-roads. St. Andrew's, the Norman church, stands on a rise amidst generally flat country, so its spire can be seen at a distance. Churcham Court, the "big house", is close by. Early in the nineteenth century, there were about a dozen houses and farms scattered out from the Birdwood cross-roads, with "a settlement of cottages" around the Coppice and the former common land. The Churcham division of the parish had seventy-four houses sheltering 327 people. A "carrier's cart provided transport for infrequent visits to Gloucester"—about six miles from Birdwood cross-roads to the Cathedral—and brought out goods which were not available locally. Otherwise, the roads and lanes were largely silent.[15]

Although he was himself able to write, it seems unlikely that any of Richard Hook's ten children—who were born between 1821 and 1846—had much in the way of formal education. In 1818, "there was no school in the Churcham half of the parish", though "the poor were said to desire the means of education." By 1833, there were two church Sunday schools and "a boarding school where 22 children were educated at their parents' expense." By 1847, there had been some further improvement, as the parish then had "a number of small dame schools."[16] The Hook men and boys, in the eighteen-thirties and forties, were agricultural labourers, working for local farmers. School attendance was not then compulsory; farmers wanted child labour; and labouring people badly needed the wages which their children could earn.

Not only could labourers not afford to *pay* for their children's education but the very presence of their children in a schoolroom, rather than out in the fields, was a burden added to an already precarious existence. So where free schools *were* available, boys and girls tended to turn up when farm work was slack and to stay away at other times, especially at haymaking and harvesting. Weeding, bird-scaring, stone-picking, and such jobs as minding sheep and pigs, could be done at a remarkably early age—as early as five. "School-life . . . was usually little longer than a year or two," even with irregular attendance, and by the age of ten, it was over entirely.[17]

Richard Hook could obviously not have afforded to send any of his children to a boarding school but perhaps he sent some of them, at least, to a Sunday school. "Few of the Anglican [Sunday] schools aimed at anything more than the ability to read the Scriptures" (and it does seem that, amongst poor children generally, the ability to read was learned more easily and often than the ability to write). Dame schools provided very variable education—at best, nothing beyond the most elementary levels of reading, writing and arithmetic; at worst, little more than "child-minding"—and the "dame" in charge had to be paid.[18] It therefore seems unlikely that the Hook children would have been sent to a dame school. The outcome was that when Henry, the V.C.-man's father, married in 1849, two days after his twenty-first birthday, he was unable to sign the register. (His bride, and the two witnesses, also had to make their marks.) The bride was Ellen Higgs, who also came from a labouring family in Birdwood. The two families evidently made an effort to do things in style and the marriage was held at St. Mary de Lode, near Gloucester Cathedral.[19] Ellen Hook, as she now became, had been baptised at Churcham on the 20th of February 1831 but little else is known about her, though she lived to a great age. She bore six children, survived two husbands, and outlived her first child—her soldier son— by sixteen years.[20]

This boy was born at Birdwood on the 6th of August 1850. He was baptised in the parish church of St. Andrew's simply as "Alfred", a fact which has caused endless confusion.[21] It was said that he always liked to be called "Harry", and he certainly adopted his father's name, Henry, in the Militia, the Regular Army, the Rifle Volunteers and the British Museum.[22] Yet, for many years, he also used "Alfred", not in conjunction with Henry but as a solitary Christian name. He led a "double life", and these two names came to symbolise his separate worlds.

2.

Hook (as he will now be called) was born into the richest country in the world. Its "superabundance of capital" and "extraordinary supplies of gold" were said to be matched by "the increasing comfort and wealth of the mass of the people."[23] But unfortunately "the mass of the people" did not include the agricultural labourers. Although they then "formed the largest single occupational group in the country", their position was very far from comfortable.[24] In part, this was due to the agricultural depression at the end of the French wars, but the plight of labourers was aggravated by the well-known "Enclosures" (or fencing-off) of common land. Distress and discontent in rural areas led to disturbances—mainly in East Anglia—during 1816 and again in 1822. The burning of corn-ricks, and the breaking-up of threshing machines (which were held to increase unemployment), became the manifestations of this unrest.

In the late summer of 1830—when Hook's father was two years old—the labourers staged their "Last Rising." They burned and destroyed a good deal of property (including some workhouses), and made demands for higher wages and also for food, drink and money to be given "on the spot."[25] Rioting in Gloucestershire was limited to the area around Cirencester, well to the south of the district where the Hooks lived. During four days in November, twenty-five threshing machines were smashed and there were five cases of "incendiarism": as a result, twenty-six people were later imprisoned and twenty-five transported to Van Diemen's Land (Tasmania).[26] In general, the four months of rioting, spreading across the country from east to west, greatly alarmed the government. When all the sentences handed down by the courts had been either commuted or confirmed, nineteen labourers were hanged, 481 (including two women) transported, and 644 sent to prison. Never again was such turmoil seen in the English countryside.[27]

It was in the aftermath of this rioting and retribution that Hook's father began his working life. The six years from 1837 to 1842 have been described as "the grimmest period in the history of the nineteenth century." The "good harvests and the trade boom came to an end, and . . . the country was plunged into a prolonged depression".[28] In the countryside, the early eighteen-forties were remembered as a time of "terrible struggle . . . We worked night and day just for existence."[29] When Henry and Ellen Hook were married, two years before the Great Exhibition, the country was again prosperous and conditions for agricultural labourers had begun to improve.

The term "labourer" is rather misleading, as experienced men were expected to do "an enormous variety of jobs", some of which would now be called "semi-skilled." They could "be called upon to set seeds, to hoe, to weed, to mow, to make hurdles, to cut chaff, to spread dung, to thresh, to hedge and ditch and even to help maintain the farm roads." Men who were in charge of animals were considered to be doing more skilled and responsible work and so they were paid more and given longer terms of employment. There was a further division between labourers who were regularly employed by a farmer and the so-called "casual men." The position of "casual men" was obviously more precarious but even those who were employed by the year were "often laid off in wet weather" without pay. Apart from such involuntary breaks, farm labourers not only slogged away for long hours, in almost all weathers, but sometimes suffered crippling wounds from scythes or machinery, for which there was no compensation. Yet in spite of all this, some of the best of the labourers "had no inclination to change; they were what one might describe as real sons of the soil, the love of the land and agricultural work seemed inbred and part of their being."[30]

The overwhelming mass of labourers were generally thought to have extremely poor prospects. (Their one certain prospect, if they lived long enough, was an old age made miserable by rheumatism.)

This view was challenged by the famous Victorian naturalist, Richard Jefferies, who said that they had "very good opportunities of rising" but that most of them lacked the ambition to rise. He described a ladder of advancement: labourer to "head-carter or head-fogger" [cattle-feeder]; to under-bailiff and then bailiff of a farm; and finally to tenant farmer.[31] This progression was similar to a private soldier becoming a colonel: it could certainly be done but seldom was done, in practice.

After their marriage, Hook's parents set up their own household in Birdwood. (Richard Hook—a widower for the second time—was living with his three youngest children.[32]) Most labourers either had a cottage "tied" to their job or else rented one at between a shilling and two shillings a week (usually paid yearly, at Michaelmas). Smaller cottages, with one room up and down, could be had for as little as sixpence or ninepence. There was considerable contemporary concern over labourers' cottages, which could look idyllic in summer—with roses around the doors—but were too often tumble-down and insanitary.[33] The cottages were lighted by tallow candles or "rushlights" and also by the fire. Sometimes, the candle would be put out, to save money, and fire-light would be relied on in the main room. At least when Hook was born in the Birdwood cottage, he was the first child, so there would have been no overcrowding.

A table published in the year of his birth, giving the weekly wages of labourers in the various counties, places Gloucestershire at joint-bottom (with Suffolk and South Wiltshire). The wage was seven shillings, exactly half of the highest rate and half-a-crown below the average.[34] (Single labourers, in those days, always earned a shilling or two less than married men.) This was *basic* pay and any labourer who was wholly dependent on seven shillings a week would have been very hard pressed indeed. There were three legal ways of supplementing this wage. Those men who had the necessary skill could earn "piecework" pay at such jobs as hedging and ditching. Then, for six or seven weeks each year, extra long hours could usually be worked at haymaking and harvesting.[35] In later years, old labourers recollected that "they sometimes reaped corn till 9 or even 10 o'clock at night by moonlight, and slept in the fields for a few hours till they could commence again at dawn."[36] Finally, there were gifts or "allowances" from individual farmers. A labourer from the adjoining county of Herefordshire, looking back to the middle of the century, said:

> A man could get a bag of wheat at market price from the farmer, and if he wanted a pig he could buy it from the farmer and pay for it in instalments. Broth and milk were given to the

children "graciously" in the old days, and if a man was kept late he was given supper. The men had as much cider as they liked then.[37]

But a farmer, talking about the same era, remarked significantly: "After Arch came [*i.e.*, the National Agricultural Labourers' Union, in 1872] they [the labourers] had more money and less perquisites." There were also two illegal—but widespread—means of supplementing wages, especially in hard times: poaching and taking vegetables from the fields.[38]

During Hook's childhood, we can therefore imagine that his father would have earned more than seven shillings a week but that life would still have been far from easy. His mother bore the usual steady succession of children: Mary (1852); James (1855); Henry Daniel (1857); Ellen (1860); and Emily (1863). Like many country-women, she also went into the fields to earn more money for her family. (The Census of 1861 actually gives her occupation as "Ag: Lab.") A labourer's wife, in later years, remembered work in the fields as "dreadfully hard . . . I would rather stand at the wash-tub all day long than do that work again." The rate of pay for women was around sixpence or a shilling a day.[39]

Hook would have had few "treats" as a child but country children had one great advantage over poor children in the towns. For half the year at least, they had the fields as a playground and could go birds'-nesting, paddle in brooks, climb ladders to hayricks and benefit in general from the open air. When he was six, a parish school was opened north of the old road, to serve both Bulley and Churcham, and he may have attended for a time. The days of compulsory education were still far off, but there are signs in his later life that he did have some formal education, if not very much. In 1861, the Census enumerator found him at work as a "Wood Cutter", his schooldays evidently over. But as a farm-worker says in *Akenfield*: "No one liked being young then as they do now [1969]; they wanted to get it over with."[40]

Virtually no labouring family could afford to apprentice its children to a trade or craft, but a father would teach his sons any skills which he had learned by his own experience.[41] Hook's father was a woodcutter for part of his life, and he may have trained his eldest son in a woodman's work. Woodmen were one of the many classes of labourers: they cut the bark from trees ("barking"), and "lopped" trees for fuel or timber, as well as felling them. Hook was entered as a "Woodman" when he was admitted to Gloucester Hospital, with a "sprained ankle", in September 1865: the only recorded incident of his boyhood.[42]

8

While he stayed with his parents, he and his father (and, later on, his two brothers) would have had very similar daily routines. One of the most sympathetic observers of village life said that a labourer's lot was "a twelve hours' day, and without any prospect of holiday as long as one lives."[43] The hours were usually from six in the morning until six in the evening, except that "in haymaking or harvest time they are expected to remain till the job in hand that day is finished, often till eight or half-past."[44] As it was a six-day week, the farmer paid his men on Saturday evening. By the time that Hook began work, the loose, knee-length smock-frock was being worn less and corduroy trousers, with a short corduroy or tweed jacket, were becoming the mode. A labourer wore his shirt without a collar, but often with a muffler; and almost every type of headgear was seen in the fields, especially caps. Boots were heavy and cumbersome, "with steel tips, plates and hobnails all over the sole"—a good preparation for army life![45]

Farmers usually sat down to midday dinner, while their men were eating a lunch brought with them in the morning. The labourer's main meal was therefore at the end of the working day, at about seven o'clock.

In the [eighteen-] "forties," "fifties," and "sixties", it is evident that the amount of food eaten by the labourers' families was barely sufficient in some localities. In the winter, the season when food was most required, the labourers and their families in the low-wage districts [including Gloucestershire] often had to live on poor diet . . . [and] as the husband had necessarily to have the largest share of the food, and also the most strengthening diet, such as pork and bacon, the women and children frequently suffered from insufficient nourishment.

In the "thirties," "forties," and "fifties," the principal diet of the agricultural labourers was wheaten bread or other food made from flour. Barley bread was, however, frequently eaten in the western counties . . . Other articles of diet were bacon, pork (the latter frequently salted), cheese, dripping, lard, milk, potatoes, onions and other vegetables. The high price of tea prohibited much being drunk. Fresh meat (beef or mutton) was seldom eaten . . .

In the low-wage counties the monotony of the bread diet was relieved by eating it soaked in broth or spread with dripping or lard. Toast water was often taken in lieu of tea. Skim milk or butter-milk was also drunk. Bacon or pork was, as a rule, eaten on Sundays only; and, at times when this could not be obtained for the Sunday dinner, potatoes were eaten with melted butter or grease.

In some of the western counties potatoes, swedes, and cheese made from skim milk formed a considerable portion of the diet. A good deal of cider was given free to the labourers in these counties by the farmers.[46]

This dismal diet began to improve in the eighteen-seventies but, even at the end of the century, "in the low-wage counties," fresh meat was seldom eaten more than once a week.[47] Still, most families could expect two breaks a year from the monotony of their meals: at harvest time, "when a substantial harvest supper would normally be provided"; and at Christmas, when "the local gentry or the farmers frequently provided gifts of meat, clothing or coal for their workers."[48]

Sunday was a day of rest, and the farmers gave their men Christmas Day off, but otherwise there were no paid holidays. Nor were there any entertainments or amusements, in the modern sense. Richard Jefferies, writing in 1874, pronounced starkly: "The alehouse is the terrible bane of the labourer." It was, he said, avoided by the "genuine agricultural labourer [who] goes early to bed. It is necessary for him, after the long toil of the day, on account of the hour at which he has to rise in the morning."[49] Yet most of the men did use the village inn, or alehouse, not only to "refresh their throats" but because

> utterly unaided by arts or any contrivances for amusements, they make entertainment for themselves . . . in an existence so empty of other pleasures, the pleasures to be derived from company are held precious. The scheme of living would be very desolate without that consolation . . .[50]

This "scheme of living" was generally accepted because working people—as shown in their autobiographies—then had "a sense of patient resignation to the facts of life, the feeling that human existence is a struggle and that survival is an end in itself."[51] Of course, not everyone had this "sense of patient resignation"—like Joseph Hook, some became restless. This restlessness seems to have to come upon his nephew after he, too, had reached the age of eighteen. He went down to Monmouth and enrolled in the Militia.

The only known photograph of Ellen (or Eleanor), Hook's mother, taken c. 1891. The girl is one of her grand-daughters, Gertrude Wintle, in whose house she died.(Courtesy, Mrs. Patricia M. Davis.)

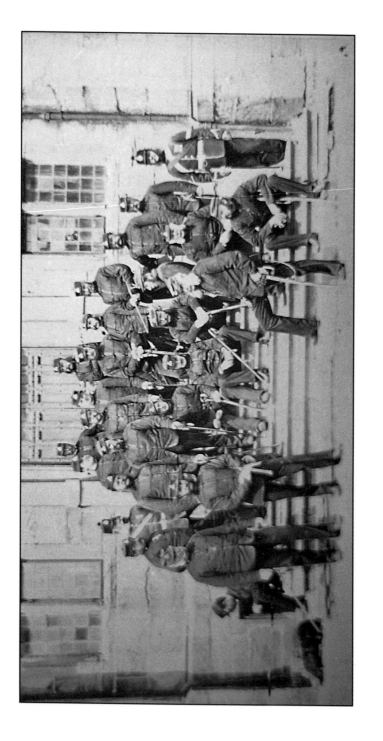

Group of Militiamen on the steps of Castle House, Monmouth, 1868. Lt.-Col. Vaughan is at the right front, leaning on his sword. (Courtesy Regimental Museum, Monmouth.)

Aston Ingham Parish Church, Herefordshire, where Hook was married on Boxing Day, 1870.
(Photograph by Mr. Norman R. Hook, 2000.)

Hook as he would have appeared in the last few months of his Regular Army service, wearing his good conduct stripe and marksman's badge. (He would not have been wearing the South Africa medal, which he was awarded early in 1881.) This photograph was taken at a studio in Camden Town, London, N.W., probably late in 1881 or in 1882. The corporal is not identified. (Furness Collection.)

NOTES

1. The quotation is from "Where our Heroes may be Seen", in *The Success*, 10 August 1895.
2. James, the son of Christopher and Mary Hooke, was baptised on 21 April 1691. For the legend connecting Agincourt and Rorke's Drift, see Appendix A.
   Except where otherwise stated, the genealogical details in this chapter are taken from the family tree prepared in 1986 by Patricia M. Davis, Hook's great niece. Mrs. Davis most kindly supplied a copy to the present writer, together with copies of many supporting documents which are in the Gloucester Record Office.
3. Will of James Hook of Oxenhall, signed on 20 January 1764 and proved on 14 September 1765 (1765/136, Gloucester Record Office). Oxenhall is north of Newent and near to Crookes Park (mentioned in Appendix A); "Alfred Hook V.C." by George Webb, in *Gloucester Journal*, 11 October 1980.
   Much of the material for Webb's article was supplied by Stephen Collins, a Gloucester man who was at that time writing a life of Hook. Although this biography has not apparently been published, the article is valuable in giving the "local view" of various controversial matters.
4. James Hook (1723-1788) and Elizabeth Hulet (1709-1783) married at Churcham in 1748 and both are buried there.
5. "Henry Hook, V.C.: Rorke's Drift Survivor & B.M. Attendant" by Barry C. Johnson, in *Colonnade: Staff Magazine of the British Museum*, No. 13, November 1967 (cited hereafter as *Colonnade*).
   The information about Hook's personal life, in this article, came from his daughter, the late Mrs. Letitia Bunting, who said that Hook "spent his early working life on his father's farm."
6. James Hook's "copyhold estate" is described in the Enclosure Award for Churcham, 11694, dated 1 September 1804, pp. 25-26 (Gloucester Record Office). On the O.S. map for 1922-23, "Hook's Farm" is shown to the north of the railway line (which still exists). The farmhouse had already been pulled down when the "traditional brick and timber barn" was auctioned in 1987. (Information and photographs supplied by Patricia Davis, with letter of 23 November 1999.) The "Hooks Farm" which appears on current maps, between Ley Court and Denny Hill, is different property entirely.
7. James Hook (1754-1829) married Elizabeth Harper (1755-1796) at Westbury-on-Severn in 1773. He married Mary Hodges on 27 May 1797.
8. "Power of Attorney to Surrender Copyhold Premises at Churcham," signed by James Hook on 10 June 1822. The copyhold was regranted to William Vernon. (D936 E/151, Gloucester Record Office.) On 25 March 1829, Administration of James Hook's "Goods Chattels and Credits" was granted to his daughter, Sarah Watkins. (1829/72, Gloucester Record Office.)
9. The marriage took place at the Church of St. Mary de Lode, Gloucester on 4 July 1820.
   The dates of birth of Richard Hook and of Mary Kear (20 February 1799) are given, with those of their children, on an unheaded scrap of paper in the Furness Collection. The dates of the children are: James—3 January 1821; John—2 April 1822; Hariett Sarah—7 November 1823; Joseph—5 February 1826; Henry—26 May 1828; and Arabella—9 February 1831.
   This paper, written in a 19th-century hand, appears to be an authentic family record. All the years of birth are those given by Mrs. Davis, based on her independent research; except that she was unable to trace the birth or baptism of Hariett Sarah Hook.
10. They were: William (1840); Ann (1842); Eliza Ann (1844); Maria (1846).
11. Record of Service of 2246 Private Joseph Hook (WO97/1638, Public Record Office).
12. Barrett, C.R.B. (ed.) *The 85th King's Light Infantry* (London: Spottiswoode & Co.

11

Ltd., 1913), pp. 290, 300-12 & 322.
13. The marriage took place at St. Mary de Lode, Gloucester, on 24 October 1839. The groom gave his occupation as "Labourer", as did his father-in-law, William Trigg. But Richard signed his name, while his bride, and the two witnesses, had to make their marks. Fanny, who is described on the certificate as a "Spinster" of "full age", died in 1848 and is buried at Churcham.
14. Information from the Poor Rates valuation of 1841 (supplied by Patricia Davis). The remains of the Coppice can be seen today, stretching from the "King's Head" along the old road to the outskirts of Huntley.
15. Elrington, C.R. and Herbert, N.M. (eds.) *A History of the County of Gloucester* (Vol. X of *The Victoria History of the Counties of England:* Oxford University Press for the Institute of Historical Research, 1972. Cited hereafter as *Victoria History*), pp. 11-18 & 27; "A brief history of the parish of Churcham, Bulley and Birdwood" by Madge Shorland, in *Forest of Dean Mercury*, 31 May 1968.
16. *Victoria History*, X, p. 28.
17. Horn, Pamela, *The Victorian Country Child* (Kineton: The Roundwood Press, 1974), pp. 72-75 & 94; Platts, A. and Hainton, G.H., *Education in Gloucestershire: A Short History* (Gloucester: Gloucestershire County Council, 1954), p. 46.
18. Horn, Pamela, *The Victorian and Edwardian Schoolchild* (Gloucester: Alan Sutton, 1989), pp. 11-13.
19. Marriage certificate of Henry Hook and Ellen Higgs, 28 May 1849. (The witnesses were William and Mary Higgs.) The bride's father, Thomas Higgs, is shown on the Poor Rates valuation of 1841 for Birdwood. His occupation, "Labourer", is given on the marriage certificate.
20. In later years, she replaced "Ellen" with "Eleanor"; and also gave various ages, all of them to her advantage! But the baptismal record, the marriage certificate and the information which she gave to the Census enumerator in 1851 seem conclusive. (See Chapter VIII, n.15.)
21. Birth certificate and baptismal record. The baptism took place on 1st of September. Mrs. Davis believes that Ellen had a brother called "Alfred", two or three years younger than herself, and that she named her eldest son after this brother. (Patricia M. Davis to the present writer, 18 April 1999.)
    Considerable confusion also exists over his date of birth and this is discussed at Appendix B.
22. *Colonnade*, p. 11.
23. Caird, James, *English Agriculture in 1850-51* (London: Longman, Brown, Green, and Longman, 1852), p. 496.
24. Burnett, John (ed.), *Useful Toil: Autobiographies of Working People from the 1820s to the 1920s* (London: Routledge, 1994), p. 5.
25. Hobsbawm, E.J. and Rudé, George, *Captain Swing* (London: Lawrence and Wishart, 1969), p. 35.
26. *Ibid.*, pp. 199, 202 & 247-49.
27. *Ibid.*, pp. 262-63. There were occasional disturbances after 1830, usually marked by rick-burning. Fifteen such fires were recorded in Gloucestershire as late as 1844-45. (*Ibid.*, p. 285.)
28. Harrison, J.F.C., *Early Victorian Britain, 1832-51* (London: Fontana, 1988), p. 24.
29. *The Hungry Forties: Life Under the Bread Tax: Descriptive Letters and Other Testimonies from Contemporary Witnesses* (London: T. Fisher Unwin, 1904), p. 116.
30. Horn, Pamela, *Labouring Life in the Victorian Countryside* (Stroud: Alan Sutton, 1987), p. 61; Mingay, G.E. (ed.), *The Victorian Countryside* (2 vols., London: Routledge & Kegan Paul, 1981), Vol. 2, pp. 507, 509 & 518; Grey, Edwin, *Cottage Life in a Hertfordshire Village* (first pub. in 1934; new. ed., Harpenden: Harpenden and District Local History Society, 1977), p. 224.
31. Jefferies, Richard, *The Toilers of the Field* (first pub. in 1892; reprinted, London: Macdonald Futura, 1981), pp. 152-53.
32. Census returns for 1851. Maria, the youngest child of his second marriage, had

died in 1850. Richard Hook died in the workhouse at Westbury-on-Severn on the 3rd of April 1871.

33. Horn, Pamela, *Joseph Arch, 1826-1919: The Farm Workers' Leader* (Kineton: The Roundwood Press, 1971), pp. 34-35. Chapter 3 of this biography gives a valuable summary of the labourers' conditions at the time when Hook was working on the land.

34. Caird, *op. cit.*, pp. vii, 40-42 & 512.

    A description of farming in the Vale of Gloucester in 1850 is in "Farming in Gloucestershire" by John Bravendar, in *The Journal of the Royal Agricultural Society of England*, Vol. XI (1850), pp. 147-51. He says that farms were then small—"the great majority scarcely reaching 150 [acres]"—and believes that the "proportions of grass and arable land" were "about equal." He found the typical Vale farmer "in possession of orchards of apple and pear-trees, from the produce of which he manufactures cider and perry."

35. Horn, *Joseph Arch*, p. 27.

36. "Agricultural Wages in England and Wales during the Last Fifty Years" by A. Wilson Fox (1903), reprinted in *Essays in Agrarian History* (Newton Abbot: David & Charles, 1968), Vol. II, p. 166.

37. *Ibid.*, p. 139.

38. *Ibid.*

39. Horn, *Joseph Arch*, p. 29; *The Hungry Forties*, p. 116.

40. *Victoria History*, X, p. 28; Census return for 1861 showing his sister Mary (aged 8) and his brother James (7) as "Scholars", *i.e.*, attending school; Blythe, Ronald, *Akenfield: Portrait of an English Village* (London: Allen Lane, The Penguin Press, 1969), p. 88.

41. Horn, *Victorian Country Child*, p. 124; Mingay, *The Victorian Countryside*, Vol. 2, p. 508.

42. Gloucester "Hospital Admisions", 10 September 1865, Ward 5. (Gloucester Library. Copy supplied by Mrs. Patricia Davis.)

43. Bourne, George [*i.e.*, George Sturt], *Change in the Village* (first pub. in 1912; reprinted, London: Gerald Duckworth & Co. Ltd., 1955), p. 68. Bourne is much more appreciative of the labourer's life and character than Jefferies, who wrote particularly from the farmer's standpoint.

44. Jefferies, *op. cit.*, p. 66.

45. Horn, *Labouring Life*, pp. 32-34.

46. Fox, *art. cit.*, pp. 141-42.

47. *Ibid.*, p. 142.

48. Horn, *Joseph Arch*, p. 38.

49. Jefferies, *op. cit.*, pp. 67-68.

50. Bourne, *op. cit.*, p. 49.

51. Burnett, *op. cit.*, p. xiv.

Chapter II

IN "THE POPE'S OWN": 1869-74

1.

There were three principal military forces during Hook's lifetime: the Regular Army, the Militia and the Volunteers. Many men served in one of them, and some in any two of them, but Hook was unusual in serving in all three.

The Militia is often referred to, by its more sentimental historians, as the "Constitutional Force" or "the People's Force."[1] There is something to be said for this sentiment, as the Militia existed, in some form or other, long before there was anything like a standing army. Many militiamen probably shared the regret of B.S. Sargeaunt at seeing "the old constitutional force, after so glorious a career, dispersed and exterminated under the Territorial Scheme of the year 1908 . . . for the Militia has beyond doubt been the backbone of the military system of the country for the past thousand years and longer."[2] Yet the Militia, for nearly all its history, had a strong element of "liability", or compulsion to serve, which was lacking in the Regular Army and also, of course, in the Volunteer forces.

The origins of this liability go back to the "fyrd" of Anglo-Saxon times, which developed into the medieval "General Levy", when there was an "obligation of able bodied men to render service within the boundaries of their own districts, and in the event of invasion or rebellion, march to any part of the country to serve as directed."[3] The regiment which Hook joined had rather obscure origins in Tudor days, when counties were expected to muster a "Trained Band", officered by the gentry. Although its modern historian gives a date— 1539, in the reign of Henry VIII—at which Militia in Monmouthshire definitely existed, it would not have been in a form recognisable to Hook and his contemporaries.[4] This came in 1660, with the Restoration, when

14

great changes took place in the military system of the country. Knight service, the feudal levy and their incidents were finally abolished; the organization of the "general levy", of which the "train-bands" were a part, into "the Militia" was completed, and the foundation of the present regular army was laid.[5]

The actual regiment of Monmouthshire Militia dates from 1660. Although "the basis of service remained the possession of property . . . it was now generally recognised that those of wealth would not serve personally and that the basic manpower would consist of hirelings and substitutes."[6] From this stage, four essential features remained unchanged during the two centuries before Hook enrolled: officers and men alike spent most of their time in civilian pursuits; there was a small amount of annual training; in emergencies, the Militia was called out for active service (or, in the technical term, "embodied"); and, when in training or embodied, was under martial law. The regiment was embodied during the Seven Years War and the War of American Independence; but during the first of these conflicts, the general system of raising militiamen was entirely changed. Men in every parish, aged between eighteen and fifty, were now to be chosen by ballot "to serve for three years, or provide a substitute." (There were "numerous exceptions" to those liable for the ballot; and all officers continued to be appointed by the lords lieutenant of their counties.) The modern view is that the Militia Act of 1757 "threw the main responsibility for Home Defence onto the shoulders of that section of the population who had not the means to purchase exemption."[7] The phrase "home defence" is significant, as successive governments were unwilling to employ militia regiments outside the United Kingdom, although in war time they actually encouraged *individual* militiamen to transfer to the Army for service overseas.

This was brought out during the French Revolutionary and Napoleonic Wars, when the Monmouthshire Militia was embodied for nearly thirteen years but only crossed the sea to go to Ireland. At the same time, it contributed over three thousand men to the Regular Army. Apart from its service in Ireland—when sentries were fired at and "several men were killed in small scuffles"—the regiment marched around a good deal in Wales and southern England, "suppressing riots" and escorting prisoners of war.[8] If there was not much glory in such duties, the long struggle against Napoleon is seen in retrospect as "the most important and interesting period in the history of the [Militia] force generally."[9]

After Waterloo, the force descended abruptly into its "dark ages." Annual training was dispensed with and the ballot was suspended. With the end of so long a war there was an obvious need for financial retrenchment; and the government could rely on the Yeomanry (volunteer cavalry) to deal with civil commotion. The Royal Monmouthshire Militia (R.M.M. for short), which had mustered seven companies during the war, was reduced to four companies when it "came out for training for twenty-one days in September 1821, and again in 1825." Six years later, a riot over Enclosures in the Forest of Dean brought out "the Adjutant and fifty men, inadequately clothed and armed."[10] This was the last activity for over twenty years. All "militia stores (arms, clothing, &c.) were transferred from the counties to the Board of Ordnance" in London, except for the arms of the permanent staff in each county town. At Monmouth, the staff comprised the adjutant and four or five N.C.O.s (all Regulars), who were, in effect, left in charge only of the orderly room, the Colours and the big drum.[11]

The Militia was at last revived after Louis Napoleon's *coup d'état* of 1851. By an Act of the following year, the government sought to raise 80,000 men, aged between eighteen and thirty-five, to serve for five years and to train for three weeks each year. Compulsion was tacitly abandoned, as "the ballot would only be applied if voluntary enlistment failed."[12] This was essentially the system which prevailed when Hook enrolled seventeen years later.

Throughout the dormant years, Militia officers had continued to be appointed and promoted. In the R.M.M., a very striking figure joined as a captain in 1836, rose without effort to major, and was promoted to lieutenant-colonel in the summer of 1853. This was John Francis Vaughan, who dominated the life of the regiment for a quarter-of-a-century after its reactivation. Colonel Vaughan enjoyed only a local celebrity but his son, Herbert, became a cardinal and succeeded Manning as Archbishop of Westminster.[13]

The Vaughans were squires of Courtfield, a manor house standing in a loop of the Wye, six miles from Monmouth. After the Reformation, they "maintained the old faith and loyalty to Rome," becoming Popish recusants, supporters of Charles I and, in two cases, Jacobites during the "Forty-Five." They were fined, imprisoned and subjected to double land-tax, but persisted in the dangerous practice of hiding priests. The future colonel was spared these particular excitements, as he came of age in 1829, the year of Catholic Emancipation. He kept up the family traditions in less dramatic ways; for instance, urging "his officers to contribute towards the rebuilding of the Catholic Church in St. Mary Street [Monmouth]."[14] One result of his zeal for the old faith was that the R.M.M., during his long ascendancy, was dubbed "the Pope's Own." He was remembered by fellow-Catholics outside the regiment as "very frank, energetic, with perhaps little comprehension for weakness of any sort . . . a model of sincerity and directness . . . well known for his cheerfulness and at times caustic humour."[15] As a young man, he had wanted to be a professional soldier, and only an unexplained "difficulty" blocked his entry into the Army, causing him to spend his life as a country gentleman and amateur soldier.[16]

Hook's future commanding officer was said to be:

> In the Mess-room an example of courtesy and general hospitality; in the Orderly Room a just and dignified magistrate; in the Field an energetic and skilful commander . . . a born leader of men.[17]

He went only once into the field, when the R.M.M. was embodied for the Crimean War in 1854. The officers, perhaps inspired by Vaughan, proposed to equip the regiment for overseas service by raising £5,000 between them. This offer to serve as a unit overseas was refused, so Vaughan left his men in Newport and set off for the Crimea himself. He was attached as a supernumerary to the Royal Welsh Fusiliers, and was joined by many of the Monmouth militiamen who transferred to the Army. Vaughan observed closely, formed characteristically strong opinions and had lunch with Lord Raglan, but whether he ever commanded troops in action seems doubtful. He left a more enduring mark with *The Soldier in War and Peace: Suggestions for Arming and Training Light Infantry, with Observations on Recruiting,* by Lt. Col. ————, published in 1855. In this anonymous booklet, he shows himself to have been well ahead of his time in general military thought. He questions whether "cumbersome and conspicuous Colours" ought any longer to be carried in battle and attacks such "useless labour" as "perpetual pipe-claying and polishing." In the chapter on recruiting, he compares the soldier's shilling unfavourably with pay in the Navy and calls for an increase to "one and sixpence a day", with fewer stoppages. If he had had a Regular commission, he might eventually have joined Sir Garnet Wolseley in reforming the Army; but, as it was, he returned home and resumed command of his militiamen.[18]

2.

The R.M.M. was not again embodied until the Boer War. In 1877, it ceased to be Light Infantry and became Engineers: not surprisingly, Colonel Vaughan then retired. During those twenty years between the Crimea and the regiment's transformation, there was a "long afternoon" of quiet routine, in which four distinct elements played their part.

The first two elements were permanently based at Monmouth. There was the staff, consisting of the adjutant, on secondment from the Army, and the quartermaster, musketry instructor, drum-major, orderly-room clerk, hospital sergeant, several other sergeants and the drummers.[19] Then there was the band, which was prominent in the social life of the town giving, for instance, "summer concerts on the Castle Square."[20]

The third element comprised the officers (other than the adjutant and quartermaster). In the Army, able N.C.O.s could win commissions, but this was never part of the Militia system. Militia officers had to be "gentlemen" in much more than the technical sense posited in *Queen's Regulations*: they were selected from the local gentry and there was no question of merit intruding from the ranks, nor even from "the new commercial and professional classes." In times of national emergency, "a gentleman was able to gain the prestige of military service without the dangers and discomforts of active service in the Regular Army."[21] This patriotic motive could hardly apply in times of peace, but the attractions of wearing uniform are perennial. To the extent that Monmouth had "a season", it was when the officers were together for annual training, and their support at "Chippenham", the local race course, was particularly appreciated. Although Castle House had been used as regimental headquarters since 1852, it had no officers' mess, so the two-dozen officers boarded at one of the town's hotels, often the "Beaufort Arms." This was good business for the hotel, but when the landlord of the "Beaufort" allowed the officers "to play billiards outside legal hours", he found himself in trouble with the magistrates.[22]

The last element was the N.C.O.s and men. Here, two questions arise: who were these auxiliary soldiers and why did they enrol? In the first of their five years, R.M.M. recruits were expected to come to Monmouth for a fortnight of "preliminary drill" before "the old hands" joined them for twenty-seven days of "annual training." Once the men had reported, they were subject to martial law until sent back to their homes. They were given a ten-shilling bounty; five shillings in "bringing money"; and a shilling as a "fee for attesting."[23] Their pay was a shilling a day during drill and training but, even apart from any stoppages, the shilling was not "all found." The regiment had no barracks or canteen, so the men had to be billetted about the town. Landladies charged fourpence a day, so a third of the men's pay disappeared in lodging costs.[24] Clearly, these terms and conditions would never attract "black-coated" workers—clerks, shopkeepers and their assistants, or anyone who ran a small business. The only interest which the middle classes took in the R.M.M. was to listen to the band and write to *The Beacon* to complain about the men's behaviour.

"The seasonal nature of the annual training programme . . . was designed with rural needs in mind: training took place before harvest." This allowed agricultural labourers to come in to Monmouth for training; but it seems likely that many of them were "casual men", who had no regular employment with a particular farmer. Conversely, the "non-seasonal pattern of industrial work created difficulties over absence for militia service." In the two years between the regiment's reactivation and the Crimean War, rather less than half of the 644 men who enrolled described themselves as labourers and 155 were in mining and heavy industry (most of them "colliers" or "coal-miners"). There were also fifty-seven craftsmen (mainly, shoemakers and tailors), thirty-seven artisans (blacksmiths, sawyers, masons and carpenters); ten with "rural skills" (grooms, saddlers and ostlers) and sixteen who were either unemployed or else in very small occupational groups such as hawkers and chimney-sweeps. Giving these figures, the regimental historian adds the dead-pan remark: "One individual described himself as a 'housebreaker.' " Perhaps the authorities thought that a spell under martial law would reform him![25] By 1874, when Hook's five years expired, the R.M.M. was having difficulty in filling its ranks, and only seventy-eight of the 264 men recruited had an industrial occupation. The Rifle Volunteer movement was flourishing and the government tended to regard "the militia's main role . . . as a recruiter" for the Army.[26]

It seems clear that the R.M.M. was crowded with poor men—but *pay* can hardly have brought them from their farms and mines to earn 8d. a day net, for a month each year. Nor can patriotism have been a motive: there was no national emergency during the twenty years in question. There must have been more cogent reasons: the broad attractions of military life; an urge for some respite from the numbing tedium of their daily lives; or both.

3.

No. 4454 Henry Hook—5'6" in height; occupation, "Labourer"; giving his age as 18 years and 9 months—began his "preliminary drill" on Monday, the 10th of May 1869.[27] He and about 120 other recruits were drilled by sergeants of the permanent staff on the square in front of Castle House. Going up Castle Hill from Agincourt Square, in the centre of the town, the present-day visitor comes out on to the same parade ground, with the seventeenth-century House to the right and the ruins of the Norman castle ahead. The River Monnow is

19

beyond the ruins, curving round towards the Wye, the two rivers enclosing all the older parts of the town.

Monmouth is surrounded and pressed in by green, wooded hills and, in Hook's time, had a population of barely five thousand. Something like a fifth of these people then lived along Monnow Street and in the courts and yards which had been built behind this thoroughfare in the early part of the nineteenth century. The street slopes up from the Monnow to join Agincourt Square: "wide in the middle and gated at each end, [it] was an ideal market area." There must have been plenty of mud, dust, clutter and strong smells. Many of the lodgings for the 600 men who needed accommodation once the regiment was fully assembled were in this part of town, convenient for Headquarters. For landladies, innkeepers and shopkeepers with rooms to let, this was the busiest time of the year. Every device was employed to make beds available, "to the dismay of the teachers who lost most of their girls. The [school] log books frequently refer to their absence while, for six weeks, they helped their mothers with the Militia, one girl having sixteen men lodged in her home."[28]

The Militia authorities did their best to keep order in these crowded lodgings, but there were some lively times. In June 1869, Cornelius Hayes, of No. 6 Company, was sentenced to five days in the cells "for Fighting in his Billet and breaking Jugs the property of the Landlord."[29] (The cells used by the R.M.M. were evidently in the local gaol; and the Officer of the Day visited them during his tour of duty.[30]) May of 1871 was specially notable for disturbances in billets: one man was drunk and refused to go to bed when ordered to do so by an officer; another was "awarded 24 hours cells for Fighting in his Billet and making use of highly improper language"; while Cornelius McKeown, of "H" Company, was first fined 7/6 for breaking one of the landlord's tables and then came up again, a few days later, for "being out of his Billet after Tattoo and Fighting in his Billet." McKeown was sent to the cells for six days. A Regimental Board tried three men in the following April for "Drunk & Fighting in his Billet"; one of them also drew his bayonet but was let off with a fine of seven and sixpence.[31]

These cases bring out the point that billets were, under military law, regarded strictly as substitute barracks. "Last Post" was at 10 P.M. and the men were expected to be in their lodgings by "Tattoo", presumably half-an-hour earlier. (The calls were no doubt sounded outside Headquarters; and Bugler Pittway was once "awarded 12 Hours Cells for being absent from Sounding the Bugle at 5 P.M."[32]) The system seems to have been that a piquet marched round the town so that the Roll could be called at the various billets. Absence from Tattoo Roll Call was an offence and was often aggravated by other misconduct, as when four privates were fined five shillings each for being "Absent from their Billets at 12.30 A.M. . . . and fighting." William Morgan, of No. 4 Company, forfeited 7/6 for being "out of his Billet after Tattoo 24th [May 1870] being Drunk and preventing a prisoner being taken to Guard Room." If a man missed an evening Roll Call, his absence might become prolonged. William Meredith— of No. 2, the Company to which Hook was assigned—forfeited his entire bounty (ten shillings) for being "Absent from his Billet at Tattoo 21" [May 1870] not returning till 4 P.M. 23rd."[33] If a militiaman was present at Roll Call but left before he was due to attend the first parade next morning (6.30 A.M.), he was guilty of "breaking out of his Billet." In one exceptional case, two privates of No. 7 Company broke out and were either caught by the police, or handed over by the piquet, and were charged additionally with "Theft." The magistrates sent them down for three months "with hard labour."[34]

In and out of billets, drink was the main problem. The town was reputed to have "one public house for every eighty-two inhabitants" (but also a flourishing temperance movement)! Regimental Orders are occasionally enlivened by such entries as "Refusing to quit the Crown Public House when ordered" (fined 7/6); and, less creditably, "Attempting to steal Beer from the Landlord of the Rope Makers Arms" (fined 5/-). A more curious case, punished by a half-crown fine, was: "Absent from Hospital at 9 A.M. 6" [June 1870] found in Redstreak Public House."[35] Drinking was obviously not confined to private soldiers; but it was very unusual that two sergeants should be reduced to the ranks in the same month: one "for being drunk and absent from Tattoo Roll Call the 5 May 1872"; and the other "for being Drunk while at Musketry"—an alarming incident, perhaps. The corporals were more likely to be in trouble. During Hook's years of service, one was reduced for being "Drunk in Hospital"; another for being "Drunk on Parade"; and four more were reduced for other offences, including absence from parades.[36]

The frequent absences from parades must often have been related to the drinking. In May 1871, Colonel Vaughan lost patience, and the following Order was published:

> There being so much irregularity in the men absenting themselves from Parade—The Commanding Officer warns the men that all future offences for absence from parade will be dealt with by a Regimental Board.[37]

Only a fortnight earlier, an Order had been issued which hints at a "dodge" adopted by some of the men to become "casuals" while their companies were away at the Butts. A "casual" would presumably have

21

to be found some light and not very exacting duty while he recovered from the previous evening's drinking. The Order reads:

> Any man absenting himself from any parade whilst undergoing a course of Musketry Instruction and thereby becoming a casual, will be handed over to a Regimental Board.[38]

These Boards, comprising one of the majors and several other officers, held their sessions in the Reading Room at Castle House and were kept busy. They had wider powers than the commanding officer and imposed an enormous number of fines and stoppages. *Courts-martial* were much less common and could inflict such sentences as "hard labour", as in the case of Horatio Page, of "G" Company, who was sent to Usk Gaol to serve fourteen days at hard labour for being absent for six days.[39]

While the Regimental Orders illuminate the more lurid and amusing aspects of Militia life, they also bring out the routine which was going on, hour by hour, as the eight companies were trained. In 1869, the "old hands" came up on the 24th of May. Some of them were either ill or else had deteriorated physically since the last training: these men were sent back home or even "permanently discharged." Parades began next day, at 6.30 and 10.30 in the morning, and 3 o'clock in the afternoon. Also on the first full day, a ceremony was ordered which, while perfectly understood at the time, is now obscure: "The Credit of the Regiment will be cried down tomorrow [25th] through out the Town." The best guess is that the Town Crier went through the streets to proclaim the start of annual training, although few citizens can have missed the arrival of several hundred men during the previous day.[40]

In the first week, most of the parades must have been devoted to drill. Marching and wheeling "like a wall" was much admired, and a good deal of practice was necessary to bring militiamen up to this sort of standard. Sunday brought a day off, apart from "Divine Service" and an afternoon Roll Call. There was no escaping the parades for Divine Service: "Roman Catholics at 8.45 A.M.; all other denominations at 10.40."[41] On the second Monday, the routine changed to allow for musketry instruction and target practice, by companies and sections, on Militia Field. The recruits fired blanks while the "old hands" were given "Ball practice"—but with a medical officer present. The middle two Saturday mornings were given over to kit inspections. "Men must have every Article complete in their Knapsacks": "1 Forage Cap, 1 Shell Jacket, 1 Shirt, 1 pair Socks, 1 Holdall, 1 Blacking, 4 Brushes, 1 Sponge, 1 Towel." Needless to say, there was punishment for those "failing to carry the above mentioned

Articles."[42]

In both drill and musketry, the regiment was now preparing for the competitive events and the climax of annual training. During the third week, the men's shooting was classified. The results were said to be "good, 479 men being classified in the first period, while over 51 per cent. became second-class shots, and nine obtained the good shooting prize of 25s."[43]

The culmination of every annual training was an inspection of the regiment by a Regular officer. This was neither a purely ceremonial occasion, nor one of pageantry, as the men paraded in "Heavy Marching Order" and were issued with "10 rounds of Blank Ammunition." It was, rather, a critical examination of auxiliaries by a professional soldier and was, in 1869, "a very long one." The inspecting officer was "again" Lieutenant-Colonel Sir Edward Campbell, and he was accompanied by the Duke of Beaufort. "His Grace went down the ranks and addressed the Regiment, which acquitted itself well. The luncheon was followed by an unusually large dance, and the Duke gave a dinner to the officers at the Beaufort Arms in the evening."[44]

It was not a coincidence that a duke turned up at a Militia inspection. He was lord lieutenant of the county; but there had been a close—and, at one time, a proprietorial—connection between the Dukes of Beaufort and the R.M.M. since 1684. This connection explains why Colonel Vaughan was able to lunch with the commander-in-chief in the Crimea: Lord Raglan was a son of the fifth duke. It was the eighth duke who attended the parade in 1869; and the ninth duke was to appear briefly in the last few months of Hook's life.[45]

The inspection by Sir Edward Campbell had been made on Tuesday, the 16th of June. It was nearly time for the men to be "settled with" and to "leave Headquarters" but, before that, they had to undergo a more functional inspection:

The 10.30 parade [on 18 June] will be in Shell Dress with Knapsacks, Small Kits and dress Clothing inside for inspection of Officers Commanding Companies (Chaco [*i.e.*, shako] to be carried in hand) who will assess Wilful damage, or Clothing in dirty condition, at the following rates

	d.
Dress Tunic	6
Trowsers	6
Shell Jacket	3
Summer Trowsers	6
Towels each	1

This will be charged to the men by Captains of Companies in his Accounts.[46]

Next day, the regiment dispersed—leaving behind, in the Cells, Cornelius Hayes (who had broken his landlord's jugs) and another unfortunate private who was caught taking someone else's tunic from the company stores.[47]

4.

Two months before the R.M.M. was due to reassemble for the next annual training, Hook went to headquarters to see the adjutant. He

expressed a wish to be transferred from the Royal Monmouthshire Militia to the Royal South Gloucestershire Militia in consequence of having employment and become a resident at Huntley near Gloucester.[48]

The adjutant had no objection to this transfer but either his opposite number made a difficulty or else there was some other official bar. Hook remained in the R.M.M. for his full five years.

The ancient village of Huntley is about two miles west of Birdwood. Its main street is the road to Ross-on-Wye, and the present-day visitor, coming from Birdwood, sees a number of buildings which were certainly there in Hook's time. On the right, a line of old cottages almost adjoins the "Red Lion", formerly a coaching inn, which the Victorians used for auctions and public meetings as well as for a hostelry. Further on, is the Church of St. John the Baptist, in red sandstone, with its adjacent parish school. Across the road, surrounded by high brick walls, stands an Elizabethan house then occupied by the rector. The squire's house, concealed from the road by conifer trees, lies behind the church, as it was the original rectory. The visitor may have the impression that the countryside around Huntley is largely unspoiled; but there were formerly "many lovely trees and orchards" which have since been cut down.

In mid-Victorian times, the population of Huntley was about five hundred: enough, it seems, to support both a "Benevolent Society" and a "Friendly Society." There were a few shops and little businesses, but most of the men were employed by tenant farmers. Many of the labourers had their cottages on common land up on Huntley Hill and Bright's Hill, beyond the church. These two wooded hills—to the left and right of the road—form a half-circle, screening the village on its western side. Both hills were Enclosed in 1870. It seems quite likely that work connected with the Enclosures brought Hook to Huntley; but whatever he was doing there must have allowed him to walk across to Monmouth that spring to resume his military training.[49]

The regiment had hardly assembled before there was a "sad accident":

> Buglers Helps (the big drummer), William Williams and Phillips, with A.H. Goss, son of the Quarter-Master-Sergeant, were upset on the river at Boys Rocks, near Vaga Cottage. Williams and Goss were drowned. They were buried on the 20th [May] with military honours.[50]

Even without this disaster, the deaths late in April of two local notables—Lady Dunraven and John E.W. Rolls—caused the cancellation of "the usual luncheon and dance" and of other "festivities."[51] (Colonel Vaughan had married into the Rolls family.)

The men were not unduly dispirited. Churchgoers were scandalised when a fight broke out "between two girls and two militiamen over a free seat in the gallery"; the outcome is not recorded![52] Routine was much as before; but the nine best shots competed "for the Regimental Prize of £1..0..0. extra, the winner of which will be the best shot in the Regiment." The best shot would thus win a total of £2..5..0. He turned out to be Private John Jenkins, who made "the remarkably high score of eighty points, as compared with fifty-seven, the score of the best shot of the previous year."[53]

This year, the inspecting officer was

> the well-known Colonel, the Hon. J.J. Bourke, commanding the 88th Regiment. He pronounced the parade movements to be good, and strongly impressed upon the Regiment that it was as important for soldiers to be clean and well turned out and orderly in the streets as to be well drilled.[54]

Colonel Burke's dictum would have been warmly applauded by the crustier residents of Monmouth. This letter to *The Beacon* was published a couple of years after Hook's service but it well represents the kind of complaint which was made against the men:

> Sir,—Allow me to ask why are the Militia allowed to assemble at the bottom of the Castle Hill, and for some yards along the paving, to the discomfort of ladies, who are bound to pass along the middle of the road through the mud, while these men in uniform stand laughing and jeering. Cannot something be done

to remedy this nuisance—are the police powerless? Have you no bye laws that will meet the case? I confess it would be difficult to get the names and summon them; but something might be done at head quarters. Why do their officers pass by and seeing such an assemblage on the pavement, receive the salutes, and walk on without ordering the men on their parade ground? Cannot military police be formed from their own staff? I enclose my card, and beg to remain your obedient servant,

C.D.J. [55]

March 21st, 1876.

A glimpse of how some of the men spent their leisure on Sundays—after Church Parade—is given in this item of "Local Intelligence" for the same year:

It was represented to the magistrates on Thursday that a great desecration of the Sabbath took place at the Chippenham Gate, on the various quays, and other places, by the Militia men playing at pitch and toss, which was a very annoying sight to persons passing by, and who wished to keep the Sabbath in a proper manner. The small number of police in the town were unable to stop it, although the Militia men left off when they saw a "blue coated" man appear, they invariably commenced again directly he was gone.[56]

In 1871, the regiment was again inspected by Colonel Burke. He found that

the drill was admirable, but he was not impressed by the turn-out of the Regiment. His remarks were resented by the local press, which pointed out, very justly, that men from the pits could not in a few weeks acquire bright and fresh complexions, and that, though appearing dirty, they were really perfectly clean. Anyone knowing the appearance which men's faces and hands acquire in certain trades, will appreciate this.[57]

5.

However much the more respectable residents might complain about the Militia, there was nothing short of consternation in the town when it was learned that annual training was to be moved thirty miles to Brecon. (The Monmouth and Brecon Militias had been amalgamated during the Napoleonic Wars but had separated again in

1820.) It seems that this new arrangement was a minor part of Cardwell's reform of the Army—the most contentious feature of which was the abolition of commissions by purchase—and in this forgotten local incident, it can be seen why the business of reform wore Cardwell down.

The news reached Monmouth about a month before training was due to begin in 1872. Captain Noel, who later became adjutant of the R.M.M., gives the sense of dismay:

> A special meeting of the Town Council was held on the 21st March, to protest against the Regiment being moved away. Under Mr. Cardwell's scheme the Monmouth were to train at Brecon, the Somersetshire in the Forest of Dean. This was considered especially hard, as it was stated that Monmouthshire supplied more men to the [Regular Army] depôt at Brecon than the counties of Brecon, Hereford and Radnor put together. The County Members [of Parliament] were memorialised, and it was pointed out how good a drill ground Chippenham Mead would be for brigade purposes, and what convenient ground was available in the Forest and about Trelleck for manoeuvres, and it was suggested that the old county gaol could easily be converted into barracks.
>
> The Mayor (Major A. Rolls) went to London, and saw Sir John Ramsden [M.P.] and Mr. Cardwell . . .[58]

When the mayor returned, he reported to another special meeting of the town council. At the War Office, he had presented the memorial to Cardwell and

> told him as strongly and forcibly as he possibly could the melancholy results which would ensue to the town if the Militia were removed; and explained that the situation was far more favourable for military manoeuvres and encampments than at Brecon. Mr. Cardwell had promised that he would see to the matter and take it into consideration and had promised to communicate with him as soon as anything final had been arranged; but nothing positive had been decided upon respecting the distribution of the forces. His Worship proceeded to state [to the council] that he had heard upon excellent authority that they need not make themselves uneasy about the removal of the Militia, as they could not be removed for two or three years at the least.[59]

The "melancholy results" which the mayor predicted were no doubt economic—the Militia spent a good deal of money in Monmouth.

But all was well: the regiment mustered on Castle Hill at 4 o'clock on the 22nd of April and everything was much as usual. Routine was enlivened early in May when

> some practical joker locked a wedding party in St. Thomas' Church. As they could not get out, and failed for some time to attract attention, they suffered what must have seemed a long imprisonment. This was laid down to the Militia, of course [as Captain Noel remarks wearily].[60]

The regiment again faced an inspection by Colonel Bourke, when its two wings, each under a major, "manoeuvred against each other." This year, "under a new regulation he [the inspecting officer] was not permitted to address the men"—perhaps one of Mr. Cardwell's more welcome reforms? Despite his unaccustomed silence, the colonel "appeared to be well satisfied."[61]

Hook had now taken part in four annual trainings. As his service was due to expire on the 11th of May 1874, and he would not be called out that spring, the training for 1873 would be his last. Despite Cardwell's tenure at the War Office throughout these years, it must have seemed that the spring weeks of training were set in an immemorial mould. Yet wherever the inspiration came from, 1873 was to be quite different from the preceding years.

It was presumably thought that the men ought to have some "camp training"—the nearest they could get to actual life in the field—and the obvious site for a camp was the Forest of Dean, a few miles east of Monmouth. Two "evil prognostications" were raised against this idea. In the first place, it was argued that "camping out" would reduce the number of new recruits—an important point now that the ballot was dead. Then Headquarters received a memorial from the Coleford magistrates advising against a camp near their town because "the Foresters entertained great hostility towards the Militia, and it would probably cause serious disturbances."[62] This was an echo from forty years earlier, the time of the Enclosure riot. The military authorities decided to ignore both prognostications.

As the recruits were not to go under canvas, they

> came out on the 17th of February [1873] for 83 days' preliminary drill [at Monmouth]. ... They were inspected on the 9th May, by Colonel Wodehouse, commanding the Depôt at Brecon ... [and] sent to their homes next day.[63]

Nine days later, the "old hands" mustered as usual on Castle House Square and were sent to their billets for the night. At half-past six next morning, they were issued with arms and given "a portion of the pay at the rate of 8d [per day]." (The deduction of fourpence was probably to pay for their rations in camp.) It was also ordered that "Officers Commanding Companies will make arrangements for their Men to have their dinners previous to the parade falling in", in "heavy Marching Order", at 12.30 P.M. The band was present and played "The Girl I left behind me" and "Auld Lang Syne" as the regiment marched away.[64]

It soon became clear that the R.M.M. was no longer seen in the Forest as an agent of repression. Quite the contrary:

> . . . the village of Staunton was decorated, and at Coleford the road was spanned with evergreens and flowers, while flags were hung out, and festoons bearing the inscriptions, "Welcome to the Monmouthshire Militia," "Welcome to the defenders of our Queen and Country," "Welcome to our country's defenders," and "Welcome to the Forest of Dean."[65]

An advance party had already put up tents at Coleford Meend, a piece of open ground in the forest beyond the town. The daily routine was much the same, but a canteen was opened and smoking in the tents was "strictly prohibited." The historic town of Coleford was at hand but some of the men evidently pined for the larger attractions of Monmouth, five or six miles away across the Wye. At any rate, after a week or so Colonel Vaughan cautioned them that

> Any men found in Monmouth without a pass will be apprehended and dealt with for absence without leave the Punishment being Court Martial or 168 hours [*i.e.*, 7 days] Cells.[66]

Still, Vaughan must have been relieved that, while he and the regimental boards had to deal with the usual defaulting, relations with the Foresters remained harmonious. When the troops passed through Coleford, on their return march, they again "received a very gratifying reception." At the town hall, an address testifying to "the general good conduct" of his regiment was presented to Colonel Vaughan

> printed in gold, and attached to it, in book form, were nearly 200 signatures, representing the clergy, magistrates, learned professions, and trading and operative classes of the town and neighbourhood.

In response, the colonel protested that it was "not usual for the service to make long speeches" but "three hearty cheers" were given before

29

the regiment moved on.[67]

> The troops had a very wet home journey, rain falling most piteously on the way, and, on reaching Monmouth, few there were with a dry skin. [It was the 12th of June!] The Regiment arrived at the Castle about half-past six, the thoroughfares through which they passed being lined with people. On the way the band played the airs, "When Johnny comes marching home," "Home, sweet home," &c., and had the Regiment been returning from a long and victorious campaign a much more exciting effect could not have been produced. Arrived at the Castle Hill, they were speedily dismissed for the night [to their billets].[68]

This was the end of the first phase of Hook's military career. There had been plenty of drinking—as there always has been in army life—but sober men like Hook learn to accommodate themselves to this. The fighting in billets seems to have been tipsy horseplay rather than real violence. Apart from the fight over the church seats— which was not apparently tried by the regiment or the magistrates— there seems to have been no bad behaviour towards women. And from the strictly military standpoint, there had been no serious insubordination. Hook must on the whole have found the experience congenial.

NOTES

1. Both terms are used by George Jackson Hay, in *An Epitomized History of the Militia* (London: "United Service Gazette" Offices, 1905).
2. Sargeaunt, B.E., *The Royal Monmouthshire Militia* (London: The Royal United Service Institution, 1910), pp. 43-44. This is a chronicle, dealing year by year with the regiment's history, and has much valuable detail.
3. "The Militia—An Outline History", an introductory chapter to *Welsh Militia and Volunteer Corps. 2: The Glamorgan Regiments of Militia* by Bryn Owen (Caernarfon: Palace Books, 1990), p. 21. See also: *The Amateur Military Tradition 1558-1945* by Ian F.W. Beckett (Manchester: Manchester University Press, 1991), which represents the best modern research on the Militia and Volunteer forces.
4. Watson, Graham, *Militiamen and Sappers* (Monmouth: Published at the Castle, 1996), pp. 12-26. This is the only account to bring the regiment's history down to the present day. See also the details of "Musters in Wales" for 1539 given by Hay, *op. cit.*, p. 86.
5. Noel, W.F.N., *Some Records of the Royal Monmouthshire Militia* (Monmouth: printed at the "Beacon" Office, 1886), p. 10. This scarce book, printed no doubt at Captain Noel's expense, gives the fullest account of the regiment during Hook's service. The author was adjutant from 1881 to 1886.
6. Hay, *op. cit.*, p. 226; Sargeaunt, *op. cit.*, p. 45; Beckett, *op. cit.*, p. 50 (for the quotation). "Royal" was added to the regiment's title in 1804.
7. Noel, *op. cit.*, p.11; Beckett, *op. cit.*, p. 63; Owen, *op. cit.*, p. 22. Under this Act, the

Militia was to consist solely of infantry.

8. Sargeaunt, *op. cit.*, pp. 80-133; Kissack, Keith, *Life in the Militia . . . 1778-1810* (n.d., but on sale at the Regimental Museum, Monmouth), p. 3. This is a very graphic, and often hilarious, account of the regiment in those days.
9. Owen, *op. cit.*, p. 22.
10. Sargeaunt, *op cit.*, pp. 103 & 136; Kissack, Keith, *Victorian Monmouth* (Monmouth: The Monmouth Historical and Educational Trust, [1988]), p. 84.
11. Noel, *op. cit.*, p. 12; Sargeaunt, *op. cit.*, p. 137; Kissack, *Victorian Monmouth*, p. 84.
12. Beckett, *op. cit.*, pp. 147-48.
13. See *Cardinal Herbert Vaughan* by Robert O'Neil (Tunbridge Wells: Burns & Oates, 1995), which has an unusual amount of family background.
14. Watson, *op. cit.*, p. 56.
15. O'Neil, *op. cit.*, p. 17.
16. *Ibid.*, p. 16.
17. Kissack, *Victorian Monmouth*, p. 199.
18. Sargeaunt, *op. cit.*, pp. 142-48; Kissack, *Victorian Monmouth*, pp. 84-87; Lt. Col. ——— [*i.e.* J.F. Vaughan], *The Soldier in War and Peace: Suggestions for Arming and Training Light Infantry, with Observations on Recruiting* (London: Burns and Lambert, 1855) pp. 12 & 31-36.
19. Sargeaunt, *op. cit.*, pp. 150 & 301.
20. Kissack, *Victorian Monmouth*, pp. 132, 139 & 154; Noel, *op. cit.*, p. 72.
21. The two quotations are from Watson, *op. cit.*, pp. 41 & 63.
22. Kissack, *Victorian Monmouth*, p. 181, Noel, *op. cit.*, p. 75; Watson, *op. cit.*, p. 56.
23. These were the payments made to Hook but no doubt they applied generally. ("Enrolment Account of the Royal Monmouth Militia" for 1869-70, in WO 13/ 1534, Public Record Office.)
24. *The Monmouthshire Beacon*, 8 February 1873; Watson, *op. cit.*, p. 53.
25. *Ibid.*, pp. 53-54. (At pp. 53 & 63, Watson emphasises the "conspicuous . . . absence" of the middle classes).
26. *Ibid.*, p. 63.
27. "Enrolment Account," cited at n. 23; "Training Pay List of the Disembodied Militia" (in WO 13/1534, Public Record Office).
28. Kissack, K.E., *A Walk Around Monmouth* (broadsheet issued by the Monmouth Historical & Educational Trust, 1992); Kissack, *Victorian Monmouth*, pp. 2-5 & 88. As for the numbers of men who poured into the town each spring, Sargeaunt (*op. cit.*, p. 156) gives "719 of all ranks" when the regiment was fully assembled in 1871. From this total would have to be deducted for billetting purposes the officers and permanent staff; and also those men who lived in Monmouth. According to Watson, (*op. cit.*, p. 54), 72 of the town's residents enrolled in the years 1852-53. The figure of about 600 needing a billet for annual training therefore seems reasonable for Hook's years.
29. "Royal Monmouth Light Infantry Militia: Regimental Orders, 1868-72", in the Regimental Archives, Great Castle House. (Cited hereafter as "Regt. Orders.") Orders for 17 June 1869.
30. Regt. Orders, 10 May 1871.
31. *Ibid.*, 22, 23, 27 & 29 May 1871; 24 April 1872. The companies had originally been numbered 1 to 8; but in 1871, the system was changed and they were lettered "A" to "H".
32. Regt. Orders, 22 April 1872.
33. *Ibid.*, 6 June 1870; 24 & 25 May 1870.
34. *Ibid.*, 28 May 1870. This case was important enough to be noted by Sargeaunt (*op. cit.*, p. 155).
35. Kissack, *Victorian Monmouth*, pp. 1 & 65: Regt. Orders, 7 June 1870; 19 & 29 May 1871.
36. *Ibid.*, 15 June 1869; 29 May 1871; 6 & 7 May 1872.
37. *Ibid.*, 27 May 1871.

38. *Ibid.*, 10 May 1871.
39. *Ibid.* 1 May 1872.
40. Noel, *op. cit.*, p. 72; Regt. Orders, 24 May 1869.
    The present writer is indebted to the late Bryn Owen for the suggestion about the Town Crier, as none of the published sources explain the ceremony of crying the "Credit of the Regiment."
41. Regt. Orders, 29 May 1869.
42. *Ibid.*, 29 May, 9 & 10 June 1869; 27 May 1870.
43. Sargeaunt, *op. cit.*, p. 154. No names are given.
44. *Ibid.*, p. 155; Regt. Orders, 15 June 1869; Noel, *op. cit.*, p. 73.
45. For the ninth duke, see Chapter XIII, n. 14.
46. Regt. Orders, 17 June 1869; Sargeaunt, *op. cit.*, p. 155.
47. Regt. Orders, 18 & 19 June 1869.
48. R.J. Hickman to Adjutant, Royal South Gloucestershire Militia, 15 March 1870, in "Adjutant, Royal Monmouthshire Militia: Letter Book, 1865-72", Regt. Museum.
49. This account of Huntley owes most to a typescript in the Gloucester Public Library. The author, Mary N. Hamlen, originally collected "the memories of some of the older inhabitants of our village for a W.I. Scrapbook." Her 300-page manuscript, dated 1 January 1981, has great charm and nostalgia, and is full of valuable detail, but it has not yet found a publisher. It has no title but appears in the Library catalogue as [History of Huntley], Item No. 45959.
    The population of Huntley is given as 516 in the *Gloucester Journal*, 22 March 1873; and the *Journal* has items on the Enclosures in the issues for 12 February & 23 July 1870, and 10 February 1872.
50. Noel, *op. cit.*, p. 73.
51. *Ibid.*
52. Kissack, *Victorian Monmouth*, p. 93.
53. Regt. Orders, 1 June 1870; Sargeaunt, *op. cit.*, p. 155.
54. Noel, *op. cit.*, p. 73. (Training in 1870 lasted from 16 May to 11 June.)
55. *Monmouthshire Beacon*, 25 March 1876.
56. *Ibid*, 6 May 1876.
57. Noel, *op. cit.*, p. 74. (Training in 1871 was from 8 May to 3 June.)
58. *Ibid.*
59. *Monmouthshire Beacon*, 6 April 1872.
60. Noel, *op. cit.*, p. 74.
61. *Ibid.*, p. 75; Sargeaunt, *op. cit.*, p. 157. (The regiment dispersed on 18 May.)
62. Noel, *op. cit.*, pp. 75 & 77. The "prognostication" about the number of recruits was completely disproved, as 150 assembled for preliminary training in 1874, twenty more than in 1873.
63. *Ibid.*, p. 75. Wodehouse also made the usual inspection of the regiment, in camp, on 11 June. (*Ibid.*, p. 76.)
64. Regt. Orders, 19 May 1873; Noel *op. cit.*, pp. 75-76.
65. *Ibid.*, p. 76.
66. Regt. Orders, 28 May 1873.
67. Noel, *op. cit.*, pp. 76-77, for the text of the memorial and Vaughan's reply.
68. *Ibid.*, p. 77. The men were sent home on Saturday, 14 June.

Chapter III

HENRIETTA'S STORY: 1870-77

This is a story never before told. Henrietta Hook was Henry's daughter from his first marriage. She never knew her father, as he went away in the Army.[1]

1.

Henrietta's story really begins in the Parish Church of Newent in 1843. Here, on the 17th of December, John Jones married Anne Sysum.

The bride was a "minor", having been born in 1827 at Kilcot, a hamlet in the parish of Newent. Her bridegroom was four years older and had been born in the city of Worcester. The groom's father was also called John Jones, and both father and son are described as "Labourers." The Sysums were a large and long-established family in the Gloucestershire area; but the social standing of the branch in "Henrietta's story" was much the same as that of the Jones family. The bride's father, Thomas Sysum, had been born in 1791 at Aston Ingham, just across the Gloucestershire border in Herefordshire. In 1815, he married Comfort Phillips, a native of Newent who was two years his junior. Anne Sysum was the fifth of what became a big family—her parents had nine, possibly eleven, children—and her father, and two of her brothers, who appear in the Census of 1851, are shown as "Road Labourers." At her wedding, she and her bridegroom, and the two witnesses (who seem to have been neighbours), all had to "make their marks" in the marriage register. The reason for this emphasis on the very modest circumstances of the Jones and Sysum families will soon become apparent.[2]

John Jones and Anne Sysum were living at Gorstley Common (now spelled without the "t"), west of Kilcot and northwest of Aston Ingham. They had come in to Newent, the nearest town, to be married in the grand old church which still dominates the town

33

centre. "The 14th century tower with its stately spire, and the chancel with its Gothic windows, are attached to a great nave in the style of the late 17th century, familiar to us from Wren's churches in London, but rare indeed in the depths of the country."[3] The couple returned to the border region of Gloucestershire and Herefordshire, where it seems almost certain that they spent their entire married lives.

Charlotte, their first child, had been born three weeks before the wedding; and a son called John followed about four years later. By that time, they had moved to Kilcot, on the main road out of Newent to the west and less than two miles from the town. What appears to have been their third child was born on the 14th of August 1849 and christened Comfort after her grandmother.[4] She was evidently given some education and could at least sign her name by the time of her own marriage. Still, the Newent area was one of the poorest parts of Gloucestershire; and her childhood was probably no more prosperous or comfortable than the lives of the Hook children who were growing up at Birdwood.[5]

No-one now knows when or where Hook met Comfort Jones.[6] In 1870, the year of their marriage, he was working at Huntley, four miles from her home at Kilcot; but the banns were called at Aston Ingham, which is recorded as the place of residence of both bride and groom "at the time of marriage." Four months later they were living in the parish of Newent (almost certainly at Kilcot); and it seems unlikely that they ever did live at Aston Ingham, except in a purely technical sense during the statutory fortnight before the banns could be called and then during the period of the three Sundays on which they were actually called. The bride may have wanted to be married at Aston Ingham, as her Sysum grandparents had been married there and had lived in the parish for about ten years afterwards.

Aston Ingham was and is a parish of cottages scattered amongst fields, woods and orchards. It has no village "core", and the parish church—together with Aston Court, the manor house—stands close to the Gloucestershire border. This twelfth-century church is small and dark but has a notable lead font which secures it a mention in the guide books.[7] The natural setting—even 130 years after the wedding—is quiet, beautiful and remote from the world. Here, on Boxing Day of 1870, Hook (calling himself "Alfred") and Comfort Jones were married by the Rector. Hook made his mark, as also did the two witnesses, John Jones and Mary Sysum (possibly the bride's aunt). The bridegroom gave his occupation as "Workman."[8] At that time, amongst cottage people, "honeymoon holidays were never thought of . . . the young couple would not be able to afford it . . . The wedding festivities were . . . generally held at the home of the

34

bride's parents . . . [where there would be] a good substantial meal, with, as a rule, plenty of beer for those who drank it (and there were few who didn't) and maybe a bottle or two of home-made wine wherewith to drink the healths of the newly wed." A home-made wedding cake was usually cut later, at the evening meal.[9]

Boxing Day that year was on a Monday and it seems likely that Hook returned to work next day. In retrospect, it can be seen that he had reached the turning point of his life. If his marriage had succeeded, he would probably have remained a labourer in rural Gloucestershire and would now be forgotten.

2.

His marriage did not succeed. Some recollections of Comfort have come down from her youngest daughter and they seem to give the key to her character. She was "a hard-working woman" but "very strict", wanting her own way and "ruling with a rod of iron."[10] Hook was no doubt a young man in love, but had he been rather older than twenty, he might have realised, before it was too late, what was ahead of him. The question of exactly what went wrong is complicated by the fact that, only a few months after the wedding, Comfort's parents were living with the couple. The Census returns for 1871 show Hook as "Head of Family", with John and Anne Jones as "Boarders." Four members of the Sysum family were living close by: Elizabeth, one of Comfort's younger aunts, and her three children, all boarders of a labourer called Jennings. Whatever differences arose between the Hooks, it might be supposed that Comfort would have had the support of the Joneses and of some of the Sysums.

There is a tradition in Henrietta's family that Hook married "to improve his lot in life", and that the Joneses "felt that he only married their daughter with an eye to getting his hands on the farm they owned." Not surprisingly—*if it was true*—they "never grew to like him."[11] This is a curiously similar tradition to the story about the Hook family farm which he is supposed to have worked on before he joined the Army and which was allegedly sold, without his knowledge, while he was serving in South Africa.[12] Neither of these "farms" seem to have had any existence outside family lore. There had been a Hook farm at Oakle Street forty years earlier; and there was a farm—perhaps even two farms—in the Wood family, into which Henrietta herself married, twenty years after her father's marriage. The Wood family is described later on; but, for the moment, it can

35

be asserted confidently that those members of the Jones and Sysum families who became closely related to Hook by marriage were labouring people, much like himself.

The Hooks had three children: Raymond, born at Kilcot on the 29th of October 1871; Henrietta, born on the 19th of September 1873, also at Kilcot; and Julia Ann, born at Gorsley on the 16th of May 1876. When they were baptised, Raymond was given the middle name "John" (which he used in later life) and Henrietta was given a first name, "Mary" (which she never used.)[13] Kilcot's most prominent building, the Inn, comes later into Henrietta's story; but the exact whereabouts of the family home in the early eighteen-seventies is unclear. It would have been a rented cottage, becoming progressively more crowded as Raymond and Henrietta had to be accommodated with the four adults. "Overcrowding" was possibly the reason for the move to Gorsley.

This parish lies about a mile west of Kilcot, along the main road to Ross-on-Wye. On the south side of the road, there are two Victorian buildings which, together with the vicarage just to the north, would have marked the centre of Gorsley in the Hooks' time. Christ Church is the Anglican church and its school-house is a little farther along the road. This was the school which all the Hook children were to attend. Just beyond the school-house is a cross-roads and the road which leads to the south passes through a small area, at another cross-roads, which was called "Mount Pleasant."[14] Standing at this lower cross-roads, and looking northeast across the fields, the low tower of Christ Church is clearly seen. In the opposite direction lies Aston Ingham church—out of sight through trees and over meadows but not much more than a mile away.

Julia Ann Hook spent most of her life in Gorsley and Kilcot. During the Second World War, travelling by bus along the Ross road, she pointed out to her grandchildren the cottage at Mount Pleasant where she, and her brother and sister, had been brought up. This cottage lies roughly lengthways to the road and had at that time a tin-roofed extension or outhouse along the back, facing the road. Although it has been much improved and renovated in recent years, the brickwork and tiled roof are much as they would have been in the eighteen-seventies and no doubt essentially the same as in 1839, when the cottage was known as "John Rudge's House and garden." The stairs originally faced the front door and the rooms were small, with low ceilings.[15] In these rooms, Hook's marriage came to a smash.

Although there are no anecdotes from these years, Hook preserved a newspaper cutting which has tantalising implications. In January 1885, he attended the annual dinner of his Volunteer company ("H", of the Bloomsbury Rifles) and was presented with a prize.

Captain Fourdrinier [his company commander] remarked upon the example set to the Company by Corporal Hook, who, originally a member of the corps, and who had obtained such a distinction as the Victoria Cross in serving his country, had come back to his old corps, and obtained a prize for the highest attendance at drill.[16]

The words "originally a member of the corps"—*if true*—can only mean that Hook was in London, serving with the Bloomsbury Rifles, *before* he entered the Army in March 1877. His last training commitment with the Militia had been in June 1873, and Julia Ann was presumably conceived in August 1875. Between those dates, he could have found work in London and tried his hand at another form of part-time soldiering, the Volunteers. This would help to explain his decision, after he left the Army, to move to London and give up country life altogether. Hook has not marked the cutting and no other evidence, or oral tradition, has been found to support Captain Fourdrinier's remark. On balance, it seems likely to be true. Hook's three absences on Militia training, after his marriage, may in themselves have been "a bone of contention" between Comfort and himself, and he may have gone to London to escape from domestic life or perhaps to see whether he could find more congenial work. It might then be conjectured that he returned to Gorsley before the late summer of 1875, to give his marriage "another chance." Supposing all this to be true, the interlude in London may itself have led to circumstances causing him to try a more drastic remedy.

When he eventually petitioned for divorce, Hook alleged:

> That in the months of December 1876 and in the months of January and February 1877 the said Comfort Hook at Newent in the County of Gloucester on numerous and divers occasions committed adultery with William Wedley who is now [1896] dead.[17]

This man appears to have been born at Kilcot on the 4th of February 1854, making him over four years younger than Comfort. He came from a Newent family and his father was an agricultural labourer. More significantly, the Wedleys were neighbours of the newly-wed Hooks although, when the Census was taken in April 1871, William was not at home.[18]

As so little is known about Comfort, and as her side of the story was left unrecorded, she should obviously be given the benefit of every reasonable doubt. Hook's petition was not defended and he never had to establish at law the truth of his allegation. His petition was really based on an entirely different claim, for which he had irrefragable proofs; and he may have put in the Wedley matter in case he was asked in court why he had left his family and joined the Army.

There were several broad reasons why men enlisted in the Victorian Army. In the first place, they might be "down and out" in wintry weather, giving rise to the contemporary maxim that "Jack Frost is the best recruiting sergeant." Or they might be fit young men, attracted by the prospects of travel or adventure. Or, again, there might be some national emergency which would cause patriotic men to enlist; but nothing occurred between the Crimea and the Boer War which would have led a married man, with children, to enlist for patriotic reasons alone.[19] Finally, the Army was a refuge for men who had personal or family troubles. Once they had taken the oath, they were "Soldiers of the Queen" and the Army enfolded them entirely. All the anxieties and discords of civilian life fell away —the more so if they were posted overseas, where about half the infantry was serving at any one time.

There seems no doubt that it was this last reason which applied in Hook's case: he came to think that life in camp and barracks would be more bearable than life with his family and his in-laws. This decision would have been made easier by his interest in military life and perhaps by his uncle's example. Whether he planned the move in advance, or whether it was a sudden resolve, brought on by a quarrel, no-one can now say. Quite possibly, it was the latter, as he told a friend, many years later, that he had walked all the way from his home to Monmouth, in order to enlist.[20] In imagination, the slamming of the door, as he set out, can be heard down the years.

And so it was true that Henrietta "never knew her father", as she was well under four when he left the cottage at Mount Pleasant.

NOTES

1. "Henry Hook, V.C.: The Hero of Rorke's Drift", presented by Vernon Harwood. A Radio Gloucestershire documentary programme "originally broadcast on 21st January 1996." The quotation was read from an anonymous notebook, left near the Visitors' Book in Churcham Parish Church but since removed.
2. Marriage certificate; Census returns for Newent, 1841, 1851 & 1871; Registers of Baptisms for Newent, 1815-44 (Gloucester Record Office).
3. Tomlinson, K.M. (ed.), *The Church of St. Mary the Virgin, Newent* (Newent: Perpetua Press, 2000), p. 3.
4. Birth certificates for Charlotte and Comfort Jones (John's certificate has not been found); Census returns for 1851.
5. Horn, *Joseph Arch*, p. 32, quoting a report that in 1867-68 many families in the Newent area had "nothing but bread from one week's end to another."
6. Mrs. Letitia Bunting, Hook's youngest daughter by his second marriage, told the present writer that her father had married before he enlisted in the Army but she

appeared to have no details whatever. Her brief remarks on the first marriage are given in *Colonnade* (pp. 12 & 15-16). She told much the same story to the late Norman Holme, who published it in *The Silver Wreath: Being the 24th Regiment at Isandhlwana and Rorke's Drift, 1879* (London: Samson Books, 1979), p. 87.

In preparing *Rorke's Drift and the British Museum: The Life of Henry Hook, V.C.* (London: The Johnson-Taunton Military Press, 1988; cited hereafter as R.D. & B.M.), the question was reconsidered. No evidence had by then come to light to support the oral tradition, so the unfortunate conclusion was reached (p. 56) that "such a marriage seems most improbable." Since then the present writer has spoken to, and corresponded with, several descendants of Hook's two daughters by the first marriage; and the valuable information and impressions which they gave are used later on. But no evidence or tradition has survived amongst these relatives as to how or when Hook met Comfort Jones.

7. Watson, Margaret, *The History of Aston Ingham* (Ross-on-Wye: Chimes Pub. Inc., 1991), pp. 5 & 13-14.
8. Details from the marriage certificate.
9. Grey, *op. cit.*, pp. 155-58. Grey's evocative account of rural weddings at this period applies particularly to his native village of Harpenden; but many of the details which he gives would hold good for the Victorian countryside generally.
10. Reminiscences of Mrs. June Dutton (née Matthews), grand-daughter of Julia Ann Hook, in conversations with the present writer, July 2000, and in a written account dated 26 August 2000. Mrs. Dutton lived with her grandmother at Kilcot from the late 1930s. She heard about the early days of the family and met Hook's other two children, Raymond and Henrietta.

      There is unfortunately no recollection of Comfort Hook's appearance, and no photograph of her seems to have survived.
11. This tradition was told to the present writer by Mrs. Heather Warman-Johnston, a great grand-daughter of Henrietta Hook. (Telephone conversation on 29 September 2000 and letter dated 3 October 2000).
12. *Colonnade*, p. 15; Holme, *op. cit.*, p. 87.
13. Birth certificates; Registers of Baptisms for Newent, 1871-74. (The baptismal and Census records in this chapter were supplied by Mrs. Patricia Davis.)
      In an anonymous, hand-written chart of the Hook family a "1st Marriage" is shown, but the only name given is a daughter called "Elizabeth." No such daughter is known to have existed. (This chart is in 7407-83-433, the National Army Museum File on Hook compiled by Canon W.M. Lummis. Cited hereafter as "Lummis File.")
14. The name "Mount Pleasant" is now preserved by one house at the lower cross-roads; otherwise, it seems to have gone out of use.
15. Information from Mrs. June Dutton (who saw the cottage from the bus); and from Mrs. Alison Arnold who, with her husband, owns the renovated house, now called "The Crescent." Mr. & Mrs. Arnold very kindly showed the present writer part of the interior, when he called in July 2000; and Mrs. Arnold (letter of 14 August 2000) sent photographs of the cottage as it had appeared in 1982. The building was extended by about a third, probably early in the 20th century, and the division between the original cottage and the new work can clearly be seen.
16. *Volunteer Service Gazette*, 7 February 1885 (cutting in Furness Collection). Hook's service in the Volunteers is fully covered in Chapter X.
17. See Chapter XII for a full account of these proceedings. The present writer has been informed privately that Wedley emigrated to Canada.
18. Birth certificate; Census returns for 1861 (showing William as a "Scholar" of 7) and for 1871 and 1881 (when he was not with his family).
19. During the "Eastern Question" or "Balkan Crisis", the Russo-Turkish War broke out in April 1877, a month after Hook had enlisted; and the Reserves were not recalled to the Colours until April 1878.
20. This was told to the present writer by Mrs. Pat Kitto.

Chapter IV

LIFE IN THE RANKS: 1877

Ever more expensive books tell us that the British soldiers of the Zulu, the 2nd Afghan, and the 1st Boer Wars came from "the least respectable sections of the working class"; that the principal factor in leading them to enlist was unemployment; that drunkenness and venereal disease were endemic among them; and that some 60% were illiterate or barely literate. . . .

The real challenge facing those who aspire to write about the Victorian army is this. How was this "socially expendable" material, officered by moneyed flâneurs who "rarely saw the men for whom they were responsible", and practically untrained to boot, transformed into the heroes—for that is what they were—who stood, fought, and died to a man at Isandhlwana along with those same officers; held Rorke's Drift; marched to, took, and held Kabul; who, facing an appalling end at Maiwand, charged, all eleven of them, into the entire Afghan army; who, after the slaughter at Laing's Nek "marched back in as good order and with as erect and soldierly a bearing, as when (the 58th) marched out"?[1]

1.

This challenge, made recently by a retired officer, can hardly be shirked by a biographer of one of the men who "held Rorke's Drift." Colonel Murray is understandably concerned about the depiction of late-Victorian officers, and this question should be considered before facing the problem of whether their men were really " 'socially expendable' material."

In the first place, most officers had some private means. With a few exceptions in the Guards and the Household Cavalry, they were by no means England's wealthiest sons but they needed money for two reasons: before 1871, most commissions in the infantry and cavalry, up to and including the rank of lieutenant-colonel, were purchased; while the pay of officers was so low that it was difficult (in the more fashionable regiments, impossible) to meet mess bills and the necessary social expenses without a private income. Those few officers who were commissioned without purchase tended to serve in India or else had to struggle hard "to make ends meet." Nor did the composition of the officer corps change significantly *after* 1871. Officers had always been drawn very largely from landed families, and the abolition of purchase failed to bring in candidates even from the urban middle classes, much less from the working classes.[2]

The only general point which needs to be made about officers who had purchased their commissions is that they were "considered to have financial claims on, or vested interests in . . . [their positions] in the Army."[3] Sir Evelyn Wood tells a story about the frame of mind which having such a "vested interest" could induce. Major Hackett— "a pillar of the regiment", blinded at Kambula, in the Zulu War— had earlier asked Wood to use his influence

> to stop what he regarded as the craze for examining officers like himself, nearly forty years of age. He pointed out the injustice of expecting old dogs to learn these new tricks, and argued that as he had bought his commission without any liability to be examined for promotion, it was unjust to exact any such test from him now.[4]

"Flâneur" means "a lounger or saunterer, an idle man about town." Officers who were stationed overseas, especially on active service, obviously had little chance to play the flâneur, even if they wanted to; and this accounted for about half of the combatant officers at any one time. Many of those who were serving in the Home Counties enjoyed the London "season", and those who were well connected could be seen at country-house parties; but very few officers could fairly be stigmatised as "flâneurs." The very reverse was actually the case, as memoirs of the period make clear. They were primarily out-of-doors men, with a life-long enthusiasm for all kinds of sports and games; so much so that the reader of these autobiographies may find the zeal displayed for fox-hunting and tiger-shooting almost overpowering. Still, Sir Bindon Blood—a tremendous tiger-shooter— was no doubt right in claiming that "polo and . . . most sports and pastimes, particularly . . . the pursuit of dangerous game" helped to "train 'eye and hand' and to give a man the coolness and self-confidence in action that is so essential to the soldier."[5]

A related characteristic was their dislike of office work. This complaint by Hallam Parr, a Zulu War officer, is quite typical:

On arrival at Maritzburg [Natal, in 1881] I found myself the

41

assistant to the Chief Staff Officer, and for some weeks worked from morn to dewy eve in a stuffy office surrounded by piles of foolscap . . .

However, Sir Redvers Buller stood my friend, and got me into the open air again . . .

To my delight I was sent to take charge of the Remount Establishment at my old station at Fort Napier.[6]

Parr's enthusiasm for remount service (and he was an infantryman) brings out his devotion to horses, which he shared with many other officers.

Because of their country's position in the world, and their own position in the country, it was a golden time to be a British officer. Writing at the end of the Great War, Charles À Court Repington— an officer in late-Victorian times and later a well-known military correspondent—describes in a striking passage the intense patriotism of his brother officers:

Looking back now I understand a little better that the history and the glories of England, enshrined in the traditions of countless families, sank unconsciously and without schooling into our youthful minds, and remained there imperishably engraved upon the tablets of our hearts. We learnt to believe that the English were the salt of the earth, and England the first and greatest country in the world. Thus England became the real and true love of our lives. Our confidence in her illimitable powers, and our utter disbelief in the possibility of any earthly Power vanquishing her, became a fixed idea which nothing could eradicate and no gloom dispel.[7]

There can be little doubt that this was the general view and that those officers, such as Sir William Butler, who had a more radical or "internationalist" outlook, were in a small minority. Butler tells us, in his autobiography, how the end of his career was blighted by his unorthodox opinions over South Africa.[8]

The more ambitious officers pushed their way into the many campaigns and field forces to win brevet promotions and make names for themselves; but it was not in the least a *studious* officer corps. Sir Hugh McCalmont, who was commissioned in 1865, writes that: "Soldiering was a less serious business in those days before the Franco-German War [1870] than it has come to be since"; but even in the eighteen-eighties it was felt at Staff College that "the Army generally remained averse to study." Major Hackett told Wood that "all he wanted was to be left alone, and not troubled with books." Perhaps this reluctance to study is best summed-up by Sir Neville Lyttelton, an Etonian who became "the first Chief of the General Staff."

*Henrietta Wood (left) and Julia Ann Matthews (Hook's daughters
by his first marriage), photographed in Birmingham c. 1900.
(Courtesy, Mrs. June W. Dutton).*

Hook's only son, Raymond, photographed c. 1900 in coachman's dress. (Courtesy, Mr. Cecil Berrington.)

The building at Gorsley, Glos., which housed Christ Church School, attended by Hook's three children by his first marriage. (Photograph by Mr. Norman R. Hook, 2000.)

The Kilcot Inn, between Newent and Gorsley, which had a part in Hook family history.
(Photograph by Mr. Norman R. Hook, 2000.)

Describing his battalion of the Rifle Brigade in about 1868, he remarks: ". . . for too many of us [officers] soldiering was not a profession, only an occupation."[9]

"An occupation" calls for practical training, but this could be limited, even if thorough. Lyttelton describes how, in 1870, "we were under the command of a veteran of the old school; we hardly ever did anything outside the barrack square, but at marching past, firing exercise and bayonet drill we were A.1." A couple of years later, when some manoeuvres were held, "though there were many shortcomings there were traces of a new order of things.[10]

This leads to the question of *how* training was conducted, particularly in the eighteen-seventies, when Hook was serving. Fortescue, the historian of the Army, in discussing how "the entire military system had been turned upside-down" after the Crimean War, says: "Two relics of the old system alone remained, long service for soldiers and purchase for officers. The former was swept away in 1870, the latter in 1871." While Fortescue seems to regret this "knell of the old British Army," he sees some gains: "Gradually, too, the training of the men, which under the old order had been chiefly the business of the adjutant, was transferred to the captains and subalterns of each company . . ."[11] The old system, as he found it in 1865, is denounced by Hallam Parr:

In peace-time officers were allowed to do but little work and were suffered to have no responsibility. In regiments (with very few exceptions) the work and responsibilities connected with the drill, discipline, feeding, and well-being of the men was almost entirely carried on by the Commanding Officer in connection with the Adjutant, the quartermaster, and the sergeant-major working through the various troop sergeant-majors or colour-sergeants. . . .

The teaching of the men was done by specialists. The Adjutant, assisted by the sergeant-major, taught the drill; the Musketry Instructor taught rifle-shooting, or rather saw that the regulation number of rounds were fired according to orders issued from the School of Musketry.

. . . it was often hard for a young officer joining, as he had little or no work to do, not to get into loafing, idle, if not disreputable ways.[12]

In 1872, Parr became adjutant of his battalion and tried to alter the system; but soon a new commanding officer arrived

who wished that every responsibility and initiative should be concentrated in the hands of the Colonel, the Adjutant, the

43

quartermaster, and the sergeant-major of the battalion, while the company officers were ignored, or had merely little tiresome bits of irresponsible work to do. No wonder in those days officers took but little interest in their work.[13]

When Sir William Robertson enlisted in 1877, on his way "From Private to Field-Marshal", he was trained under the adjutant system, which was quite popular, in one sense, as "the other officers were able to enjoy increased facilities for leave." By the time he was commissioned in 1888, "this system was rapidly passing away. Troop and squadron officers [he was a cavalryman] were now being made really responsible for the training and administration of their commands. . . ."[14] As Hook also enlisted in 1877, it seems likely that he, too, was trained under the old system and not by the officers of his company. Under those conditions, would he have "rarely seen" the officers who were "responsible" for him?

In January 1871, "A Staff-Sergeant" published an article on "How to Make the Army Popular" and says of relations between officers and men:

> A soldier is only brought in contact with his superiors officially. He sees his commanding officer on parade; his company officers visit his room, too often to find fault with some very trifling irregularity. If he has some temporary ailment and goes to hospital, he sees the surgeon, who possibly tells him there is little wrong with him. On Sunday he is marched to church, and, in all probability, hears a regimental sermon, as it is called, wherein the chaplain sets forth the heinousness of the slightest neglect of the Queens Regulations . . . There are many officers who do take a personal interest in their men, and study their welfare; but they are the exception, not the rule.[15]

Horace Wyndham was a "toff" who enlisted in 1890, for obscure family reasons, and became a sergeant before "buying himself out." His entry in *Who's Who* lists many publications, including *The Queen's Service*, an amusing and instructive book about his experiences "in the British Infantry at Home and Abroad." On his appointment as lance-corporal, he was taken before his company commander:

> I very much doubt if Captain Semple knew my name at the time, or as far as that went, those of half his Company. As officers are so constantly on leave, and, when doing duty, see so little of their men, this was not unnatural. Unless a man is continually distinguishing himself by being brought before him as a prisoner, a Company officer seems to find great difficulty in remembering one from another. His opportunities for really

44

knowing them are not many. He commands a Company on parade, where the men are simply referred to by the numbers which they happen to be temporarily occupying in the ranks, and occasionally goes round a barrack-room.[16]

If these "voices from the ranks" seem biased, we can turn again to Sir William Robertson, looking back on his "early days":

> In not a few regiments his officers saw little or nothing of him [the soldier] except when on parade . . .; they showed no interest in his personal concerns, and sometimes did not even know his name, although he might have been under their command for weeks. It was realised by some inspecting officers that this state of affairs was not what it should be, from the professional standpoint alone, and I have heard the most absurd replies given when troop officers have been asked to tell them a man's name, or what length of service he had. The great thing was to give an answer of some sort and give it quickly, whether it might be the right one or not.[17]

It may well be that many men thought little about this remoteness of their officers, accepting that it was part of the system. Hallam Parr tells how

> On the dreary long parades under the Adjutant, when I was dreaming of the last pretty face, or of the last gallop with the hounds, Holt or O'Sullivan [both old soldiers] would delicately rouse me to a sense of responsibilities by gently nudging me, whispering, "Change your flank, sir."[18]

Penn Symons, one of the historians of the 24th Regiment, wrote of Michael Minehan, who was at the defence of Rorke's Drift: "Minehan was a great pal of mine; he was right-hand man, front rank of B Company, who knew his drill well and had often kept me straight."[19]

Perhaps there are glimpses in these two stories of "the bond of union . . . between officers and men" which Fortescue strongly believed to have existed in both the Old and the New Army. He must certainly be right in saying that "work in the field . . . always draws all ranks nearer to each other."[20] On active service, "officers had to rough it quite as much as the men, with the exception of a few more luxuries to eat and drink."[21] They were also expected to lead by personal example. Sir William Butler, writing about the Gordon Relief Expedition of 1885, says almost casually: "Our officers, mounted and on foot, did not dismount nor take cover, for at that date it had not become the order or the habit to do so."[22] Here was the supreme test. In the natural order of things, regimental officers would make some tactical mistakes or misjudgements; but if their courage failed, or if they let their men down in battle, they knew that, at best, there would be persistent mutterings against them and that, at worst, their careers would be ended.

So much for the officers: now for the men.

2.

Henry Hook (No. 1373) "was enlisted at Monmouth for the 25th. Brigade on the 13th. March 1877."[23]

Most recruits seem to have had a drink or two with the recruiting sergeant in the local pub, and a talk with him about service life, before accepting the legendary shilling. There were two further stages before a civilian became a soldier: medical examination and swearing in (called "attestation"). A man could "change his mind after receiving the shilling, and escape the service by paying £1, called 'smart money', before being attested." To allow for "a change of mind", there was an interval of at least twenty-four hours between taking the shilling and attestation.[24]

As Hook evidently had no "second thoughts", he was brought before a magistrate, probably with some other recruits, took the oath of allegiance and "kissed the book." (The future Socialist writer, Robert Blatchford, remembered kissing "a greasy Prayer-book tied with string" when he enlisted!) Hook joined for "short service"—six years with the Colours and six in the Reserve—the only alternative at that time being twelve years of Army service. In attesting, he had to answer a standard set of twenty questions, the sixth of which was: "Are you married?" The "Proceedings on Attestation" in his case have never come to light, but it seems probable that he answered "No." There is an equal probability that he admitted to the recruiting sergeant that he was married and was advised to say that he was single, if he really wanted to enlist.[25]

The Army's attitude to married soldiers was strictly utilitarian. It was an Army nearly all of whose regiments spent long years in India or in the colonies, often on active service and in unhealthy climates. Such duties demanded single men—or at least men who were prepared to *attest* that they were single. A few men in each battalion were given permission to marry by their colonel. The wives of these soldiers were said to be "on the strength" and they, and any children, were given married accommodation with their husbands and such services as free medical attention. There was an element of utilitarianism even in these "official" marriages, as the wives were paid to act as laundresses for the officers and men. No other wives had any official standing and no provision was made for them or for their children. A soldier had the usual obligation to maintain his wife and children, and he could make an allowance to his family through stoppages from his pay. Yet it was extraordinarily difficult for a wife who was not getting a voluntary allowance to *enforce* her rights at law, and once her husband was ordered overseas, this difficulty became a practical impossibility. If a husband attested that he was single; changed his name (as from Alfred Hook to Henry Hook); and was moved by the Army away from his home town or county, the chances of his wife being able to gain a maintenance allowance were extremely remote. (And the Army never permitted a compulsory allowance of more than 3d. a day from the pay of a private.) There is a legend that Hook made some sort of allowance to his family before he was posted abroad, when it stopped, but there is no real evidence on this point.[26]

His physical description was:- Height: 5ft. 6¼ in.; Complexion: "fresh"; Eyes: "blue"; Hair: "brown". He gave his age as "23 8/12 Years"; but *should* have given it as 26 years and 7 months. The age which he had given on enrolment in the Militia suggested that he was born in February 1850; but he told the recruiting authorities, in effect, that he was born in August 1853. The Army at that time was recruiting men between the ages of eighteen and twenty-five but it made no attempt to check the age of any likely recruit.[27] Agricultural labourers had always been esteemed, for not altogether flattering reasons given by Fortescue:

> They were not, as a rule, so keen-witted as those drawn from the towns, but they were, generally speaking, strong, healthy, docile, steady, stable and trustworthy, and blessed moreover with good eyesight and alert observation.[28]

It seems probable that either Hook knew that he was over-age or that the helpful recruiting sergeant—who had a financial interest in the outcome—advised him to be under twenty-five.

So Hook was enlisted. He could not have guessed it but (to use one of General Gordon's expressions) he was "boarding the tram of the world." The tram was to take Recruit Hook to an entry in *Who's Who*.

47

"Our first lesson in the Depot had been of our apartness from life." This had been the experience of T.E. Lawrence, when he enlisted in 1922, but it would have applied with greater force to a recruit in 1877. The overwhelming impression of "apartness", once a recruit had passed through the barrack gates, could be put another way: "Civilians may have two lives, the soldier has one; away from his work, the worker is a private person; but the soldier is a soldier day and night."[29]

The gates through which Hook would have passed were at the depot of the 25th Brigade. Under the Localisation Act of 1873

> all the infantry battalions were affiliated in pairs, and localized for the purposes of recruiting and training, in brigade areas, . . . normally in each double-battalion regiment, one battalion should be abroad and one at home. The latter would supply the former with drafts of trained men until it relieved its sister battalion overseas. The Militia and auxiliaries were included in the localization scheme in that together with the two line battalions they comprised the "brigade", and were attached to the same headquarters, called the "brigade depot."[30]

The area of the 25th Brigade comprised the counties of Cardigan, Radnor, Brecon and Monmouth, and its depot was at Brecon, in mid-Wales. The two line battalions of the brigade were the 1st and 2nd Battalions of the 24th Regiment: the 1/24th was then in South Africa and the 2/24th was at Dover Citadel. Before Hook and other recruits to the brigade were assigned to one of these battalions, they were sent to the depot for training. The barracks at Brecon were, and still are, on the outskirts of the town, on the main road to Abergavenny, and they now house the regimental museum.[31]

The recruits would have been taken first to their barrack-room and introduced to the corporal in charge. J.E. Acland-Troyte—an Oxford graduate who enlisted in 1873 and wrote of his experiences in *Through the Ranks to a Commission*—describes the room into which he was shown:

> [It was] very lofty and well ventilated, three large windows and a good fireplace. Barrack-rooms are all furnished much alike. . . . The walls were whitewashed, and the floor bare boards; there were tables in the centre, sufficient for all the occupants of the room to sit down to at once, and wooden forms to correspond. Generally a hanging shelf over the table, on which are kept all the plates and basins, one of each being provided

for each man in the room. The iron bedsteads are arranged all round, the heads against the wall, and they are made in two parts, so that during the day one half can be run in or closed up under the other, thus giving much more free space to move about in. The mattress is rolled up, pillow inside, and kept fastened with a strap, the two blankets and two sheets folded up very neatly, and placed on top of the rolled mattress, which is stood against the head of the bed, occupying about half of the bedstead when closed up. The remaining half (on which the rug or counterpane is laid) serves for the men to sit on. As a rule there is a space of about three or four feet between the bedsteads, and a man next a window is generally best off.

All round the rooms, over the heads of the beds, are iron shelves, and hooks just below, each man having that part of the shelves immediately over his own cot. All the soldiers' worldly possessions are kept on these shelves, and have to be arranged with scrupulous tidiness. The knapsack and other accoutrements are put on the hooks, and the rifle generally stands in a little place made for it close to the head of the bed. Very often if a man has near his cot a piece of spare wall he will hang up pictures or photographs, which gives the room a more comfortable appearance, and, provided it is done tidily, it is never objected to. The other articles of common property in the room are a hair broom, mop, long-handled scrubber (for cleaning the wood floors), a hand scrubbing brush (for cleaning tables and forms) two tin dishes, on which the dinner is brought in, two tin pails, two wooden buckets, and a big iron coal box, also two coal trays, *i.e.* square wooden boxes used for carrying coal about in, but generally kept in the room for throwing any litter into.[32]

Sir William Robertson makes some more down-to-earth remarks:

The brown bed-blankets were seldom or ever washed; clean sheets were issued once a month; and clean straw for the mattresses once every three months. Besides the beds, the only other furniture consisted of four benches and two deal tables. The men polished their boots on the former, and the latter were used for cleaning the remaining articles of kit as well as for dining-tables. Tablecloths there were none, and plates and basins (paid for by the men) were the only crockery, the basin being used in turn as a coffee-cup, tea-cup, beer-mug, soup-plate, shaving-mug, and receptacle for pipe-clay with which to clean gloves and belts.[33]

"A Staff-Sergeant" remembered with distaste "an offensive wooden tub [for urine] brought into the rooms at night, in defiance at once of health and decency." Yet it would be unfair to end on this note, as there is no doubt much truth in Correlli Barnett's caption to the photograph of a barrack-room in 1875: "Austere though it was, it was a better lodging than many recruits had ever known in their lives."[34]

These descriptions show that barrack-rooms then served as dining-rooms, as well as bedrooms and living quarters. "The regulation meals were coffee and bread for breakfast; meat and potatoes for dinner, with soup or pudding once or twice a week; tea and bread for tea. If a man wished to have supper . . . he had to purchase it from the barrack hawkers or canteen."[35] Horace Wyndham's first meal in barracks was one o'clock dinner, which he recalls with fastidious horror:

Presently the shrill notes of a bugle reached our ears. "There goes the cook-house; come and give us a hand, some of you," cried one of the men. . . .

About ten minutes later this man [the orderly-man of the day], with a couple of assistants, reappeared, bearing with them some baked beef in a dish, and a tin-full of boiled potatoes. This was placed on a table, and while some one arranged a plate for each man in the room the remainder cut up the meat and shared the potatoes.

According to barrack-room custom, meat is not cut into slices, it is hacked into lumps. Again, instead of placing a moderate portion by way of a first helping on each plate, every particle is cut from the bone and served out as far as it will go. . . . The same quaint system is in force with regard to the vegetables, or any other extra that may be provided. A lump of coarse salt is raked out of the dust on the shelf overhead, and a basin containing mustard is added. The Orderly-man inspects the various portions in order to satisfy himself that they are all of approximately the same size. When he is satisfied on this point, he gives the order "Take 'em away," and all hands promptly seize the plates which please them most, and, sitting down to the table, fall to with a vengeance. . . .

I shall never forget the juggling feats that they performed with their knives, or the manner in which they would take lumps of meat from their plates, and for greater convenience cut them up on the bare table. Their fingers, too, in many instances played so important a part in this operation that knives and forks were rendered almost superfluous. . . .

Soon after the commencement of dinner the door was thrown open by a Corporal, who shouted " 'Tchun!" in so fierce a tone that I quite thought that something alarming was going to occur. It was, however, simply his manner of notifying the impending approach of the Orderly-officer. Following

closely behind him came this personage.
"Any complaints?" he inquired interrogatively.
"None, Sir," replied the Orderly-man.[36]

Wyndham's account of his first breakfast brings out a curious feature of the regulations:

> A tin pail-full of coffee and a pound of bread per man, with a small allowance of butter, formed the menu. The coffee and butter were provided by means of a compulsory stoppage of threepence per diem, which is made from each man's pay . . . This deduction has also to supply tea, sugar, salt, potatoes, flour, &c., as none of these articles are included under the heading of "free rations."[37]

The daily "free rations" consisted only of "¾ lb. beef or mutton, reckoned before cooking, and with bone, and 1 lb. of bread." Everything else was called "groceries" and recruiting placards—without defining "groceries"—stated that such items had "to be paid for by the soldier." Still, Wyndham and Acland-Troyte—both used to upper-class meals—commend the "excellent quality" of the Army's bread, which Wyndham thought was "in all probability, vastly superior to that which he [the average recruit] has been in the habit of receiving prior to his enlistment."[38] Acland-Troyte also found the meat ration to be "decidedly good" but "it only comes to about twelve mouthfuls a day" and (addressing his upper-class readers) he adds: "I suppose people of our class eat a great deal more meat than the lower classes." He makes another "class" point:

> Soldiers have a curious habit of never drinking anything at dinner. They often get a pint of beer before dinner, and all except the abstainers pay a visit to the canteen directly afterwards; but they apparently have no wish to drink until the eating part of the business is all over. [And he observed that] The young recruits generally eat all they can get hold of; but the older men don't really want as much as they can get.[39]

On the same day as his arrival at the depot, or perhaps a few days later, the recruit was taken to the Quartermaster's stores to be fitted with his uniform and supplied with the articles of kit which the Army called "necessaries." Acland-Troyte describes this ritual:

> The kit is given to the soldier free of expense at first; but he must keep it up in a proper state of efficiency for himself, with the exception of the cloth clothes and boots, and certain articles of equipment . . . viz. rifle, knapsack, waist-belts, etc., gaiters,

greatcoat, and chako [later, helmet]. If these are damaged or worn out before the proper time, the soldier will have to pay for them, otherwise they are no expense. In 1873 the regulation about cloth clothes was three pairs of trousers in two years (one pair every year, and an extra pair alternate years), and the tunics—a cloth tunic every two years, and a serge tunic every year. If these are not kept tidy and clean a man will be ordered to buy new ones. . . . The rest of the "necessaries" are (in addition, *i.e.*, to the two pairs of boots and cloth clothes and articles of equipment mentioned above), two coarse flannel shirts, three pairs of thick socks, a pair of braces, a pair of worsted gloves, glengarry cap, comb, razor and shaving-brush, knife, fork, spoon, a brass button stick and polishing-brush (used for cleaning buttons, badges, etc.), box of blacking, two boot brushes, a clothes brush, a small sponge for use with pipeclay, and a Bible and Prayer-Book . . . a tin canteen, which is carried on the knapsack, and on service is used for eating or drinking out of, and the top or lid is fitted with a folding handle, so that it can be used for cooking purposes . . . [and] a rough canvas bag. . . .

I was very much surprised on first joining to see how much cleaning and polishing and pipeclay, etc., was necessary. Men seemed always at it . . . [and] they always call it "soldiering."[40]

This is a rather bland account, as Wyndham remarks that, while the Army did replace boots and items of uniform the soldier's

first supply of brushes, shirts, socks, towels, &c., had . . . to last him for the whole of his service. . . . As a matter of fact, the most economical soldier is from time to time called upon to purchase fresh supplies of these articles, while the careless and untidy are seldom out of the Quarter-master's books for several of these items. . . .

The boots, invariably known as "ammunitions", are, as far as material goes, of good quality, but they are terrible to march in. They are enormously heavy, and the soles are so plentifully studded with hob-nails that they seem to be almost armour-plated.[41]

Perhaps even before his visit to the stores, the recruit would have begun his training. "Until he has passed his recruits' drill he does no guard duty nor fatigue work, but is kept steady at squad drill, etc., school, and gymnasium." A typical day might be:

Turn out of bed at 6, and, after a short wash and making up bed, parade, 6.30-7.30; breakfast at 7.45; then sit round table and peel potatoes, etc., for dinner; time for general polishing

up of person and clothes; parade, 9.30, for an hour; and . . .
another parade about 11.30; dinner, 12.45: parade, 2.30; tea,
4.30; . . . besides these hours of drill, recruits must go to school
[after the afternoon parade] until they can pass an examination
in reading, writing, and the four simple rules of arithmetic.[42]

Although he had served in the Volunteers, Acland-Troyte

found the manipulation of the rifle harder than I expected,
such absolute precision has to be acquired, and the "time" of
each motion of the rifle has to be learnt by heart, so to speak;
every man in the regiment must know, without thinking or
watching, the exact time of working, so that every movement
of the hand or arm may be done (begun and finished) together.[43]

It was only after they had been "dismissed from recruits' drill" that
soldiers were "handed over to the sergeant-instructor in musketry to
be taught to shoot."[44]

From tea until the roll was called at 9.30 p.m., the recruits were
left to their own devices but they had to spend a lot of time in learning
to clean their kit. "Lights out" was sounded at 10.15 and the gas-jets
were then extinguished to mark the end of the official day. On
Sundays, although recruit training was suspended, the bugle rang out
"at frequent intervals from morning till night": there was no respite
from this insistent feature of Army life.[45]

After a week, the recruits would receive their first pay. John
Fraser—who, when unemployed, enlisted during the same year as
Hook—says of a soldier's pay:

The pay of a private soldier was one shilling a day, paid weekly,
with a monthly final settlement. Compulsory deductions
amounted to threepence for food, . . . halfpenny a day for
washing shirt, towel, and socks once a week; also threepence
for hair-cutting by the company barber, one of the men, . . .
As the kit issued on joining from the Quartermaster's stores
needed renewing, the necessary articles were supplied from
the same source but on payment. "Barrack damages" too, might
amount to fourpence or sixpence a month. At the most a man
would get a pound net each month. Out of that sum had to
come any wants, amusements, expenses, or what not. But it
was far more money than I, for one, and probably most of us,
had ever had at our own disposal.[46]

There was also "deferred pay" of 2d. a day, paid in a lump sum
after a man had left the Army or joined the Reserve. At the end of
recruit training, some men could earn "extra duty pay"; and, after

two or three years, many began to draw "Good Conduct Pay." Despite all the stoppages, Acland-Troyte was convinced that "great numbers of soldiers do save." He compared the position, "as regards money, of soldiers and civilians" and summed-up the advantages of a soldier's life:

> The free ration of bread and meat, comfortable lodgings also free, boots and cloth clothes every year, education if necessary, and a good hospital. 2dly, The certainty of all the above; 3dly, As a private, plenty of spare time; 4thly, A holiday or furlough of one month a year, with full pay all the time, and an extra sixpence a day in lieu of the free ration.[47]

Robert Blatchford, who enlisted in London and trained at Cowes, says that

> They kept us as recruits pretty busy. . . . But we were young, and the air was good. And the gymnastics, the drilling, and regular hours and plain food began to tell. In a few weeks we were straight and smart, and stood and moved lightly. In the bronzed, alert, upright young soldiers no one could have recognised the mob of assorted ragamuffins who had . . . [enlisted with him].[48]

This description would apply, in some respects, more to townsmen than to countrymen, but it brings out what the Army intended to achieve by keeping the recruits "pretty busy." Training usually lasted for three months but men who had served in the Militia or the Volunteers had an advantage and could be "passed by the adjutant" before the three months was up. It seems that Hook did only two months at the Depot: on the 11th of May, he was posted to Dover, to join the 2nd Battalion of the 24th Regiment.[49]

4.

The 24th was an ancient regiment, having been formed in March 1689 for service in Ireland. It missed the Battle of the Boyne but was at the siege of Limerick. The Duke of Marlborough was its Colonel for two years and it served under him at Blenheim, Ramillies and Malplaquet. A less glorious episode was the regiment's surrender at Saratoga during the War of American Independence. The sphinx which figured so prominently in the regimental badge was gained in the Egyptian campaign against Napoleon in 1801. A second battalion was formed during the Napoleonic Wars and called "the Peninsular

Second Battalion." After the fall of Napoleon, the 24th reverted to one battalion, which was in India from 1846 to 1861. During these years, at Chillianwallah, "one half of the men and two-thirds of the officers were killed or wounded."[50]

A new second battalion was raised in June 1858 and Hook's Army career was spent in this unit. On Christmas Day of the following year, when the battalion was at Aldershot, a canteen quarrel broke out with men of the Tower Hamlets Militia. It turned into a serious affray which subsequently brought the Duke of Cambridge to the scene. The Commander-in-Chief told the battalion that he would like to send it to hell but would send it to Mauritius, instead! Once out of the country, the 2/24th remained abroad for thirteen years.[51]

Since 1782, the 24th Regiment had had the county title of "2nd Warwickshire", and throughout Hook's service the regimental march was "The Warwickshire Lads."[52] The Localisation Act of 1873 had given it a depot in Wales and four Welsh counties as a recruiting area. When, in July 1881, the regiment became "The South Wales Borderers", its increasing "Welshness" was confirmed. This sequence of events explains the extraordinary confusion over whether the regiment was Welsh or English, and whether Rorke's Drift was held by Welshmen or Englishmen. The facts had become so obscured by 1968 that Sir Brian Horrocks could describe Rorke's Drift as "a typically staunch Welsh performance."[53] Popular "history" has reinforced this impression. For instance, in David Rattray's lectures on the Zulu War, Hook is given a Welsh accent, although he would have spoken in the soft and slow tones of the Gloucestershire countryside.[54]

The late Norman Holme published a table showing the "Nationality of the Defenders of Rorke's Drift Serving in the 24th Regiment" which should set all doubts at rest. Of the 122 members of the regiment present, there were 49 from England; 32 from Wales; 16 from Ireland; 3 from overseas; 1 from Scotland; and 21 of unknown origin.[55] Most of the defenders belonged to "B" Company, 2/24th, the company to which Hook was assigned. The surviving records of the company's N.C.O.s and men are very variable in their detail. As published by Holme, the records of some (particularly the V.C.-winners) fill a closely-printed page while others extend only to a few lines. Keeping in mind the incompleteness of these records, it is still possible to compose a "profile" of "B" Company, as it was in Hook's time, which will give a fairly accurate impression of what it was like to be part of the company.[56]

The company commander when Hook joined, and until the autumn of 1878, was Captain Alfred Godwin-Austen. He came from a notable family. His grandfather, a general; his father, a geologist;

and his eldest brother, a soldier and surveyor, all have entries in the *Dictionary of National Biography*. The elder brother had served in the 24th before transferring to the Indian Army; and a younger brother, Frederick, was a subaltern in the 2nd Battalion. Alfred Godwin-Austen was born in 1844 and had been commissioned from Sandhurst, by purchase, in 1862. In 1875, he transferred to the 24th as a captain. He was a bachelor, who appears to have been one of the less ambitious members of his family.[57]

There was a corporal in another company who became probably the most famous N.C.O. in the regiment's history. This was Frank Bourne, the son of a Surrey farmer, who had enlisted in 1872, at seventeen, apparently against his father's wishes. It was not until the 2/24th reached South Africa that Bourne—during April 1878—rose three grades to become colour-sergeant of "B", the equivalent of the present-day company sergeant-major.[58] (Colour sergeants wore above their chevrons an elaborate device of a crown and two flags and were "commonly known" in their companies as "the Flag."[59]) Bourne was the very best type of N.C.O. and he went unfalteringly on to a commission. Few N.C.O.s of those days were that steady. There was a considerable number of "reductions to the ranks" and then re-promotions amongst a particular class of men, who were seen to have the necessary qualities for corporals and sergeants. By contrast, many private soldiers remained privates, lacking either ambition or the necessary education.

Like the 2/24th as a whole, "B" Company was mainly composed of young soldiers, enlisted for short service. Of the ninety-two men whose enlistment dates are known, only fifteen were "old soldiers", in their second enlistments; while nearly half had joined during 1877. The ages of sixty-eight are given: sixteen were older than Hook but twenty-nine were five years or more younger than him. Six men were known to be married, two of them with a wife "on the strength." There was a good proportion of former Militiamen (nineteen are recorded) and eight of these had served in the R.M.M. By current standards, only two of the men could be described as tall—they were 5 ft. 10¼ in.—and most were between 5 ft. 4 in. and 5 ft. 6 in., making Hook of good average height. Soldiers at that time were expected to keep their hair neat, though not particularly short, but had to grow moustaches.

On attesting, a recruit was asked "What is your Trade or Calling?": he was *not* asked whether he was actually employed. There are thus no figures to show whether unemployment *was* "the principal factor" in enlistment; but official enquiries during the second half of the century "continued to record the view that the pressure of necessity drove men into the army."[60] The late Frank Emery thought that "many were forced to enlist by the severe economic recession through which Britain was passing in the 1870s, and quite a few of them could write a decent letter."[61] For "B" Company, the "trades" of fifty-five men are known, of which thirty were town or agricultural labourers. Of the rest, only three would have been described as "black-coated" workers; they had been clerks. There was a miscellany of other occupations: three grooms, three porters, two colliers; and other jobs with only one representative, ranging from a "compositor" (a skilled man) to a chimney sweep. These figures correspond well with national statistics for 1877, a year in which 62% of those enlisting were labourers; 28.5% were artisans or mechanics (skilled men); and only 6.9% were clerks or shopmen ("black-coated" workers).[62] The company—like the Army as a whole—can be seen to be overwhelmingly working class and very largely drawn from the *unskilled* working class. This is *not* to say—returning to Colonel Murray's "challenge"—that these men came from "the least respectable sections of the working class." There was a "contemporary gulf" between "the 'rough' and the 'respectable' poor", the characteristics of the "roughs" being "swearing, cruelty, drunkenness, vulgarity and violence." Undoubtedly there had been many of the "rough poor" in the "Old Army", and it was one of the aims of "short service" to encourage the enlistment of a better type of recruit. Lyttelton recalls that, during the eighteen-sixties, commanding officers had been allowed "to dismiss really bad characters, and we got rid of a lot." Then, in 1870, "a very good batch of recruits joined us." A few years later, Acland-Troyte found that "in every regiment there are some men who are distinctly bad characters of the lowest type, mere 'gaol-birds' . . . but it is not generally known how entirely these men are left to themselves, and avoided by all respectable soldiers."[63]

The surviving records show that there were four "bad characters" in "B" Company (there may, of course, have been a few more) and that one of these seems to have been of that "lowest type" who gave the Army a bad name. This man—who enlisted in 1877, at eighteen—was discharged into a lunatic asylum with the remarks: "Served for 4 years, including 2 years in South Africa. Character bad and dirty. . . . Has appeared in the defaulter book on ten occasions; twice convicted by court martial."[64] In this, as in the other three cases, the main difficulty was "intemperance." Drunkenness, on or off duty, accounted for nearly half of the "crimes"—as the Army called offences of all kinds—recorded against the men of "B" Company. There were three desertions; four cases of insubordination; five "absences"; and one instance of "disgraceful conduct" (perhaps sodomy) for which the offender was sent to prison in Natal. All the other recorded "crimes"—thirty in all—were such peculiarly military offences as "losing a pair of boots" or being "In bed at 7.00 a.m."

In short, it hardly seems to have been a very disorderly company, and this is to some extent confirmed by the number of men who had "good conduct badges" (reverse chevrons worn at the bottom of the sleeve). One badge was awarded after two years without any *serious* fault and brought a penny a day in extra pay; a second could be earned after five years, with twopence a day extra; and so on, up to six. It was a peculiar system, as men could lose badges for a "crime"; regain one or more; lose them again and regain them once more, their pay going up or down accordingly. The system is demonstrated by the sixty men of "B" Company for whom full records survive: forty-six were awarded one or more badges but twenty-four of them lost badges at one time or another. Perhaps it was rather too easy to gain and regain these badges but the authorities probably thought that their award, and the extra pay, were good for morale.[65]

The books mentioned in Murray's "challenge" are said to "tell us . . . that drunkenness and venereal disease were endemic" in the ranks. They were both serious, but gradually diminishing, problems; but the first was a disciplinary matter, usually punished by a fine, while the second carried no apparent stigma. A soldier who contracted the disease was admitted to hospital and given "mercury treatment" but his service "character" was not affected. In the Army at home, "never less than one man in ten, and for most of the period [1859-99] one in five or an even higher proportion, underwent treatment each year."[66] Four men in "B" Company, all privates, are known to have been treated. One of them (treated twice) emerged with a character of "fair, habits intemperate"; another ("Found to be suffering from Venereal Disease of the Heart. Discharged as unfit for further service") was given a character of "temperate and steady"; a third (several times treated for "Primary Syphilis") was discharged with a character of: "Conduct temperate, good." The fourth man's "character" is missing.[67] Even allowing for the incomplete records, it seems that "B" Company was no worse in this respect than the Army as a whole: perhaps it was better.

Lastly, comes the question of literacy. Frank Emery said: "I would argue that at least half of the N.C.O.s and private soldiers serving in Zululand [in 1879] were capable of scribbling some kind of letter from that campaign."[68] It would not have been at all shameful to have been amongst the other half, as not until 1870 did the state set up education authorities and another ten years passed before elementary schooling was made compulsory. Standards could hardly be much higher in the army than in society at large; though, curiously enough, the military authorities had been making efforts to educate soldiers and their dependants for over a century before the state took the education of its citizens in hand. Regimental schools had been run unofficially until 1811, when all commanding officers were ordered to establish schools "for the instruction of young soldiers and the children of soldiers." The instruction of these "young soldiers" was at the same time made rather haphazard by a judge's ruling that: "It is no part of the military duty to attend a school, and to learn to read and write." Voluntary instruction was therefore resorted to until after the Crimean War, when the Articles of War were amended to make it an offence "for a soldier to absent himself from school, *if ordered to attend.*"[69]

By the time of Hook's enlistment, all recruits had to attend an Army school for five hours a week, in the hope that they would gain the fourth-class certificate of education. The first-class certificate made its holder eligible for a commission; the second and third classes were necessary for promotion to sergeant and corporal, respectively; but the fourth class merely relieved its holder from any further attendance at school. For the fourth-class certificate, a soldier had "to copy a few lines of easy words and to do a few simple sums"; but many men "were unable or perhaps unwilling to pass the examination for this certificate." The official statistics for the Army in 1877 show that 0.6% of the men held the first-class certificate; that 12.1% had the second class; 13.6%, the third class; and 22.4%, the fourth class. The remaining 51.3% had no certificate.[70] It follows that, in this year of Hook's enlistment, nearly three-quarters of all men in the ranks were ineligible for any kind of promotion (except to lance-corporal, which was technically only an appointment). Yet such statistics are relative; the prospects of advancement for unskilled workers in civil life were probably worse; and few of them, in 1877, would have done any better in the examination room.

In "B" Company, the records show that, during their careers, ten men gained a second-class certificate; five, a third class; and fifteen, a fourth class. The incompleteness of the records may do the company an injustice; and once it went on active service, early in 1878, its education would have been in abeyance.

5.

The 2/24th had a change of C.O. a few weeks after Hook joined, when Lieutenant-Colonel Henry J. Degacher assumed command. He was born in France in 1835 and pronounced his name as D'gahsher. He had served briefly in the Crimea as a young officer (in the 16th Foot) and had recently been in South Africa as second-in-command of the 1/24th.[71] A look through the list of Degacher's officers shows many names now familiar only to close students of the regiment. Two of the subalterns became exceptions: Bromhead for Rorke's Drift; and Penn Symons for his historical work and for his death, as a lieutenant-general, in the first days of the Boer War. Churchill, who had met him in India, wrote: "So Sir Penn Symons is killed! Well, no one would have laid down his life more gladly in such a cause [a sentiment very resonant of that time] . . . Everyone talked of Symons, of his energy, of his jokes, of his enthusiasm." And Churchill remarked on how "intensely popular" Symons had been with "the private soldiers."[72]

The battalion had been at Dover since 1875 but on the 21st of June 1877, it moved to Chatham. This large and important naval and military station teemed with sailors, marines, engineers and infantrymen. It was the headquarters of the Royal Engineers and housed the School of Military Engineering, where newly-commissioned Engineer officers were given practical training. Lyttelton found Chatham "a bad place for young soldiers, no proper training ground and much temptation in the town." The troops had to be marched eight miles to Gravesend for musketry practice.[73]

During his brief time at Dover, Hook would already have settled into the normal routine of a battalion. Depots were "at best very dull places for recruits, where they have only a few non-commissioned officers and grumbling old soldiers to mix with": by contrast, life in a battalion was much more diverse, interesting and lively.[74] He would have become "a duty man", the subject of a caustic passage in Blatchford's "Life in the Army":

> Duty means work. It means guard, which implies eight hours of sentry-go; it means picket, a most dismal duty; and it means all kinds of "fatigues", from grass-picking on the gravel square to washing up dishes in the officers' or sergeants' mess.[75]

Acland-Troyte, the future officer, agreed that there was too much guard duty:

> . . . it is in some places the chief duty a soldier has to do; and one might almost say that a standing army is required purely to furnish guards and sentries, the time between whiles being kindly given to the commanding officer to teach his men what he can in the way of manoeuvring and shooting. This happily is not the case everywhere; to be continually going on guard is most depressing and monotonous, besides being in many places very fatiguing;
> . . . Any default or neglect is magnified into a serious crime by its having occurred "on guard", and the "guard-mounting

parade", or inspection of the men before they march off to their respective stations, is the severest test a soldier will have to undergo as to his powers of keeping his clothes and accoutrements clean and smart. A spot on his waist-belt, or a badly-folded coat, will without doubt entail on the offender "an extra guard," . . .[76]

By contrast, Acland-Troyte found piquet duty "very easy":

About a dozen men or so . . . with a corporal and sergeant, have to parade about dusk with their side-arms, but no rifles, and patrol the streets, going along very slowly, staying out about half-an-hour or an hour, then returning to barracks. Probably they will have to go out again just before "tattoo", returning shortly after the time that all men have to be at home. The duties of the piquet are simply to keep order in the streets, to take charge of any drunken soldiers, or any that may be out after proper hours. The duty lasts for twenty-four hours, and during that time the men composing the piquet are not allowed to leave the barracks except on duty (parades, etc.), so that they may be ready whenever wanted.[77]

Despite the guards, piquets and fatigues, there was still plenty of drill in a battalion's routine: three parades a day in Acland-Troyte's experience, beginning with "setting-up drill" at 6.30 a.m., which consisted of:

extension motions and running drill; about twenty minutes of the former and ten minutes of the latter. Old soldiers are excused the running, but this half-hour's work before breakfast is most useful although rather hard. An English soldier is supposed to be able to run a thousand yards without stopping, and to be able to do the bayonet exercise with vigour at the end of it.[78]

Even in civilian life, the concept of a "weekend" had not then been thought of; but military routine in garrison was different on Saturdays and Sundays. On Saturdays:

Instead of the usual 6.30 A.M. setting-up drill, the whole of the barrack-rooms were thoroughly scrubbed and washed, the shelves swept, windows cleaned, etc. Then at 10 A.M. the parade [in place of an hour's drill] was "kit inspection", at which every man had to show his regulation kit . . . The various articles are arranged, according to a prescribed form, on the soldier's bed; and every man, however employed, must lay out

61

his kit for inspection at least once a month. There is usually also on Saturdays the medical inspection, at which the men stand in a row, with their coats off, their shirt sleeves rolled right up, their boots and socks off, and their trousers turned up to the knees. The doctor then walks down the rank and sees that the men are clean, etc.[79]

On Sundays, there was no drill but church parades took its place. Acland-Troyte took a particular interest in this aspect of Army life. Church parades, he says

> are always in the morning, and men have a choice of three sorts of religious exercise—viz. the Church of England, commonly called the Church party, the Romanists, usually called the Catholics; and the Wesleyans or Chapel party. When a recruit enlists he is asked what he belongs to; and having made his choice, he has to stick to it. In my Regiment the Church party was the most popular. The band always played us to church and back, and very often led the singing, the brass instruments not being used in church. For some reason these church parades are very unpopular; whether men simply think it no use or waste of time I don't know, but they will always get off if they can. Yet, on the other hand, men continually go to an evening service, and I have often heard them say they like to go to church once on a Sunday. Whilst service is going on men almost always behave quietly and properly, but seldom kneel. They join pretty well in the singing and responses, and listen to the sermon quite sufficiently to discuss it afterwards, which seems a common practice.[80]

There is no record of what religious "party" Hook belonged to; but as he, and his parents and grandparents, were all married in Anglican churches, it seems likely that he was at least nominally "Church of England" and would have marched behind the band on Sunday mornings.

In his chapter "Sunday in Barracks", Wyndham describes the aftermath:

> When the service is over and the troops have marched back to barracks the remainder of the day is at their own disposal [unless they are on guard or piquet duty]. A considerable number devote it to visiting their friends in town, &c. On fine Sunday afternoons the streets in the vicinity of barracks are always more or less thronged by soldiers and their friends of the opposite sex, who muster in force outside the gates, waiting for the appearance of their swains at two P.M. prompt.

In the barracks there is not much going on. The Canteen is closed for the greater part of the afternoon, but makes up for it by doing a roaring trade at night.[81]

From an upper-class perspective, private soldiers in garrison were seen as having "plenty of spare time", with probably five evenings a week free from any duty. Wyndham thought that "the average soldier . . . accustomed to work from six in the morning until six in the dewy evening [before his enlistment] . . . enjoys a very much larger and more liberal amount of leisure than most people are aware of."[82] The authorities hoped rather piously that Army libraries and reading rooms would "encourage the soldiery to employ their leisure hours in a manner that shall combine amusement with the attainment of useful knowledge." All the main garrisons had libraries and these rooms were a boon to the better-educated soldiers: one of them remembers that "my particular retreat was the library, where I was almost certain to find peace to write my letters home." Many barracks had a recreation room, where "all sorts of games were provided—draughts, chess, backgammon, cards and two or three bagatelle tables."[83] Smoking was allowed in this kind of room and also in the canteen. After four-o'clock tea in the barrack-rooms:

> Most of the men went to the canteen which was open from six till nine. They sat there at tables and drank beer at fourpence a quart, and yarned with that ease and colour which is so often found in companies of men bound together by propinquity and similarity of occupation. Occasionally, after a good deal of good-natured chaff, one of us would go, half unwillingly, to the stage at the end of the room and sing a song. On the whole we behaved ourselves, for there was a sergeant or corporal always in the canteen to check irregularities of conduct.
> We weren't restricted to the canteen for our fun, for non-drinkers might try the coffee-bar for "door-steps", buns and tobacco, or we might ramble into the grocery bar to replenish our stock of oddments— pipe-clay, matches, soap, and blacking.[84]

Wyndham noticed that while "soldiers very seldom go out in the afternoon . . . by eight o'clock comparatively few men are left in the barrack-rooms." Those who were not in a canteen or recreation room were "out about the town"—in theatres, music-halls or "publics" (where the "publicans attract soldiers very much by engaging a singer or two, or perhaps a dancer, whose performances are held in the public room, and no charge for admission"). The idea of landlords "attracting" soldiers is at odds with the indelible impression created by the publican in Kipling's "Tommy", who exclaims: "We serve no

63

red-coats here." The "Staff-Sergeant" whose views have already been quoted wrote in 1870: "Soldiers of respectable parentage, when on leave or furlough, must wear plain clothes, if they wish to visit many persons or places where their presence in uniform would not be tolerated . . . . True, a great improvement has taken place in this respect since the Crimean war, but the old feeling of aversion to military men still exists." In *Sixty Years in Uniform*, which is a fine tribute to the Army of that time, John Fraser tells how his father would sooner have had him "out of work for the rest of my life" than become a soldier. There was clearly a very bad "folk memory" from an earlier time (though certainly from a time within living memory in 1877) and it was probably still assumed by many people that a red coat was merely a smart disguise for the "rough poor". Drink was undoubtedly a problem—as it always had been in standing armies—yet in garrison towns there must have been many publicans and music-hall owners who thrived on the soldiers' pennies, perhaps relying on piquets to keep order, if necessary.[85]

"The more quietly disposed men" could spend their evenings in a "soldiers' home." Whether it was a coincidence, or whether Chatham was an exceptionally "bad place", the "movement to create 'soldiers' homes' had been inaugurated at Chatham in 1861, when the Wesleyan Charles Henry Kelly opened a little club-house in a basement, with a reading room, a chapel, and minimal sleeping quarters." The impetus behind this movement was Christian philanthropy. "Should a fresh arrival enter the reading-room to have a look at the evening paper he will certainly be made welcome. He will also have a tract pressed upon him." If he stayed, he was likely to be invited into the chapel to join in what the worldly Wyndham calls "knee-drill." Although soldiers found these "homes" comfortable, and in some respects an agreeable change from barracks, no alcoholic drinks were served and "the most innocent description of popular literature was rigorously tabooed."[86]

The "sleeping quarters" at the Chatham home were no doubt intended for the use of soldiers who had a "pass" to be out of barracks for a night (or up to forty-eight hours). These passes were officially described as "an indulgence to be granted to soldiers of a good character" but they seem to have been issued quite readily. Barrack-rooms were noisy places—"men continually lost their tempers over mere trifles"—and "the more quietly disposed men" would have welcomed the chance to spend a night or two away.[87]

During the months of November to March, the Army was also generous in granting "furloughs", as leaves of absence were called. Men of good character, who were out of debt and had a complete kit, could apply for up to a month's leave and draw part of their pay in advance. In late January 1878, when the 2/24th was suddenly ordered to the Cape, "many of the men were on leave" and had to be sent "letters of recall."[88] It seems highly unlikely that Hook was amongst them or that he had applied for leave during that "furlough season." He would not have wanted to go back to Mount Pleasant, and a long stay at his parents' house in Monmouth might have seemed ill advised. Perhaps he would have wished to avoid Christmas in barracks by taking a short furlough but the round journey to Monmouth and back was about three hundred miles across country.

Christmas dinner was "a great institution in all regiments."

> The officers, or at any rate the captains, give money to their companies, and the canteen fund is also drawn on, so that a substantial repast may be provided; wine and beer are on the table, and the rooms decorated with the most artistic taste. At dinner time the captains and their subs. [subalterns] visit their own companies, and go through the ceremony of drinking a glass of wine with their men, the officers' health being given in an appropriate speech, by some man who is selected by his comrades as having the necessary power of eloquence. The unfortunate Colonel, who goes all through the barracks, has to submit to eight or ten speeches, ...
>
> Dinner over, the majority of the men settle down to enjoy themselves in any way they like, and are not interfered with at all by the non-commissioned officers. If they like to drink too much they can do so, ...[89]

Wyndham says that he left his first Christmas dinner in the Army "about the time that beer as a substitute for gravy was being poured over the goose, and sought relaxation in the town." Some colour-sergeants tried to prevent "very open breaches of discipline" by sending in a couple of barrels of beer to the men of their companies and then locking the barrack-room doors! There was no Boxing Day holiday and men who had been brought in by the piquets for celebrating too well in the town would appear at the orderly room in the morning to face a colonel less benign than he had been the day before.[90]

Christmas Day interrupted another feature of life during the winter months: "route-marching." The idea was "to accustom the troops to carrying their packs, as they would have to do constantly on active service." The eight companies of a battalion would parade in mid-morning "in full marching order", including rifles, and tramp out along the roads near its garrison "for five or six miles and home again, with a rest or two on the way." There were two or three marches a week, "in all sorts of weather", and the troops "had to keep strictly in the ranks the whole time." In Acland-Troyte's regiment, "plain marching out" was varied by days in which, after marching a few miles, the men were "posted as the sentries or outposts of an imaginary army."[91]

The theme of preparation for active service brings us back to Murray's "challenge" and to the elements which moulded batches of working men into reliable, and on occasions heroic, soldiers. There was the "apartness" of Army life, inducing that "sense of true comradeship" which Lord Wavell thought was "the supreme gift of the military life"[92]; the discipline and ordered routine; the training, rigorous if rather narrow; and, particularly in the field, the personal example of the officers. There were the barrack-room "lessons" appreciated by Wyndham: "The barrack-room is undoubtedly a rough school, but it is a thorough one, and lessons of self-control and self-reliance are to be learned there which will everywhere prove invaluable."[93]

Colonel Murray himself brings out the importance of the "regimental spirit", which he says is "rarely defined." No doubt it had a good deal to do with the fact that a regiment was a substitute for "home life", its incidents, experiences and preoccupations becoming those of each individual soldier. The workings of this "spirit" can be glimpsed in a Battalion Order issued to the 2/24th at Pietermaritzburg on the 30th of September 1878, after the campaign to be described in the next chapter:

> The Commanding Officer thinking that the N.C. Officers and men of the battalion would be glad to send home to their friends some account of the hard work they have lately gone through, has had the Battalion Records of the late War in Kaffraria printed . . . for private circulation.
>
> These records, chiefly compiled from official despatches, are but a small page to add to the history of a regiment that bears so many glorious scrolls on its colours, but experience has been gained by all, experience which may soon be put to the test, when the Commanding Officer knows well, he will be able to reckon with still more confidence, on a successful issue to the endeavours of every man in the battalion, to keep the good name and fame of the old Corps, well to the front.[94]

6.

It was on the 21st of January 1878 that "a telegraphic despatch" was received from London "ordering the Battalion to be held in immediate readiness for embarkation for the Cape of Good Hope." The 2/24th was given ten days to pack after its five years in England. At a personal level, this could be "a rather ruthless business, for unmarried soldiers were not allowed to take with them any goods other than those they could carry on their backs." With the "exception of a very few", the furlough men had returned to Chatham by the 1st of February, when the battalion left for Portsmouth "in two special trains." The strength was 24 officers; 87 N.C.O.s; and 762 privates and drummers.[95]

At Portsmouth, they boarded the "Himalaya", a troopship which had become well known during the colonial campaigns. It was about a quarter-of-a-century old and had been a P. & O. liner before being sold to the Admiralty during the Crimean War. Embarkations for India and the colonies were frequent and had some standard features: the arrival of a general to make a brief inspection and wish the troops "good-bye"; the more functional appearance of a sergeant of Marines at the gangway to "tell off" the men into "messes" of about fifteen; and eventually the playing of "Auld Lang Syne" as the ship slipped away from the shore. The "horrors" of troopship life were familiar in the service; and it was an officer going out to the Zulu War, a year later, who described his men as being "stowed below like so many sardines in a box."[96] What was most complained about was "the stifling heat and stuffiness" of the troop-decks and the "washing arrangements":

> . . . when at half-past five o'clock the wash-house was opened, it immediately became thronged with a crowd of men trying to get in, and with others who, having completed their ablutions, were equally trying to get out.[97]

On troopships, military and naval life went on in a curious correlation: bugle calls regulated the military day, much as on land, but "piercing whistles" reminded the troops that there was also a naval day going on around them The outlines of the military day were:-

Reveille at 6 a.m.: "stow hammocks; bedding for
   airing taken on deck."
Breakfast between 7 and 7.30, when: "The day watch will go on
   deck clean. The watches below will clean their
messes and troop decks, and then themselves, after which all
but the mess orderlies and troop deck swabbers go on deck,
and remain there till after the inspection [by the ship's captain]."
Roll-call parade at 10 a.m.: "All the troops, except the cooks and
   mess orderlies, fall in on upper deck for inspection.
The military officers of the day inspect troop decks and messes
to see they are clean and in order."
Dinner at noon and a pint of porter issued at 12.30.
Sweeping of messes and decks at 1 p.m.
Supper at 4.30 p.m.

67

Decks cleared for the night at 8 p.m.
"Lights out" at 8.15: "Every man to be in his hammock."
("Lights out" for officers in the saloon was at 11 o'clock.)[98]

When they were not sweeping or swabbing, the troops could

> spend the day as they pleased—usually in lying about the deck, smoking, reading and playing cards. With reference to smoking, it should be explained that this is everywhere strictly forbidden except on deck, and then permitted only during certain hours. The signal to light up is most appropriately the sounding by the bugler on duty of the call "Commence firing", while "Cease firing" means pipes out.[99]

During a voyage lasting five weeks, there was plenty of time for all but the least imaginative of men to wonder what their chances would be on active service. The young Churchill, describing his experiences on the Northwest Frontier, found that:

> The first time he [the soldier] is under fire he imagines himself to be in great danger. He thinks that every bullet is going to hit him, and that every shot is aimed at him. Assuredly he will be killed in a moment. If he goes through this ordeal once or twice, he begins to get some idea of the odds in his favour. He has heard lots of bullets and they have not hurt him. He will get home safely to his tea this evening, just as he did the last time.[100]

In *Told from the Ranks* (published in 1898, the same year as Churchill's book), some of the soldiers themselves make brief comments about their experiences under fire. Harry O'Clery, in his chapter "Facing the Zulus", says:

> It was my first appearance on a battlefield. We were told by our officers to keep ourselves cool and steady, and fire low; and I tried not to get carried away by the excitement, but it's not so easy, when you know that each puff *may* mean a dose of death to you or the man next you.[101]

Two other men bring out the excitement of being in action: "the whole fight was so exciting that we took no heed of time or hunger"; and "I shall never forget the excitement of driving the enemy from their stronghold."[102]

One question which has since become of compelling concern would not have troubled them. A reviewer of one of Emery's books of soldiers' letters remarked that what he "might have touched upon is the theme of racial superiority from which so many Victorians drew their inspiration. How did men in the ranks feel about it all?"[103] The answer is surely that "men in the ranks" were still Victorians and, although they held a rather low position in their own society, this sense of "racial superiority" was in the very air which they would have breathed from childhood. As working men, it may not have been their "inspiration", but it was accepted as part of the natural order and conditioned their attitudes to native peoples. This is brought out by Private Frank Richards in *Old-Soldier Sahib*, his account of soldiering in India and Burma in the first years of the twentieth century: "Every British unit I came across . . . handled the natives in the same manner . . . They had to realise that they were our inferiors." In introducing the second edition, Robert Graves says: "As for his opinions on the proper treatment of Asiatics—he [Richards] would not have been the authentic Tommy Atkins if he had held others."[104] Soldiers in Africa, twenty or thirty years earlier, would have held the same opinions. They could, for instance, admire the fighting prowess of the Zulus—"they were like lions and not afraid of death"—but this could be accommodated within the soldiers' general view of things.[105] Victorian "men in the ranks" often used the phrase "old England"—words which seem to resonate both pride and affection— and, in some important respects, their view of the world was much the same as that of their officers.

The "Himalaya" arrived off East London, in what was then called "British Kaffraria", on the 9th of March. Landing at East London was then "a very slow, and even a dangerous operation on account of the bar" but, that day, conditions were favourable for a crossing and "B and C companies under Major W.M. Dunbar were landed at once in surf boats."[106] It was thus on the 9th of March 1878 that Hook set foot on what was to be the land of his fame.

NOTES

1. " 'Scum of the Earth' " by David Murray, in *Soldiers of the Queen*, No. 85, June 1996, p. 24.
2. Spiers, Edward M., *The Army and Society, 1815-1914* (London: Longman, 1980), pp. 23-25; Harries-Jenkins, Gwyn, *The Army in Victorian Society* (London: Routledge & Kegan Paul, 1977) pp. 44-45.
3. Parr, Sir Henry Hallam, *Major-General Sir Henry Hallam Parr . . . Recollections and Correspondence . . .*, ed. by Sir Charles Fortescue-Brickdale (London: T. Fisher Unwin Ltd., 1917), p. 71.
4. Wood, Evelyn, *From Midshipman to Field Marshal* (2 vols., London: Methuen & Co., 1906), II, p. 64.
5. Blood, Sir Bindon, *Four Score Years and Ten* (London: G. Bell & Sons Ltd., 1933), pp.

   21-22.
6. Parr, *op. cit.*, p. 161.
7. Repington, Charles À Court, *Vestigia* (London: Constable & Co. Ltd., 1919), p. 21.
8. Butler, Sir William, *An Autobiography* (London: Constable & Co. Ltd., 1911), Chapters XXI-XXIII.
9. McCalmont, Major-General Sir Hugh, *The Memoirs of . . .* ed. by Sir. C.E. Callwell (London: Hutchinson & Co., 1924), p. 30; Lyttelton, Sir Neville, *Eighty Years: Soldiering, Politics, Games* (London: Hodder & Stoughton Ltd., [1927]), p. 54.
10. *Ibid.*, pp. 66 & 70.
11. Fortescue, J.W., *A History of the British Army* (13 vols., London: Macmillan & Co. Ltd., 1899-1930), XIII, pp. 560 & 563.
12. Parr, *op. cit.*, pp. 65-66.
13. *Ibid.*, p. 87.
14. Robertson, Sir William, *From Private to Field-Marshal* (London: Constable & Co. Ltd., 1921), p. 31.
15. "How to Make the Army Popular" by "A Staff Sergeant", in *The Saint Pauls Magazine*, Vol. VII, January 1871, p. 373.
16. Wyndham, Horace, *The Queen's Service* (London: William Heinemann, 1899) p. 152.
17. Robertson, *op. cit.*, p. 155.
18. Parr, *op. cit.*, p. 71.
19. Holme, Norman, *The Noble 24th: Biographical Records of the 24th Regiment in the Zulu War and the South African Campaigns, 1877-1879* (London: Savannah, 1999), p. 352.
20. Fortescue, *op. cit.*, XIII, p. 562.
21. *Told from the Ranks: Recollections of Service during the Queen's Reign by Privates and Non-Commissioned Officers of the British Army*, collected by E. Milton Small (London: Andrew Melrose, 1898), p. 100. Another soldier (p. 170) remembered that: "The officers used to sleep inside the waggons, and were, so far, a little more comfortable than the rank and file [who slept under the waggons], but even they were roughing it."
22. Butler, *op. cit.*, p. 326.
23. "Parchment Certificate" of Discharge, dated at Gibraltar, 25 June 1880 (in Furness Collection).
24. Wyndham, *op. cit.*, pp. 2-9; Blatchford, Robert, *My Life in the Army* ([London:] The Amalgamated Press Ltd., [1910]), pp. 4-8; [Acland-Troyte, John Edward], *Through the Ranks to a Commission* (London: Macmillan & Co., 1881), pp. 10-13.
25. Hook's "Record of Service", incl. the Attestation Proceedings, is missing from the Public Record Office; but a typical "Record" of the period is reproduced in Holme, *op. cit.*, pp. 370-72; Wyndham, *op. cit.*, p. 271; Trustram, Myna, *Women of the regiment: Marriage and the Victorian army* (Cambridge: Cambridge University Press, 1984), p. 32.
26. *Ibid.*, pp. 30-31 & 62; "A Staff-Sergeant", *art. cit.*, p. 269; Reminiscences of Mrs. June Dutton (as cited in Chapter III).
27. Details from "Parchment Certificate" (cited at n. 23); Spiers, Edward M., *The late Victorian army: 1868-1902* (Manchester: Manchester University Press, 1992), p. 123.
28. Fortescue, *op. cit.*, XIII, p. 8.
29. Lawrence, T.E., *The Mint* (Harmondsworth: Penguin Books, 1978), p. 41; White, A.C.T., *The Story of Army Education, 1643-1963* (London: George G. Harrap & Co. Ltd., 1963), p. 28.
30. "The Effect of the Cardwell Reforms in Army Organization, 1874-1904" by Brian Bond, in *Journal of the Royal United Service Institution*, Vol. CV, No. 620, November 1960, pp. 515-16.
31. Paton, George; Glennie, Farquhar; Penn Symons, William, *Historical Records of the 24th Regiment, from its Formation, in 1689* (London: Simpkin, Marshall, Hamilton, Kent & Co., 1892), p. 194.
32. Acland-Troyte, *op. cit.*, pp. 15-17.
33. Robertson, *op. cit.*, p. 4.
34. "Why the Army is Unpopular" by "A Staff-Sergeant", in *The Saint Pauls Magazine*,

Vol. VII, December 1870, p. 245; Barnett, Correlli, *Britain and Her Army, 1509-1970* (Harmondsworth: Penguin Books, 1974), plate no. 22.

35. Robertson, *op. cit.*, p. 4.
36. Wyndham, *op. cit.*, pp. 22-24.
37. *Ibid.*, p. 31.
38. *Ibid.*, pp. 31-33; Acland-Troyte, *op. cit.*, pp. 30 & 37.
39. *Ibid.*, pp. 32-33.
40. *Ibid.*, pp. 22-25.
41. Wyndham, *op. cit.*, pp. 26-28.
42. Acland-Troyte, *op. cit.*, pp. 21 & 29-30.
43. *Ibid.*, pp. 49-50.
44. *Ibid.*, p. 49; Blatchford, *op. cit.*, p 30.
45. Acland-Troyte, *op. cit.*, p. 22; Wyndham, *op. cit.*, pp. 42-43, 53 & 64.
46. Fraser, John, *Sixty Years in Uniform* (London: Stanley Paul & Co. Ltd., 1939), pp. 47-48.
47. Acland-Troyte, *op. cit.*, pp. 182-92.
48. Blatchford, *op. cit.*, pp. 21-22.
49. Acland-Troyte, *op. cit.*, p. 49; Holme, *Silver Wreath*, p. 87.
50. Paton, Glennie & Symons, *op. cit.*, pp. 1-156.
51. *Ibid.*, pp. 190-94; Adams, Jack, *The South Wales Borderers* (London: Hamish Hamilton, 1968), p. 80.
52. Paton, Glennie & Symons, *op. cit.*, p. 75; Holme, *Noble 24th*, p. 5.
53. Adams, *op. cit.*, p. 7.
54. Mr. Rattray's 3-part lecture has been given annually in London since 1994, and the present writer heard the part on Rorke's Drift in June 1998. The individual parts are available on tape and, as far as Rorke's Drift is concerned, the tape is preferable for historical accuracy. Hook is very prominent, and on the tape he has 29 mentions: Lord Chelmsford has 35.
55. Holme, *Noble 24th*, p. 383.
56. *Ibid.*, pp. 321-69.
57. *Ibid.*, p. 105.
58. *Ibid.*, pp. 279 & 324. See also: "Colour Sergeant Frank Bourne of Rorke's Drift" by Stephen Benson, in *Soldiers of the Queen*, No. 19, November 1979, pp. 12-14. At his death in 1945, he was believed to be the last survivor of the Rorke's Drift garrison. There is a blue plaque at the house in Bromley where he lived in retirement.
59. Wyndham, *op. cit.*, p. 19.
60. Skelley, Alan Ramsay, *The Victorian Army at Home: The Recruitment and Terms and Conditions of the British Regular, 1859-1899* (London: Croom Helm, 1977), p. 248.
61. The quotation is from a review by Emery in *Soldiers of the Queen*, No. 18, September 1979, p. 14.
62. Skelley, *op. cit.*, p. 297.
63. Harrison, Brian, *Drink and the Victorians* (London: Faber & Faber, 1971), pp. 23-24; "Why the Army is Unpopular" by "A Staff-Sergeant", *art. cit.*, p. 242; Lyttelton, *op. cit.*, p. 66; Acland-Troyte, *op. cit.*, p. 302.
64. Holme, *Noble 24th*, p. 366.
65. Acland-Troyte, *op. cit.*, p. 261; Skelley, *op. cit.*, p. 320 (where nearly half the privates in the Army are shown to have had at least one badge in 1878).
66. *Ibid.*, p. 54.
67. Holme, *Noble 24th*, pp. 327, 331, 355 & 357-58.
68. "Soldiers' Letters: How Much Edited, How Many Written?" by Frank Emery, in *Soldiers of the Queen*, Vol. IV, No. 15, p. 14.
69. White, *op. cit.*, pp. 18-39.
70. *Ibid.*, p. 40; Skelley, *op. cit.*, pp. 94-95 & 311.
71. Holme, *Noble 24th*, p. 102; Jackson, F.W.D., *Hill of the Sphinx: The Battle of Isandlwana* (London: Westerners Publications Ltd., 2002), p. 8.

72. Churchill, Winston S., *The Boer War: London to Ladysmith via Pretoria* [and] *Ian Hamilton's March* (London: Leo Cooper, 1989), p. 6. For the list of officers, see Paton, Glennie & Symons, *op. cit.*, p. 209.
73. *Ibid.*, p. 208; Lyttelton, *op. cit.*, pp. 67-68.
74. Bond, *art. cit.*, p. 519.
75. Blatchford, *op. cit.*, p. 50.
76. Acland-Troyte, *op. cit.*, pp. 75-76.
77. *Ibid.*, pp. 74-75.
78. *Ibid.*, pp. 50-51.
79. *Ibid.*, pp. 51-52.
80. *Ibid.*, pp. 108-11.
81. Wyndham, *op. cit.*, p. 69.
82. Acland-Troyte, *op. cit.*, pp. 25 & 74; Wyndham, *op. cit.*, p. 44.
83. Skelley, *op. cit.*, p. 93; Fraser, *op. cit.*, p. 51; Acland-Troyte, *op. cit.*, p. 63.
84. Fraser, *op. cit.*, p. 50.
85. Wyndham, *op. cit.*, p. 50; Acland-Troyte, *op. cit.*, p. 61; "Why the Army is Unpopular" by "A Staff-Sergeant", *art. cit.*, pp. 243-44; Fraser, *op. cit.*, p. 42.
86. "Religion and Nationality in the Mid-Victorian Army" by H.J. Hanham, in *War and Society*, ed. by M.R.D. Foot (London: Paul Elek, 1973), p. 169; Skelley, *op. cit.*, p. 164; Wyndham, *op. cit.*, pp. 84-85.
87. *Ibid.*, p. 77; Acland-Troyte, *op. cit.*, pp. 113-14 & 198.
88. *Ibid.*, p. 119; Paton, Glennie & Symons, *op. cit.*, p. 208.
89. Acland-Troyte, *op. cit.*, p. 120.
90. Wyndham, *op. cit.*, pp. 74-79.
91. *Ibid.*, pp. 37-38; Acland-Troyte, *op. cit.*, p. 107.
92. Wavell, Earl, *Soldiers and Soldiering* (London: Jonathan Cape, 1953), p. 126.
93. Wyndham, *op. cit.*, p. 281.
94. "Battalion Order" prefixed to *Historical Records of the 2nd Battalion, 24th Regiment for the Kaffir War of 1877-8* ([Pietermaritzburg, Natal: privately printed by "the Press of the 1st Battalion", 1878]), and cited hereafter as "Historical Records."
   The account of this campaign published in Paton, Glennie & Symons, *op. cit.*, pp. 208-19 is an abridgement of pp. 5-27 of the privately-printed pamphlet and the text has been given some literary "polish".
95. *Historical Records*, pp. 5-6; Fraser, *op. cit.*, p. 76.
96. Rogers, H.C.B., *Troopships and their History* (London: Seeley Service Ltd., 1963), pp. 105-06; Acland-Troyte, *op. cit.*, pp. 215-20; Wyndham, *op. cit.*, pp. 122-23; Montague, W.E., *Campaigning in South Africa: Reminiscences of an Officer in 1879* (Edinburgh: William Blackwood & Sons, 1880), p. 13.
97. Wyndham, *op. cit.*, p. 127.
98. Wolseley, Sir Garnet J., *The Soldier's Pocket-Book for Field Service* (4th ed., London: Macmillan & Co., 1882), p. 218.
99. Wyndham, *op. cit.*, p. 132.
100. Churchill, Winston S., *The Story of the Malakand Field Force* (1st. ed., 1898. Reissued, London: Leo Cooper, 1989), p. 184.
101. *Told from the Ranks* (as cited at n. 21), p. 166.
102. *Ibid.*, pp. 103 & 139.
103. Review by Victor Neuburg of Emery's *Marching over Africa* (1986), in *Journal of the Society for Army Historical Research*, Vol. LXV, No. 263, Autumn 1987, p. 147.
104. Richards, Frank, *Old-Soldier Sahib* (1st ed. 1936. 2nd ed., London: Faber & Faber Ltd., 1965), pp. 142-43 & p. 7. (Graves's foreword).
105. The quotation is from *The Red Soldier: Letters from the Zulu War, 1879* by Frank Emery (London: Hodder & Stoughton, 1977), p. 101.
106. *Historical Records*, p. 6.

Chapter V

SOUTH AFRICA—1

War on the Frontier: 1878

1.

It was a time when Britain was "the dominant Power" in Southern Africa. All of the territory which became the Union and, later, the Republic, of South Africa, was either under some form of British rule or was a British "zone of influence." Other European powers were, of course, in Africa but the "Scramble" for the continent had then hardly begun.[1]

The Dutch, who had been the original colonisers, lost the Cape during the Napoleonic Wars and it was "confirmed in British hands in 1815", after Waterloo. What became Cape Colony (often called the "Old Colony") had been "conquered and held for strategic reasons", as the harbours of the Cape peninsula were "important links on the trade route to India, the most profitable of all British possessions." Since 1872, Cape Colony had enjoyed "responsible government", a species of "home rule", and it included the northeastern frontier region of British Kaffraria. Further to the north were the colonies of Natal and Griqualand West; Basutoland, which was then governed from the Cape; the Kingdom of Zululand; and the Boer Republics of Orange Free State and the Transvaal (the latter annexed as a colony, for a few years, from 1877).[2]

The border regions of South Africa have been compared with the American frontier. The similarities—the "rough and ready" nature of life outside the few towns, the struggles for land and natural resources, and the raids and incidents leading to wars and military campaigns—were offset by two marked differences:

First, by the end of the nineteenth century, when the frontiers had closed and whites had established hegemony, the survivors

73

of the indigenous peoples of the United States amounted to fewer than one half of one per cent of the total population, whereas the Bantu-speaking peoples were still a large majority of the population of Southern Africa. Second, white settlers in North America rarely used Indian labour, whereas from an early stage the white Southern African economies depended on the labour services of indigenous people as well as imported slaves.[3]

The long series of "Indian Wars" on the American frontier had its counterpart in "the hundred years' war between the Whites and the Xhosa" on the Eastern Cape Frontier, and in the Zulu War. The Xhosas were a sedentary people and they fought for their land and their large herds of cattle, as well as for their political independence from the Dutch and the British. They were "much more numerous" than the whites "but ill-armed, and without any central authority." Xhosa chiefs had individual authority but although they "sought again and again to secure solidarity among themselves", and with neighbouring native peoples, "they failed in both aims."[4]

The "hundred years' war" began in 1779, under Dutch rule and, up to 1877, there had been eight component wars, which contemporaries collectively called the "Kaffir Wars." In his modern history of these conflicts, John Milton explains that

> The word "Kaffir" (also "Kafir", "Caffre") . . . is a word (however spelt) which is today offensive to those to whom it is applied. Of Arabic origin, in which language it meant "unbeliever" or "heathen", it was used by Arab slave traders to denote the African tribespeople upon whom they preyed. . . . The Xhosa, as the first African tribe to come into contact with the Dutch colonists in southern Africa, were, inevitably, called "Kaffirs", and for a long time the word specifically identified the Xhosa and their country [*i.e.* Kaffraria].[5]

The word is avoided here, except in contemporary quotations.

One of the best of the contemporary accounts is by Captain Molyneux, a British staff officer who served in the Ninth War of 1877-78. He observed that the Xhosa

> is a splendid man physically, but weak in the arms, for he only attends to the cattle and milks the cows, while the women do such field-work as is necessary. The men's dress in hot weather is nothing at all; in cool weather skins or blankets are wrapped round them; the chiefs wear an ivory band round the arm above the left elbow. Married women wear a skin kilt always; unmarried girls are content with a string and bunch of beads;

all wear necklaces and bangles. Their huts are like beehives; there is a very small opening, no chimney, and a fire-place in the middle of the floor; a collection of huts is called a kraal. . . .

[Their wealth] consists in cattle. . . . The milk is put in skins, soured, and drunk almost in lumps. Mealies and Kafir corn are their cereals, and from the latter they make Kafir beer, which is drunk grains and all. . . .

[Their weapons] are one short broad-bladed stabbing assegai, half-a-dozen long, tapering, throwing assegais, a knobkerrie, or club, and now generally a gun; perhaps an old Tower musket dated 1835, a trade "gas-pipe" gun, or sometimes an Austrian rifle with two triggers. Out of these they fire iron potlegs, slugs, stones, or any heavy thing that will go down; and the musical notes of the various missiles in a Kafir fight is a thing to hear.
. . . The throwing assegai of the Kafir will wound seriously at forty yards; the *coup de grâce* is given with the stabbing assegai in the abdomen . . . there are very few good shots among them . . . [and] as a rule a Kafir with his assegai and knobkerrie is more to be dreaded in the bush than the one with a gun.

The fellow has a hide like a rhinoceros; the wait-a-bit thorn, that tears pieces out of your clothes, merely makes a white scratch on his bronze or reddened skin. His movements are therefore unheard; you may be surrounded by a crowd of Kafirs in the bush, and unless you have come across their spoor you may be quite ignorant of their proximity till, with a rush, a red form with a quivering assegai appears within a few yards of you. Then your coolness and your fire-arm, Snider-carbine, or Winchester-repeater for choice, decides if you are to be ripped open or not.[6] [Of course, only an officer or a colonial volunteer could realistically have a "choice" of fire-arm.]

As against the "total war" practiced by the Zulus, warfare with the Xhosas was "limited and certain conventions were respected by both sides. Women and children were not intentionally killed." Molyneux found the Xhosa warriors "plucky enough by daylight" (but never "of any use at night") but they were very elusive for regular troops to bring to a decisive action. An officer prominent in the Sixth and Eighth Wars said that they "can move in an hour a distance it requires soldiers three; they have neither front nor rear nor commissariat; they can assemble like magic and disperse like a mist."[7]

2.

On the 2nd of October 1877, Sir Arthur Cunynghame, commanding the British forces at the Cape, reported to London:

Small native war on the [River] Kei. Have command of all troops. Am collecting certain British troops from Natal and Cape Town. Have ordered half battery from St. Helena. Quiet at present within the [Cape] Colony. Local forces show excellent spirit.[8]

There was little hint in this despatch that the Ninth War had already started and was to last for nearly a year.

A month earlier, Sir Bartle Frere, the Governor and High Commissioner at the Cape, had arrived at King William's Town, in British Kaffraria. He was at once called on by "the Town Council, the Chamber of Commerce for British Kaffraria, and a large deputation of the principal farmers of the frontier districts." It became clear to Sir Bartle that "almost the whole population of this flourishing town, and rich frontier district, was in a state of most genuine apprehension and alarm"; and his "assurances that the war seemed to be only an inter-tribal quarrel, and not likely to affect the British territory, were listened to with incredulous impatience." The Governor was urged to "take measures to remove all occasion for such 'scares' in future, since otherwise no amount of prosperity on the Frontier would render life tolerable."[9] The Eighth War had ended as long ago as 1853 and no doubt the colonists had thought that "such scares" belonged to the past.

"King", as it was known in the local slang, was the "chief town" of British Kaffraria and the headquarters of the 1/24th, whose colonel, R.T. Glyn, commanded on the Eastern Frontier. One of his subalterns wrote privately that Glyn was "as good a little man as ever breathed" but that he had "a monomania" for hunting with hounds.[10] He did well under Sir Arthur Cunynghame but had a hard time under Cunynghame's successor, Lord Chelmsford, who lacked confidence in him. It was at the barracks in King William's Town that Sir Bartle Frere now established himself for the next seven months, messing with the officers of the 1/24th and conducting the business of South Africa from his quarters. When he finally returned to Government House at Cape Town, he sent his "old friends round the mess table" a small silver box for cigars as "a souvenir" of those times.[11]

The "inter-tribal quarrel" which brought on the war was initially between the Galekas and the Fingos. Later, the Gaikas were drawn in. The Galekas were "the 'parent' or senior section of the Xhosa nation" and Galekaland lay to the east of the Great Kei River, which flows into the sea about sixty miles northeast of King William's Town. The Fingos were located to the northwest, on the same side of the Kei but divided from the Galekas by a smaller river. They were "an acquisitive and industrious people", of uncertain origin, who had been driven into Xhosa country by the Zulus. Although they were "accepted" by the Xhosas, they had been without property or local kin and so had a "low status in Xhosa society." Cunynghame put it more trenchantly: the Fingos were "the former slaves of the Kafirs, but who now, under our rule, had assumed an independent position. The Kafirs could not bear to see those who had been formerly treated as their dogs now free and independent." The Fingos had fought alongside the colonists in the Seventh and Eighth Wars and had "prospered under white patronage." In short, they had abandoned their original Xhosa patrons, who saw them as "disloyal", and relations between the two peoples became "increasingly more embittered."[12]

By 1877, Galekaland was "all but surrounded by British territory" where it was not bounded by the Indian Ocean, but the Galekas were still a military force and their chief, Kreli, was regarded by the colonial authorities as "the greatest source of frontier insecurity." Five years earlier, Kreli had led a successful attack on a neighbouring tribe and neither the Cape government's Frontier Armed and Mounted Police (F.A.M.P.), nor British troops, had intervened. The memory of this raid, and of the apparent indifference of the whites, lodged in the minds of the more restless amongst the Galekas.[13] Then

> on the 3rd of August 1877 a marriage feast was held at the kraal of Ngenga, a Fingo residing within the borders of Fingoland, adjoining Kreli's country. At this feast were a number of the neighbouring Galekas who had joined the Fingos by special invitation; these at the close of the day retired peacefully to their homes across the Ganua or Butterworth River.
>
> It happened, however, that another party of Galekas, under two petty Chiefs . . . came from a distance, and without invitation joined in the wedding festivities. In the evening when the invited guests retired, it was suggested to . . . [these chiefs] that they should also retire; they demanded more beer, and refused to leave. A collision ensued, in which, from all we have been able to gather, the Galekas were the aggressors. This was resented by the Fingos, who, overpowering the Galekas, drove them across the boundary, wounding the two Chiefs, and inflicting such injuries on one of their followers that he died from his wounds during the night.
>
> Six days after this occurrence the Galekas assembled in large force, and entered Fingoland at five different points, sweeping off the stock from a number of Fingo villages, consisting of 140 head of cattle and about 600 sheep and goats, wounding two of the Fingos.[14]

This was the origin of the Ninth War. The Galekas were by no means united for war and Kreli himself—despite his fearsome reputation—seems to have been undecided. He was a survivor of the two previous wars and had "an awful sense of foreboding" as "the war party" amongst his people began their raids into Fingoland. The Fingos were British subjects and some of the colonial officials saw a chance to impose colonial rule on Galekaland and snuff out its rather tenuous independence. Those Galekas who had expected the whites to stand aside, as they did in 1872, were soon disabused. Sir Bartle Frere, being on the spot, was able to investigate the disturbances in person but Kreli avoided a meeting with the Governor. Colonel Glyn's adjutant was sent across the Kei to report "on the true state of affairs." The "Government Agent with [the] Fingos" and the "Resident with Kreli" formed a commission of enquiry but their proceedings were "constantly interrupted by alarms that Galekas were coming to attack the Fingos."[15]

On the 2nd of September, the local inspector of the F.A.M.P. reported to his commandant that, although there appeared to be "quite a lull", he did not "see how the Government can wink at the fact of the Galekas having crossed the boundary last Wednesday in such numbers, and attacked the Fingos."[16] Raiding was soon resumed, and the "inter-tribal quarrel" became irrevocably a frontier war on the 26th of September

> when the police for the first time came into collision with the Galekas who were in large numbers, attacking the Fingos at the Gwadana [mountains, Fingoland].
> The Fingos and the 100 men of the Frontier Armed and Mounted Police, after a short engagement, retired before the overwhelming masses of the Galekas, one officer and six men of the Frontier Armed and Mounted Police being killed; this slight success on the part of the Galekas greatly elated them, and the most exaggerated accounts were sent about among the native tribes with a view to secure their aid and co-operation.[17]

Three days later, a Galeka army, about eight-thousand strong, appeared at the Police Camp of Ibeka, in Fingoland. Commandant Charles D. Griffith had 180 Europeans (with three guns and some rockets), together with about two thousand Fingos; and he was given ample warning of the attack. The Galeka tactics—advancing in close formation—were fatal and they were "repulsed with great loss." There were no European casualties and only "very slight" Fingo losses.[18]

This is the stage at which General Cunynghame sent his despatch about the "small native war." It was technically true that he had "command of all troops" but he was not in charge of actual operations in the field. Apart from the Imperial troops, consisting largely of the

1/24th and the 88th Regiment, there was available the F.A.M.P., the Volunteers, the Burghers and the Native Levies (including the Fingos). Mounted Volunteers and Burghers drew five shillings per day, with rations, and those on foot, four shillings with rations. Because of the enormous disparity between these rates of pay and their own pay, the British Regulars called the civilians "Five Bob Colonials"; but it was the Colonials, the Police and the Levies who, for the next two or three months, did the fighting across the Kei. All that the Regulars were given to do was to guard the line of the river, so protecting the frontier of Cape Colony from the hostile Galekas. It was Commandant Griffith who was in effective control of operations, due to "political arrangements" made between the Governor and the Prime Minister of the Cape, J.C. Molteno. Relations between the "responsible government" of a colony and the Imperial authorities were, in general, always likely to be rather prickly; but Molteno regarded British troops as "slow, clumsy, costly and unsuited to local conditions." The compromise reached between Frere and Molteno was therefore that Sir Arthur Cunynghame should be appointed "overall commander of both British and colonial forces but with the assurance that he would not interfere with the handling of the actual campaign."[19]

Griffith was unable to repeat his success at Ibeka by bringing the Galekas to another general engagement. He appeared to have cleared Galekaland by early November; but the hostile Galekas had merely withdrawn to "the wild broken country" along the Bashee River, which formed the eastern border of their territory with Bomvanaland. By the end of December, many of the Gaikas of Cape Colony had "openly taken up arms against the Government." The Gaikas were located northeast of King William's Town and their chief was Sandilli. Born in 1821, he had been a chief since he was twenty and had two well-known characteristics: he had a withered left leg and rode a white horse. Like Kreli, he had fought in the last two wars but it was during the second part of the present campaign that he achieved his apotheosis and became the legendary figure which he remains today.[20]

Even before the Gaika eruption, Cunynghame had become critical of the Colonial forces whose operations he had been forbidden to control. He learned that the F.A.M.P. "having done some service in this war, in a rugged and difficult country, complain of the state of their horses, which are sadly reduced in numbers. The Burgher Mounted Volunteers, a useful body of men for this war, have returned to their homes, ... All the assistance now therefore that I am receiving from the Colony is that of less than 200 foot volunteers, a large portion of whom have this day [19 December] notified their intention to return home, and the Frontier Armed and Mounted Police now in the front do not much exceed 400 men." The general explained to the Secretary of State for War that what he saw as the failure of the campaign was due to the "extremely faulty organisation of the Colonial forces, reserving to themselves the privilege of being *daily* soldiers, returning to their homes whenever it suited them so to do, and also to the fact of the supplies, especially ammunition, not having been forwarded so regularly as would enable the Commandant in command [Griffith] to continually employ his troops." Feeling that "circumstances have very much altered . . . for the worse", Cunynghame asked that "two regiments should be sent at once to the Cape" (and one of these turned out to be the 2/24th).[21]

A few days before this request, Frere had himself concluded that, as "an appeal for fresh [Colonial] volunteers was not likely to produce the number of men . . . which was required", it was necessary to send British troops across the Kei and that these troops "could only serve under officers holding Her Majesty's commission." A column of Imperial troops crossed the river on the 8th of December and Colonel Glyn established himself at Ibeka and took "command of the whole of the Transkei [*i.e.*, the region east of the Kei]." Another British officer commanded the frontier west of the river (the Ciskei). A field force of four columns was organised to clear Galekaland and began its operations under Glyn in the last few days of 1877.[22] On the Colony's side of the river, the year ended with what Frere called "two very brilliant affairs" when the Gaikas "were attempting to cut off the communication between the railway and King William's Town." Behind the brilliance, the official despatches give facts of a kind which were readily seized upon by critics of short service. Major Moore, of the 88th Regiment, who commanded in both engagements, reported that his detachment, "boys though they are, not one of whom had ever seen an enemy before . . . behaved admirably. They repelled attack after attack from large bodies advancing from every direction, charging with a cheer when called on, and held final possession of their well-contested hill-top. Their fire, however, was very wild. . . ." His colonel explained to higher authority that "some of the men engaged had never fired, and that others had only been put through a recruit's course . . . I am of opinion that the mere handful of young soldiers could only have been made to stand as firmly as they did by such conspicuous courage and cool daring as Major Moore showed during the whole time of the [second] action, the least wavering would have been fatal."[23]

During the early weeks of the New Year, Colonel Glyn continued his operations in Galekaland, with his own battalion prominently engaged. On the 13th of January, his mixed force of infantry, artillery, F.A.M.P. and Fingo Levies attacked a strong body of Galekas and Gaikas, who made "a resolute stand for three-quarters of an hour before they began to retreat. They were followed until darkness compelled the troops to return to camp." A sympathetic modern writer says that: "The battle of Nyumaga had been a severe defeat for the Xhosa, and they now dispersed into the depths of the Tyityaba [a valley off the Kei]."[24] Here, the two chiefs, Kreli and Sandilli, reached a ruinous decision: they would storm a fortified camp which had been established by Captain Russell Upcher, of the 1/24th. (The place was then usually called Quintana but is now known as Centane Mountain.)[25] Upcher had prepared what the regimental history describes as "shelter-trenches . . . dug on the lines traced out for a fort." On the day of the attack, the 7th of February, he had fourteen officers and 422 men (including two companies of his own battalion), 140 Fingos, one nine-pounder, one seven-pounder, and a Naval Brigade rocket tube. He was opposed by between four and five thousand Galekas and Gaikas who, "feeling that the result of this engagement would finally decide their fate, fought with more bravery and desperation that they had ever before manifested." Yet during five hours of fighting in front of the post, and in the hills and bush beyond, they never seem to have got closer to the earthworks than about four hundred yards. The artillery and rifle fire of the troops inflicted heavy losses—the contemporary figure of almost four hundred dead seems to be generally accepted—while the white casualties were two wounded. The Fingos lost two killed and seven wounded. Captain Upcher was promoted brevet major and warmly praised for his "signal success."[26]

This was the decisive battle in Galekaland. Kreli and most of his followers crossed the Bashee and took refuge in Bomvanaland. Sandilli and his people, with "their few remaining cattle", recrossed the Kei and eventually disappeared into the Amatola Mountains, northwest of King William's Town.[27]

During January, there had been some curious goings-on in the town. Molteno came up from Cape Town and determined that the Colony should establish "its own quite separate military structure for a campaign within the Ciskei." In short, that it should "run its own war or at least that part of it fought on its own colonial soil." Griffith was accordingly appointed Commandant-General of Colonial forces while Cunynghame, who was in the Transkei, was ignored and given no information about operations which were "carried out with ruthless vigour" in the Gaika location. The Governor, who was still at the barracks, refused to accept this "attempt to set aside Sir Arthur Cunynghame" and thought that the operations under Griffith were "rash, ill-timed, and ill-considered enterprises, entailing much needless expenditure of life, and calculated to protract and extend than to terminate and limit the spread of the war fever." Frere called on

Molteno, and one other minister, to resign and, when they refused, he dismissed the entire ministry. The resulting change of ministry, so the Governor claimed, "restored the unity of action" for the remainder of the war.[28]

At much the same time, the authorities in London were concluding that Cunynghame's "want of cordiality with the [Molteno] ministry" should be remedied by his own recall. Communications between London and the Cape were still very slow in 1878 so, by the time the news of Sir Arthur's supersession had reached King William's Town, the ministry had itself been superseded. The new Commander of the Forces at the Cape was Lieutenant-General Thesiger (later, Lord Chelmsford). He arrived at King William's Town on the 4th of March and "assumed command the same day."[29] When the 2/24th landed a few days later, they found that the war was being conducted by a new general, in a new theatre of operations.

3.

In South Africa, as at Chatham, the 2/24th wore the famous red coats of the British infantry: the term "red coats" was often used as a noun—so many redcoats—to mean Imperial soldiers. The undress frock coat worn on active service was of rough red serge, unlined and with a leather thong inside the collar. There were five brass buttons down the front, a brass button on each epaulet, and a brass hitch for the brown leather belt and pouch. The 2/24th's frocks had green collars but there was no decoration on the sleeves. Trousers were of dark blue and the "foreign service" helmet, without ornament, was usually worn in the field (although the well-known photograph of "B" Company, taken after Rorke's Drift, shows the men in glengarry caps). Molyneux observes that: "The white helmet and accoutrements of the Regulars show at great distances even in the bush. They should be coloured with coffee or boiled mimosa-bark, and when wanted for parade again can be pipe-clayed up as neat as ever."[30] The staining of helmets became common during the Zulu war.

It was not an age in which comfortable dress was much esteemed, either in civil or military life. "Shirt-sleeve order" was then unknown for soldiers, even in the hottest weather, except sometimes on fatigues or off-duty. This apparently led the Africans of Kaffraria to think that "the British soldier entered the world attired in a red coat"! In his journal of the campaign, Major Crealock twice mentions troops being "hurried off" into action "in their shirt sleeves", but these occasions were obviously so unusual as to be worth recording. Officially the only concession that seems to have been made to the South African climate came under the heading of "Sanitary Precautions": "On the march, when the heat is oppressive, the men should be allowed greater freedom about the neck, by opening the tunic and shirt."[31]

In this campaign, and in the Zulu War, the infantry was armed with the Martini-Henry breech-loading rifle and a long socket bayonet. The Martini-Henry weighed 9 lbs., was over 4 ft. long, and "was sighted up to 1,000 yards." It was said to be a "real man-stopper"—very useful in the colonial wars, where it was an object to prevent warriors "charging home" with clubs and spears—but its recoil caused the troops themselves "many a sore shoulder."[32]

Regulations for Field Forces in South Africa show what kind of rations were issued during the Zulu War; and the troops were probably fed in much the same way during the preceding campaign. The basic daily diet was meat (1¼ lbs. fresh or 1 lb. salt or preserved); bread (1½ lbs. fresh or 1 lb. biscuit or flour); and vegetables (½ lb. of fresh potatoes or onions; or 1 lb. of other fresh vegetables). If only preserved vegetables were available, an ounce of lime juice was to be served out, to prevent scurvy. Small amounts of coffee, tea, sugar, salt and pepper were also issued. Finally, there was provision for extra rations of coffee or cocoa and "bread stuff" when troops marched at night or had "to be under arms before daybreak." Most of the men smoked pipes and they could buy tobacco from the Commissariat at 3d. a stick "from twelve to sixteen sticks on the average weighing one pound." During the Eighth War, a remarkable order was once given to troops in the bush: "halt, lie down and smoke your pipes"—a ruse to confuse the enemy![33]

The climate of the Eastern Frontier, in which the 2/24th operated for the next three months, must have been exacting for a battalion just arrived from England. They went into the bush at a season of "excessive heat" by day and "chilling thunderstorms" by night. By the end of March, the rains had "nearly ceased" but "the nights were becoming cold, and the dews heavy, and the alterations of temperature were very sudden and trying to the constitution." It was these "atmospheric changes" which, in the opinion of the Deputy Surgeon-General, caused enteric fever (*i.e.*, inflammation and ulceration of the intestines). At first, it was "of a mild character" but "as the month of May advanced, this disease everywhere began to assume a more serious type, and no place was free from it . . . [it] was the true autumnal fever . . . [and] the young soldiers, three [those?] under 24, were especially attacked, and the two regiments lately arrived in the country, viz., the 2/24th and 90th, appeared more liable to it than others." It is not known whether Hook—who was then in his 28th year—was attacked by this fever; but, by the end of the campaign, "the general state of health" of the troops was reported

"Sketch Map to illustrate the Gaika Rebellion", i.e., the fighting in the Ciskei in which the 2/24th was engaged in 1878.
(From Midshipman to Field Marshal *by Sir Evelyn Wood, 1906.*)

to be "favourable."[34]

There is, in fact, no knowing how Hook "got along" during this campaign. The plain truth seems to be that no-one asked him. After his return to England, everyone wanted to know about Rorke's Drift; and it was in giving what was probably the last interview of his life that he made his only recorded remark about the Ninth War. This is a casual reference to "the whiz and rip of the assegais, the spears . . . of which I had had experience during the Kaffir Campaign of 1877-78."[35]

The nearest we can get to what it was like to fight the Gaikas is by generous use of the *Historical Records of the 2nd Battalion*, mentioned earlier. These *Records* often refer to "B" Company and as we read about the Company, we are reading, in effect, about Hook's own experiences.

"As fast as trains could be provided", all the companies but "D" were sent from East London to King William's Town. By the 14th of March, these seven companies had marched out of the town and were in the mountains to the northwest. Due largely to the terrain and to the type of warfare, Colonel Degacher never had the full battalion under his command: it was divided into detachments of varying strengths, under himself, the two majors (Dunbar and Black) and sometimes under captains. From close observation, General Thesiger was able to provide the authorities at home with a telling description of the terrain:

It is bounded on the north and west by the Kologha range of mountains, a continuation of the Amatolas, and by the Keiskama River, on the south by the road running from Izeli to Middle Drift, and on the east by the main road from King William's Town to Stutterheim.

In this country, which has an area of about 286 square miles, from the 11th March to the 29th May 1878 the mass of the rebels held out. It is one of extraordinary difficulty, owing to its mountainous character, to the scarcity of cart roads, and to its being covered with dense forest for about two-thirds of its area.

There are, at distances of 17 miles apart, but two roads practicable for carts crossing this mountainous district, from south to north, . . . but there were no roads traversing it from east to west. Two roads had therefore to be constructed, . . .

The timber in the bush is large and the undergrowth in parts almost impenetrable, but the chief difficulty for the passage of troops lies in the fallen trees, the detached rocks, the rugged river beds, and the entanglements of creepers. The few valleys that exist are as a rule deep and narrow. Their sides are covered

85

with dense bush, and seamed with numerous ravines (or kloofs as they are called in South Africa) which form the favourite hiding place of the Kafir.

These ravines, which are often found even in the open ground on the tops of the mountains, render lateral communication, even by footmen, most difficult and very often impossible. They are often many miles in length, are filled with rocks and boulders tossed about in wild confusion, and trees tied together by monkey ropes and other creepers, the whole affording admirable cover for a clever skirmisher like the Kafir.

The highest hill tops are rounded and for the most part free from bush; at a distance they appear to be smooth and undulating, but on a nearer approach they are found to be intersected by rocky watercourses, and their surface broken by boulders and treacherous from bogs.

The under features connected with this higher ground slope away gradually at first until they reach the forest zone, where they either finish abruptly in a craggy precipice, or form huge buttresses with precipitous sides, buried in a maze of tangled bush.

When I arrived at King William's Town, . . . a Colonial force under Commandant-General Griffith, C.M.G., was operating on the Thomas River [which flows into the Kei] against the Gaika rebels under their Chief Sandilli who after the battle of Quintana had returned to their own country, commonly known as the Gaika location ["a poorly defensible plane situated between the Amatolas and the Kei river"].

On the 10th March, about midnight, information reached me that Sandilli and a large following [estimated at 800], after having been severely handled by the above-mentioned force, had managed to slip past between two of the columns, and had escaped [south] into the Perie Bush.

This bush, though well known in the Colony by name, proved on inquiry to be a complete "terra incognita" . . .

Immediate steps were taken to protect the country in the immediate neighbourhood of the bush from plunder by establishing a cordon of posts around it, varying in strength according to their relative importance.

By the 17th March, . . . the cordon was complete, and on the following day we made our first attack.[36]

During the first part of his campaign, Thesiger's attacks consisted of combined movements of troops, Volunteers and Fingos. His plan was that there should be concentric "drives" into the bush by several columns, the Gaikas being driven towards "outlets" which would be blocked, usually by Regular infantry. He had initially nearly three thousand men, of which less than six hundred were Regulars. The

Regulars were untrained in bush warfare—and, as Molyneux says, "with their clothes, their great helmets and their boots", it was hard for them "to move through the bush at any pace"—while the Colonials were equally untrained in disciplined operations.[37]

At the end of the war, Thesiger complained that the local newspapers had "systematically denounced us all as quite ignorant of the manner in which to conduct Colonial warfare"; and a recent editor of his military papers remarks on the general's apparent reluctance "to adapt European strategy to colonial conditions."[38] Thesiger certainly had no experience of colonial warfare, nor had he set foot in Southern Africa before February 1878. He had served in the Crimea as a junior officer, and in the later stages of the Indian Mutiny as colonel of the 95th Regiment; but his experience of commanding troops in the field was extremely limited. He was essentially a staff officer who had risen in the Army on that account. His "inside" view of the Abyssinian expedition of 1868, conducted by Lord Napier of Magdala—one of the "model" campaigns of the Victorian age—was no doubt valuable, and Napier was impressed by the ability and energy of his staff work. Yet none of this had really prepared Thesiger for the chief command at the Cape, in difficult times. His heart was in India, where he had served for fifteen years and had married: in the Army slang of the day, he was an "Indian" rather than an "African." It was not surprising that it took him a few weeks to "adapt to colonial conditions."

To return now to the first day of operations. The column of Colonel Evelyn Wood was to be "the directing force in the attack", with the support of two columns under colonial commandants. In front of Wood and to his right, the Volunteers and Fingos under Commandant Brabant spotted at daybreak a herd of cattle—too strong a temptation "for indisciplined men"! Without waiting for Wood, they "went on at once" and fell into a Gaika ambush. After ten men had been wounded and some horses lost, Brabant's column broke up. On the left, Commandant Frost "tried to send help, but his men were stopped by a kloof." During a day of confusion, detachments of the 2/24th were deployed in an extended arc from east to west, with "B" and "C" Companies on the extreme left. These companies "formed part of the attacking columns", while other companies were "waylaying" paths coming from the bush. "B" Company climbed "the Rabula heights" in support of Brabant, only to find (as it was euphemistically put) that Brabant's men were "coming out of action." After staging their successful ambush, the Gaikas had also gone, so "the company bivouacked for the night on the heights." The general reported, in some bafflement, that "it became apparently impracticable to carry out the original plan of advance."[39]

Still, a modified "advance" was made by Colonel Wood on the following day. "B" Company

> descended to a lower plateau, and skirmishing through the bush towards the edge of the krantz [a steep, bare, rocky slope] overlooking Haynes' Mill, drove the rebels before it; at nightfall returned to occupy the bivouacking ground of the previous evening. The next day it had to remain inactive on account of the thick mist which enveloped the whole of the mountains, and on the 21st beat the bush back to Baillie's Grave [a post to the south of their position on the 18th].[40]

This was the end of the first combined movement. Thesiger had moved up to direct an attack in person but found to his dismay "the Volunteer forces retiring from the plateau: difficulties in obtaining rations was the reason given, besides that many of the volunteers were desirous of leaving for their homes, their term of engagement being about to expire."[41] Apart from "fresh levies of Volunteers", the general felt that he needed many more Fingos to search the bush. The new colonial government agreed that he should have "a reinforcement of 1,000 Fingos, raised in Fingoland itself", and he postponed a "grand attack" until their arrival. Instead, on the 28th of March, he began a more limited operation with the idea of "surrounding the position of Sandilli in the Peri, and endeavouring to beat the bush, and drive him from his lair." The general set up his headquarters on "Mount Kempt, a high bleak mountain to the north of the Buffalo Poort and overlooking the whole of the country towards King William's Town."[42]

> As on the previous occasion, the attack was commenced from the Keiskamma valley [to the west of Mt. Kempt], and B & C companies again ascending the heights from that side, were engaged in all the operations which then took place. H.E. [His Excellency] the Lt. General, from Mount Kempt, witnessed these two companies beating through three separate clumps of bush on the plateau beneath him, and afterwards personally complimented them on the "admirable manner" in which this had been done.
> The rebels having been driven from the plateau, they were confined to the bush of the Buffalo Poort, but this Poort is of such an extent, that more men were required to beat it, . . . the troops in the mean time were employed in waylaying [paths] and cutting roads through the bush.
> The Transkei Fingoes having arrived, the Buffalo Poort was driven on the 5th April, when 1,777 Fingoes, led by European

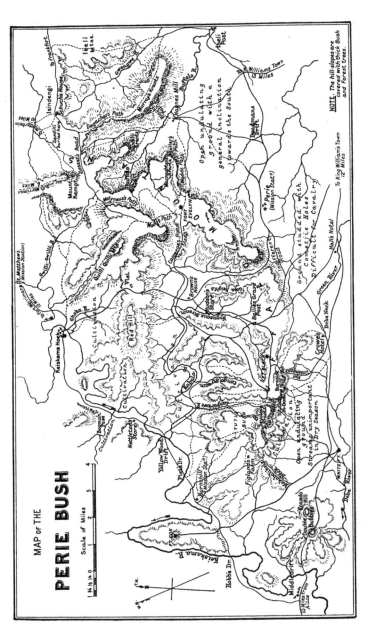

MAP OF THE

PERIE BUSH

"Map of the Pirie Bush," in which the 2/24th served during the second half of the 9th Frontier War. (From Midshipman to Field Marshal by Sir Evelyn Wood, 1906.)

officers, were sent into it. On this day the various paths cut through the forest, and all points of egress, were lined by the companies and Colonial Volunteers. Only a few Kaffirs were seen and almost all of them killed.[43]

Two of the general's staff officers say that there was considerable firing by the Fingos to little effect. The casualties were: eleven Gaikas killed; one Fingo killed and one wounded. From his position south of the Buffalo Poort, the general thought from the noise that Sandilli was making a stand and, when given the facts, asked in astonishment: "What on earth have you been shooting at?" Sandilli could afford this loss, as he was himself being substantially reinforced. Several chiefs in the Ciskei, whose followers had been "for some months restless", now (as Thesiger put it) "openly declared themselves against us." The most prominent of these chiefs was Seyolo, "whose renown as a warrior dated from his exploits in the 8th frontier war." Seyolo had with him between 1,200 and 1,500 men who— after being "heavily engaged" with Volunteers of the Diamond Field Horse—took "refuge in the thick bush near the mountain called the Intaba Ka N'Doda . . . at the south-west extremity of the Buffalo range." The general was given this news just as the "drive" in the Buffalo Poort was ending for the day, and "orders were at once issued for a concentration of forces round the Intaba Ka N'Doda." As part of this redeployment, "B" and "C" Companies made "a forced march to Baillie's Grave [east of the mountain] with Colonel Wood's force."[44]

On the 6th [of April] the rebels were attacked and defended themselves well, they made an obstinate stand and repulsed the 1st division of the 'Transkei Fingoes, but at this moment Colonel Wood's force appearing on high ground in rear of them, the bush was cleared. . . .

During the night of the 6th the rebels broke away in different directions, but about 7 a.m. on the 7th a body of 150 to 200 passing near Baillie's Grave into the Perie Bush, A, B & C companies moved out to intercept them, the Tutu Bush [north of the mountain] was driven and 44 Kaffirs were killed amongst whom were two chiefs. A Company lost Private J. Collins who was shot whilst skirmishing in the bush [apparently the first man of the 2/24th to be killed in the campaign.].[45]

This is how the events of those two days are described in the battalion's *Records*. They were observed less favourably by Major Crealock, the general's military secretary. In his journal entry for the 6th of April—after grumbling about Commandant Brabant's reluctance to carry out his orders and "move off" in support of Colonel Wood—he writes:

> Soon after we moved off [*i.e.*, the general and Crealock, after 11 a.m.] with two companies of the 24th, and 2 guns. Molyneux rode down to Brown's House [north of Baillie's Grave] to bring up another company ["B"] of the 2-24th under Capt Austen. They never appeared until the day was over and required two pert messages.[46]

In his entry for the following day, Crealock is equally critical:

> At 8 a.m. news that some [of Seyolo's men] were there slipping through within a mile of our camp was brought. Two companies of the 2.24th hastened up to intercept them there but were too late than to do more than cut off a few who went back into the Bush. These companies under Capts Tongue and Austen ["A" & "B"] by some mistake after having been extended in the bush at 10 a.m. remained halted until 3 o'clock; they lost one man [Collins], but their want of enterprise lost much valuable time.[47]

It would be difficult to get at the truth of these two incidents involving "B" Company. Thesiger and his staff may have become increasingly irritable over the difficulties of co-ordinating the movements of Volunteers, Fingos and Regulars; but there was "almost universal dislike of Crealock as a person and . . . general criticism of his abilities and influence as an officer."[48]

Thesiger returned to King William's Town; and four companies of the 2/24th, including "B", were assembled there under Colonel Degacher. "At this critical point of the campaign," so the general reported, "active operations had to be almost entirely suspended for 24 days owing to the departure of nearly all the Colonial forces to their homes on the expiry of their three months' engagement." At the same time, the Transkeian Fingos made an involuntary departure. They were judged to have failed on the 5th of April and, next day, "though gallantly led in many instances by their officers, showed no aptitude or inclination for bush fighting. They had to be withdrawn a little before sunset, having expended nearly all their ammunition, and having inflicted very small loss on the enemy." The catalogue of their military vices was completed by "mutinous conduct and plundering propensities." The general sent them back to Fingoland.[49]

An "entirely fresh force of Volunteers and native levies" was raised; and King William's Town for a time seethed "with men in every shade of uniform, and in every possible condition from perfect sobriety to beastly drunkenness." Even without this influx, "King" was no longer the pleasant frontier town which it had been before the war. It had become overcrowded and pestilential: "a scene reminiscent of the Great Plague was the 'dead cart' which did a daily round accompanied by two constables with fixed bayonets." Fortunately for the Regular troops and their families, the "Military Reserve" was beyond the town. On this "large tract of land", the barracks and other buildings "were of white-washed brick or stone, had thatched roofs and were solidly built." Here, the 2/24th's women and children had been quartered since the battalion's arrival from England. The three-weeks' suspension of operations would have been as agreeable for them as for the men of the four companies who came in from the bush.[50]

This homely interlude ended on the 29th of April, when the companies marched back to Baillie's Grave to take part in another "combined attack." The general had "ascertained without doubt that nearly all the rebels were massed in the Zanyorkwe Valley and the Intaba Ka'ndoda bush [the valley is immediately north of the mountain], and he intended to surprise them there." Four columns converged on "the objective point", three under Regular officers (Colonel Wood, Lieutenant-Colonel Degacher and Major Redvers Buller) and one under a Colonial commandant.[51]

> Lt. Colonel Degacher's force consisting of five companies of the 2-24th [including "B"] and 4 7-pr. guns was to occupy the ground near the Intaba ka' N'doda where the guns were to be placed in position. C company, Lieut. Williams was to accompany the Frontier Light Horse . . . to a ridge between Zanyorkwe and Congo valley. Colonial corps were placed all round the valley, between the regulars.
>
> By 5 a.m. the Forces were in motion, and by 6-15 a.m. as it was getting light, Colonel Degacher's force occupied the heights round the Intaba ka' N'doda.
>
> The rebels were already on the move, and it was difficult to account for their subsequent behaviour unless they were completely surprised. When the Artillery opened a well directed fire, a large number of the enemy moved in a south-westerly direction towards the point where Colonel Wood's right column was advancing, and another portion descended into the valley towards the position occupied by Lt. Colonel Degacher's force.
>
> About 6-45 a.m. heavy firing was heard from Colonel Wood's direction, and from the hurried movements of the Kaffirs who had gone that way, it was evident an engagement was taking place, and one that gave them encouragement, for they advanced and retired more than once towards and into the

bush which concealed Colonel Wood's advance but at 7-30 the column was seen to emerge from the bush; not without loss however, as the 90th L.I. lost Lieutenant Saltmarshe and four men killed, and Captain Stevens and three men severely wounded.[52]

At about 8 a.m. the flag signallers of C company requested permission for the company to descend into the valley. This was granted, and the company was re-inforced by B company from Lt. Colonel Degacher's force, Major Wilsone Black went with it, and joining C company they worked their way up to the high ground on the opposite side, engaged and inflicted heavy loss on the enemy. On this occasion, Kaffir women facilitated the escape of the men by forming up in front of them, preventing our men from firing. From this time till sunset the Zanyorkwe valley was steadily worked through. Two companies, A and G searched part of the Eastern side of the valley, which the Fingoes under Commandant Maclean had left unbeaten, under the plea of excessive fatigue, and these companies were afterwards strengthened by E and half of H joining them in the bush.

Towards dusk, the day's work having been satisfactorily concluded, the troops returned to their original posts. . . .

The following morning at 4 a.m. heavy firing was heard in the direction of Baillie's Post, Bt. Major Chamberlin's company ["E"] was sent out towards it when it was found that a party of Kaffirs, endeavouring to break into the Buffalo range, had stumbled on a Fingoe camp in the dark. At daylight, two companies and two guns R.A. under Major Black, together with some Colonial troops searched the bush from this spot to the Intaba ka' N'doda.

On this day, (1st May) an order was received to send a company with 2 7-pr guns to Isidengi [to the northeast of the Buffalo Mountains]. A Company under Captain Tongue was ordered to march the following morning and on the 3rd [May] it was followed by B company; at the same time Major W.M. Dunbar was ordered to proceed to Isidengi to take command of this detachment.

In fact, it was soon found that the rebels had completely left the Zanyorkwe valley for the Buffalo range; . . .[53]

Therefore, at daybreak on the 8th of May four columns, under the same officers as before, "advanced to attack the enemy in the bushes of the Buffalo Range."

A & B companies under Major Dunbar were to operate from Mount Kempt with a column commanded by Major Buller, C.B., and descending to a lower plateau, attack from the north

93

-west. . . . [During the morning they] rushed several positions held by the Kaffirs who fled to the thick bush opposite.

About 11 a.m. whilst the two companies were resting in the open, they were fired on by a party of Kaffirs who had approached unseen through the long grass from the adjoining bush. This attack was promptly repulsed as were two others later in the day.

On the following day (9th) the western portion of the Buffalo Poort Bush was searched, A & B companies again descended from Mount Kempt to drive the bush. On this occasion Captain Godwin-Austen was slightly wounded.[54]

How Godwin-Austen was shot by one of his own lance-corporals is recounted by Frank N. Streatfeild, Commandant of the Fingo Levies (described by Molyneux as "that best of good fellows"):

Captain Austen, of the 2-24th, had a most marvellous escape in the course of the day. He was getting down some rocks with some other men, one or two of my officers among the number, when a rifle behind him exploded. The bullet passed across his back, cutting his tunic all to pieces for a foot or more, breaking his flask into shivers, and leaving a rather nasty gash, though not deep, in his back, from which he suffered for some time. I refrain from saying who fired the shot, for of course it was a mistake; but the owner of the rifle which went off ought not to have had a cartridge in at the time.[55]

In later years, "the owner of the rifle" met his former captain at a regimental reunion and they "discussed the affair on a friendly basis."[56] This was remarkably forgiving of Godwin-Austen, as he went home on sick leave and so missed the Zulu War.

In the battalion's *Records*, these "drives" of the 8th and 9th of May are described as "the last combined movement that was made", and little more is said about the campaign except to detail the movements of various detachments. For the next two months, "A" and "B" Companies continued to operate from Mount Kempt, under Major Dunbar, "experiencing much rough and bitterly cold weather." During May, two forts were built in the Buffalo Mountains. Fort Black (named after Wilsone Black, of the 2/24th, who was making a reputation as a particularly energetic officer) was near the Intaba Ka N'doda, commanding "the route usually followed by the rebels in their periodical migration from the Buffalo Range Bush to the Tutu and adjoining bush country." Fort Evelyn (named after Colonel Wood, who was credited by the general with having "been mainly instrumental in bringing the war to a speedy close") was on the Gozo Heights, south of Mount Kempt, and was intended "further to obstruct the free circulation from bush to bush of the bands of rebels."[57]

In his review of the war, Thesiger summarises the operations during May and June:

> From the 9th to the 29th May the troops under Colonel Evelyn Wood gave the rebels no rest.
>
> Day after day, and at last, night after night, small columns of Imperial and Colonial troops, starting from different points, explored the bush in all directions, until they knew it as well as the Kafirs themselves.
>
> The rebels were continually surprised, their horses and cattle were captured, their food destroyed, and at last they could find in that vast extent of bush no single place of safety.
>
> They made their final stand in the rocky ground under Sandilli's Krantz [east of the Buffalo Poort], and when driven from that stronghold they dispersed, never to rally again.
>
> On the 29th of May a chance shot mortally wounded Sandilli, and the operations in the Perie Bush came to a close.
>
> During the time the above-mentioned successful operations were being carried on the troops in other directions were not idle.
>
> The rebels who had returned to the Schelm Kloof [in the Kroome Mountains, about 40 miles northwest of the Intaba Ka N'doda] were successfully attacked by the Colonial troops in the Fort Beaufort District, and shortly after Tini Macomo and his two brothers having been taken prisoners all anxiety in that quarter finally ceased.
>
> The rebels under Seyolo, who had succeeded in reaching the Fish River Bush [about 30 miles southwest of King William's Town], were not left for long undisturbed; numerous patrols were at once pushed through that difficult country, and Seyolo having been killed his followers left the locality and dispersed in all directions. ...
>
> Resistance, in fact, has entirely ceased on the part of the rebels, and they are now only struggling for bare existence.[58]

On the 12th of June, a table was issued giving the casualties on both sides since Thesiger assumed command. The Gaikas had lost 1,298 killed ("actually counted on the field"); 89 "found wounded"; and 175 taken prisoner. The Imperial and Colonial forces had lost 7 officers, 9 privates and 47 native levies killed; and 6 officers, 25 privates and 78 levies wounded. During the full course of the war, the Gaikas and Galekas had had 3,680 men killed: John Milton remarks that "never before had the Xhosa been so thoroughly beaten ... [and they] would never again go to war over the land."[59]

Something should be said about the death of Sandilli, especially as it is a fair assumption that Hook witnessed the chief's curious burial. As befits a legendary figure, some of the circumstances surrounding his death are disputed, though not apparently the fact that he died at the hands of the Fingo Levies. In a skirmish with Sandilli's party, the Fingos had two men killed and four wounded, but seventeen Gaikas were killed and their chief was hit in the right side by a Snider bullet. Sandilli's body was not amongst those "counted on the field" nor was it discovered until ten days later, on the 7th of June. The chief's remains were then "strapped on to the back of a horse and taken to the military camp at Isidenge", east of Mount Kempt, where Commandant Frederick X. Schermbrucker had a formal identification and "post-mortem" carried out.[60]

Schermbrucker reported the sequel to the military authorities:

> In accordance with instructions I had the dead body of Sandilli decently and properly, but without any military consideration, buried at Isidenge this morning at 11 o'clock [9 June].The interment was witnessed by all the European forces in the camp, by a number of Imperial troops from Mount Kempt who passed through here on patrol under command of Major Dunbar at the time of the burial, and by about 500 Fingos . . .[61]

Much of interest is omitted from this austere report. Although there was no "military consideration—that is, no firing of volleys or sounding of the "Last Post"—the troops from "A" and "B" Companies of the 2/24th, the Volunteers and the Fingo Levies were formed into a square around the grave. Commandant Schermbrucker was a notable man on the frontier, who later became prominent in Cape politics, and he took charge of the proceedings. "He spoke no eulogy of the dead man, but rather drew attention to the fact that he had been a rebel against his Queen and had suffered the fate of a rebel." After the interment, Schermbrucker spoke even more plainly. Sandilli's grave had been dug "between the graves of two white troopers . . . both of whom had been killed in the fighting around Isidenge in the early months of 1878" and, referring to this juxtaposition, the Commandant observed: "That will keep the Blackguard quiet."[62]

"A" and "B" Companies remained at Mount Kempt for another month after these rites, but

> The positions held by the Battalion were gradually handed over to the Colonial Forces, and by the 12th July, 7 companies were assembled together in one camp on an open site in the Buffalo Poort Bush for the purpose of drill and refitting, both of which, from the rough work gone through were much

required, but the Battalion had not been here long before a telegram arrived on the 21st ordering immediate embarkation for Natal, where a war against Chetewayo, King of the Zulus was threatening. . . .

Leaving women and children and all heavy baggage at King William's Town, the Regiment [*i.e.*, Battalion] "strength as under"

3 Field Officers
5 Captains
10 Subalterns
3 Staff
5 Staff Sergts
34 Sergeants
29 Corporals
15 Drummers
663 Privates

embarked by half-battalions at East London on the 24th and 26th July and disembarking at Durban, where it remained a few days, marched on Pietermaritzburg which it reached on the 6th August, 1878.[63]

This brings to an end the 2/24th's own record of its campaigning during the last of the Cape Frontier Wars.

NOTES

1. Much of this section of the chapter is based on *A History of South Africa to 1870*, ed. by Monica Wilson and Leonard Thompson (London: Croom Helm, 1982).
2. *Ibid.*, pp. 273, 325, 331, 369 & 382.
3. *Ibid.*, p. 15.
4. *Ibid.*, pp. 241 & 250; Thompson, Leonard, *A History of South Africa* (Revised ed., New Haven: Yale University Press, 1995), p. 126.
5. Milton, John *The Edges of War* (Cape Town: Juta & Co. Ltd., 1983), p. ix.
6. Molyneux, W.C.F., *Campaigning in South Africa and Egypt* (London: Macmillan & Co. Ltd., 1896), pp. 34-37. Compare this with Milton's description (*op. cit.*, pp. 11-14).
7. Wilson & Thompson, *op. cit.*, pp. 242-43; Molyneux, *op. cit.*, p. 85; Lehmann, Joseph H., *Remember You Are an Englishman: A Biography of Sir Harry Smith, 1787-1860* (London: Jonathan Cape, 1977), p. 338.
8. Much of this section is based on those British Parliamentary Papers issued under the general heading of "Correspondence Respecting the Affairs of South Africa", in the series of "Command Papers" published by H.M.S.O. The quotation here is from *C. 1961*, 1878, p. 92.
9. *Ibid.*, p. 80.
10. Coghill, Patrick, *Whom the Gods Love . . .: A Memoir of Lieutenant Nevill Josiah Aylmer Coghill, V.C.* (Halesowen: printed for the author, 1968), p. 38.
11. Paton, Glennie & Symons, *op. cit.*, p. 207.
12. Crealock, John, *The Frontier War Journal of Major John Crealock, 1878: A Narrative of the Ninth Frontier War . . .* ed. and introduced by Chris Hummel (Cape Town: Van Riebeeck Society, 1989), pp. 6-8. (Hummel's introduction gives the modern view of

the causes of the Ninth War and is fully documented.); Thompson, *op. cit.*, p. 75; *C. 2144*, 1878, p. 200.

13. Crealock, *op. cit.*, p. 8 (Hummel's intro.).
14. Brownlee, Charles, "Sketch of Present War, Its Origins and Progress." This account was written by the "Resident Commissioner Native Affairs" at Frere's request, who forwarded a copy to London on 4 August 1878. It was printed in *C. 2220*, 1878, pp. 87-101. (Cited hereafter as "Brownlee".) The passage quoted is at pp. 87-88.
15. Crealock, *op. cit.*, p. 10 (Hummel's intro.); Brownlee, p. 88.
16. *C. 1961*, 1878, p. 85.
17. Brownlee, p. 91.
18. *C. 1961*, 1878, p. 112; Milton, *op. cit.*, p. 259.
19. *C. 1961*, 1878, pp. 113-14 & 211; Crealock, *op. cit.*, pp. 11-12 (Hummel's intro.).
20. *Ibid.*, pp. 11-12 & Appendix A; Brownlee, p. 96; Milton, *op. cit.*, p. 261.
21. *C. 2000*, 1878, pp. 47-48 & 88.
22. *Ibid.*, pp. 48 & 78; Crealock, *op. cit.*, p. 12 (Hummel's intro.); Paton, Glennie & Symons, *op. cit.*, p. 199.
23. *C. 2000*, 1878, pp. 142-46.
24. Paton, Glennie & Symons, *op. cit.*, p. 201; Milton, *op. cit.*, pp. 266-67.
25. This decision was taken because "the crops had failed" and ammunition "was in short supply." Upcher's camp was known to "be well provisioned with guns, ammunition and food." (Milton, *op. cit.*, p. 267.)
26. *Ibid.*, p. 269; Paton, Glennie & Symons, *op. cit.*, pp. 202-03; Brownlee, p. 97; *C. 2079*, 1878, pp. 111 & 147-53.
27. Brownlee, p. 97; Milton, *op. cit.*, pp. 269-72.
28. *Ibid.*, p. 270; Crealock, *op. cit.*, p. 13. (Hummel's intro.); *C. 2144*, 1878, pp. 198-99.
29. *C. 2144*, 1878, p. 206; *C. 2100*, 1878, p. 52 (The Hon. F.A. Thesiger succeeded to his father's peerage in October 1878.)
30. Wilkinson-Latham, Christopher, *Uniforms & Weapons of the Zulu War* (London: B.T. Batsford, 1978), pp. 23, 32 & 38; Molyneux, *op. cit.*, pp. 38-39.
31. Crealock, *op. cit.*, pp. 51, 65 & 77; *Regulations for Field Forces in South Africa* (1st ed., 1878), para. 116.
32. Wilkinson-Latham, *op. cit.*, pp. 56-57.
33. Paras. 46, 47 & 52 of the *Regulations*; "British Troops and Savage Warfare, with Special Reference to the Kafir Wars" by Colonel Gawler, in *The Journal of the Royal United Service Institution*, Vol. XVII, No. LXXV, 1873, p. 930.
34. *C. 2144*, 1878, p. 257.
35. "How They Held Rorke's Drift", from the Narrative of Sergeant Henry Hook, V.C., in *The Royal Magazine*, February 1905, (cited hereafter as *Royal Magazine*), p. 343.
36. This passage is from Thesiger's despatch of 26 June 1878, reporting to the Secretary of State that the war had been "virtually brought to a close." In the version printed in *C. 2144*, 1878, pp. 247-48, the paragraphs are numbered. The quotation about the Gaika location is from a note by Hummel (Crealock, *op. cit.*, p. 91).
37. Molyneux, *op. cit.* pp. 37 & 49-51.
38. French, Gerald, *Lord Chelmsford and the Zulu War* (London: John Lane, The Bodley Head, 1939), p. 33; Laband, John P.C. (ed.), *Lord Chelmsford's Zululand Campaign, 1878-1879* (Stroud: Alan Sutton Publishing Ltd. for the Army Records Society, 1994), pp. xxv & xxxiii.

    French's book is the nearest approach to a biography of Chelmsford but is mainly an apologia for his conduct of the Zulu War. The best sketch of his career and character is in Laband's Introduction to the selection of documents in *Lord Chelmsford's Zululand Campaign*. Whatever may have been Chelmsford's limitations as a soldier, he was a decent and honourable man. The venomous traducing of his character in what was advertised as "Zulu: the True Story" (B.B.C.2 "Timewatch", 24 October 2003) is unbelievably shoddy, as well as being untrue. (See also Chapter

VI, n. 57.)

39. *C. 2144*, 1878, pp. 19-28; Molyneux, *op. cit.*, pp. 51-53; Milton, *op. cit.*, p. 274; *Historical Records*, pp. 10-14.
40. *Ibid.*, p. 14.
41. *Ibid.*, p. 12.
42. *Ibid.*, p. 14; *C. 2100*, 1878, p. 91; *C. 2144*, 1878, p. 249; Molyneux, *op. cit.*, p. 60.
43. *Historical Records*, pp. 15-17. Molyneux (*op. cit.*, p. 43) describes a poort as "the lower end of a kloof" and a kloof as "literally a chasm, what would be called a canon in the Western States of America."
44. Molyneux, *op. cit.*, pp. 63-65; Crealock, *op. cit.*, pp. 16, 35 & 57; *C. 2144*, 1878, p. 249; *Historical Records*, p. 17.
45. *Ibid.*, pp. 17-18.
46. Crealock, *op. cit.*, p. 59.
47. *Ibid.*, p. 67.
48. *Ibid.*, p. 2 (Hummel's intro.).
49. *Historical Records*, p. 18; *C. 2144*, 1878, p. 249; Molyneux, *op. cit.*, p. 70; Milton, *op. cit.*, p. 275.
50. *C. 2144*, 1878, p. 250; Milton, *op. cit.*, p. 275; *Historical Records*, p. 27; Gon, Philip, *The Road to Isandlwana: The Years of an Imperial Battalion* (Johannesburg: Ad Donker, 1979), pp. 92 & 150-51.
51. *C. 2144*, 1878, p. 250; Molyneux, *op. cit.*, pp. 76-77.
52. The 90th Light Infantry was Evelyn Wood's regiment. He gives an unforgettable account of Saltmarshe's death, and of his own relations with this young officer, in *From Midshipman to Field Marshal*, I, pp. 316-17.
53. *Historical Records*, pp. 19-21.
54. *Ibid.*, pp. 22-25
55. Streatfeild, Frank N., *Kafirland: A Ten Months' Campaign* (London: Sampson Low, Marston, Searle & Rivington, 1879), pp. 226-27.
56. Information from Mr. F.W.D. Jackson, who interviewed Godwin-Austen's son in 1958.
57. *Historical Records*, pp. 25-26; *C. 2144*, 1878, p. 84.
58. *C. 2144*, 1878, p. 250.
59. *Ibid.*, pp. 239 & 253; Milton, *op. cit.*, pp. 281-82.
60. Crealock, *op. cit.*, pp. 163-67. (This is Hummel's analysis of the "controversy and legends" relating to Sandilli.)
61. *C. 2144*, 1878, p. 193.
62. Gon, *op. cit.*, p. 166; Milton, *op. cit.*, p. 279; Crealock, *op. cit.*, pp. 25 & 166.
63. *Historical Records*, pp. 26-27. The company ("G") which was not at the Buffalo Poort camp had been sent to East London.

Chapter VI

SOUTH AFRICA—2

Rorke's Drift: 1878-79

1.

During the three months that the battalion was in camp at Pietermaritzburg, Hook took the pledge. In what was almost certainly the first interview which he gave after his discharge from the Army, he said: "I joined the Good Templars at Pieter Maritzburgh, and kept that pledge as long as I remained in that country. . . . I was sorely tempted to break the pledge the day I got the [Victoria] cross—even the officers offered me drink, but I firmly refused; I had not even been in the habit of drinking my allowance of rum; I gave that away." He repeated this two years later; but, in 1898, in a brief account of Rorke's Drift which appeared in *Answers*, he seems to contradict himself:

> . . . after the fighting was over, and the usual daily ration of rum was served out, he put in an appearance with the rest, pannikin in hand.
> "What!" exclaimed the sergeant, in surprise. "You here!"
> "Yes," replied the hero. "I feel as if I could do with a drop after *that*!"[1]

He was by no means the only member of the 24th Regiment to join the Templars in South Africa. Sergeant Daley, writing a few months later to the widow of another sergeant of the 2/24th who had been killed at Isandlwana, says: "About ten of the Templars are lost altogether." Daley names six of the "Brothers" who had "joined our lodge since we arrived in South Africa" and who were amongst those killed in the battle. He touchingly assures the widow, Mrs. McCaffery, that he and her husband had "been great comrades since

I joined the Order, always going to the lodges together, walking and talking about matters when we got settled down again and able to attend a lodge regular once more."[2] There had been branches of the Templars in Britain for ten years and the brotherhood combined temperance with a certain amount of ritual. Officers tended to be Masons; and the Templars—like the Odd Fellows, which Hook joined later—would have been essentially a working man's order but giving much the same sort of rather mystic exclusiveness.

Pietermaritzburg was the capital of Natal and, apart from Durban, the only town in the Colony "of any significant size." Anthony Trollope, the novelist, had stayed there "for a day or two" in 1877 and liked it "very much." He described it as

> a town covering a large area of ground . . . I do not know that it contains anything that can be called a handsome building;—but the edifices whether public or private are neat, appropriate, and sufficient. The town is surrounded by hills, and is therefore, necessarily, pretty. . . . It contains only a little more than 4,000 white inhabitants, whereas it would seem from the appearance of the place, and the breadth and length of the streets, and the size of the shops, and the number of churches of different denominations, to require more than double that number of persons [but] . . . the deficiency is made up by natives, who in fact do all the manual and domestic work of the place.[3]

Alan F. Hattersley, in his *Pietermaritzburg Panorama*, remarks that the "more prosperous households had large establishments of Zulu servants. These servants were more dependable and more faithful than the houseboys of to-day [1938]." Photographs of the period show what appears to be a frontier town, but "Officers of the Executive Government were expected to wear morning coats with tails"; "Early Victorian fashions were still followed by Pietermaritzburg women in the 'seventies and early 'eighties"; and their houses were "overcrowded with small furniture and knick-knacks."[4] No wonder that Natal, as a whole, struck Trollope "as being peculiarly English, in opposition to much of the Cape Colony which is peculiarly Dutch."[5]

The 2/24th spent its time at Pietermaritzburg "busily employed in drilling and refitting", and taking part in several field days under Lord Chelmsford (as Thesiger should now be called).[6] Godwin-Austen had gone home and Lieutenant Gonville Bromhead had succeeded to the command of "B" Company. His brother officers called him "Gonny" or "Gunny." He was thirty-three, the son of a Lincolnshire baronet and an Irish mother, who had served for four years as an ensign and seven years as a lieutenant. He was one of those officers—

101

rather looked down on by the ambitious—who are content to spend their entire careers in the same regiment. A group photograph in the Regimental Museum shows him amongst the 1st-class shots of the 2/24th; and even critical contemporaries described him as "fearless", "cheery" and "a great favourite in his regiment"—all admirable qualities in a regimental officer.[7]

Until 1965, it was not widely known that Bromhead was deaf; and in an account of the colonial wars, published a few years later, Byron Farwell asserts that "he ought not to have been in the army at all."[8] No doubt Major Farwell was thinking of his own time but Bromhead's deafness would have caused no surprise in the Victorian Army. The Victorians had a good deal to put up with in the way of illness, pain and disability, and their attitudes were necessarily quite different from those which have developed since the coming of the Welfare State and the advances in medicine over the past fifty years. Evelyn Wood—the most successful officer during the Zulu War— was said by a contemporary to be "very deaf"; and Lyttelton tells an anecdote about Lord Kitchener's brother

> an excellent brigade commander [in the Boer War], but very deaf. On one occasion a Long Tom shell burst about 50 yards off when I was talking to him and he said guardedly, "I thought I heard a shell," one of the few he did hear.[9]

Bromhead's deafness would never have become an issue but for his role as the second senior combatant officer in the defence of Rorke's Drift. That engagement thrust him into the lurid lights of publicity—always welcome to some but disconcerting to those who have never sought its attractions. One result of unwanted fame was that Bromhead's intelligence was soon questioned (although a feature of deafness is that the failure to hear may be mistaken for a failure to understand). At least five contemporary criticisms have survived but they remained unpublished until recent times. The first, chronologically, is in a letter which Lieutenant George S. Banister, 2/24th, wrote to his father. Banister was with the column which relieved Rorke's Drift, and he "found old Gunny as cheery as ever" amidst "a scene of awful confusion." Later,

> The Colonel [Degacher] took me aside and said "I promised you the I of M'ship [Instructor of Musketry] and it is still yours as I never go back on my word, but I should like to do something for Bromhead, and it is about the only thing he is fit for, so would you let him have it, and take instead the Adjutantcy?" I told him I did not care for the Adjutantcy and had always looked forward to the other thing, but that under the circumstances I

would not for worlds stand in Bromhead's light.[10]

Next come the remarks of Lieutenant Henry T. Curling, R.A., in a letter to his mother. He was a survivor of the Isandlwana disaster and "his nerves were a good deal shaken." Writing from Pietermaritzburg on the 28th of April, he says:

> It is very amusing to read the accounts of Chard [commanding officer during the defence of Rorke's Drift] and Bromhead. They are about the most commonplace men in the British army. . . . Bromhead is a stupid old fellow as deaf as a post. Is it not curious how some men are forced into notoriety.[11]

In his home letters during 1879, Curling several times bewails his failure to gain promotion; and it must have been gall and wormwood to find "a stupid old fellow" of his own rank not only being promoted but also being awarded the V.C.

Probably the best-known reflection on Bromhead is in a letter which Major C.F. Clery—Principal Staff Officer of No. 3 Column, in the first invasion of Zululand—wrote in May to Lady Alison, wife of the Chief of Intelligence at the War Office. Telling her that he "will have a little gossip", he amply fulfils expectations:

> Bromhead is a great favourite in his regiment and a capital fellow at everything except soldiering. So little was he held to be qualified in this way from unconquerable indolence that he had to be reported confidentially as hopeless. This is confidential as I was told it by his commanding officer [Degacher]. I was about a month with him at Rorke's Drift after Isandlwana, and the height of his enjoyment seemed to be to sit all day on a stone on the ground smoking a most uninviting-looking pipe. The only thing that seemed equal to moving him in any way was any allusion to the defence of Rorke's Drift. This used to have a sort of electrical effect on him, for up he would jump and off he would go, and not a word could be got out of him. When I told him he should send me an official report on the affair it seemed to have a most distressing effect on him. I used to find him hiding away in corners with a friend helping him to complete this account, and the only thing that afterwards helped to lessen the compassion I felt for all this, was my own labour when perusing this composition—to understand what it was all about. So you can fancy that there was not one who knew him who envied him his distinction, for his modesty about himself was, and is, excessive.[12]

Clery's outpourings to Sir Archibald and Lady Alison caused a friend, who read them at the time, to point out that: "Throughout the letters there is not one word of kindly appreciation of the services of anyone else [during the Zulu War]."[13] Clery was, though, an admirer of Sir Garnet Wolseley—who had not then arrived in South Africa—and he seems to have been a disappointed "candidate" for inclusion in Wolseley's influential "Ring."

Two prominent members of the Ring were Wood and Buller, who greatly enhanced their reputations in Zululand. After the War, they were invited to Balmoral and their visit was recorded by Sir Henry Ponsonby, the Queen's Private Secretary. Most of their remarks about Rorke's Drift concern Lieutenant Chard; but they were also disparaging about Bromhead (though probably only from hearsay):

> Bromehead [sic] was fearless but hopelessly stupid. They could understand Chard & Bromehead bravely resisting to the death—but that they should have actively ordered any defence was impossible.[14]

On the 11th of September—the day after Ponsonby wrote his account—Sir Garnet Wolseley made this entry in his journal:

> The troops paraded [at Utrecht] at 9 a.m. & I gave away two Victoria Crosses, one to Major Bromhead 24th & the other to Private [Robert] Jones 24th Regt.—I have now given away these decorations to both the officers who took part in the defence of Roorke's [sic] Drift, and two duller, more stupid, more uninteresting even or less like Gentlemen it has not been my luck to meet for a long time.[15]

Wolseley also "gave away" a Cross to Hook, so more will be said about him later; but three points should be made here: Firstly, he was the Army's leading intellectual—as well as its youngest and best-known general—and, measured against him, many officers would have seemed "dull" and "stupid." Secondly, he was a vehement critic of the praises and rewards which were generously bestowed on the defenders of Rorke's Drift. And lastly, Wood, before his return home, had given Wolseley his own unflattering opinion of Chard and Bromhead.[16]

The cumulative effect of these assessments of Bromhead may overwhelm even a sympathetic reader; but after all the discussions about Rorke's Drift at Balmoral, one courtier wrote that: "Bromhead . . . had of course great influence over his own men, and kept them in their places or moved them about, controlled their fire with great judgment." One matter of substance should also be corrected. Major Clery says that he observed Bromhead writing an "official report"—although the true "official report" on Rorke's Drift was naturally written by Chard—but no such report has survived. On the 15th of February, Bromhead did write to Colonel Degacher bringing to his notice the six men of "B" Company whose names form the original list of V.C. winners. Perhaps Clery meant this letter which, as published, is perfectly lucid; but at least three other letters by Bromhead are known to exist. They cancel out altogether the assertions that he was stupid—they are quite simply not the letters of a stupid man.[17] That Bromhead was not an outstanding officer is evident; but that he was the object of at least some envy and resentment is equally apparent. The fact that his colonel thought that something should be done for him, after Rorke's Drift, shows that on that occasion—the great day of his life—Bromhead had done the regiment full credit.

2.

On the last day of 1878, Sir Garnet Wolseley was in Cyprus, hoping that he would not be there much longer if there were to be wars in Afghanistan and Zululand:

> When I was in Natal [in 1875] I took notes in preparation for an invasion of Cetewayo's territory. Thinking then I should have a command when the war, which everyone in South Africa knew and felt must come off sooner or later, did take place. With his 40,000 men armed with fire-arms he will be no mean enemy.[18]

If Wolseley had been taking notes as early as 1875, Lord Chelmsford was "turning his attention to 'impending hostilities with the Zulus' " before he had quite finished with the Ninth Frontier War.[19] Nor was this premonition of war with the Zulus confined to officers of high rank. Throughout the Frontier War, Arthur Harness, an artillery major, had "constantly reiterated" in his letters home "his expectation of moving to Natal to prepare for war against the Zulu nation."[20] The old history of the 24th Regiment, compiled by three of its officers, states plainly that war with the Zulus was "a foregone conclusion, and in point of fact a mere question of time."[21] This feeling that the war was "a foregone conclusion" must have filtered down to the ranks long before "hostilities" actually began.

There were three main differences between the war which had just ended and the one which was now expected. In the first place, the military had made no preparations for what grew into the Frontier War. Secondly, that war had merely "broken out" and, eventually, it "fizzled out"; while the Zulu Kingdom—like a European power—

was given an ultimatum which, as no-one expected it to be accepted, was tantamount to a declaration of war. The ultimatum was delivered on the 11th of December 1878 and "hostilities" followed immediately after it expired, a month later. Thirdly, as Wolseley had foreseen, there was a planned invasion of Zululand, aimed at the destruction of its capital, Ulundi. When that had been achieved, the war was deemed to be over and a "settlement" was imposed by the victors. Such formality and symmetry were greatly in contrast to the "shapelessness" of the fighting in Cape Colony.

The celebrated ultimatum was issued by Sir Bartle Frere without the knowledge or consent of the home government, and its consequences have therefore usually been held to be "Frere's war."[22] He had been asked to go to South Africa to bring about a confederation of the various territories along the lines of the Canadian federation and, if he succeeded, he was to have been its first governor-general. Frere was extremely able, determined and experienced but there was, in fact, no true analogy between South Africa and Canada and he soon found that the difficulties were much greater than either he or the Colonial Secretary had reckoned with. By the time he had been at the Cape for a year, he had become convinced not only that the Zulu Kingdom was one of the main obstacles in his path but that its king, Cetshwayo, was at the head of "a widespread combination against the white man."[23] He saw the Zulu military system and its redoubtable army as a "standing menace", especially to Natal, which had a long and exposed border with Zululand. It was necessary, he decided, "to settle with the Zulus", hence the ultimatum, with its impossible demand that the Zulu army should be disbanded.

Up to the early part of October 1878, the Colonial Office appeared to give him its rather unenthusiastic support; but

> At this point Disraeli [Prime Minister since 1874], who had been "extremely dissatisfied" by the [9th] Cape-Xhosa War, seems suddenly to have become aware that a new and more serious war now threatened in South Africa.[24]

On the 7th of November, the Colonial Secretary wrote to Frere

> that matters in Eastern Europe & India [which had been occupying Disraeli's attention] . . . wear so serious an aspect that we *cannot now have a Zulu war in addition to other greater and too possible troubles.*[25]

This letter, which has generally been interpreted as a "veto" on war, reached the proconsul on the 13th of December—two days *after* his ultimatum had been delivered to the envoys of Cetshwayo.[26] Frere felt that there could be no going back; and, indeed, his gamble on a quick and decisive campaign would probably have succeeded if he had had the services of Wolseley, who was a master of the "small wars" of that era (especially of their logistics). But Frere had, instead, the services of Lord Chelmsford and both men were ruined.

3.

Several weeks before the ultimatum was even delivered, the 2/24th was moving north towards the frontier. The Tugela River, which debouches into the Indian Ocean; and then the Buffalo River, which flows into the Tugela, formed the borders between Natal and Zululand. The route to these rivers from Pietermaritzburg lay over roads which were "little more than 'mud-hole tracks.'" Three companies left the town at the end of October; and "the remainder of the battalion [including "B" Company] followed soon after, under Major Dunbar . . . and encamped at Greytown.[27]

Dunbar's troops were joined by a battery under Major Harness, who wrote home:

> Our old friends the 2nd Battalion 24th Foot are here, and their band met us and played us in. This is rather a pretty little village, hilly ground all round, and we are encamped about a quarter of a mile from the village, but there is nothing to induce one to go into it. Yesterday the band played for the entertainment of the inhabitants. . . . We have had a fair amount of rain lately and the grass looks a little green; but when not raining it is very hot.
> . . . The cooking is a great difficulty as the fires will not keep alight.[28]

He was still complaining about the rain in early December:

> The hot winds which we always have whenever it does not rain have something of the effect upon one that the Malta sirocco has. The rain comes regularly every afternoon with heavy thunderstorms. . . .
> The 1st Battalion of the 24th [four companies only] marched in here yesterday [1st December]; they precede us to Helpmekaar and go on tomorrow. . . . Colonel Glyn will be in command of the whole force at Helpmekaar, but the general [Chelmsford] will be there himself mostly, I fancy.[29]

What Harness meant by "the whole force" was the 3rd (or Centre)

Column, which was assembling at Helpmekaar for the invasion.[30] Helpmekaar was on a "broad, well-watered plateau" twelve miles from Rorke's Drift, the point on the Buffalo River where the Column was to cross into Zululand.

It would seem that the elevated, windy position of Helpmekaar, with its cold nights, made it freer than normal from the Natal bane of horse-sickness . . .

Throughout December the encampment grew with the arrival of the other units that were to make up the Centre Column, and by early January the two lone houses at Helpmekaar had quite disappeared in a sea of white tents and government stores.[31]

As Christmas approached, the 2/24th—now reunited under Degacher—was still at Greytown, about forty-five miles in a straight line to the southeast. Permission had been given for it to remain there over Christmas Day but

owing to a message which had come in from the Border, to the effect that Cetywayo was calling in his men for the different regiments, Colonel Degacher had decided on sending four companies of the 2-24th to Helpmakaar at once, . . . the waggons were got ready in good time with serviceable oxen, and, headed by their band, the four companies, under Major Dunbar, marched out of town at 11.30 [on Christmas Eve].[32]

"B" Company was part of Dunbar's wing of the battalion. Although Hook left no account of this Christmas march, one of the corporals described it as "the worst I have gone through since I have been out here":

We had sixteen miles to go the first day, and got to camp at about six o'clock p.m. The second day we started at five o'clock in the morning; we went eleven miles, crossed the River Mooi, all down hill, and got there about ten o'clock. We had our breakfast and Christmas dinner after we had crossed, at the other side, a dinner that was not fit for a dog to eat—at least, the meat we had dogs would not eat it; it was bullocks that had died on the side of the road and were then cut up for us. . . .

At three o'clock the same day we left the Mooi River, marching twelve more miles, that was altogether twenty-three miles that day; to make it worse we had to go through a wood seventeen miles long. At eight o'clock that night we got to the River Tugela, and it was that dark we could not see one another, and raining in torrents, and we had to sleep on the ground wet through without anything to put under or over us [as the waggons had fallen behind]. . . . We slept that night, got up the next morning at five o'clock, and commenced to cross the river at six, and we had not done until four in the afternoon. We then pitched tents and slept there for the night. We started the next morning at four o'clock and went eight miles; halted, had breakfast and dinner, and started again at three, marched ten more miles and got to camp at seven-thirty at Sands Spruit, . . . We had a rest there the next day. Sunday we marched at five and had a worse hill to go up than the one on the first day, but not so long. We got to the camp at Helpmakaar about five o'clock in the evening, and was played into camp by the band of the 1/24th Regiment who were there before us. They had a nice bit of dinner ready for us, and did all our work for us when we got in.[33]

Dunbar's wing spent only about a week at Helpmekaar before moving down to Rorke's Drift. Private Jobbins, of "B" Company, told his parents:

We arrived at Rorke's Drift on the 6th [January] and we were allowed one hour for dinner, and mount our duty, which we were on 24 hours, and not even time for a smoke at times; so I can assure you that it is not all sugar out here.[34]

Frere's ultimatum would expire at midnight on the 10th of January. By the day before, "4,709 men, 302 waggons and carts, and 1,507 oxen and 116 horses and mules" were waiting at Rorke's Drift, where a supply depot and field hospital had been set up.[35] The stores and hospital obviously had to be guarded and, during the 10th, Bromhead was told that his company had been detailed for this duty. No evidence has come to light to show how or why the decision was reached, or if it was generally resented by the men of "B" Company (although Bourne, their colour-sergeant, later remarked that "at the time I was bitterly disappointed"). Only in retrospect did this assignment assume any importance and it was probably "a routine posting."[36]

The post of Rorke's Drift was about half-a-mile from the drift (or ford) of the Buffalo River, and the Army had taken over the only two buildings which stood on the site. "Both buildings were of rough stone packed with dagga [an African plant], roofed with thatch." One was the old store of a trader, James Rorke—this explains why the Zulus called the engagement the "fight at Jim's"—which in recent years had been used as the church of a Swedish Mission. Under the supervision of Assistant Commissary W.A. Dunne, the building reverted to a storehouse:

The quantity of Supplies to be stored was very large and my

109

work was very arduous, . . .

Heavily laden ox-waggons constantly came and went, accompanied by the usual yelling, whip cracking, and bellowing; piles of corn bags, biscuit boxes, etc. rose up; detachments of troops were continually arriving and pitching their tents—all the bustle of a large camp and depôt was apparent.

The tents of "B" Company were behind this store.[37]

The second building was the eleven-room house of the missionary, which was turned into a hospital and became the scene of Hook's best-known exploits. Despite the number of rooms, it was only about sixty feet in length and the rooms at the back and sides were small (in some cases, as Hook remembered, "so small that you could hardly swing a bayonet in them"). The two main rooms were at the front, shaded by a verandah and facing a dirt road and fruit garden. Surgeon James H. Reynolds, and three men of the Medical Department, fitted up one of the front rooms as an operating theatre, used a corner room for medical supplies, and cleared the remaining rooms "for patient's beds, and storage of their kit and rifles." The verandah, "screened with army blankets . . . became home to a number of patients, presumably convalescents." By the 22nd of January (the day of the Zulu attack), Reynolds had "some thirty six patients listed in his admissions book, . . . [including three who] were receiving treatment for wounds received in action."[38]

The post was invulnerable to attack while the troops of the Centre Column remained nearby, on the Natal side of the river. Even when the column crossed into Zululand, a few hours after the ultimatum expired, it remained close to the river until the 20th of January. That day, Lord Chelmsford marched about ten miles into the interior and camped at Isandlwana, the place which was to be "always with him" as long as he lived. To Commissary Dunne, the post at Rorke's Drift now seemed "silent and lonely." Apart from Bromhead's company, the only organised force "left behind" was a company of the Natal Native Contingent under a white officer, Captain Stephenson. (As Stephenson was not an Imperial officer, and so could not command Imperial troops, his nominal seniority to Bromhead was immaterial.) When Hallam Parr saw the post, the morning after the defence, he thought that

A worse position could hardly be imagined. Two small thatched buildings, about thirty-nine yards apart, with thin walls, commanded by rising ground on the south and west, completely overlooked on the south by a high hill. On the north side an orchard and garden gave good cover to an enemy up to within a few yards of the houses.[39]

The weakness of the position was apparent to Bromhead, who told Penn Symons that he had twice asked permission from Chelmsford's staff to put the post "in a state of defence". When permission was refused, he was nevertheless "so persuaded of the danger" that "he made up his mind what to do if occasion should arise." (Hook, in one of his lesser-known accounts, says that "it was really Lieut. Bromhead who arranged the hastily-organised defence.") Permission to fortify the post may have been refused because the staff knew that orders had been sent to Captain Rainforth, of the 1/24th, to march from Helpmekaar, with his company, and build a fort at the Drift, where there were "two large Ponts." Under curious circumstances, Rainforth never arrived, so neither the drift nor the post was "in a state of defence." Despite his concern, Bromhead was not actually the senior officer left at the post, as Major Henry Spalding, of the 104th Regiment—who was in charge of part of the line of communications—had his tent there and signed the Camp Orders.[40]

On the 19th of January, the relative "silence and loneliness" was slightly disturbed by the arrival of Lieutenant Chard and five men of the Royal Engineers. Like the assignment of "B" Company to guard the post, Chard's arrival there had no significance which was apparent at the time. Chard has an entry in *The Dictionary of National Biography* solely because, three days later, in Major Spalding's absence, the command of Rorke's Drift devolved upon him and he held it against the Zulu attack. No-one could pretend that his career would otherwise justify such a distinction, but Chard—like Bromhead—has been subjected to criticism of such virulence that the enquiring person is bound to wonder at its cause.

John Rouse Merriott Chard was a year younger than Bromhead, a Devon man from the prosperous middle classes, with an elder brother in the Army and a younger one in the Church. He attended grammar school and then entered "The Shop" (The Royal Military Academy at Woolwich), where officers of the Engineers and Artillery were trained. The two-and-a-half year course consisted of both practical and theoretical subjects, including fortification. As it had never been possible to "purchase" into these scientific corps, there could be no question of the intelligence and ability of those who successfully passed through "The Shop." Chard was commissioned into the Royal Engineers in 1868 and was stationed in Malta and Bermuda (where he was employed on dockyard fortifications), as well as in England. The Engineers were a combatant corps but he had not yet been on active service when he was posted to South Africa at the end of 1878.[41]

With one exception, the same officers who excoriated Bromhead did the same with Chard. Here is the disgruntled Curling, writing to his mother in April 1879: "Chard is a most insignificant man in appearance and is only 5 ft 2 or 3 in. in height."[42] Next in order comes the letter from Major Clery to Lady Alison:

> Well, Chard and Bromhead to begin with: both are almost typical in their separate corps of what would be termed the very dull class. . . .
> Chard there is very little to say about except that he too is a "very good fellow"—but very uninteresting.[43]

On the 16th of July, Chard had the misfortune to meet Sir Garnet Wolseley, whose journal entry reads:

> I presented Major Chard R.E. with his Victoria X: a more uninteresting or more stupid-looking fellow I never saw. Wood tells me he is a most useless officer, fit for nothing.[44]

After Rorke's Drift, Chard was promoted captain and brevet major; and on the 2nd of August, his old company commander wrote privately:

> Chard got his orders to leave the 5th Company for good and departed yesterday. He is a most amiable fellow and a loss to the mess, but as a company officer he is so hopelessly slow and slack. I shall get on much better without him . . . Chard makes me angry, with such a start as he got, he stuck to the company doing nothing. In his place I should have gone up and asked Lord Chelmsford for an appointment, he must have got it and if not he could have gone home soon after Rorke's Drift, at the height of his popularity and done splendidly at home. I advised him, but he placidly smokes his pipe and does nothing. Few men get such opportunities.[45]

In this letter, the fizzing exasperation of Captain Jones at Chard's apparent indifference to fame and ambition is only too evident.

When Wood and Buller were at Balmoral, Ponsonby recorded that

> They spoke to me about Rorke's Drift. They could not conceive why Chelmsford did not fortify it. The defence was brilliant and stubborn. But the puzzle to them was—who was the man who organised it—for it showed genius and quickness neither of which was apparently the qualification of Chard.

A dull heavy man who seemed scarcely even able to do his regular work. One day Wood sent him to clear some ground and when he arrived later found nothing done and Chard asleep. Another day he was sent to find a ford & make it passable. Fearing his man and that a halt might be inconvenient to the Army Wood rode forward. Found Chard quite helpless—he didn't seem to take in clearly what a ford was—and had done nothing. Wood ordered his man to do it—Yet Chard's despatch was a good one.[46]

These incidents with Wood—which obviously lost nothing in the telling—belong to the *second* invasion of Zululand.

In October, Chard was himself summoned to Balmoral. He charmed the Queen with his "modest, unassuming demeanour": she presented him with "a valuable Waterkloof diamond ring" and asked him to write her a personal account of Rorke's Drift. He had made a lasting impression and, at the time of his death in 1897, the Queen sent a laurel wreath with a card inscribed: "A mark of admiration and regard for a brave soldier. From his Sovereign."[47] One of the courtiers—writing, oddly enough, to Wood—gives his own opinion of Chard:

He explained the defence of Rorke's Drift to the Queen, Prince Leopold, the Grand Duke of Hesse, and Princess Beatrice in the Queen's private room, and did it all very clearly and modestly. After dinner he did likewise to us in the billiard room on the table, where store and hospital were books and boxes, and mealie-bags and biscuit tins were billiard balls. . . .

He is not a genius and not quick, but a quiet, plodding, dogged sort of fellow who will hold his own in most of the situations in which, as an Engineer officer, his lot may be cast.[48]

Chard lived longer than Bromhead, reaching the rank of colonel, and holding two posts as "Commanding Royal Engineer." After his death, Colonel R.H. Vetch wrote in the *Royal Engineers Journal* that:

Few military incidents in history had a greater effect at the time, or will, for all time, remain a more memorable instance of gallantry and tenacity . . . and the fact that a young subaltern of engineers, of no very conspicuous ability, rose to the occasion, and was the hero of the gallant defence of the post . . . is one that has made the Corps proud of Chard, who had done it honour . . .

This "damning with faint praise" is perpetuated in a recent, semi-official work, *The Sapper VCs*; but, paradoxically, Chard is the best-remembered of the Corps's fifty-five V.C. winners and is depicted on both the dust-jacket and the title-page in a detail from Lady Butler's painting. [49] What Chard and Bromhead were alike in lacking was the "push" not only of Wolseley's Ring (which was composed of quite exceptional officers) but of such men as Jones and Curling. Yet if their critics were right, it seems strange that *both* the combatant officers at Rorke's Drift were so "hopelessly slow" and "hopelessly stupid" but that the post was held for twelve hours against odds of about forty to one!

Two explanations were quickly found. In the first place, it was held to be "essentially a soldiers fight"; and, in fact, Bromhead told Godwin-Austen (then at Brecon) that "the Company behaved splendidly and as our ammunition held out we kept them [the Zulus] back till daylight."[50] Clery—having earlier reported to Sir Archibald Alison that "a most brilliant defence" had been made—later wrote to Lady Alison, in a back-handed way, that:

> The fact is that until the accounts came out from England nobody had thought of the Rorke's Drift affair except as one in which the private soldiers of the 24th behaved so well. For as a matter of fact they all stayed there to defend the place for there was nowhere else to go, and in defending it they fought most determinedly.[51]

Months after the war had ended, Wolseley was scribbling away on much the same theme:

> ... & it is monstrous making heroes of those ... who shut up in the buildings at Roorke's [*sic*] drift could not bolt & and fought like rats for their lives which they could not otherwise save.[52]

This phrase is curiously similar to Hook's "We were pinned like rats in a hole"; but Wolseley was prejudiced against both battalions of the 24th and thought it "ridiculous" that so many awards should have been made to the regiment "owing to Ellice's interest at the Horse Gds."[53] (He meant Sir Charles Ellice, the Adjutant-General, who had commanded the 2/24th in the early eighteen-sixties.)

The second explanation—which was also put forward at the time and has become increasingly fashionable since—is that "the man who worked hardest in defence of Roorke's Drift Post was the Commissariat officer."[54] Again, these are Wolseley's words but of course he had no personal means of knowing and presumably relied on Wood's opinion (which was itself based on hearsay).[55] The "Commissariat officer" was James Langley Dalton, who was actually a civilian serving under Dunne with the appointment of Acting Assistant Commissary. He died eight years later, leaving only a brief account of the defence (in response to a request that he should describe the role of Surgeon Reynolds).[56] Dalton was a Londoner of forty-six, who had served for twelve years in the 85th Regiment, reaching the rank of sergeant before transferring to commissary work. He retired in 1871 and, as he had been stationed at the Cape during his infantry service, he returned there to settle in civil life. On the outbreak of the Ninth Frontier War, Dalton had volunteered for commissary duty; and it has been suggested that "his good working relationship with Glyn [at the Ibeka supply camp] may have been a factor which led to his appointment at Rorke's Drift."[57]

Dalton was a tall, bearded man and no doubt had the "presence" and force of character of a former N.C.O. and of an experienced frontiersman. The men of "B" Company are said to have "raised a deafening cheer" when they saw him standing in the crowd as the battalion marched through Pietermaritzburg at the close of the campaign. Corporal Lyons, in a newspaper, said that "Mr. Dalton . . . deserved any amount of praise"; but there is no mention of him during Colour-Sergeant Bourne's B.B.C. interview.[58] Hook gave six quite substantial accounts of Rorke's Drift without even referring to Dalton, only to bring him in quite fulsomely during his last and longest version. Dalton was certainly prominent in the defence and set a fine example before he was wounded; but one *ex-parte* book credits him with having "dominated the scene" and with being "the leading personality."[59] There was another expansive civilian whose striking appearance and exploits made him a "personality" in the modern "media" sense: Padre George Smith. He is "reported to have thus corrected the men for cursing whilst the fight was at its height. "Don't swear men, don't swear, but shoot them boys, shoot them."[60] The intensity of the action, the confusion of night fighting, and the fact that only two combatant officers were present, all gave plenty of scope for displays of initiative by these brave and energetic civilians. It detracts nothing from them to point out that they had scant authority and bore no responsibility.

More important as far as Dalton is concerned is the assertion—made soon after the action and now repeated almost as a matter of course—that it was he who "originated the defence" or "devised all the rapid arrangements for the defence."[61] If this was the whole truth, it would take much of the credit for the defence from Chard and Bromhead, and the idea is obviously consistent with the caricatures of both officers. But, of course, the truth is not that simple.

Chard was at Rorke's Drift because Lord Chelmsford had directed that "an Officer and a few good men of the RE, with mining implements, etc., should join the 3rd [Centre] Column as soon as possible."[62] When he arrived, he found that the column was camped on the far bank of the Buffalo River but he and his men pitched their tents on the Natal side. One of the ponts in the river needed repair and his sappers began putting it into working order. During the evening of the 21st of January, he received orders for his men to join the column—then at Isandlwana—but his own position was left unclear. He consulted Major Spalding and got permission to go with his sappers to Isandlwana next morning and find out whether he should remain with them. When he reached Chelmsford's camp, he could see that Zulus were "moving on the distant hills"; and, by that time, the general himself had left on his ill-starred reconnaissance-in-force. Chard learned that his own duties "lay on the right [Natal] bank of the River Buffalo", so he rode back to the Drift. There, he was handed Spalding's "Camp Morning Orders" detailing seven men of Bromhead's company, and "50 armed natives", to guard the ponts until the expected arrival of Captain Rainforth's company. He rode on to the post itself and had the interview with Spalding which became so memorable in retrospect:

> [I] pointed out to him that in the event of an attack on the Ponts it would be impossible with seven men (not counting the natives) to make an effective defence. . . . Major Spalding told me he was going over to Helpmakaar, and would see about getting it [Rainforth's company] down at once. Just as I was about to ride away he said to me "Which of you is senior, you or Bromhead?" I said "I don't know"—he went back into his tent, looked at an Army List, and coming back, said—"I see you are senior, so you will be in charge, although, of course, nothing will happen, and I shall be back again this evening early."[63]

In his account for the Queen, Chard says that he then went down to his own tent, "had some lunch comfortably, and was writing a letter home," when news was brought from across the river that the camp at Isandlwana was "in the hands of the Zulus and the army destroyed." This was at about 3.15 p.m.[64] Almost at the same moment, "a messenger arrived from Lieutenant Bromhead . . . [asking Chard] to come up at once." The "armed natives" had left earlier and the ponts were guarded only by a sergeant and six men of "B" Company. After giving some orders to the sergeant, Chard galloped up to the post: Major Spalding had left at two o'clock, so Chard was now in charge of both the post and the ponts.

Apart from Bromhead, there were two other Imperial officers at the post, Surgeon Reynolds and Commissary Dunne. At about the time when Chard was lunching alone, Bromhead and Dunne were lunching together. In his "Reminiscences", published thirteen years later, Dunne describes the sequel:

Bromhead and I were resting after luncheon under an awning which we had formed by propping up a tarpaulin with tent poles; everything was peaceful and quiet, when, suddenly, we noticed at some distance across the river a large number of mounted natives approaching, preceded by a lot of women and children and oxen. We were going down to find out what they were, but had not gone many steps when we were called back by one of the men who said that a mounted orderly wished to see the officer in command. Turning back at once we met a mounted man in his shirt sleeves riding hurriedly towards us. His first words were "The camp is taken by Zulus!" . . . we soon gathered the truth that . . . the Zulus, flushed with victory, were advancing to attack our post.

Dalton, as brave a soldier as ever lived, had joined us, and hearing the terrible news said "Now, we must make a defence!" It was his suggestion which decided us to form a breastwork of bags of grain, boxes of biscuit, and everything that would help to stop a bullet or keep out a man. An ox-waggon and even barrels of rum and lime juice were pressed into the service.

Bromhead at once ordered the men to fall in; outposts were thrown out, tents were struck, ammunition was served out, and the work of putting up the barricade was begun by all hands. Other preparations were also made: a water barrel was filled and brought inside, and several boxes of ammunition were opened and placed in convenient places. . . . Chard had now come up from the river and heartily superintended the progression of the fortification, making many improvements.[65]

In this account, Dunne has forgotten Dr. Reynolds and in *his* official report of the defence, Reynolds forgets Dunne! The doctor had not been lunching but had, instead, climbed the Oscarberg, the hill overlooking the post. This was at about 12.30 p.m. when, as he wrote, "we were surprised at Rorke's Drift by hearing big guns in our neighbourhood." Even from the hill, he was unable to see "the scene of action" but eventually four horsemen appeared below, "galloping in the direction of our post." Reynolds thought that they "might possibly be messengers for additional medical assistance" and he "hurried down to the hospital and got there as they rode up."

They shouted frantically, "the camp at Isandlana has been taken by the enemy and all our men in it massacred, that no power could stand against the enormous number of the Zulus, and the only chance for us all was by immediate flight." Lieutenant

Bromhead, Acting Commissary Dalton, and myself forthwith consulted together, Lieutenant Chard not having as yet joined us from the pontoon, and we quickly decided that with barricades well placed around our present position a stand could best be made where we were.

In other words, removing the sick and wounded would have been embarrassing to our movements, and desertion of them was never thought of.

Just at this period Mr. Dalton's energies were invaluable. Without the smallest delay, which would have been so fatal for us, he called upon the men (all eager for doing) to carry the mealie sacks here and there for defences, and it was charming to find in a short time how comparatively protected we had made ourselves. Lieutenant Chard arrived as this work was in progress and gave many useful orders as regards the lines of defence. He approved also of the hospital being taken in, . . . [66]

Chard says, in describing his arrival:

Lieutenant Bromhead had, with the assistance of Mr. Dalton, Dr. Reynolds and the other Officers present, commenced barricading and loopholing the stores building and the Missionary's house, which was used as a Hospital, and connecting the defence of the two buildings by walls of mealie bags, and two wagons that were on the ground. The Native Contingent, under their Officer, Captain Stephenson, were working hard at this with our own men, and the walls were rapidly progressing. . . . I held a consultation with Lieutenant Bromhead, and with Mr. Dalton, whose energy, intelligence and gallantry were of the greatest service to us, and whom I said in my [official] report at the time, and I am sure Bromhead would unite with me in saying again now [to the Queen], I cannot sufficiently thank for his services. I went round the position with them and then rode down to the Ponts where I found everything ready for a start [back to the post], Ponts in midstream, hawsers and cables sunk etc.[67]

These eyewitness accounts bring out what is easily forgotten in the froth over "personalities": that whatever others might do or suggest, Chard, as commanding officer, *alone* bore the *responsibility* for the defence.

4.

The Zulus who had overrun Lord Chelmsford's camp were using

the same methods, and largely the same weapons, as their people had been using for the past seventy years. If the British Army had tended towards conservatism since Waterloo, "Zulu military thinking . . . [was also] of the most conservative kind." The application of this "thinking" gave the Zulus three clear victories in their war against the British but it also brought them heavy losses on nearly every field, so that even Isandlwana came close to being a pyrrhic victory. On the same day, the "extraordinary bravery and persistence" of their attack on Rorke's Drift led to "insupportable" casualties, without the solace of success.[68]

It was the sheer courage of the Zulus, throughout the war, which most impressed the British soldiers and this comes out strongly in their letters home. One sergeant wrote: "I confess that I do not think that a braver lot of men than our enemies in point of disregard for life, and for their bravery under fire, could be found anywhere." A colour-sergeant, recalling old times, gives a vivid glimpse of the difference between expectation and reality: "our 'school' at Chatham, over one hot whisky, used to laugh about these niggers, but I assure you that fighting with them is terribly earnest work, and not child's play."[69]

The "basic traditional weapon" of the Zulus was the spear, or assegai, of which the most deadly type was "the short-handled stabbing-spear . . . only used at close quarters, when an underarm stab—normally aimed at the abdomen—was followed without withdrawing by a rip." Two or three "throwing-spears with long shafts" were also carried: "well balance in flight", these were effective at up to about thirty-five yards. Some warriors also favoured a wooden club (knobkerrie), or "a battle-axe with a crescent blade," for close fighting. For defence, they had a shield of cattle-hide "two-thirds of the man-height size" used in earlier times.[70]

Only about half of the Zulu army was equipped with a gun of any kind. Twenty thousand firearms were reckoned to be in Zululand at the outbreak of war: "500 superior British breech-loading rifles, a further 2,500 good rifles like the percussion Enfield, and 5,000 second-hand ones. The balance were inferior weapons, mainly muskets." The number of warriors who were good shots and "familiar with modern firearms" was very small—"probably a few hundred." In consequence, the Zulus "seldom made full use of their firearms or developed new tactics which would have exploited their potential more effectively." This was strikingly evident at Rorke's Drift, where the best they could do was to "lay down a heavy volume of totally inaccurate fire, and hope that some of it struck home." The object of Zulu tactics—as in the days before they had any firearms—was still to get to close quarters with stabbing spears. To Hook, and the

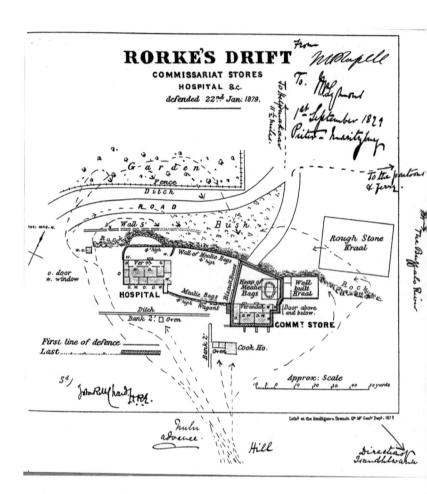

Chard's map of Rorke's Drift, with the signature of Captain Penn Symons at the top right and his date of 1st September 1879.

other defenders of Rorke's Drift, they may have appeared to be advancing in "one black mass" but they actually made good use of the ground.[71]

The three or four thousand warriors who attacked the post had formed the Zulu reserve at Isandlwana and had not been in action. Their commander, Prince Dabulamanzi—described as "the king's over-confident and aggressive half-brother"—afterwards "admitted that he was chagrined at having missed the fighting at Isandlwana and 'wanted to wash the spears of his boys' " (which they themselves wanted to do). Dabulamanzi led "his boys" across the river with the idea of raiding into Natal "as far as the foot of the Helpmekaar heights", returning with some cattle and "with honour vindicated." It was the sight of "kwaJim", lightly defended and apparently easily taken, which soon diverted him from this raid. There was a general belief at the time that the successful defence of "kwaJim" saved Natal from "a wild wave of savage invasion." Few now believe this—the Colony was saved from some burning and pillaging; and Lord Chelmsford from the loss of more men and supplies—but of course the contemporary perception is important and no-one can really know what would have followed if Rorke's Drift had been sacked.[72]

It was "a warm, sunny day with a gentle, cooling breeze just stirring the grass." Hook was "preparing the tea for the sick at the out-of-door cooking place, just at the back of the hospital." At the same time, Frederick Hitch was "cooking the tea for the Company."[73] The reason why these two men, who were to win the V.C. that day, should have been cooking as the Zulus approached was that the Army had very few trained cooks. The privates of a battalion were assigned to this work by roster, as with any other duty; but, unfortunately for Hook, his name rhymes with "cook." It has been too much of a temptation for at least one popular narrator to repeat the phrase "Hook the Cook" and then to express surprise that he was "given a rifle" to help in the defence.[74]

For the rest of his life, Hook was asked about his exploits at Rorke's Drift. At first, he was reluctant to talk but, with experience, he became increasingly practised at telling his story. As historical evidence, his accounts have two obvious limitations. In the first place, as he was becoming more articulate, the events which he was describing were becoming more distant in time. Secondly, as he wrote none of the accounts himself, he was dependent to an extent on what his interviewers wanted to know; what they (or their sub-editors) decided to publish; and how accurate they were in taking down what he said. (It is hardly reassuring to find that the report of his first interview gives his Christian name as "William".[75]) Against this, he was a truthful man and, when his accounts are compared, it can be seen that the variations are consistent both with the common vagaries of memory and with the disadvantages of depending on interviewers. There is also the fact—brought out by Ian Knight in his analysis of the fight in the hospital—that Hook was the "only one of the participants [who] left an account that is anything like detailed."[76] The question is: which of Hook's narratives is to be preferred? The one usually reprinted or quoted from was "gleaned" three or four months before Hook's death and twenty-five years after the event.[77] In 1891—twelve years after the event—*The Strand Magazine* had published a much shorter account, less dramatic and without dialogue. It has no editorial interpolations and purports to consist only of what Hook told the interviewer. This is used here as the basis for what Hook saw and did, with the addition of an incident which he had described earlier, and some explanatory notes.

Between three and four in the afternoon, when I was engaged preparing the tea for the sick at the out-of-door cooking place, just at the back of the hospital—for I was hospital cook—two mounted men, looking much exhausted, and their horses worn out, rode up to me. One was in his shirt sleeves, and without a hat, with a revolver strapped round his breast; the other had his coat and hat on. They stopped for a moment and told me that the whole force on the other side of the river had been cut up, and that the Zulus were coming on in great force. They then rode off. I immediately ran to the camp close by and related what I had heard. We were at once fallen in and set to work to strengthen the post by loopholing the windows of the buildings, and to make breastworks of biscuit boxes and mealie bags.[78] About half an hour later [in fact, over an hour later] the Zulus were seen coming round a hill, and about 1,200 yards off. We were then told off to our posts. I was placed in one of the corner rooms of the hospital. [There were five more privates, with Hook, defending the hospital.]

About this time Captain Stevens [*i.e.*, Stephenson] and all his men [of the Natal Native Contingent], except one native and two Europeans, non-commissioned officers, deserted us, and went off to Helpmakair [*sic*].[79] We were so enraged that we fired several shots at them, one of which dropped a European non-commissioned officer. [The garrison was thus reduced to 139 of all ranks, including civilians and the sick.] From my loophole I saw the Zulus approaching in their thousands. They began to fire, yelling as they did so, when they were 500 or 600 yards off. They came on boldly, taking advantage of anthills and other cover, and we were soon surrounded. More than half of them had muskets or rifles. I began to fire when they were 600 yards distant. I managed to clip several of them, for I had an excellent rifle, and was a "marksman." I recollect particularly one Zulu. He was about 400 yards off, and was running from one anthill to another. As he was running from cover to cover, I fired at him; my bullet caught him in the body, and he made a complete somersault. Another man was lying below an anthill, about 300 yards off, popping his head out now and again to fire. I took careful aim, but my bullet went just over his head. I then lowered my sight, and fired again the next time he showed himself. I saw the bullet strike the ground in a direct line, but about ten yards short. I then took a little fuller sight, aimed at the spot where I knew his head would come out, and, when he showed himself, I fired. I did not then see whether he was struck, but he never showed again. The next morning, when the fighting was over, I felt curious to know whether I had hit this man, so I went to the spot where I had last seen him. I found him lying dead, with his skull pierced by my bullet.

The Zulus kept drawing closer and closer, and I went on firing, killing several of them. At last they got close up, and set fire to the hospital. There was only one patient in my room with a broken leg, and he was burnt, and I was driven out by the flames, and was unable to save him. At first I had a comrade [Private Thomas Cole], but he left after a time, and was killed on his way to the inner entrenchment. When driven out of this room, I retired by a partition door into the next room, where there were several patients. For a few minutes I was the only fighting man there. A wounded man of the 24th came to me from another room with a bullet wound in the arm. I tied it up. Then [Private] John Williams came in from another room, and made a hole in the partition, through which he helped the sick and wounded men. Whilst he was doing this, the Zulus beat in the door, and tried to enter. I stood at the side, and shot and bayoneted several—I could not tell how many, but there were four or five lying dead at my feet. They threw assegais continually, but only one touched me, and that inflicted a scalp wound which I did not think worth reporting; in fact, I did not feel the wound at the time. One Zulu seized my rifle, and tried to drag it away. Whilst we were tussling I slipped in a cartridge and pulled the trigger—the muzzle was against his breast, and he fell dead. Every now and again a Zulu would make a rush to enter—the door would only let in one man at a time—but I bayoneted or shot every one. When all the patients were out except one [Private John Connolly], who owing to a broken leg could not move, I also went through the hole, dragging the man after me, in doing which I broke his leg again. I then stopped at the hole to guard it, whilst Williams was making a hole through the partition into the next room.

When the patients had been got into the next room I followed, dragging the man with the broken leg after me. I stopped at the hole to guard it whilst Williams was helping the patients through a window into the other defences. I stuck to my particular charge, and dragged him out and helped him into the inner line of defences. [This is one of the incidents depicted in de Neuville's painting.] I then took my post behind the parapet where three men had been hit just before. One of these was shot in the thick part of the neck, and was calling on me all night to shift from one side to the other. On this side the blaze of the hospital lighted up the ground in front, enabling us to take aim. The Zulus would every quarter of an hour or so get together and make a rush accompanied by yells. We let them get close, and then fired a volley—sometimes two. This would check them and send them back. Then after a time they would rally and come on again. About 3 a.m. day began to break, and the Zulus retreated. A party, of which I was one, then volunteered to go across to the hospital, where there was a water cart, and bring it in to the inner enclosure, where there was no water, and the wounded were crying for it. When the sun rose we found the Zulus had disappeared. We then went out to search for our missing comrades. I saw one man kneeling behind the outer defences with his rifle to his shoulder, and resting on the parapet as if he were taking aim; I touched him on the shoulder, asking him why he didn't come inside, but he fell over, and I saw he was dead. I saw several others of our dead ripped open and otherwise mutilated. Going beyond the outer defences I went, as I have said before, whither I had killed the man at whom I had fired three shots from the hospital. Going on a little further I came across a very tall Zulu, bleeding from a wound in the leg; I was passing him by when he made a yell and clutched the butt of my rifle, dragging himself on to his knees. We had a severe struggle which lasted for several seconds, when finding he could not get the rifle from me, he let go with one hand and caught me round the leg, trying to throw me. Whilst he was doing this I got the rifle from him, and drawing back a yard or two, loaded and blew his brains out. I then was fetched back to the fort, and no one was allowed to go out save with other men. Then several of us went out together, and we brought in several wounded Zulus. By this time it was about eight or nine o'clock, and we saw a body [of Zulus] coming towards us; at the same time Lord Chelmsford's column came in sight, and the enemy retired.[80]

Lord Chelmsford, soon after he arrived, called me up to enquire about the defence of the hospital. I was busy preparing tea for the sick and wounded, and was in my shirt-sleeves, with my braces down. I wanted to put on my coat before appearing in front of the General, but I was told to come along at once, and I felt rather nervous at leaving in such a state, and thought I had committed some offence. When Lord Chelmsford heard my story he praised me and shook me by the hand.[81]

Lord Chelmsford had spent the night at what, a few hours earlier, had been his headquarters camp. During the day, his reconnaissance had become aimless and it had ended in a belated forced march back to Isandlwana. There, seeing "a big flame . . . [which] burst out from where Rorke's Drift post was thought to be", he was tormented not only by the destruction of his own camp but by the fear that the depots at Rorke's Drift and Helpmekaar would also be lost. He resumed the march before there was enough light for the men of his column to see clearly the wreckage and carnage about them. As his troops neared Rorke's Drift, "all thought: 'Again too late!' for heavy smoke was rising from the house [hospital] and Zulus were seen retiring from it, but . . . to our intense relief however, the waving of hats was seen from the inside of a hastily-erected entrenchment."[82] It must be a question *whose* relief was the most intense—the garrison's or the general's! As Lord Chelmsford shook hands with its defenders, the legend of Rorke's Drift was born.

NOTES

1. "How he Won his Victoria Cross," an article which appeared in an unidentified West-country newspaper on 21 May 1881. Reprinted as Appendix C; "The Victoria Cross: How, Where, and by Whom Won", in *Rare Bits*, c. 1883; "What Becomes of V.C. Heroes", in *Answers*, 22 January 1898. (Cuttings in Furness Collection.) The story in *Answers* seems to be the original version of the one given in Michael Glover's *Rorke's Drift* (1975), p. 123.
2. Emery, *op. cit.*, p. 103.
3. Trollope, Anthony, *South Africa* (originally pub. in 2 vols., 1878. Reprinted, Gloucester: Alan Sutton Pub. Ltd., 1987), I, pp. 208-09.
4. Hattersley, Alan F., *Pietermaritzburg Panorama* (Pietermaritzburg: Shuter and Shooter, 1938), pp. 81-89.
5. Trollope, *op. cit.*, I, p. 186.
6. *Historical Records of the 2nd Battalion, 24th Regiment, for the Campaign in South Africa, 1877-78-79; Embracing the Kaffir & Zulu Wars* (Secunderabad: privately printed, 1882). The part headed "The Zulu War" has separate pagination numbered 1-58. (Cited hereafter as "Zulu War".) The quotation is at p. 1.
7. *Army List* for 1878; Summary of career in: Lummis, William M., *Padre George Smith of Rorke's Drift* (Norwich: Wensum Books Ltd., 1978), p. 85.
8. The exposé was made by Donald R. Morris—*The Washing of the Spears* (American ed., 1965; British ed., London: Jonathan Cape, 1966), pp. 264 & 317—but there is no reason to believe the other remarks which he makes about Bromhead; Farwell, Byron, *Queen Victoria's Little Wars* (London: Allan Lane, 1973), p. 231.
9. Lyttelton, *op. cit.*, p. 235. The remark about Wood was made by Sir Henry Ponsonby (see n. 14, below).
10. Banister to his father, Rorke's Drift, 27 January 1879 (typescript in Regt. Museum).
11. *The Journal of the Anglo Zulu War Historical Society*, December 1999, p. 29.
12. Clarke, Sonia, *Zululand at War, 1879* (Johannesburg: The Brenthurst Press, 1984), p. 131 (letter dated 16 May 1879).

13. *Ibid.*, p. 271. The friend was John F. Maurice, the writer on military science and a member of Wolseley's "Ring."

14. "Observations on the Zulu War, 1879" by P.H. Butterfield, in *Africana Notes and News*, Vol. 26, No. 1, March 1984, p. 8. (This paper is based on Ponsonby's letters at Windsor Castle.)

    For an outline of Wolseley's Ring—and its rival, Roberts's Ring—see *Buller's Campaign* by Julian Symons (1963), pp. 3-21.

15. Wolseley, Sir Garnet, *The South African Journal of, 1879-1880*, ed. with an introduction by Adrian Preston (Cape Town: A.A. Balkema, 1973), p. 112. In the introduction, Wolseley is compared to Field Marshal Montgomery; but he had no popular nickname, like "Monty" and, despite his general celebrity, was somewhat distant from his troops.

16. *Ibid.*, p. 57.

17. Emery, Frank, *Marching over Africa: Letters from Victorian Soldiers* (London: Hodder and Stoughton, 1986), p. 84; parts of Bromhead's letter to Degacher are reprinted in Chapter VII; his letter to Hook, dated 30 September 1881, is in *R.D. & B.M.*, p. 39; part of a letter written to his sister soon after Rorke's Drift is given in French, *op. cit.*, p. 113; and his letter to Godwin-Austen, dated 19 February 1879, is in the Regt. Museum.

18. Wolseley, Sir Garnet, *Cyprus 1878: The Journal of . . .*, edited by Anne Cavendish (Nicosia: Cyprus Popular Bank Cultural Centre, 1991), p. 164.

19. French, *op. cit.*, p. 40.

20. Clarke, Sonia, *Invasion of Zululand, 1879* (Johannesburg: The Brenthurst Press, 1979), p. 35.

21. Paton, Glennie & Symons, *op. cit.*, p. 223.

22. "It was Frere's war, but the blame he incurred for it in England was . . . a good deal more than he deserved."—Coupland, Sir Reginald, *Zulu Battle Piece: Isandhlwana* (London: Collins, 1948), p. 42; "The war was therefore emphatically Frere's war."—Blake, Robert, *Disraeli* (London: Eyre & Spottiswoode, 1966), p. 669.

    The complicated controversy over the origins of the Zulu War, has been reduced here to the barest outline. See Chapter XIII, "Events Leading up to the Zulu War," in *A History of Natal* by Edgar H. Brookes and Colin De B. Webb (Pietermaritzburg: University of Natal Press, 1965); and, on Frere's side, the only biography: Martineau, John, *The Life and Correspondence of the Right Hon. Sir Bartle Frere* (2 vols., London: John Murray, 1895). More correspondence is in: Worsfold, Basil, *Sir Bartle Frere* (London: Thornton Butterworth, 1923).

23. Goodfellow, Clement Francis, *Great Britain and South African Confederation, 1870-1881* (Cape Town: Oxford University Press, 1966), p. 159. This is the standard work from the Imperial viewpoint; and for the Zulu side, see Laband, John, *The Rise & Fall of the Zulu Nation* (London: Arms and Armour Press, 1997). Published in South Africa as *Rope of Sand* (1995), this splendid and detailed work, scrupulously fair and balanced, concludes (pp. 211-12) that while "there is no doubt that as the crisis intensified and war loomed, Cetshwayo was in search of allies against the British, . . . [he] found that when it came to war he had to face the British alone."

24. Goodfellow, *op. cit.*, pp. 160-161.

25. *Ibid.*, p. 161.

26. Of its seven demands, "the king's inner council reportedly were prepared to acquiesce to all the terms of the ultimatum—except the fundamental ones relating to the abolition of the *ibutho* system [*i.e.*, regiments formed according to age and marital status] . . . [which] could never be conceded except at the point of the sword." (Laband, *op. cit.*, pp. 201-02.) Of course, Frere knew that this system—on which the whole of Zulu society rested—*was* fundamental and that its abolition would not therefore be conceded.

27. "The War, Natal and Confederation" by Bill Guest, in *The Anglo-Zulu War: New Perspectives*, ed. by Andrew Duminy and Charles Ballard (Pietermaritzburg: University of Natal Press, 1981), p. 55; "Zulu War", p. 2.

28. Clarke, *Invasion*, pp. 48 & 50.
29. *Ibid.*, pp. 53-54.
30. There were originally five columns, all under colonels; but No. 5 (Rowlands), on the Transvaal border, took no part in the war; and No. 2 (Durnford) joined No. 3 on 22 January and was largely destroyed at Isandlwana. No. 1 (Pearson) and No. 4 (Wood) were respectively to the south and north of the Centre Column.

    For the composition of the Centre Column, see Jackson, *op. cit.*, p. 7. As Mr. Jackson says in his Introduction, this book is "a much expanded, and therefore largely rewritten" version of his well-known 3-part article, "Isandhlwana 1879: the Sources Re-examined" (1965), and can be recommended as by far the best account of the battle from the Army's standpoint. The Zulu perspective is given in Laband, *op. cit.*, pp. 217-29.
31. Laband, J.P.C. and Thompson, P.S., with Henderson, Sheila, *The Buffalo Border, 1879: The Anglo-Zulu War in Northern Natal* (Durban: Dept. of History, University of Natal, 1983), p. 36.
32. Norris-Newman, Charles L., *In Zululand with the British Throughout the War of 1879* (London: W.H. Allen & Co., 1880), p. 26.
33. Corporal Brown's letter to his wife, dated 29 December 1878, first appeared in *The Dover Express,* and is reprinted in Emery, *Red Soldier*, p. 62. The march is described more briefly in: Lloyd, W.G., *John Williams, V.C.: A Biography* (Bridgend: Printed for the Author, 1993), pp. 21-22.
34. *Ibid.*, p. 22.
35. Laband, Thompson & Henderson, *op. cit.*, p. 40.
36. Narrative of Isandlwana and Rorke's Drift, compiled by W. Penn Symons from the results of his enquiries at the time (in Regt. Museum). This manuscript is described by Frank Emery in *The 24th Regiment at Isandlwana* (1978), a pamphlet in which "selected passages" are printed; Holme, *Noble 24th*, p. 280; " 'Cruel Slaughter and Bloodshed': Some Reflections on the Battle of Rorke's Drift" by Ian Knight, in *The Journal of the Anglo Zulu War Historical Society*, June 1998, p. 52.
37. Laband, Thompson & Henderson, *op. cit.*, p. 40; "Reminiscences of Campaigning in South Africa, 1877-81" by W.A. Dunne, in *The Army Service Corps Journal*, February 1892, pp. 286-87; Knight, Ian, *Nothing Remains but to Fight: The Defence of Rorke's Drift, 1879* (London: BCA, 1993), p. 45. (There are at least five book-length accounts of Rorke's Drift but this is by far the best and most detailed analysis.)
38. *Ibid.*, p. 37; *Royal Magazine*, p. 342; Stevenson, Lee, *The Rorke's Drift Doctor: James Henry Reynolds, V.C.* . . . (Brighton: Lee Stevenson Publishing, 2001), pp. 62-70. The three men were apparently wounded during the skirmish at Sihayo's kraal, on 12 January, the Centre Column's first engagement.
39. Dunne, *art. cit.*, p. 287; Knight, *op. cit.*, p. 44; Parr, *op. cit.*, p. 123.
40. Penn Symons Narrative; "The Victoria Cross . . . From Rorke's Drift to the British Museum", in *The* [London] *Morning Leader*, 11 November 1897; Jackson, *op. cit.*, p. 11.
41. *Dictionary of National Biography*, Supplement, Vol. I (1901). The entry is by Col. R.H. Vetch, R.E., who gives no personal details or characteristics for Chard, except to remark on the "simplicity and modesty" of his official report of Rorke's Drift; *Red Earth: The Royal Engineers and the Zulu War, 1879* (Catalogue of a "Special Exhibition." Gillingham: Royal Engineers Museum, [1996], pp. 17-18; Kenworthy, J.C. (compiler), *The South Africa Wars, 1877 to 1879: The Somerset Connection: Part 1— Lieutenant John Rouse Merriott Chard* . . . (Combe St. Nicholas, Somerset: "amended and updated, March 1994.") This is the only biography of Chard and takes the form of a 33-page foolscap script which the compiler appears to make available as a computer print-out. Pages 1-8 deal with Chard's life before, and during, the Zulu War.
42. *The Journal of the Anglo Zulu War Historical Society*, December 1999, p. 29.
43. Clarke, *Invasion*, p. 131.
44. Wolseley, *South African Journal*, p. 57.

45. Emery, *Red Soldier*, p. 241.
46. Butterfield, *art. cit.*, p. 8.
47. Kenworthy, *op. cit.*, pp. 8, 19 & 24. The fine print prefixed to the text shows Chard wearing what is believed to be the Queen's ring.
48. Emery, *Marching over Africa*, p. 84. The letter was written by A.F. Pickard.
49. Napier, Gerald, *The Sapper VCs: The Story of Valour in the Royal Engineers and its Associated Corps* (London: The Stationery Office, 1998), pp. 86-94 (incl. quotation); 286.
50. Penn Symons Narrative; Bromhead to Godwin-Austen, 19 February 1879 (in Regt. Museum).
51. Clarke, *Invasion*, pp. 81 & 131.
52. Wolseley, *South African Journal*, p. 257.
53. *Royal Magazine*, p. 344; Wolseley, *South African Journal*, p. 256.
54. *Ibid.*, p. 57.
55. Butterfield, *art. cit.*, p. 8. Wood and Buller told Ponsonby, in September 1879, that they believed that the defence was "actively ordered" by "a Commissary named Dalton." No doubt they had said the same to Wolseley, when he arrived in South Africa in June.
56. The text of Dalton's account is given in Stevenson, *op. cit.*, p. 108.
57. Lummis, *op. cit.*, p. 86; "The Dalton VC" by Ian Knight, in *Soldiers of the Queen*, No. 45, June 1986, p. 12.

    In the B.B.C. "Timewatch" programme (mentioned at Chapter V, n. 38), Dalton takes over the command from Chard and Bromhead but is denied due credit because of class distinction! The absurdity of this proposition is self-evident, as seven of the Rorke's Drift V.C.s were awarded to working men (privates and corporals); three to commissioned officers; and the other to Dalton himself, a civilian with officer status. In fact, the official citation actually describes Dalton as an "Officer" and gives him full credit for his part in the defence.
58. Bennett, Ian H.W., *Eyewitness in Zululand: The Campaign Reminiscences of Colonel W.A. Dunne, CB, South Africa, 1877-1881* (London: Greenhill, 1989), p. 181. (A different version of "B" Company's appreciation of Dalton is given by Molyneux, *op. cit.*, p. 207); Holme, *Noble 24th*, pp. 279-82 & 291.
59. Bennett, *op. cit.*, pp. 125-26.
60. Wolseley, *South African Journal*, pp. 92-93.
61. Bennett, *op. cit.*, p. 182 (quoting the *Natal Witness* for 16 October 1879); Harford, Henry, *The Zulu War Journal of . . .*, ed. by Daphne Child (Pietermaritzburg: Shuter & Shooter, 1978), p. 40. In 1879, Harford was a subaltern attached to the 3rd Natal Native Contingent. He was not at the defence of Rorke's Drift nor is his account strictly a "journal." (See the remarks of Jackson, *op. cit.*, p. 81.)

    Hook preserved a cutting, headed "Rorke's Drift Heroes", from *The Westminster Gazette* for 3 November 1897, in which a British Museum Reader, F. Reginald Statham, took the occasion of Chard's death to assert that "there can be little doubt that the idea of making the post defensible with the aid of the commissariat stores . . . originated with Assistant-Commissary Dalton." Statham then devotes a paragraph to Hook, although he was sorry to say that he had forgotten "this man's name." (Furness Collection.)
62. Chard's account of the defence of Rorke's Drift written for Queen Victoria and submitted on 21 February 1880 (reprinted in Holme, *Noble 24th*, pp. 270-78; quotation at p. 270). This description of his actions—much fuller than in his official despatch—seems not to be disputed.
63. *Ibid.*, p. 272.
64. Jackson, *op. cit.*, p. 42. The battle for the camp had opened at about midday and was in its last stages when the news reached Chard.
65. Dunne, *art. cit.*, pp. 289-90.
66. Reynolds's report is printed in Stevenson, *op. cit.*, pp. 163-67.
67. Holme, *Noble 24th*, pp. 272-73 (account for the Queen).

68. Laband, *op. cit.*, pp. 34 & 238.
69. Emery, *Red Soldier*, pp. 172-73 & 186.
70. Laband, *op. cit.*, pp. 36-37.
71. *Ibid.*, pp. 40 & 181-82; Knight, " 'Cruel Slaughter and Bloodshed' ", p. 50; Hook's letter to his mother, printed in *The North Wales Express* for 18 April 1879 (reprinted in Emery, *Red Soldier*, p. 135).
72. Laband, *op. cit.*, pp. 231-33 (including the statement that "Cetshwayo had made it very clear to his army that . . . it was his policy to fight only in defence of Zulu soil"); "Address by the Mayor of Durban to the . . . 2nd Battalion of H.M. 24th Regiment" (text in Holme, *Noble 24th*, p. 309); Yorke, Edmund J., *Rorke's Drift, 1879* (Stroud: Tempus, 2001), pp. 135-37 (for a restatement of the contemporary view).
73. Jackson, *op. cit.*, p. 23; Hook's account in *The Strand Magazine*, Vol. I, May 1891, pp. 548-50 (reprinted below); Hitch's account, reprinted in Holme, *Noble 24th*, pp. 284-85.
74. Acland-Troyte, *op. cit.*, pp. 47-48, where the system is explained. In his battalion, each company provided one cook for the kitchens, who did duty for a month. "At the head of the cooks there is a sergeant specially trained at Aldershot."; Adams (*op. cit.*, p. 101) refers to Hook as "one of the cooks" but should have known better.
75. See n. 1, above.
76. Knight, *op. cit.*, p. 91. The general question of the reportage of Hook in the contemporary press is discussed in Chapter XI.
77. *Royal Magazine*, pp. 339-48. Both Holme (*Noble 24th*, pp. 285-89) and Emery (*Red Soldier*, pp. 124-31) reprint most of the text, with comments.
78. In the *Royal Magazine* (1905), Hook says: "Lieutenant Chard rushed up from the river, about a quarter of a mile away, and saw Lieutenant Bromhead. Orders were given to strike the camp and make ready to go, and we actually loaded up two wagons. Then Mr. Dalton, of the Commissariat Department, came up, and said that if we left the drift every man was certain to be killed. He had formerly been a sergeant-major in a Line regiment, and was one of the bravest men that ever lived. Lieutenants Chard and Bromhead held a consultation, short and earnest; and orders were given that we were to get the hospital and storehouse ready for defence, and that we were never to say 'die' or 'surrender.' "
But in *The Morning Leader* (11 November 1897) he had said: "The company might have escaped by themselves, but to attempt a retreat to the next post, 12 miles off, with the sick and wounded would have been madness. 'We should have been surrounded and cut up,' Mr. Hook remarks, 'before we had got a mile away.' The only thing was to fight it out there to the last; and fight it out they did. . . . Lieut. Chard, the senior officer, was down at the river when the news came, and it was really Lieut. Bromhead who arranged the hastily-organised defence. We threw up a barrier of biscuit boxes and mealy bags, and with our only two wagons managed to make a respectable square. . . ."
79. In *Royal Magazine* (p. 340), he says that the Contingent "bolted in a body", and this seems to be the general impression.
80. The following incident in the hospital is only described in one of Hook's accounts (*Rare Bits*, c.1883): " . . . in the hospital I had my top coat and a rug. A young Zulu—he was only about twenty—stole this, and was making off with them when he was disabled, and I came and caught him with my things. I clubbed my rifle, brought it down with all my force on his head, and smashed—not the Zulu's skull, but the stock of my rifle all to pieces. He lay quiet for about five minutes and then began to wink his eyes a bit, so I gave him the contents of the barrel in his head, and finished him off."
81. Hook's grandson, Mr. H.E.R. Bunting, has in his collection Vols. II & III of *Tristram Shandy* and these "tiny volumes" are said to have been carried by Hook "in his tunic pocket throughout the battle." ("Henry Hook V.C.—Hero of Rorke's Drift" by George Henderson, in *Gloucestershire: the County Magazine*, March 1987, p. 23.)
82. "Zulu War", pp. 20-22.

Chapter VII

SOUTH AFRICA—3

"The Buffalo Border": 1879

1.

Penn Symons was one of the first of Chelmsford's officers to reach the post. He found "some of the defenders hysterical, others waved their caps and cheered. All were begrimed with powder, blood, smoke and smuts. . . . Bromhead was cool and collected. His first thought was to issue rations and get breakfasts cooked for the column."[1]

There is another recollection of Bromhead that morning. Lieutenant Mainwaring was with the six companies of the 2/24th which had been on Chelmsford's reconnaissance and which now (with "B" Company) comprised what was left of the column's regular infantry. Mainwaring recalled:

> I shall never forget seeing Gonny Bromhead . . . come out to meet us as we formed in quarter column outside the gate. He told me afterwards he felt as if he was walking on air as he never expected to see daylight again.
>
> After giving me some food Bromhead took me round the scene of the fight. In front of the verandah outside the hospital and near the two blue gum trees the Zulu bodies were lying three deep.
>
> Gonny especially pointed out one young Zulu Induna with a plume head-dress, telling me that he was a very gallant man, and had headed a charge three times.
>
> "But we got him the third time" he added.
>
> Inside the hospital he pointed out the burnt remains of Sergt. Maxwell [*i.e.* Robert Maxfield] who I knew well—a good fellow.[2]

There is a glimpse of Chard as the responsibilities of commanding officer passed from him: "In wrecking the stores in my wagon, the

Zulus had brought to light a forgotten bottle of beer, and Bromhead and I drank it with mutual congratulations on having come safely out of so much danger."[3] He then returned to his duties as an Engineer.

Lieutenant Banister wrote that:

> . . . the General and all our force had to remain here that night, so that in spite of being very nearly done by all our past exertions every soul had to work like a horse cleaning up the place and enlarging the extent of the defences. Zulus were known to be in the vicinity so it was imperative that things should be something like shipshape before dusk.[4]

The Natal Native Contingent was

> the last to get in, and for some time it was quite impossible to keep the men in hand. They were all round the surroundings of the Fort in a second, crowding about the Zulu dead who were lying thick everywhere, partly, no doubt, from curiosity but I dare say some may have been looking out to identify friends or relations as many of the Natal Kaffirs are refugees from Zululand.[5]

Perhaps there is a hint here to support the contemporary claim that at first "the panic and confusion were fearful"[6]; but the men of the Contingent were soon put to "most necessary duties" under Hallam Parr. The dead Zulus had to be buried quickly—it was the South African summer—and as many men "as could be supplied with picks and shovels were set to work to dig pits."[7] Parr found that

> natives have a great repugnance to touching a dead body, so the soldiers [of the 2/24th] had to do this part of the work. If we had had a few carts, or even horses, our labours would have been much lightened, but the dead Zulus had either to be hauled by "reims" (ropes of hide) over the ground, or carried in rough stretchers.
> It was disagreeable work handling the dead, naked bodies, with many awful looking wounds.
> The men worked hard and cheerfully, and we soon got the immediate neighbourhood of the entrenchment clear of dead bodies.[8]

Hook mentions these burials but he implies that the men of "B" Company were spared this "disagreeable work."[9] His figure for the burials—351—is the one usually given; but many other Zulus were either mortally wounded or were found some distance from the post and killed. An episode described by Commandant "Maori" Browne (in memoirs thought to be rather unreliable) seems to have happened, if not exactly as he recalled it thirty years later:

> During the afternoon it was discovered that a large number of wounded and worn-out Zulus had taken refuge or hidden in the mealie fields near the laager. My two companies of Zulus [of the Native Contingent] with some of my non-coms. and a few of the 24th quickly drew these fields and killed them with bayonet, [rifle] butt and assagai.
>
> It was beastly but there was nothing else to do. War is war and savage war is the worst of the lot. Moreover our men were worked up to a pitch of fury by the sights they had seen in the morning and the mutilated bodies of the poor fellows lying in front of the burned hospital.[10]

The number thus "systematically finished off", as Professor Laband puts it, was 200, bringing "the probable figure of Zulu casualties at Rorke's Drift up to about 600." Zulu warriors gave no quarter themselves and expected none in return; and their wounded, on this occasion, were stabbed or battered to death to save ammunition. The column had lost all its ammunition at Isandlwana, except for "75 rounds per man in the pouches", while the garrison of Rorke's Drift had fired off so much during the defence that, by the early morning, a last determined attack by the Zulus would have carried the post.[11] Mainwaring says that:

> It was not for several days that the ammunition waggons were seen approaching from Helpmakaar. Great was the cheering by the garrison who could not have been greater pleased if they had been granted a special issue of grog.[12]

Apart from this "finishing off" of the wounded, there were undoubtedly a few discreditable incidents at the post itself. Lieutenant Smith-Dorrien—who escaped from Isandlwana and reached Helpmekaar—went down to Rorke's Drift the next day to resume his duties as a transport officer. He had erected a gallows-like structure for drying ox-hide and was presently startled to see two Zulus hanging from it. Major Clery accused him "of having given the order" but Smith-Dorrien was exonerated

> when it was found that it was a case of lynch law performed by incensed men, who were bitter at the loss of their comrades. Other incidents of the same sort occurred in the next few days before law and order were re-established.[13]

One of these luckless Zulus may have been the prisoner taken to

132

Bromhead by Private James Ashton, of "B" Company. Ashton said that he had been told "to get the hell out of here with him" and—Ashton added—"I did."[14]

A more serious charge was made a year later:

> A few Zulus prisoners had been taken by our troops—some the day before, others previous to the disaster at Isandhlwana, and these prisoners were put to death in cold blood at Rorke's Drift. It was intended to set them free, and they were told to run for their lives, but they were shot down and killed, within sight and sound of the whole force. An eye-witness—an officer—described the affair to the present writer [Frances Colenso], saying that the men whom *he* saw killed numbered "not more than seven, nor less than five." He said that he was standing with others in the camp, and hearing shots close behind him, he turned, and saw the prisoners in question in the act of falling beneath the shots and stabs of a party of our men.[15]

Miss Colenso adds that "the number of prisoners thus killed is said to have been about twenty" and that the men responsible belonged to the Native Contingent. Like her father, the Bishop of Natal, she was zealous in the Zulu cause but there seems no reason to doubt that she reported faithfully what she had been told.

Hallam Parr also rushed out a book in 1880, and the Colensoes were no doubt amongst the "persons" denounced in this passage:

> There seemed at one time in South Africa a persistent endeavour of some persons to spread rumours pointing to the cruel and brutal treatment by our soldiers of any Zulus who fell into our hands. What end such rumours had, it is hard to understand.[16]

Parr contends that the Zulu wounded "would have been put an end to, according to native custom"; and it should be said in defence of the Native Contingent that if they also "put an end to" some unwounded Zulus, they had suffered heavily at Isandlwana.[17]

The white casualties at Rorke's Drift were officially reported as fifteen killed and twelve wounded but two of the wounded died within a few days.[18] Towards the close of his last interview, Hook said:

> As for our own comrades, we, who had fought side by side with them, buried them. This was done the day after the fight, not far from the place where they fell, and at the foot of the hill. Soon afterwards the little cemetery was walled in and a monument was put up in the middle. The lettering was cut on it by a very clever bandsman named Mellsop, who used bits of broken bayonets as chisels. He drew a capital picture of the fight. Those who had been killed in action were buried on one

side of the cemetery, and those who died of disease on the other side. A curious thing was that a civilian named Byrne, who had taken part in the defence and was killed, was buried outside the cemetery wall. I don't know why, except that he was not a regular soldier.[19]

Byrne had been "a civilian clerk" working for Commissary Dunne and Dunne recalls that "early in the fight Mr. Byrne was shot through the head." There seems to be some doubt whether he is, in fact, buried outside the cemetery wall; but, according to Chard, there had at first only been "a fence around, and a rough wood cross over, the graves."[20]

Lieutenant Curling, like Smith-Dorrien, had got through to Helpmekaar and, hearing the next afternoon that what remained of the Centre Column was at Rorke's Drift, he rode there and arrived "just as it was getting dark. . . . A [Zulu] spy was hanging on one of the trees in the garden and the whole place was one mass of men."

Large numbers of Zulus were appearing in the hills all round and a strong fortification had been made round the farm. We lay down round the parapets but although there were several alarms no attack was made. None of us had any blankets and the men had not even their greatcoats. The General and staff were no better off and as the night was cold we felt it much. The General started off at daylight for PeterMaritzburg . . .[21]

Lord Chelmsford reached the town on the 26th of January, "so changed and worn with anxiety and sleeplessness as to look many years older, and to alarm Frere lest he should break down." Frere had already heard the news and "saw at once how fatal the disaster was to all hope of a speedy end to the war." He nevertheless

urged that the third column should advance again from Rorke's Drift and take up a position near Isandhlwana, so that at least the dead might be buried. But he urged in vain and for four months their bones lay whitening in the sun.[22]

Chelmsford had already decided that little could be done until reinforcements were sent out from England. This was certainly true of the Centre (or third) Column, which he now left actually—rather than nominally—in the hands of Colonel Glyn. On the 3rd of February, he wrote privately to Glyn:

I am afraid your troops will be very tired of sitting still & doing nothing, but there is no help for it—Send the mounted corps to Wood as soon as you can, so as to enable him to act offensively.[23]

Glyn's force was divided into two. What the general called "the mounted corps", and the remnants of the artillery, joined two companies of the 1/24th and half-a-company of Engineers at Helpmekaar. Seven companies of the 2/24th, and the other half of the Engineer company, garrisoned Rorke's Drift. Chelmsford had ordered the disbandment of the Native Contingent; but its white officers and N.C.O.s stayed on at Rorke's Drift and were "given the N.E. corner of it to hold" and "all the reconnoitring and patrolling work."[24] This abrupt disarming and dismissal of the Contingent, whose men had begun to desert and "admitted their moral terror" of the Zulus,

> precipitated the desertion of the black hospital bearers and Pioneers, and left the British garrison at Rorke's Drift without any black auxiliaries for outpost duty and the other more menial military tasks.[25]

These losses were to a slight extent balanced by the arrival, on the 29th of January, of the half-company of Engineers and by a routine draft of forty-four N.C.O.s and men for the 2/24th. Chard put the Engineers to work replacing the "mealie-bag walls" by

> a strong stone-walled enclosure, loopholed all around. The new wall took in the storehouse (now roofed with tarpaulins) and the cattle kraal, and was just under eight feet high, except where it faced the Oskarberg and rose to two storeys, with a banquette made of planks.[26]

The draft was distributed amongst the companies; and "G" (which had been entirely lost at Isandlwana) was reconstituted by transfers and from the draft. Amongst the transfers, Hook was assigned to the new "G" Company. The men of the draft were soon saying that "they would rather be in the depot at Brecon than be out here"; and all accounts agree that for some weeks conditions at Rorke's Drift were extremely unpleasant and unhealthy.[27] The *Historical Records of the 2nd Battalion* (printed in 1882 and marked "Confidential") by no means overstate the plight of the garrison:

> At first it seemed that very few of the men would be left fit for duty, for the battalion had nothing but what it stood in, everything even to great coats, had been lost; there were no tents, no covering of any kind; all that officers and men had to shelter them from the bitterly cold sleet and rain which fell nightly converting the enclosed space occupied into a slough of liquid mud, was their

thin kersey frocks [tunics]. It is not to be wondered at therefore if the morning's sick list increased alarmingly; to make matters worse, the medicines having been burnt with the hospital, all that remained at the disposal of the medical officers was contained in the small "field companions" they had carried with them into the field. The staff on leaving had promised to remedy this, but by some mistake the medicines were put into a slow Cape wagon, instead of being sent by a man on horseback, and it took weeks before this much-needed relief came to hand.

Energetic measures were taken for the safety and sanitation of the post. Whilst the greater part of the men were occupied in replacing the mealie-bag parapets by a good stone wall, another party was employed in continually cleaning and scraping the ground, till at last nothing was left but the bare rock. This was a great comfort however, as saving the men from the mud. With all our precautions, it nevertheless speaks volumes for the healthiness of the climate of Natal, that during a stay of about three months, the battalion only lost one officer—Lieutenant Reginald Franklin—and twelve men by death, and two officers and thirteen invalided. A good supply of tarpaulins was luckily found in the Commissariat stores; these were used to make "lean-to-shelters" for men and officers. There was certainly little room, but all huddled together and this gave warmth. Cooking pots and canteens of course there were none, but a hungry man thrown on his own resources will soon find means to cook his food, and the old camping ground by the river was ransacked for cast away meat and marmalade tins, which were used for the purpose.

The great want of all was great coats, especially for the officers and men who had the look-out at night. B company had only saved a few of theirs, but about sixty corn sacks having been found, they were converted into an extempore covering for sentries, by slitting holes for the head and arms.[28]

Hook, in his first interview, speaks of wearing one of these sacks; but for a week before his transfer, he would have shared with "B" Company the privilege of sleeping

> in the attic of Rorke's house [*i.e.*, the store] with a tarpaulin thrown over the rafters (from which the thatch had been removed) to shelter them from the wet, a well-deserved honour. However, even they had their troubles in trying to keep dry, as the tarpaulin often bagged in between the rafters with a collection of water which had to be ejected, . . .[29]

A discomfort not mentioned in the *Historical Records* crops up in some of the "home letters", written during the first few weeks after the defence. The men were concerned about their personal hygiene:

not being "allowed to take our things off to get a wash", as one of them put it.[30] "Letters from Zululand" appeared in many newspapers in the first part of 1879, and an excerpt from one of Hook's letters was printed in *The North Wales Express*.[31] He wrote to his parents in Monmouth but not—it may safely be assumed—to his family at Mount Pleasant. When he was first interviewed after his discharge, he told the reporter (the "we" of this passage):

As you are aware (we saw his letters) in all my letters home, I made no allusions to any serious hardships, nor attempted to credit myself with any deeds of bravery, it being my desire not to alarm my parents. One man who was not within eighty miles of Rorke's Drift sent home a fictitious account of the battle; his letter got into the papers, and the colonel saw it; the man, who was a corporal, was tried and reduced for the offence.[32]

It seems that none of the other letters which this reporter saw have survived.

At the end of February, one of the N.C.O.s told his wife that Rorke's Drift was "raging with fever." Dr. Reynolds reported that it was "essentially bilious remittent, characterised by bilious vomiting, hepatic [*i.e.*, liver] congestion and delirium." He had himself soon succumbed to dysentery and was sent first to Helpmekaar—where conditions were equally bad but where there were more doctors—and then to Ladysmith. There, he was joined by Chard, who had become "very weak with fever", and by Dunne, who had typhoid fever.[33] All the more seriously sick and wounded seem to have been evacuated from Rorke's Drift; but some of those who remained passed their time by making a large, beaded pincushion "out of small bits of cloth from different uniforms."[34]

2.

Amidst the mud and the fever, the immemorial routine of army life went on. The pattern of the days can be traced in the one surviving "Order Book", which contains battalion, fort and column orders for the period between the 28th of January and the 4th of April.

Reveille sounded at 4.45 a.m., when the troops "fell in" and three mounted patrols left immediately "to reconnoitre for the enemy not further than a mile from the post & and then return at once & report." Blankets were collected and put away and, at 5.30, half the battalion began fatigue work. Two companies were assigned to the Engineers, who, in the early weeks, were improving the parapets of the original post. When this work was finished, by the beginning of March, a new fort was begun at the Drift. This labouring work by the 2/24th lasted for about three months. At the same time, another company was cutting wood and a fourth, under "the garrison captain", was cleaning the post and its surroundings. The fatigue parties came in for breakfast at 8 o'clock, went out again at 9, and worked until dinner time at 12.30. After the dinner hour, there was a three-hour spell of work until the "men's tea" at 5 o'clock. Meanwhile, the remaining companies were either on inlying piquet duty or were in reserve. The two companies on duty were to "remain accoutred"— wearing ammunition pouches, canteens and bayonets—and, during the night, they manned the walls with bayonets fixed ("in the event of a thunderstorm all bayonets to be unfixed for the time"). At night, the two reserve companies were "to lie down with their arms by their side."[35]

The whole battalion assembled again for evening parade, when the commanding officer went round the post. "Retreat" was sounded at 6.30 and, for the men, the rest of the evening was very dull. An order of the 30th of January laid it down that: "After evening parade no lights or noise will be allowed, any one having occasion to move about must do so as quietly as possible"; and as late as the end of March, it was ordered that: "N.C. Officers & men are forbidden to have Lights in their Tents." But most of the men were probably very tired by dusk and those not manning the walls would have quickly gone to sleep. There seems to have been no "day of rest", but the battalion always paraded on Sunday mornings for "Divine Service."

It seems clear that the lack of tents mentioned in the *Historical Records* was fairly soon remedied. In fact, Colonel Glyn has been rather unreasonably criticised for forbidding the pitching of tents outside the walls, but his fears of a sudden attack were not irrational in the light of what was known at the time. The Zulus made no further assault on Rorke's Drift itself, but small raiding parties were very active on both sides of the Buffalo River during February and, to a diminishing extent, in March. Some other precautions were taken to make the garrison secure: a "line of obstacles [was] placed round the Fort"; poles were fixed at different distances outside the walls for the "guidance of fire in case of attack"; men on piquet duty carried seventy rounds in their pouches; and no-one was allowed inside the fort once the gate had been closed in the evening. These measures are referred to in an item which appeared in the *Times of Natal* at the end of February: "We learn that a very vigilant guard against the enemy is maintained here [Rorke's Drift], and that groundless alarms are almost of nightly occurrence." A few days later, someone at the post replied indignantly:

Now, Sir, although we are ever vigilantly on guard against a possible attack (and, should it come, we have a sort of an idea how to deal with it), . . . Not the slightest symptom of an alarm either by day or night has occurred here since the departure of our native allies on the 25th January.[36]

There was much concern over sanitary arrangements. No cooking was allowed inside the walls and:

The latrine inside the Fort is not to be used during the hours the gate is open, urine tubs are provided for the use of all during the night and no one is to go elsewhere for that purpose.[37]

One man was punished for "committing a nuisance against the walls of the fort" and another for "committing a nuisance in the ranks"— a discreet way of putting things!

This leads to the question of discipline. In a cramped and isolated post, with a good deal of ill-health, little free time (and nothing to do with it, anyway), nerves and tempers were bound to fray. The "Order Book" shows that during the period of just over two months following the Zulu attack, five men were tried by regimental court-martial—a court composed entirely of officers of the battalion— and twenty-seven by the commanding officer. A large proportion of the offences consisted of "making replies" or of using "obscene" or "improper" language to N.C.O.s; "hesitating to obey an order"; or of various forms of "neglect", especially on sentry or piquet duty. One man was obviously dissatisfied with his food and was given fourteen days "Confined to Camp" for "making a frivolous complaint & throwing away his ration of bread." "Confined to Camp" was the usual sentence but, as there was nowhere to go outside of camp, these defaulters were presumably given disagreeable fatigues and "punishment drill" of the kind which always formed part of "Confinement to Barracks."

The regimental courts reduced a sergeant for "neglect of duty when Orderly Sergt"; and convicted one man of "sleeping on his Post" (a grave offence on active service) and three others in unspecified cases of "insubordination." These four privates were sentenced to be flogged: in three cases, twenty-five lashes; and in one case of "insubordination", fifty lashes (at that time, the maximum number allowed). The commanding officer "remitted the punishment" for the sleeping offence—the sentry may have been over-tired or unwell, or was perhaps of previous good character— but the other sentences were confirmed. Unlike such punishment in civil prisons, a military flogging took the form of a public example; and Hook would therefore have witnessed an age-old spectacle which was then very close to extinction.

From the time of the Napoleonic Wars—when upwards of a thousand lashes were still being inflicted—both the severity of flogging, and the number of offences for which it could be awarded, were steadily reduced. The impetus for reform came from politicians not soldiers, as both the War Office authorities, and most officers, were consistently opposed to abolition. These officers held that, without flogging, discipline would be impossible to maintain, especially on active service. Yet in spite of their opposition, by the time that Hook enlisted, flogging had in practice almost died out: there had been no instance in 1872 and only two cases in 1876. When the campaigns of 1877-79 began in South Africa, there was a startling increase: twenty-nine cases in 1878 and 545 in 1879. The number of floggings during the year of the Zulu War exceeded that for any since 1860—why this should have happened is one of the minor problems of the war.[38]

Some of the points made by Hook in his first interview—though a little garbled—offer a partial explanation:

> I only had nine months training in England before I was sent out to Zululand [i.e., South Africa] on active service; ... Many of us were over two years without knowing what it was to sleep in a bed, and often had to rabble away the mud and water from the ground before we could lie down upon it, using a stone covered with our helmets for a pillow. ... [At Rorke's Drift] we had no waterproof sheets, or top-coats—I had a mealy sack, with holes cut in it for my arms and head to go through for a top-coat, and I have seen officers, with no other. A lot of our young men could not stand it, and were invalided in the first twelve months; they were too young.[39]

In short, the conditions were severe and many of the troops sent to South Africa were inexperienced: the loss of the long-service men of the 1st Battalion, 24th, at Isandlwana, was therefore particularly unfortunate. Also, there seems to be no doubt that many of the troops who came out as reinforcements, and took part in the "second invasion" of Zululand, at the end of May, were not only inexperienced in campaigning but had heard altogether too much about the early disasters and about the ferocious fighting prowess of the Zulus. There were some panicky incidents and "false alarms"; and, by contrast, "listlessness" on the part of men not used to camp life. Some humane officers, such as Harness, were reluctant floggers; but the more conservative elements thought that objections to corporal punishment were "mere sentiment."[40] This was the view of Captain Montague, of the 94th Regiment, who in 1880 put the "retentionist" case with complete candour:

> Men of late have been educated too much for the barrack-room, forgetful that the ultimate use of the soldier is on the field, hard and rough, death-strewn, with scenes of pain around so frequent as to be unnoticed.[41]

The three floggings at Rorke's Drift, in February and March, would have taken the ritual form established by long usage. The battalion was paraded and drawn up in a hollow square, with the "triangle"—to which the prisoner was tied hand and foot—set up in the centre. Five functionaries took their places near the triangle: the adjutant, who read to the assembled companies the sentence of the court; the commanding officer, who then gave the order, "Drummer! Do your duty"; a medical officer, who was authorised to stop the flogging if life was in danger; a sergeant, who called out the number of each stroke; and a drummer, who had to lay on the strokes with a knotted cat-o-nine-tails. (Drummers had "supple wrists" and were taught how to deliver the blows in a scientific way.) At the end, the prisoner was taken down and led off to the hospital, to recover from his ordeal.[42]

The "Order Book" is not composed solely of duties and punishments. During February, "Subscription lists" were "opened in each Company in aid of the widows & orphans of those who fell in [the] 24th Regt on the 22nd Jany. 1879." In March, men in Chelmsford's Command who were in the last year of their six-year enlistments were offered a gratuity of £3 to extend their service to ten years and agree to transfer to another regiment if their own was ordered home—evidently a recognition of the need to retain seasoned troops. And in April, there was "a *Free* issue of a red night cap to each man in the Battn. from the Canteen Funds."[43]

3.

In his undated letter printed in *The North Wales Express*, Hook says: "I am now servant to Major Black (his man having been killed), and a nice gentleman he is, and I like him very much."[44] The news of Black's promotion to brevet lieutenant-colonel was published at Rorke's Drift on the 26th of March, so Hook had presumably begun his new work before that date.[45]

Wilsone Black, who was then forty-two, had a conventionally

successful career—he retired as a major-general and was knighted—yet despite a reputation for unusual energy and enterprise, he never quite achieved the prominence which he seems to have deserved. During the Zulu War, he was overshadowed by Wood and Buller and, unlike them, he was not a member of the Wolseley Ring. He was a Glaswegian, whose "shrill voice in broad Scotch" Lieutenant Harford recalls "urging his men on" in the first skirmish of the war. "Besides being a splendid soldier he was a most amusing companion [to Harford], and his fondness for bringing in lines of poetry to suit the occasion was a treat to listen to . . ."[46] Black was not only "a splendid soldier" but notably well educated and professionally qualified: he had passed through Sandhurst and Staff College, and was "acquainted" with French and German. He had been commissioned in time to serve in the Crimea with the Highlanders and to be present at the fall of Sebastopol. Most of his subsequent service had been in the 6th Regiment and it was not until the end of 1875 that he transferred, as a major, into the 2/24th. In 1869, during five years as a brigade major in Nova Scotia, he had married a Canadian lady and their two children (twins) were born there.[47]

Mrs. Black was as enterprising as her husband. When Harness met her at Greytown, in November 1878, she had missed Black by three hours, as he had just moved nearer to the border.

> She is the only officer's wife of the 2nd Battalion of the 24th who has come out to this country: all the other married men have left their wives in England. She told me that the colonel of the regiment [Degacher] did not like her for coming out and would like her still less for coming up to Greytown. This was corroborated afterwards by the colonel confiding to me that he "couldn't get rid of her; she would come wherever they went."[48]

Perhaps she stayed at Greytown—she was certainly not at Rorke's Drift—but of course all officers were entitled to a soldier-servant and her husband chose Hook.

A soldier had to agree to be assigned as an officer's servant, and there were both advantages and disadvantages in accepting. The most obvious advantage was the extra pay: "one shilling and sixpence in the infantry, but more is usually given"; and no doubt there were such occasional gifts as, say, a sovereign at Christmas. The memoirs and letters of the time abound in appreciations of soldier-servants, who sometimes stayed with the same officer for many years. Lieutenant Banister, writing a few days after Isandlwana, says: "I can even now hardly believe that poor McCracken is done for, he was my servant and such a capital fellow."[49] (McCracken had been left in the camp during Chelmsford's reconnaissance and so it seems had Black's "man".) Clearly, it was an agreeable life for a soldier who had a certain *savoir faire*, and a mutual affection could readily develop between officer and servant. The main disadvantage was that the position inhibited the prospects of promotion; but many men were, in any case, educationally debarred from such prospects. Hook, for instance, might have been appointed a lance-corporal but there is nothing to show that he would then have been qualified for promotion to corporal. The attraction for him was probably the extra money, especially if he was already thinking of "buying himself out." He was kept busy earning it, as this anecdote shows:

> [Black's voice] could be heard above the Fort calling for "H-o-o-k!" many times a day. So the men had their little joke, and whenever Hook was called for they themselves shouted for Hook and then yelled out, "I think he's hooked it, sir!", which always caused great merriment.[50]

Black was certainly very active at Rorke's Drift. Apart from his well-known exploit in recovering the Queen's Colour of the 1/24th from the river, and finding the bodies of Melvill and Coghill, who had died trying to save it, he was prominent in three patrols to Isandlwana in March and May, and in the burials of the dead during June.[51] The first two patrols to the battlefield—which he led—were quite small, consisting mainly of officers; but on the 21st of May, a very substantial force of infantry, cavalry and artillery moved out to Isandlwana. Colonel Black commanded four companies of the 2/24th, and it seems likely that Hook was with his company (then "E"). The Regimental Museum has a Bible which Hook is said to have found on the battlefield and, from Norris-Newman's eyewitness account, he would probably have had the opportunity of picking up this memento during the expedition:

> Pushing on steadily and carefully we reached the plain of Isandwhlana between 9 and 10 A.M.
> I found the whole site of the conflict over-grown with grass, thickly intermixed with green and growing stalks of oats and mealies. Concealed among these, lay the corpses of our soldiers, in all postures and stages of decay; while the site of the camp itself was indicated by the debris of the tents, intermingled with a heterogeneous mass of broken trunks, boxes, meat-tins, and their contents, with confused masses of papers, books, letters, etc., scattered in wild disorder. The sole visible objects, however, were the waggons, more or less broken up, and the skeletons of horses and oxen. All else was hidden from view, and could

only be found by a close search. ...

While the work of harnessing the horses to the best of the waggons was being actively prosecuted, all the men, except those on duty as vedettes or otherwise, were permitted to wander over the scene of the disaster; and various interesting relics were found and brought away.[52]

Some of the bodies were buried that morning; but this melancholy work was done mainly during four days late in June, under Black's supervision. He then had with him only 140 men of the 2/24th and there is no knowing whether Hook was amongst them. Soldier-servants were on a form of detached duty, and whether or not they accompanied their officers on particular occasions depended on the circumstances. The decision—if it was that definite—to leave McCracken, and other servants, behind when Chelmsford hurried off early on the 22nd of January, cost them their lives; but, in different circumstances, it might have saved them.

While these expeditions were providing some interest for the garrison at Rorke's Drift, the Engineers were building Fort Melvill "on the high ground overlooking and protecting the pont at the drift." The new fort was oblong in shape, with walls "partly of masonry and partly of dry-stone, and with two flanking towers." It was surrounded by a broad ditch. At about the time of the new fort's completion, an anonymous correspondent wrote to the *Times of Natal* describing conditions at the old post:

April 23, 1879.

Having just returned from a short visit to the celebrated but out-of-the-way corner of the world, Rorke's Drift, I venture to think a letter from me may interest some of your numerous readers. I found the 2nd bat. 24th regt. thoroughly "at home" there, after their sojourn of thirteen weeks. The officers and men look fit and ready for any amount of hard work, and as they turn out for fatigues in their red nightcaps and blue "jumpers" they give a busy and picturesque look to the laager and its surroundings. They are daily waiting for and expecting an order to move to Dundee, to join General Newdigate's Column [for the second invasion of Zululand]. Should they be kept at Rorke's Drift they tell me their hearts would break, and certainly most will agree with me that there is no regiment in the country more deserving of being sent to the front. ...

At night everyone sleeps inside the fort, and you may be sure that I felt very secure, as no less than 28 sentries watch from the walls, and besides these, four non-commissioned officers and one officer keep watch throughout the night, being relieved every two hours. The officer in command also, Colonel Degacher,

C.B., is ever nervously anxious for the safety of his little garrison, and frequently goes the rounds during the night.

I noticed that all the soldiers of the 24th regiment had pieces of bullock hide neatly fastened round the barrels of their rifles to prevent their hands being burnt by rapid firing.[53]

By the end of April, the 2/24th had again been divided into half-battalions. Four companies under Degacher moved to Dundee, while the other companies remained with Black and occupied the new fort. Hook's transfer to "E" Company, on the 3rd of April, was no doubt intended to keep him in Black's wing of the battalion.[54] By about the 19th of May, the post at the mission station had been abandoned. Three years later, "no vestiges of the old defences" of Rorke's Drift could be seen, and the "only reminder of the battle was the small cemetery."[55]

4.

For his second invasion of Zululand, Lord Chelmsford abolished the original columns and reorganised his greatly augmented forces into two divisions, with an independent "flying column." The 2/24th was assigned to the 2nd (or northern) Division, which Chelmsford accompanied. It has been assumed that he wished to avoid using his former route into Zululand, for psychological reasons, so the 2nd Division moved via Dundee and Landsman's Drift (to the northwest of Helpmekaar and Rorke's Drift).[56] There was no sign of the 2/24th being "sent to the front", so Degacher

wrote to Lord Chelmsford, expressing a hope that it was not his intention to leave the 2nd Battalion behind. To this, the following answer was received:

"My dear Degacher,—The 2nd Battalion MUST remain in charge of my base depots. I could not entrust such important posts to less experienced troops, but I am expecting the arrival of a battalion of old soldiers from home, when you may rely on my being but too glad to bring my old friends of the 2nd Battalion again to the front.

(Sig.) CHELMSFORD."

The 1st Battalion however, which had been reconstituted in a way by the two companies at Helpmakaar, young officers of the Guards and others attached pro tem for duty, and the draft already mentioned [15 officers and 526 men], composed of officers and men volunteers from every regiment in the service, all strangers to each other, being as yet 24th but in name, was sent to the front to maintain the honor of the regiment. It was perhaps a dangerous experiment.

The [2nd] battalion had to resign itself to its fate, and during the remainder of the campaign, although it did good and arduous work, it was not of an active description . . . [57]

On the 16th of June—while the 2nd Division was advancing very cautiously towards Ulundi, the Zulu capital—Chelmsford received the news that he had been superseded. Sir Garnet Wolseley—"the inevitable Sir Garnet" or "England's one soldier", as he was known to sarcastic opponents—was on his way to Cape Town. He had been vested with such extensive civil and military powers in South Africa that "he outranked all those in authority, with the single exception of Sir Bartle Frere in the Cape Colony."[58] Wolseley hastened up to Zululand, sending ahead of him urgent telegrams of instruction; but Chelmsford, in practice, ignored the fact of his supersession and went doggedly on until he arrived at last in front of the Zulu capital. There, on the 4th of July, he decisively defeated the Zulu army. The war was over and so was Chelmsford's career as a commander in the field. Whatever chance there might have been that his reputation would recover from Isandlwana had vanished on the 1st of June, when the Zulus killed the Prince Imperial of France in a minor skirmish. The Prince's death caused a stir in Europe and no British government, of either party, would employ Lord Chelmsford again.[59]

Frere was allowed to linger on with his much-reduced remit until Disraeli's government lost office in 1880, when he was recalled.

5.

Bromhead's letter commending the conduct of a corporal and five privates of "B" Company, during the defence of Rorke's Drift, has already been mentioned. He wrote:

Rorke's Drift
15th February 1879

Sir

I beg to bring to your notice the names of the following men belonging to my Company who especially distinguished themselves during the attack by the Zulus on this Post on the 22nd & 23rd January last; & whose conduct on this occasion came under my personal cognizance.

No. 1395 Private John Williams was posted by me together with Private Joseph Williams & Private William Horrigan 1/24th Regt: in a further room of the Hospital. They held it for more than an hour, so long as they had a round of ammunition left, when, as communication was for the time cut off, the Zulus were enabled to advance & burst open the door. They dragged out Private Joseph Williams & two of the patients by the arms, & assegaied them. Whilst the Zulus were occupied with the slaughter of these unfortunate men, a lull took place, during which Private John Williams—who with two Patients were the only men now left alive in this ward—succeeded in knocking a hole in the partition, & in taking the two patients with him into the next ward, where he found

No. 1373 Private Henry Hook. These two men together, one man working whilst the other fought & held the enemy at bay with his bayonet, broke through three more partitions, & were thus enabled to bring eight patients through a small window into our inner line of defence. . . . [60]

The letter concludes by describing the conduct of Privates William and Robert Jones—who were "in another ward, facing the hill"—and of Corporal Allen and Private Hitch, to whom it was "chiefly due . . . that communication with the Hospital was kept up at all." In forwarding the letter, Colonel Degacher made the recommendation that the names of the six men should be "brought by H.R.H. the Commander-in-Chief to the gracious notice of Her Majesty the Queen, and be deemed worthy of the Victoria Cross being awarded them." When these papers reached Lord Chelmsford, he sent them to the Horse Guards with the endorsement that:

I would express a hope that the gallant conduct of Lt Chard R.E. and Lt Bromhead 2/24th may be taken into consideration in view, if possible, that those two officers should receive the Victoria Cross—Had it not been for their fine example and excellent behaviour, under most trying circumstances, it may be assumed that the defence of Rorkes drift post would not have been conducted with that intelligence and tenacity which so essentially characterised it-[61]

It is possible to sense, in these remarks, Chelmsford's real gratitude to Chard and Bromhead for holding the post. In addition to well-deserved promotions, a more customary recommendation in these circumstances—and one made in Upcher's case, after Centane—would have been for the Companionship of the Bath, rather than for the V.C. The Duke of Cambridge nevertheless added their names to the list which, on the 29th of March, he submitted to the Secretary for War for "most favourable consideration." There was a delay of nearly a month before the names were sent to the Queen, together with the formal "Statement" which was published in the *London Gazette* on the 2nd of May. The other three Rorke's Drift V.C.s were announced later in the year, bringing the total to eleven out of the twenty-three awarded for the Zulu War as a whole. As is often said, there has been no single engagement since the medal was instituted in 1856 for which so many Crosses have been awarded. (Six had been awarded for the Charge of the Light Brigade.)

It fell to Chelmsford's successor to present some of these medals; and, bearing in mind Wolseley's private opinion of the 24th Regiment and of Rorke's Drift, it was not a very agreeable duty. Unlike his great rival, Lord Roberts, he had not won the V.C. himself, although he had been recommended for its award and his record in action was undoubtedly a very fine one. The best-known biography begins: "Ensign Garnet Wolseley believed that the best possible way to get ahead in the army was to try to get killed every time he had the chance."[62] The outcome was that he had been wounded several times and had "got ahead." His judgements were, in general, severe and exacting; and his attitude towards the Rorke's Drift awards was, in particular, affected by prejudice and coloured by War Office politics. At the presentation to Hook, it will be seen that he was "true to himself" in confining his remarks to generalities and in allowing the official citation to describe the actual exploits of the recipient. It seems most unlikely that Hook or anyone else—amidst the pomp of the parade—would have noticed this intellectual austerity of expression.

Five years earlier, Disraeli had described Wolseley as "a little man, but with a good presence and a bright blue eye, holds his head well and has an upright figure"—and this would still have held good.[63] In the first days of August, he was on his way to the ruins of Ulundi to meet Zulu chiefs; and the "special war correspondent" of the *Times of Natal* was sending back detailed accounts of the general's progress. Wolseley's party arrived at Rorke's Drift on the 2nd of August, finding the old post

> now altogether deserted, and although the walls still surround it which were erected after the defence, and while Fort Melville [*sic*] was being built, their strength is never likely to be tested. The little graveyard behind is, however, beautifully kept, with its two rows of graves, and one central cross "in memoriam" of all. It is surrounded by a neat stone wall and coping, ingress being obtained over a small stone stile. Fort Melville is now also unoccupied, being used entirely for holding commissariat stores,

the officers and men forming the garrison being quartered in tents just outside the *abattis*. A signalling party is kept upon the hill at the back, from which a good view of the whole of the adjacent part of Zululand is obtained.

Wolseley camped at Fort Melvill overnight. Orders were issued for a parade at 11 o'clock next morning

of the two companies of the 2-24th to enable the General to present the Victoria Cross to Private Hook, the only one here now of those entitled to it. Punctually the men were drawn up, and Sir Garnet, attended by Gen. Colley, Col. Brackenbury and Capt. Braithwaite rode up, with Col. East and Capt. Stewart— Col. Degacher, Lieut. Col. Black, Capt. Church, and Lieuts. Logan and Lloyd being the 24th officers present. A general salute was given, and then the warrant was read out referring to the occasion and bestowal of the decoration; after which Sir Garnet said: "Colonel Degacher, officers and men of the 24th Regiment,—It is always a very great pleasure to a General Officer to give away such a decoration as the Victoria Cross; but the pleasure on this occasion was doubled, as he was enabled to present it on the spot where the deed for which it was given was performed. The defence of Rorke's Drift would always be remembered in future history, and especially in that of the regiment, in which no act would ever appear which was braver, or the memory of which would be more cherished, than the Defence of Rorke's Drift, on January 22nd, 1879." The cross having been handed to the General by Colonel Brackenbury, and Private Hook called up, His Excellency pinned it on his breast himself. This concluded the ceremony, after which Sir Garnet rode down the lines, and the men were then dismissed. The man, who is a quiet young fellow, was much congratulated by his officers and fellow-soldiers. The cross has the name of its recipient engraved on the bar attached to the ribbon, and the date of the special act of bravery for which it was conferred in a small medallion on the reverse side of the cross itself. . . . During the day Sir Garnet and his Staff went over the scene of the brilliant defence, and then remained quietly in camp all day.[64]

The general wrote in his journal:

Sunday 3rd August

. . . I gave away a Victoria X this morning to a private of [the] 24th Regt. named Hook. Went over the scene of the fight afterwards. Lovely weather. . . .[65]

The recipient, near the end of his life, remarked:

It was curious, but until then I had scarcely ever thought about the V.C.—in fact we did not know or trouble much about it, although we had a V.C. man in the regiment—Griffiths they called him. He was killed, with the rest, at Isandhlwana.[66]

The medal carried with it a pension of £10 a year, paid quarterly in arrears. Hook was "admitted to pension" on the 13th of May 1879 (back-dated to the 22nd of January); and this *assured* income was very valuable to him when he returned to civil life.[67]

6.

King Cetshwayo, who had escaped from Ulundi, was captured on the 28th of August and taken to Cape Town. Even before this, the economically-minded Wolseley had broken up his predecessor's formations and sent home large numbers of troops, including the 1/24th. He had intended to keep the Second Battalion in South Africa but, early in September, he learned that the War Office had ordered it to Gibraltar.[68]

The battalion's "march of about 250 miles down country was begun on the 29th September." Pietermaritzburg was reached on the 14th of October; but Arthur Harness, who was already in the town, had written home that: "My old friend Black . . . turned up yesterday [27 September] from a long time at the 'front' ".[69] It seems almost certain that Hook was with Colonel Black and went on with him to Gibraltar, ahead of the battalion. Hook was not at Durban, on the 13th of January 1880, when the mayor presented an illuminated address to the 2/24th, shortly before its embarkation on "the hired transport 'Ontario' ". All those defenders of Rorke's Drift who were at Durban were given copies of the address; and a nominal roll was prepared of those who were not then with the battalion but who were to be sent their copies by Major Bromhead. This roll shows Hook at Gibraltar, and the "Pay Lists" place him on the Troopship "Himalaya", rather than the "Ontario."[70]

The 2/24th arrived at Gibraltar on the 12th of February 1880. It was "quartered in the casemate barracks", where "for the first time since it left Chatham on the 1st February, 1878, the battalion again had a roof over its head." It was not to remain for long on "The Rock", as orders were received at the end of July for it "to be held in immediate readiness for India."[71] Well before then, Hook had decided to purchase his discharge. He gave the reason a year later: "I was very ill when I came home and that is why I left the army."[72]

He must have made his intention known during May, if not before, as *Queen's Regulations* provided that

> commanding officers are to allow a period of thirty days to intervene between the receipt of the soldier's application and its transmission to the Adjutant-General, or other sanctioning authority, in order to afford the man sufficient time to reconsider the step he is about to take, and to withdraw his request, if on mature deliberation he shall be disposed to change his mind; and it is the duty of the commanding officer to assist the man with the best information and advice in his power on so important a point.[73]

Whatever advice Hook was offered officially—and perhaps more personally, by Black—his mind was made up. The machinery for discharge was put in motion during June, when Black was for the time being in command of the battalion. On the 21st of the month, Hook paid "the regulated compensation" of £18; and he would also have been "required to lodge . . . a sum sufficient to defray the expense of . . . [his] passage home."[74]

Colonel Black endorsed the "Parchment Certificate" of discharge:

> His conduct has been very good.
>   Granted the decoration of the Victoria Cross for gallantry at the defence of Rorke's Drift. He is in possession of one Good Conduct Badge.[75]

Hook's discharge took effect on the 25th of June 1880, when there was probably a ship at Gibraltar for the "passage home."

So Hook sailed for England. He never left her shores again; but he had been further, and seen more, than the vast majority of working people of his day.

NOTES

1. Penn Symons Narrative.
2. "Isandhlwana: January 22nd, 1879" by Brig. General H.G. Mainwaring. An account in typescript, written in 1895 (copy supplied by Mr. F.W.D. Jackson).
3. Holme, *Noble 24th*, p. 277.
4. Banister's letter (as cited in Chapter VI, n. 10).
5. Harford, *op. cit.*, p. 36.
6. Colenso, Frances E., assisted by Durnford, Edward, *History of the Zulu War and its Origin* (London: Chapman and Hall, 1880). The preface is dated 22 January 1880. The remark quoted (p. 307) is said to be by an unnamed member of the garrison; and Chelmsford is blamed for leaving the post "in utter confusion."

7. Parr, Henry Hallam, *A Sketch of the Kafir and Zulu Wars* (London: C. Kegan Paul & Co., 1880), pp. 260-61; Harford, *op. cit.*, p. 37.
8. Parr, *A Sketch*, p. 261.
9. *Royal Magazine*, p. 348.
10. Hamilton-Browne, G., *A Lost Legionary in South Africa* (London: T. Werner Laurie, 1912), p. 152.
11. Laband, *op. cit.*, pp. 237-39; Mainwaring's account (as cited at n. 2).
12. *Ibid.*
13. Smith-Dorrien, Sir Horace, *Memories of Forty-Eight Years' Service* (London: John Murray, 1925), p. 19.
14. Holme, *Noble 24th*, p. 322.
15. Colenso & Durnford, *op. cit.*, p. 307.
16. Parr, *A Sketch*, p. 263.
17. *Ibid.*, p. 265. See Jackson, *op. cit.*, pp. 63-64, for a valuable appendix on "The Native Contingent at Isandlwana."
18. Holme, *Noble 24th*, p. 269.
19. *Royal Magazine*, p. 348.
20. Dunne, *art. cit.*, pp. 287 & 292; Knight, *op. cit.*, p. 118; Holme, *Noble 24th*, p. 278.
21. Curling to his mother, 28 January 1879 (copy of typescript supplied by Mr. F.W.D. Jackson).
22. Martineau, *op. cit.*, II, pp. 276-77.
23. Original in Regt. Museum.
24. Harford, *op. cit.*, pp. 37-38; Laband, Thompson & Henderson, *op. cit.*, pp. 45-46.
25. *Ibid.*, p. 45. (Three regiments of native troops had been raised and it was the third regiment which had been with the Centre Column.)
26. *Ibid.*, p. 110.
27. Battalion Orders for 30 January 1879, in "Order Book No. 1—Rorke's Drift" (Regt. Museum). (Cited hereafter as "Order Book".); Emery, *Red Soldier*, pp. 123 & 140.
    By 1st February, there were 605 N.C.O.s and men of the 2/24th at Rorke's Drift. (Jackson, *op. cit.*, p. 10, n. 5.)
28. "Zulu War", pp. 43-44.
29. Harford, *op. cit.*, p. 38.
30. Emery, *Red Soldier*, p. 63.
31. Reprinted in *ibid.*, p. 135. It seems probable that the actual writing of Hook's letters was done for him.
32. See Chapter VI, n. 1. This appears to be the case described by Emery, *Marching Over Africa*, p. 66.
33. Emery, *Red Soldier*, pp. 63 & 141; Stevenson, *op. cit.*, pp. 97-98; Dunne, *art. cit.*, p. 338.
34. Item P.254.53, displayed at the Regt. Museum.
35. "Order Book", 28 January & 2 February 1879.
36. *Ibid.*, 28 January & 11 February 1879; Harford, *op. cit.*, p. 39; Laband, Thompson & Henderson, *op. cit.*, pp. 45, 58-59 & 110; *The Red Book* [a reprinting of contemporary reports in Natal newspapers. Pinetown, Natal: 2000], pp. 105 & 117.
    Glyn was said to be "in a highly nervous and apprehensive state"; but this was not surprising, as his regiment had just lost six companies in a few hours and he was obviously only too well aware of Chelmsford's lack of confidence in him. He moved to Helpmekaar early in March, leaving Degacher in command at Rorke's Drift.
37. "Order Book", 28 January 1879.
38. Spiers, *Army and Society*, pp. 62-63; Skelley, *op. cit.*, pp. 148-51 (who says that: "Flogging seemed about to die out, but in 1878 it was revived in all its former vigour to maintain discipline among the forces in South Africa").
    Flogging was finally abolished in 1881.

39. As cited in Chapter VI, n. 1.
40. Emery, *Marching Over Africa*, pp. 62-63; Skelley, *op. cit.*, p. 148; Clarke, *Invasion*, pp. 260-61; Montague, *op. cit.*, p. 104.
41. *Ibid.*
42. See *Follow the Drum* (an exhibition catalogue published in 1988 by the National Army Museum, Chelsea), pp. 6-8, for an account of this aspect of a drummer's duty and a photograph of a cat-o-nine-tails.
43. "Order Book", 23 February, 19 March & 2 April 1879.
44. Published on 18 April 1879.
45. "Order Book", 26 March 1879. The promotion had appeared in the *London Gazette* for 31 December 1878 but was delayed in reaching South Africa.
46. Harford, *op. cit.*, pp. 19 & 47.
47. There is no biography of Black; but there are some personal details in *Who Was Who*, Vol. I, and in a Record of Service (extending only to 1875) at WO 76/235, Public Record Office. He was born on 10 February 1837; retired in 1899; and died on 5 July 1909. He was married at Halifax, Nova Scotia, on 8 June 1869; and his children were born on 30 March 1870. The names of his wife are difficult to read on the Record of Service but the last two appear to be "Mander Baffs." See the photograph of "Black in Canadian outfit" in Jackson, *op. cit.*, p. 53.
48. Clarke, *Invasion*, p. 50.
49. Bellairs, Sir William, *The Military Career* (London: W.H. Allen & Co., 1889), p. 106; Banister to his father (as cited in Chapter VI, n. 10).
50. Harford, *op. cit.*, p. 41.
51. The Colour was found on 4 February; and Black led parties to Isandlwana on 14 March and 15 May. These patrols are described by Norris-Newman, *op. cit.*, pp. 116-24 & 179-80 and by Laband, Thompson & Henderson, *op. cit.*, pp. 60-73.
52. Norris-Newman, *op. cit.*, pp. 182-83. The Bible was presented to the Museum by the late Mrs. Bunting, in 1971 and is Item B.346.71.
53. Laband, Thompson & Henderson, *op. cit.*, p. 111; *Red Book*, pp. 180-81.
54. "Zulu War", p. 47; "Order Book", 3 April 1879.
55. Laband, Thompson & Henderson, *op. cit.*, p. 111.
56. Clarke, *Invasion*, p. 113.
57. "Zulu War", pp. 46-47.
58. Clarke, *Zululand*, p. 139; Clarke, *Invasion*, pp. 139-40.
59. *Ibid.*, pp. 114-15 & 139-41.
60. The papers referring to the awards made for the defence of Rorke's Drift are at WO 32/7390, Public Record Office. In his official report, dated 25 January, Chard mentions by name fifteen officers and men, including Hook. (The present writer has discussed the controversy surrounding these awards in *R.D. & B.M.*, pp. 30-31.)
61. Chelmsford to "Military Secretary", 23 February 1879.
    There had been nineteen Sapper V.C.s before 1879 and Chard's was the only one awarded to an Engineer during the Zulu War. The accounts given by Napier (*op. cit.*, pp. 5-80) show that the previous awards had been made for more clear-cut and defined acts of valour than in Chard's case; but the circumstances at Rorke's Drift were peculiar and, as he was himself the commanding officer, there was no-one present at the defence who was competent to make a recommendation in his favour.
62. Lehmann, Joseph H., *All Sir Garnet: A Life of Field Marshal Lord Wolseley* (London: Jonathan Cape, 1964), p. 13.
63. Disraeli, [Benjamin], *The Letters of . . ., to Lady Bradford and Lady Chesterfield*, ed. by the Marquis of Zetland (2 vols., London: Ernest Benn Ltd., 1929), I, p. 64.
64. *Times of Natal*, 11 August 1879.
65. Wolseley, *South African Journal*, p. 70.
66. *Royal Magazine*, p. 348. Private William Griffiths, of "G" Company, 2/24th, had won the V.C. in 1867.
67. Letter to Hook from the War Office, 13 May 1879; and "Certificate of Identity",

dated at Brecon, 30 December 1901 (both in Furness Collection).

68. "Zulu War", p. 49.
69. *Ibid.*, pp. 50-51; Clarke, *Invasion*, p. 177.
70. See Holme, *Noble 24th*, pp. 309-10, for the text of the mayor's address, and the nominal rolls of the defenders of Rorke's Drift who were present and absent on the occasion of the presentation. (If Hook received his copy of the address, it has not apparently survived.) The Pay Lists are at WO 16/1580, Public Record Office.
71. "Zulu War", p. 52.
72. His first interview (as cited at Chapter VI, n. 1).
73. *The Queen's Regulations and Orders for the Army* (1873), section 20, para. 47.
74. *Ibid.*, sec. 20, para. 51.
75. Certificate in the Furness Collection. Hook had been receiving a penny a day for good conduct since 31 January 1880.

       Queen's Regulations (sec. 20, para. 16) provided that "the class of education certificate" was to be entered on the "Parchment Certificate" but that "the non-possession of any . . . education certificate is not to be stated." No remark was made in Hook's case.

This is believed to be Hook's last photograph (c. 1904) and shows him as a sergeant in the 1st Volunteer Battalion, Royal Fusiliers. (Furness Collection.)

*The author in the basement of the Iron Library, British Museum,
with a Victorian book barrow. Hook worked in the Iron Library
during the first half of his service at the Museum.
(Photographed by Mrs. Joyce Millard, 1992.)*

Letter from the Treasury to the Trustees of the British Museum, 23 December 1904, awarding Hook a gratuity of £40..6..11d., on his retirement. (Courtesy, Trustees of the British Museum.)

Victoria Catherine and Letitia Jean, Hook's daughters by his second marriage, photographed in Gloucester, perhaps before they were admitted to the Royal Soldiers' Daughters' Home. Victoria, the eldest daughter, is wearing miniatures of her father's medals. (Furness Collection.)

Chapter VIII

THE MOVE TO LONDON: 1880-81

1.

All soldiers had to tell the Discharge Board their "Intended place of residence" and this was entered on each man's "Parchment Certificate" of discharge. On Hook's certificate, the place is given as: "Drybridge [Street] Monmouth, Monmouthshire." At that time, he evidently regarded Monmouth as his true home.

The tradition in his second family was that he returned to Gloucestershire to find that "the family farm had been sold, and his wife—who apparently believed that he had been killed at Rorke's Drift—had married again and moved from the village."[1] He *might* have gone to Gorsley on his way to his parents' home but, if he did, what he would have found was certainly not what this tradition records. His family was still living at Mount Pleasant, which was then a hamlet of ten households. Hook's father-in-law, John Jones, had become head of the household and his wife, daughter and three grandchildren were living with him. When the Census was taken next spring, Comfort Hook gave her occupation as "Gloveress" and her children were at school.[2] Comfort had neither re-married nor moved, but she may have disposed of some of her husband's domestic or personal possessions, as she must have felt herself abandoned. (This was perhaps the origin of the legend that *real property* had been sold.)

Comfort was bringing up her children during the years when "various Education Acts . . . [were passed] with the purpose of enforcing the attendance at school of every child over the age of five."[3] Raymond reached this age in the autumn of 1876 and Henrietta in the autumn of 1878. Both of them were sent to the Gorsley National School; but, in February 1879, they were admitted to the school at Christ Church. (Their address is given as "Scruffy

155

Street", a strange name which may have referred to the lane which leads to the west from the Mount Pleasant cross-roads.) In September 1881, they were joined by Julia, and by 1883, Raymond and Henrietta had reached Standard III (out of five Standards). All three children were then withdrawn from the school on the same day and without any reason being officially recorded.[4] There must have been a "family" reason for these simultaneous withdrawals and it could have been that the Joneses and Hooks were moving back to Kilcot (where they were living when the next Census was taken in 1891). The childrens' education *ought* to have continued until the age of fourteen—and perhaps it did—but there were "persistent breaches of the Education Acts" in rural areas until the end of the nineteenth century. One reason for these "breaches", at least until 1891, was the school fees— "only 1d or 2d per child per week in most cases", but "a major outlay" when a family with several children was going through hard times.[5]

The Jones/Hook family had one regular wage—from John Jones himself—to support three adults and three children. Mrs. Jones and the children may well have worked for local farmers at the haymaking and harvesting seasons, and there was also Comfort's income as a gloveress. Gloving was a "cottage industry" which then employed many women, and some children, in the rural Midlands. It was one of the so-called "sweated trades", in which long hours of exacting work brought sparse returns. Some gloveresses dealt with "middlemen"—local merchants or shopkeepers—but Comfort Hook sold her gloves in Ledbury market. By walking nine or ten miles each way—no doubt trudging part of the way over fields—she would have got a better price for her wares. Cottage glovers worked with pre-dressed skins but did well to make a dozen pairs of good-quality gloves per week, if they also had ordinary household duties. For a week's work, they earned something between 3/3d and 3/9d (although market and individual circumstances would have caused more variations than with wages on the land.)[6]

Her daughter, Julia, recalled that Comfort made plain, shammy-leather gloves for women, cutting out the leather and hand-stitching with "very fine one-inch needles." In the evening, Julia was given the job of threading a row of needles, ready for the morning, as her mother's eyesight was no longer good enough for such work by candle-light. (During the day, in fine weather, gloveresses usually sat out of doors to stitch, as the light would be better and kinder to their eyes.) If Julia began to fall asleep while threading, her mother "would thump her on the head with her finger containing a very heavy metal thimble saying 'I'm going to thimble pie you if you don't keep awake.' "[7]

Comfort was evidently a severe, as well as an overworked, mother but her children did have some lighter moments. When they ate gooseberries or raspberries from the garden—which were needed for jam-making—Comfort "sprinkled all the bushes with baking flour and told the children that it would kill them if they ate any more." Raymond and Henrietta were "undaunted" and got their younger sister to eat one of the berries "while they stood by to see if she died"! Yet whatever fun there may have been, these were straitened years at the cottage. As an absent husband and father, Hook dropped to a very low point in his family's esteem, and recollections of what was said about him have come down the generations. "A bit of a rogue" and "a womaniser" were typical remarks; and Julia's children and grandchildren were brought up to be ashamed of him. On the other hand, his family knew that he had won the V.C.; and one of Henrietta's grandchildren recalls that there was a photograph of Hook in their house in Birmingham, between the Wars.[8]

It must now be seen how his reputation fared in Monmouth.

2.

Henry Hook—he was never "Alfred" in Monmouth—arrived at his parents' house during the second half of July 1880. It suited *The Beacon*, and no doubt many people in the town, to regard the new V.C.-man as a local hero. His decoration had been reported under the heading "Honour to a Monmouth Soldier."[9] Now *The Beacon* announced his return home:

> Our gallant townsman's arrival at Monmouth would in all probability have been signalised by some demonstration of welcome, at all events on the part of the members of the Royal Monmouthshire Engineer Militia . . . but with characteristic modesty he informed no one of his coming, not even his own relatives.

The newspaper remarked that he was

> looking out for a situation as gamekeeper, woodward, gardener, groom, or in some similar capacity. No doubt many employers would be glad to obtain the services of a steady, prudent, resolute man such as Hook has proved himself to be, and we trust he may not be long before he is satisfactorily settled in civil life.[10]

This appropriation by Monmouth of a Gloucestershire hero was to some extent justified. Apart from his service in the Militia, his

157

parents had moved to the town during the eighteen-seventies; and the Census returns show that three other Hook families were living there in 1881. None of these families were "Churcham Hooks", but they would have added to the impression that the wider Hook family had strong roots in Monmouth. *The Beacon*'s proprietary attitude also survived into very different times. Its review of the film "Zulu" imagines Hook thinking of his "native Monmouthshire" at Rorke's Drift, and speculates that he "might never have been there at all but for a decision of Monmouth Magistrates." From another local source comes the more realistic claim that he is "remembered in Monmouth at Hook Close, Osbaston."[11]

Despite a suggestion that Hook's father "had owned a shop below the Monnow Bridge", it seems much more likely that the elder Henry had never left the land. At the time of his son's return, he was a "Wood Cutter" but the family lived in one of the oldest and most agreeable parts of Monmouth. Drybridge Street is the first road on the right beyond Monnow Bridge (on leaving the town centre) and it lies more or less parallel to the river. On the left, is Cinderhill Street, where the mother of Sergeant Maxfield "kept a small shop." Some of the houses in Drybridge Street date from the fifteenth century and the landlord—who lived at the far end, in Drybridge House— had this ancient property renovated at about the time that the Hooks were there.[12]

The younger Henry had now to recover his health—though he was never able to restore it fully—and this was hampered by poor sleep. It was again *The Beacon* which reported "that for a long time after the Zulu campaign he found it no easy task to sleep, for the recollections of what was experienced there [at Rorke's Drift] left a remarkable impression on his memory." In these circumstances, he was fortunate in finding work with the town's best-known medical man, George Owen Willis. Dr. Willis had been assistant surgeon of the Militia during Hook's service and he was for many years the medical officer at Monmouth Hospital. He was able to afford three resident servants at his house in Glendower Street, in the town centre, and presumably offered Hook the job of groom after reading in *The Beacon* that the former militiaman was looking out for work. The household which Hook joined comprised Dr. Willis and his wife, Emily; an elderly clergyman as boarder; and two young, unmarried servants: Mary Powell (26), the cook, and Catherine Harris (17), the housemaid. Grooms on country estates were then paid £18 or £20 a year, with food and accommodation provided (say, about seven or eight shilling a week). Hook could hardly have earned more than this, working for a small employer, but his duties may not have been very demanding. This appears to have been his only stint as a groom and he held the post for, at most, a year.[13]

As the winter of 1880 came on, his father fell ill with typhoid fever. He was attended by Dr. Willis but double pneumonia soon developed and he died at his home on the 29th of December. The elder Henry was buried at the nearby church, St. Thomas's, which has stood since the twelfth century at what became the junction of Drybridge Street and Cinderhill Street.[14]

3.

Within a year, both the widow and her eldest son had left Monmouth. They went their separate ways and neither of them lived in the town again. It must be admitted that the departures of mother and son are equally mysterious and are never likely to be fully fathomed.

Eleanor Hook was either a "fast worker" or else she already knew Eli Attwood, who married her ten months after her first husband's death. Attwood was a Worcestershire man, a widower of forty who was by trade a "Smith" or "Journeyman Nail Maker." He was then living in Cardiff, and the wedding took place at the city register office, from his house in the Cathays district.[15]

Hook's decision to move to London would have been made easier by the knowledge that his mother was planning to re-marry. He was still at Monmouth as late as the third week of May 1881—by late August or early September, he was in London. That April, he had told the Census enumerator that he was married, but he must have felt that his marriage was, in effect, over. There was nothing to keep him in the West-country and, if he had already spent some time in London, he would have known that he could find work and lodgings for himself. He may have grown dissatisfied with his duties as a groom or with his place in the Willis household. Perhaps the Army had made him restless, so that he could no longer settle back into country or small-town life. In any case, he was no longer the simple countryman of Gray's "useful toil . . . and destiny obscure." Already, in Monmouth, he had tasted the heady delights of being interviewed by the press, and the first of many accounts of his experiences had been published. He might have hoped that in London he could find some sort of civilian work in uniform: that he had the fondness of many men for wearing uniform is obvious. There may well have been a more direct reason in what seems to have been his wish to return to South Africa and to serve with the Cape Mounted Riflemen. (Some of the Riflemen were recruited in London.) But whatever reasons he had for his move to London, the days of "Alfred" Hook, the countryman, were over.[16]

Assuming that he travelled by train, he would have stepped from the carriage into "the vast smoky cavern" of Paddington Station. It was an age of strong and distinctive smells, and the smells prevailing at the main railway stations were of "horses and engine smoke." Flora Thompson—a country-woman coming to London for the first time, and sitting at night on the outside seats of a horse-bus—pondered "the smell and taste of the thick, moist air! What was it? It appeared to be a blend of orange-peel, horse-manure and wet clothes, with a dash of coal gas." (There was always plenty of manure and when it dried, in summery weather, the wind blew it in drifts into the gutters.) She was amazed to see "children playing in the gutter, actually playing, with so much traffic about, and at that hour!" In the Dickensian fogs—white, yellow or black—the mouth seemed to be full of coal dust, but some people found the fogs "friendly." The mud in the streets gave occupations to "shoe-blacks, registered and red-coated, at the kerbside doing a mighty job with blacking and spittle for 2d."; and to "London's crossing-sweeper of the fashionable quarters."[17]

There was a great contrast between the "rattling and rumbling" of horse-buses, hansoms, four-wheel cabs ("growlers"), dray and other goods vehicles, in the shopping and business districts, and the almost-deserted suburban roads, where "a tradesman's cart, a hawker or a hurdy-gurdy [barrel-organ], were the sum total of the usual traffic." The hawkers offered an extraordinary assortment of goods

each with an appropriate cry: "Flowers all a-blowing and a-growing", "Ornaments for your fire-stove" (unbelievably hideous streamers of coloured paper), "A pair of fine soles", bird-cages, iron-holders, brooms, brushes, and baskets.[18]

The American novelist, Henry James, returning to London from Paris, thought that

on the whole it strikes me as stuffier and duskier indoors and smuttier and damper out than ever before. As you sit in your room you seem to taste the very coal in the great clumsy fires, and when you open your windows for fresh air you admit . . . a rain of sootflakes.[19]

But he also found that

It takes London to put you in the way of a purely rustic walk from Notting Hill to Whitehall. You may traverse this immense distance—a most comprehensive diagonal—altogether on soft, fine turf, amid the song of birds, the bleat of lambs, the ripple of ponds, the rustle of admirable trees.[20]

James was an "inveterate walker" around mid and late-Victorian London, and he observed that

> The shabby quarters are too dusky, too depressing . . . There are too many gin-shops, and too many miserable women at their doors; too many, far too many dirty-faced children sprawling between one's legs; the young ladies of the neighbourhood are too much addicted to violent forms of coquetry. On the other hand, the Squares and Crescents, the Roads and Gardens, are too rigidly, too blankly genteel. They are enlivened by groups of charming children, coming out to walk with their governesses or nursemaids, and by the figures of superior flunkies, lingering, in the consciousness of elegant leisure, on the doorstep. But, although these groups—the children and the flunkies—are the most beautiful specimens in the world of their respective classes, they hardly avail to impart a lively interest to miles of smoke-darkened stucco, sub-divided into porticos and windows.[21]

When he took "the little voyage from Westminster Bridge to Greenwich", the novelist felt himself initiated

> into the duskiness, the blackness, the crowdedness, the intensely commercial character of London. Few European cities have a finer river than the Thames, but none certainly has expended more ingenuity in producing a sordid river-front. For miles and miles you see nothing but the sooty backs of warehouses, . . . They stand massed together on the banks of the wide turbid stream, which is fortunately of too opaque a quality to reflect the dismal image. A damp-looking, dirty blackness is the universal tone. The river is almost black, and is covered with black barges; above the black housetops, from among the far-stretching docks and basins, rises a dusky wilderness of masts. . . . the whole picture, glazed over with the glutinous London mist, becomes a masterly composition. But it is very impressive in spite of its want of lightness and brightness, and though it is ugly it is anything but trivial. Like so many of the aspects of English civilisation that are untouched by elegance or grace, it has the merit of expressing something very serious. Viewed in this intellectual light the polluted river, the sprawling barges, the dead-faced warehouses, the frowsy people, the atmospheric impurities become richly suggestive. It sounds rather absurd, but all this smudgy detail may remind you of nothing less than the wealth and power of the British Empire at large; . . . I don't exactly understand the association, but I know that when I look off to the left at the East India Docks, or pass under the dark hugely

161

piled bridges, where the railway trains and the human processions are for ever moving, I feel a kind of imaginative thrill. The tremendous piers of the bridges, in especial, seem the very pillars of the Empire . . .[22]

But perhaps the most compelling impression of arriving in the capital of that Empire comes in this recollection of a London girl returning after a long holiday:

The size and importance of the terminus [Paddington] might alarm a timid fellow passenger, but were nothing to us. The wet streets (for it invariably seemed to rain on our return), the reflections from the street-lamps and the shops, the utter indifference of everybody to us and our concerns—why was it fascinating even to a child? I suppose we took on that feeling of superiority to all the world, the idea of finality, that London gives. No sign-posts to other towns are to be seen. Here's London. Here you are. We were almost of the same mind as the old Cornish farm-labourer who could not be made to believe that there was anything *beyond* London.[23]

4.

Hook found work with William Cubitt & Co., the old-established firm of builders, whose offices were in Gray's Inn Road. At that time, the building industry employed "a vast number of labourers who were not organised [into unions]." Wages appear to have been 5½d an hour, usually for a ten-hour day. By working ten hours a day, six days a week, these labourers could earn about 27/6 a week; but this was an *hourly* scheme and the labourers had little bargaining power.[24]

Cubitts had a contract with the British Museum for the supply of materials and also for the services of carpenters, masons and labourers.[25] By what seems to have been pure chance, Hook was sent to the Museum as a labourer and, in this way, he entered the very institution where his fame—though hardly his fortune—could best be advanced. He was assigned to "General Cleaning" under the Clerk of Works.[26]

It must soon have occurred to him that he was part of a rather peculiar system. There were "Contractor's Labourers" paid by Cubitts (of which he was one) and also Labourers, doing much the same work, but employed by the Trustees of the Museum. These "Trustees' men" had very much greater security, as they were engaged under Treasury regulations and so were minor civil servants. To balance what was seen as much more "respectable" and permanent employment, the Trustees paid only 24/- a week for very similar hours to those worked by Cubitts' men (but this was *weekly*, not hourly, pay). Hook would have soon learned that it was possible to transfer from Cubitts' to the Trustees' service. A Cubitts' man had to be "well recommended" and if, on transfer to the Museum staff, he turned out to be unsuitable, he could be sent back to Cubitts.

This happened to a Labourer called Arthur Donn who, after becoming a Trustees' man, was "several times reprimanded and cautioned for want of punctuality of attendance." When his case came before the Trustees, Donn was "transferred to the Contractor's staff" and "his place as a Duster in the [Museum] Library" was taken by one of Cubitts' men "well recommended, and possessing the necessary qualifications."[27]

This occurred while Hook was himself hoping to become a Library Duster. At the end of September, Pulman, the Clerk of Works, recommended him "for employment under the Trustees when a vacancy may occur." He was probably told that he should submit outside recommendations; and Major Bromhead wrote from Brecon to say that "I have always found Hook an honest & sober man & that I can strongly recommend him for employment."[28] There was then a waiting period of nearly two months.

It was during this time that he was befriended by one of the most successful and unusual members of the Museum staff. George Knottesford Fortescue was three years older than Hook but was said by contemporaries to be "very young in appearance." This was certainly not due to a sheltered life. He had been removed from college by his father (the Provost of Perth Cathedral) on account of "misdemeanours" and sent into the "merchant shipping service." Sailing for the Far East in a collier, he had had "a very hard time" and ran away when his ship reached Singapore. Later on, he was able to transfer into the Royal Navy. For five or six years, in one service or another, he "made a good many voyages, [and] visited Indian, Chinese, and South American ports." During these years, Fortescue led a life quite as remote from Museum routine as Hook's had been in the Army, and only an accident brought these adventures to a close. He fell from a mast and was "badly knocked about." This happened in 1869, the very year in which his uncle, A.C. Tait, became Archbishop of Canterbury.

The significance of this piece of preferment, in his nephew's case, was that the Archbishop was always, *ex officio*, the senior of the three Principal Trustees of the British Museum (the other two being the Lord Chancellor and the Speaker of the House of Commons). Most appointments to the Museum staff were then vested in the Principal

Trustees. When he heard that his nephew had left the sea, Tait nominated him for an Assistantship (the lowest academic grade) at the Museum. Fortescue "failed in spelling" in the qualifying examination, so the Archbishop gave him "another nomination at once." This time he passed and quickly became "one of the most efficient men that the British Museum has ever had." As a colleague dryly remarked: "nepotism has its uses"![29] Although he rose to be Superintendent of the Reading Room, and later Keeper of Printed Books, Fortescue was "unacademic" but he was "very quick-witted and original [and] extremely human." Everyone noticed "the incisive vigour of his speech"—particularly, the "nautical words"—and he was "essentially a man of affairs rather than a student."

When he met Hook, he had been on the staff for eleven years and was responsible for "placing books" in the Library.[30] Either he heard that there was a Rorke' Drift man about the precincts, or he saw Hook wearing his V.C.—to Hook, at that stage, he would merely have been one of the frock-coated men of the Higher Staff, indistinguishable from the others who were running the Museum. Fortescue was described by a friend as "a ravenous cigarette smoker" and he could only have satisfied this craving, during working hours, by standing at one of the outer doors—perhaps he met Hook in this way?

However they met, the "warm-hearted" Assistant must have got the V.C.-man to confide in him and to say that he wanted to transfer to the Museum staff. Fortescue used to stay at Addington, the Archbishop's country house, where "he met all sorts of people of distinction in Church and State." It seems quite possible that he knew Lord Chelmsford, or at any rate that the Archbishop did. He evidently said that he would ask Chelmsford to recommend Hook to the Museum authorities, and Chelmsford responded:

50, Stanhope Gardens,
  Queen's Gate, S.W.

25 November 1881

Henry Hook,
  Mr Fortescue has written to me regarding your wish to obtain the place of "Inside Duster" at the British Museum, and it has given me great pleasure to be of some slight service to you by writing in your favour to the Principal Librarian [the equivalent of the present-day Director].
  The promise I made to you at Rorkes Drift I shall be always ready to keep to the best of my ability;—as I can never forget those who made such a gallant stand and behaved so nobly on

that memorable occasion—
                        Believe me always
                        Your well wisher
                        Chelmsford.[31]

It will be seen that this letter is not addressed and it was probably sent to the Museum (where there was a rack for staff letters in the Front Hall). Little is known about Hook's private life in London during the eighteen-eighties, except that in February 1882 he joined (or rejoined) the Bloomsbury Rifles. As a single man, he presumably lived in lodgings and had his meals provided by the landlady. Exactly *where* he lived in these years is a problem, but he had very sound reasons for being within walking distance of the Museum. Apart from his part-time service in the Bloomsbury Rifles, whose headquarters were only a few hundred yards from the Museum, he had to report for work at six o'clock each morning. His lodgings might have been in the Gray's Inn Road or King's Cross area; in Holborn or Bloomsbury itself; or perhaps further north, in Islington, where he certainly lived in later years,—but all this is speculation.[32]

Lord Chelmsford's letter to the Principal Librarian seems to have been decisive. From that point, things moved forward as rapidly as they are ever likely to in a great public institution. Hook was interviewed at the Principal Librarian's Office on the 29th of November and it was noted officially that he "Cannot read and write." He promised to "practice to qualify himself." As he would not, at that stage, be given any clerical duties, the test which the Office had to apply were no doubt quite basic.[33] Within a few weeks, he was considered to have qualified, and his appointment as a "Trustees' man" dated from Boxing Day.[34]

NOTES

1. *Colonnade*, pp. 15-16.
2. Census return, April 1881. Anne Jones had no occupation.
3. Horn, *Victorian Country Child*, p. 66.
4. Details from the "Admission Register" of Gorsley School, supplied by Miss Lilian James, of Culver St., Newent. Raymond and Henrietta were admitted on 17 February 1879 and Julia on 5 September 1881. All were withdrawn on 9 October 1883; and no further information about their schooling has been found.
5. Horn, *Victorian Country Child*, pp. 69, 72 & 77.
6. *Ibid.*, p. 128; Reminiscences of Mrs. June Dutton, as cited at Chapter III, n. 10; Leyland, N.L. and Troughton, J.E., *Glovemaking in West Oxfordshire* (Oxford City and County Museum Publication No. 4; 1974), p. 22; Information from Mr. Richard Bidgood, of Witney, Oxon. (Telephone conversation, 13 July 2000).
7. Leyland & Troughton, *op. cit.*, p. 10; Reminiscences of Mrs. Dutton.
8. Reminiscences of Mrs. Dutton; Telephone conversation with Mrs. Heather Warman-

Johnston, 29 September 2000; Telephone conversation with Mr. Denis A. McCarthy, a grandson of Henrietta Hook, on 1 October 2000. Mr. McCarthy, who now lives in Ireland, was brought up in Birmingham.

9. *Monmouthshire Beacon*, 13 September 1879.

10. *Ibid.*, 24 July 1880.

11. *The Beacon* carried the review of "Zulu" on 5 June 1964. Its story about Hook and the magistrates is that "he was brought before them for poaching and given the option of going to prison or joining the army." There is no evidence to support this tale.

   For Hook Close, see *Monmouth V.C.s* by E.T. Davies (Monmouth: The Regimental Museum, c. 1991), p. 1. The late Mr. Davies was aware that Hook was born in Churcham.

12. "Alfred Henry Hook, 1850-1905: Gloucestershire's First V.C." by Henry Bunting, in *Local History Bulletin*, No. 45, Spring 1982, p. 2; Death certificate for Hook's father, occupation given by his widow; *Monmouthshire Beacon*, 5 May 1905; Kissack, *Victorian Monmouth*, p. 12.

13. *Monmouthshire Beacon*, 6 May 1898; Noel, *op. cit.*, p. 106; Census return, 1881, for the Willis household; Horn, Pamela, *The Rise and Fall of the Victorian Servant* (Stroud: Alan Sutton, 1990), pp. 213-14.

   Hook was certainly living in the Willis household by 12 February 1881, as a letter from the War Office, in reply to his letter of that date, is addressed to Glendower St. He had applied for the South Africa medal, which was granted. (War Office to Hook, 18 February 1881, in Furness Collection.)

14. Information from the Death certificate and from Mrs. Patricia Davis.

15. Marriage certificate, showing that Eli Attwood and Eleanor Hook were married on 17 October 1881, in the presence of Eliza James and Fanny Bush. He gave his occupation as "Smith" (and his father, James, is also entered as a "Smith"). Although he gave his age as 36, his birth certificate shows that Eleazer Attwood was born at Cradley, near Halesowen, on 19 March 1841.

   Eleanor gave her age as 44; but as she had been entered as 20, at the Census of 1851, she was almost certainly 50 at the time of the wedding. The 1881 Census shows that in April "Ellen" Hook was living at 22, Drybridge St., Monmouth, and had a lodger.

16. See Appendix C for the interview. Can Hook really have told the reporter that Monmouth was "his native town"?

17. Flora Thompson's account of her first visit to London is in "Heatherley", included in *A Country Calendar* (Oxford: Oxford University Press, 1979), pp. 264-65; "Seventy Years Back" by H.B. Creswell, in *The Architectural Review*, December 1958, p. 403.

18. Hughes, M. Vivian, *A London Family: 1870-1900* (London: Oxford University Press, 1946), pp. 5 & 49.

19. James, Henry, *Letters*, ed. by Leon Edel (4 vols., 1974-84. Vol. II, London: Macmillan, 1976), p. 5.

20. James, Henry, "London" (1888), in *English Hours* (Oxford: Oxford University Press, 1981), p. 11.

21. James, Henry, "The Suburbs of London" (1877), in *London Stories and Other Writings* (Padstow: Tabb House, 1989), p. 222.

22. James, Henry, "London at Midsummer" (1877), in *English Hours*, pp. 94-95.

23. Hughes, *op. cit.*, p. 126.

24. Kingsford, P.W., *Builders and Building Workers* (London: Edward Arnold, 1973), pp. 109 & 123.

25. Edward A. Bond, British Museum, to Cubitts, 16 March 1880, accepting a "schedule of prices" for "the supply of labour and materials" (in British Museum Archives); Harris, P.R., *A History of the British Museum Library, 1753-1973* (London: The British Library, 1998), p. 315.

26. Memorandum by C. Pulman, Clerk of Works, dated 30/9/81, in Hook's envelope, which forms part of the series "Staff Applications & Testimonials, 1835-1935",

British Museum Archives. (All papers in these Archives are quoted by permission of the Trustees.)

27. The details of Donn's case, decided by the Trustees on 10 December 1881, are in the bound volumes of "Minutes, Reports, Letters, etc.", Department of Printed Books (now in the British Library Archives, and cited hereafter as "MRL").

The beneficiary of Donn's unpunctuality was Samuel Francis, who eventually became "Foreman of Library Dusters" and thus, for a few years, Hook's immediate superior. See *R.D. & B.M.*, pp. 43-45.

28. Papers in Hook's envelope (cited at n. 26). The full text of Bromhead's letter is in *R.D. & B.M.*, p. 39.

29. The original system of Principal Trustees, and of nominations by them, no longer survives.

30. The "Placer" of books decided exactly where each volume should be put on the Library shelves, in accordance with the classification scheme.

31. Original in Furness Collection. For Edward A. Bond, the Principal Librarian, of the same date, see *R.D. & B.M.*, pp. 39-40.

The outline of Fortescue's life, and most of the quotations, are taken from "George Knottesford Fortescue: A Memory" by Henry Jenner, in *The Library*, January 1913. The colleague who made the remark about "nepotism", and also about Fortescue being "quick-witted and original", was Arundell Esdaile, in *The British Museum Library* (London: George Allen & Unwin Ltd., 1946), pp. 367-68. It is of course possible that Hook was introduced to Fortescue by another member of the staff.

32. Both the present writer (*Colonnade*, p. 16), and the late Norman Holme (*Silver Wreath*, p. 87), followed the tradition of Hook's London family that "for many years, he lodged at Sydenham Hill, near the Crystal Palace." This would have involved a journey of nine miles to the Museum—not far by present-day commuting standards but difficult for a Victorian working man who had to begin duty at 6 a.m. The present writer now believes that this tradition hardly rings true.

33. Papers in Hook's envelope (cited at n. 26); and see also *R.D. & B.M.*, p. 40.

It seems likely that the reading and writing skills which Hook had learned at school had decayed while he was on the land and in the Army. This condition is now called "functional illiteracy"; and it is believed to affect a considerable number of people who would have had very much better educational opportunities than were available to working people in mid-Victorian times.

34. *British Museum: List of the Trustees . . . also the Establishment of the Museum Generally* (Printed by Order of the Trustees; and usually referred to as the "House List"). Hook's appointment is recorded at p. 13 of the List dated 4 April 1882. The system of nomination by the Principal Trustees did not apply to his grade. The appointment was made by the Principal Librarian and confirmed by the Standing Committee of the Trustees on 14 January 1882.

It should be noted that all the records of his long service in the Museum refer to him as "Henry Hook."

Chapter IX

"THE V.C. AT THE MUSEUM": 1882-92[1]

1.

"The British Museum is, next to the British Navy, the national institution which is held in most universal respect abroad."[2] This was said by a former Director in 1943 but it would have been equally true during Hook's quarter-century of service. He worked for the only institution which housed a national museum and a national library in the same building; and the Library, in which he spent nearly all of his time, was the largest in the world.

The length, height and grandeur of some of the public galleries of this early-Victorian pile will have been noticed by millions of visitors. More surprising is that most of the workrooms used by the Library staff were equally grand and ornate. They were also *book* rooms, in which parts of the Library were housed either around the walls or in heavy, glazed cases which jutted out to form a line of alcoves. The higher staff generally had their tables between the bookcases and under the tall windows which lighted the alcoves. Railed platforms, or galleries, ran above the bookcases and below the windows, and open book shelves between the windows were reached by walking along the galleries. There were a few small, private rooms, called studies, in which mainly administrative work was done; but most of the staff were surrounded by the Library's books, which had to be taken into the reading rooms when Readers sent for them.

To any new member of the staff, there are two distinctive sounds of Museum life which can be heard today as readily as when Hook joined. The first is the rattle of the four-inch long "house keys" as the doors of the staff rooms are unlocked. The second is the echoing crash as these high, heavy, double doors close, giving visitors a glimpse of an inner world beyond. That this "inner world" of the Museum would have been strange and novel to Hook is obvious enough. He had spent his first thirty years in the out-of-doors and now—by his own request—he was to work wholly indoors. The Museum was undoubtedly a rather dusty place when he began his "General Cleaning" and this, together with the effects of the heating and ventilation systems, caused some respiratory problems amongst the staff, as well as the "Museum headache" made famous by Thomas Carlyle. Such conditions, and more particularly the nature of his work during the first half of his service, probably did Hook no good at all; but of course not everyone was affected. His head of department, Dr. Richard Garnett, "knew nothing of Museum headaches. The atmosphere produced in winter by its hot-water pipes he used to compare for its warmth and dryness to the air of Egypt, and he seems to have found it sufficiently bracing to keep him in constant health."[3]

Then, except for his few years in the Army, he had worked for very small, private employers, sometimes perhaps "living in" and always dealing with the people who paid him. Now, he was one of a staff of 350, who were all paid by the government and subject to Treasury regulations. If he could accept the impersonal nature of such employment, he would have reached a permanent post in times when the loss of work often led to abject misery. This security of income was a priceless boon, perhaps difficult to appreciate in an age of "welfare states."

Lastly, he would be working amongst colleagues who, with a few exceptions, came from entirely different backgrounds to his own. The Museum liked to engage some ex-soldiers, as their characters were matters of official record and they were especially suitable for the uniformed posts. Yet such men were a tiny minority and they were all near the bottom of the Museum hierarchy. In its way, this hierarchy was more rigid than the Army's but it was based more on education than on class.

At its head were the Keepers and Assistant Keepers (referred to as "Officers") and the Assistants: under the Principal Librarian, these grades administered the departments and did the academic work. Below them—the N.C.O.s of the Museum—was a large body of men called "Attendants." Their formal qualifications—a knowledge of the first two rules of arithmetic and the ability to write from dictation "in a clear hand"—give no idea of the range of duties which Attendants performed in Victorian and Edwardian days, or of the range of abilities found within the grade. At the lowest level, some Attendants could expect to do little more during their careers than the fetching and carrying of books or perhaps the supervision of this basic work in a particular part of the Library. Those Attendants with a better education would eventually be given work of a more clerical nature; while those who showed distinct qualities of intelligence and initiative could expect to reach posts of considerable responsibility, for which they were given special allowances. The Attendants dressed formally, in black and white, much in the style of office clerks of the day. When on duty in the public galleries, they carried a "wand"—a long, slender stick, reminiscent of a billiard cue, which was held upright, rather as a soldier holds his rifle.

Below the Attendants was a group of people who appeared in the *House List* under the heading: "House Attendants, Servants, etc." These included the staff of the Front Hall, under the Messenger; and the Firemen, Gate Keepers, Housemaids, Ladies' Attendants, Window Cleaners, and various other grades who came under a "General Foreman." The largest category under the Foreman was "Labourers", twenty-seven of them, including Hook, and all paid at a fixed rate of 24/- a week.[4]

Surprise has been expressed that "the V.C. carried so little weight that Hook, with the special recommendation of Lord Chelmsford, could obtain only a lowly paid menial job" at the Museum.[5] He was obviously beginning in the lower grades, and his work was undeniably "menial"; but there were certain, though limited, prospects of promotion. James R. Lee, whose place Hook had filled, was promoted to Attendant after five years as a Labourer. A few others during Hook's time were given Attendantships for "exceptionally good service" as Labourers, so that he could certainly have risen from "menial" work. The official reports on Attendants are replete with words like "steady", "respectable" and "trustworthy". Hook was a model of such old-fashioned virtues and was well qualified for the promotion in many respects. What he may have lacked was the willingness to improve his education in his spare time and to push himself forward, but it seems clear that many of his leisure hours were instead devoted to the Rifle Volunteer movement.

At a higher level, the chasm between Attendants and Assistants was almost uncrossable. As with Army officers, the Assistants were regarded as "gentlemen" and were always referred to as "Mr.——", while the lower grades were known simply by their surnames. The educational qualifications demanded of the Assistants were so much higher than for other members of the staff that it was infinitely more difficult to be promoted to an Assistantship than to win a commission from the ranks of the Army. All things considered, the general prospects of advancement in the Museum were decidedly slimmer than in the Army; and Hook's "menial job" was not really so surprising as might appear at first sight.[6]

The Labourers were assigned either to one of the departments or to more general work around the building. At the time of Hook's transfer from the Contractor's staff, the largest department, Printed Books, had ten Labourers, but the Treasury had been asked to increase this number to sixteen. Well over a million books had to be dusted and the department reported that conditions had become "most unsatisfactory, in consequence of the accumulation of dust, and has given rise to complaints by persons using the books." Even apart from cleanliness, dusting the books was regarded "as an essential thing to guard against their deterioration." Some of the men were kept at this dusting all day but others had, in addition, a miscellany of different duties: "burnishing the metal work in the King's Library"; emptying waste-paper baskets; filling carafes of water; "Sweeping odd Rooms"; operating lifts; "Watching" (presumably, the public!); and perhaps most curious of all—and Hook's eventual berth—taking care of the Readers' umbrellas.[7]

While Hook was still in Monmouth, an official letter from the Keeper of his future department gives a vivid glimpse of what was expected of the Library Dusters:

> . . . some of the labourers employed as Dusters in this Dept. [Printed Books] are very remiss in their attendance here in the morning . . . Their time is properly from 6 O'Clock A.M. to 6 P.M. in the summer and to 4 P.M. in the winter . . . [but] Sometimes two of the number (there are 7 in all) do not come until 7 O'Clock, and sometimes not until 9—Occasionally one absents himself for a whole day on the plea of illness . . . a great deal is required to be done before 9 O'Clock [in tidying up the Reading Room before it opened at that hour].

The Keeper thought that "it would be a good thing to dispense with the services of at least one of these [offenders] and get some person who will attend more regularly to his duties." Still, he was a kindly man and suggested to his superior, the Principal Librarian, that the men should be given "a strong warning . . . in the first instance."[8]

The Labourers were not without complaints of their own and petitioned the Trustees "for a reduction of one hour in their day's work, when extending from 6 a.m. to 6 p.m." In forwarding this petition, the Library authorities were sympathetic, but pointed out that the request should only be granted

subject to withdrawal in the case of misconduct. It must however be understood that the men may be required to stay on special occasions and it should be arranged that one of the number stays until half past 5 in this department [Printed Books] for the purpose of closing windows.[9]

The Trustees granted this petition, so that when Hook was assigned to Printed Books, he worked only an eleven-hour day in the summer and a ten-hour day in the winter. Everyone at the Museum then did a six-day week; and, in the Labourers' case, there is no hint of any paid leave (except for four Bank Holidays). He was put to dusting full time in the famous Iron Library, which had been built around the outside of the Round Reading Room with unbroken circles of gridiron floors, and with book shelves, stanchions and stairs also in metal. The two floors and basement were topped by a glass roof, which allowed daylight to filter down through the grids. Although the authorities knew that "work carried on in the heated atmosphere under the glazed skylights of the New [Iron] Library is during summer extremely trying"[10], the skylights were believed to be essential. London was largely gas-lit but the Trustees forbade the use of gas in the Museum: they lived in enough terror of the national treasures being destroyed by fire without running the risk of them being blown up in a gas explosion! Other rooms and galleries had also been designed to take the fullest advantage of daylight, by setting large windows high in the walls (but the walls themselves were in dark colours, with reds predominating). Apart from Victorian London's uncertain daylight, staff and Readers had long been dependent on a cautious and limited use of oil lamps. A dramatic change came about in 1879, when electricity was introduced into the Reading Room. Very gradually, this newest form of lighting was extended to other parts of the building but it never reached the Iron Library in Hook's time there. During his second winter, there were "four large arc lights in the Reading Room, fifteen smaller arc lights in the Front Hall and other public rooms, and thirty-nine Swan [incandescent] lights" elsewhere in the Museum. Yet even with these improvements, as Hook and his colleagues began work early on winter mornings, and the Attendants moved about with "heavy and clumsy oil lanterns, locked and double barred", the Museum must have been an eerie place of shadows.[11]

The books were dusted manually and, in the case of heavy and bulky volumes, this work was physically demanding as well as dirty. The Dusters wore the ordinary clothes of working men, with aprons to give some protection from the dirt. But when a reporter from *Rare Bits* was unexpectedly taken to see Hook, he saw at once that there was something very distinctive about him, as above that peaceful apron was worn the narrow strip of red ribbon flanking the Zulu medal on the side nearest the waistcoat button, which I at once recognised as the outward and visible sign of the Victoria Cross.[12]

At that time, two "domestic" questions troubled many of the staff much more than they did in later years. Firstly: where were they to dry their boots and clothes in wet weather (as a good deal of walking was done by most workers in those days)? Secondly: where were they to eat their lunches in the limited time allowed (as there was then no staff canteen)? During 1883, the Attendants in Printed Books petitioned for "a room in which they may make tea and consume such articles of food as they find it necessary to bring from home." The Library authorities hoped that the Trustees would "grant this indulgence", as it was "extremely undesirable" that the staff "should be allowed to consume food in the sections [of the Iron Library] where they are at work as it attracts mice and leads to injury of the books but this cannot well be prevented unless there is a room provided for the purpose."

A decision was "postponed", so in 1886, the Attendants wrote formally to the Keeper to draw his attention "to the scant accommodation afforded us for washing and other purposes":

The lavatory adjoining the Reading Room is now in use by upwards of *sixty* attendants and we have no other place; communicating with this room there is another which is clean & light and much more spacious than the one provided for us, it is used by *twelve* of the "dusters" . . . who in addition to the superior comfort at their disposal make common use of our lavatory . . . As the "dusters" have a place *in addition*, for retirement [*i.e.*, when not on duty], we would most respectfully ask you to allow us the exclusive use of both rooms . . . [so that] we shall be enabled to dry our clothes, boots, &c. on the hot-water pipes when the weather is wet, and at the same time we should not be depriving the dusters of the privilege as they have a room with a fire in it.[13]

From this, it seems that the Dusters were doing rather well in the way of accommodation.

3.

After Hook had lived in London for a year, an unusual public event took place which obviously impressed him. Cetshwayo had been kept in more or less comfortable captivity at the Cape for three years

173

after his deposition. He made several applications "to go to England to lay his case for returning to Zululand before the Home Government" and was at last allowed to sail for London.[14] During most of August 1882, the King was staying at 18, Melbury Road, "a handsome private residence, overlooking Holland Park [Kensington] . . . temporarily acquired by the Colonial Office." Sketches in the *Illustrated London News* show him arriving in the capital dressed in a military type of braided jacket, with a peaked cap.[15]

Half-a-dozen newspaper cuttings preserved by Hook describe Cetshwayo's visits to the Zoological Gardens at Kew; to the Colonial Office in Downing Street and then to the Houses of Parliament; to Windsor Castle; and (most lavishly reported) to Woolwich Arsenal.[16] The present-day reader of these graphic but dignified accounts is struck by the respect paid to the King wherever he went and by his own bearing, so clearly bringing out his character. They emphasise, above all, the very general interest which the visit aroused. One Sunday, "a large crowd assembled at an early hour [outside No. 18], and until nightfall three policemen were required to keep the spectators 'moving on'." Several vantage points during the visit to Woolwich were "densely crowded with spectators" and there were "ringing cheers" for Cetshwayo. The Queen herself could hardly have been more enthusiastically received.

It would have been natural for Hook to have wanted to see the Zulu King, but it would have brought back very mixed memories. The hardships of the campaign could never be forgotten but nor could the satisfactions of being in uniform. For some years after he joined the B.M., he hoped to find work more rewarding and less disagreeable than dusting. What he would have liked was regular employment in uniform and, at first, he hoped also to go back to South Africa. Before he was recommended for inside work at the Museum, Hook had applied "for admission to the ranks" of the Cape Mounted Riflemen. He probably saw this force in the field during the Ninth Frontier War. The C.M.R. had missed the Zulu War but had recently suffered some losses in action in Basutoland. It had a "dual function as a police force to preserve peace and prevent crime and as a military force for the defence of the Colony." Pay was good—on joining, a 3rd Class Private drew 4/6 a day—but it was in one sense like civil employment, "the Government only issuing arms and ammunition gratis."[17] The card which Hook received, granting him an interview at the Cape "Emigration Office" in London, bears the stark phrase: "N.B.—No travelling expenses allowed." Whether he could have paid for a passage to South Africa; whether he was still fit enough for five years in the saddle on the Cape frontier; or whether he even attended the interview, are all unclear. He had been given almost two months' notice of the appointment, yet if he had passed the interview and medical examination, he would have been expected to sail for the Cape the next day![18]

In retrospect, it seems obvious that he would have had a much better chance of enrolling as a Rifleman if he had left the Army while he was still in South Africa. The country evidently attracted him, as this letter shows:

A Rorke's Drift Hero

TO THE EDITOR OF THE NATAL MERCURY

28, Back Beach, July 7.

Sir,—Referring to your notice relative to Pte. Hook, V.C. I would like to know if something could not be done for him in Natal, that would be better than the very poor post of "duster" in the British Museum. Surely Natalians will do something for one of the men to whose courage and devotion they owe so much. My father [Gregory W. Eccles], who is one of the assistant librarians in the British Museum, speaks most highly of Hook's character, and has several times asked me to try and get him something to do out here; but though I have spoken to several influential people, none of them seemed able to do anything; and seeing the above referred to notice in your paper induced me to write to you to solicit your aid in bringing Hook's case before the public. There is only one thing against him, and that is that he is quite uneducated, being unable to read or write with any facility. Trusting you may be able to do something.—I am, &c.,

W.G. ECCLES.[19]

This appeal failed and Hook turned to uniformed civilian posts. There is a groundless story that he "worked for a time as a commissionaire" at a bank in Gloucester; but the posts which he is known to have applied for were in London.[20] The only trace of one application is a rather brusque testimonial from Lord Wolseley, then Adjutant-General:

Henry Hook.
In reply to your application for a testimonial in support of your application for a situation as messenger or attendant at the Royal Courts of Justice, I can only express the hope that your gallant Service at Rorke's Drift for which you were given the Victoria Cross may be considered by those with whom rests the

selection of Candidates for the posts in question.

Wolseley
General

Horse Guards
War Office,
15 Jany. 1883.[21]

In the following year, Hook took his case to the Prince of Wales, whose interest in the Army was well known and who was also a Trustee of the Museum. That autumn, the Prince was at Abergeldie Castle, Ballater, and two letters were received there in quick succession, one of them having been "forwarded to him by Princess Christian [President of the Soldiers' and Sailors' Help Society]." Both letters were sent on to the Museum "with a view to seeing whether anything can be done for Mr. Henry Hook." It seems that Hook was applying for the post of porter at the College of Arms; but this brief flurry of Royal correspondence came to nothing.[22]

Meanwhile, Hook had entered the Volunteers shortly after joining the Museum staff, so he was at least in uniform outside of working hours. He remained a Volunteer to within a few weeks of his death, except for an apparent interval between November 1890 and April 1896.[23] No explanation for this gap is known, but it was during these years that he hoped to become a Yeoman of the Guard.

This corps, like the Volunteer movement, was (and still is) a part-time force, but membership was severely limited and carried much greater prestige. Gilbert and Sullivan, with their opera *The Yeomen of the Guard* (1888), had given the impression that the Guard was stationed in the Tower but it was actually based at St. James's Palace. (The Yeomen *Warders* do duty at the Tower.) A hint of contemporary confusion can be seen in this newspaper item:

> A candidate for enlistment in the Yeomen of the Guard, familiarly known as Beefeaters, is Henry Hook, V.C., late of the 24th Regiment, and at present an attendant in the Reading Room of the British Museum. Mr. Hook, who also wears the medal and clasp for the Zulu Campaign, and won his V.C. at Rorke's Drift, is the possessor of excellent testimonials to character and conduct, which combined with his military record, should induce the authorities to do something, in his case, to disprove the charge that the British Government never values the valour of the British soldier at a higher rate than that of sixpence [*sic*] a day.[24]

The reporter seems to think that Hook would have benefited financially from joining the Guard but the reverse was true. Pay was "nominal" and was cancelled out by the expenses incurred: for instance, when they were in attendance on the Queen for a ceremonial occasion at Windsor Castle, the Yeomen paid their own train fares and then had to "sleep in the corridors of St. James's Palace for what remained of the night."[25] Whether membership of this corps would have been consistent with Hook's work at the Museum is a moot point, as individual Yeomen had to be available for duty when called out. They had been the sovereign's body guard in Tudor times, which accounts for their gorgeous uniforms and antique weapons. In Hook's day, they were also obliged to wear beards.[26]

During the summer of 1892, Hook approached Chard, Chelmsford and Wolseley for their help in securing an appointment. (Major Bromhead had died in India.) Wolseley sent word that he would "if referred to, be happy to testify to your gallantry on service."[27] Lord Chelmsford replied:

Knaresborough Place,
Cromwell Road, S.W.

8 July 1892

Dear Mr Hook,
    I shall be only too pleased to act as your referee when you make your application to be appointed to the Yeomen of the Guard.
    If you will let me know when your application has been sent in, I will do my best to help you-

very faithfully yours
Chelmsford.[28]

Chard wrote:

Fulwood Barracks
Preston
Lancashire

11th July 1892

Dear Sir,
    I shall be very glad if any word of mine can help you in your application. Your character at the British Museum will after so long service be the best guarantee of your character as a citizen— of your devotion and gallantry as a Soldier I have already borne witness.
    I shall be very glad to hear you have been successful in your application.

Yours Truly
J R M Chard
Major R.E.

Mr. Hook V.C.)
Late 24th Regt) [29]

Hook's formal application to the War Office was made through the Regimental Depot; but no-one at any stage seems to have advised him that he would fail to meet at least two of the necessary qualifications. The official reply points out that: "not having held the rank of Sergeant, and being below the standard height (5 ft. 10 in.) His Royal Highness [the Commander-in-Chief] regrets that this man is ineligible for appointment."[30] Hook is often referred to as a sergeant but this was a *Volunteer* rank; and in his letter of application, he gives his height as "five feet seven and a half [inches]."[31] Although Hook undoubtedly met other criteria—notably, gallantry in action, good conduct and general smartness—it seems clear that he also lacked at least one "unofficial" qualification. Those N.C.O.s who were appointed Yeomen in the years after he left the Army were invariably of long service. Four Yeomen were actually appointed during 1892, none of whom had served less than twenty-one years in the Army.[32]

There was a curiously delayed sequel to this application. Hook received a card illustrated with a jolly and portly Beefeater, who was raising a tankard to Christmas. The handwritten message reads:

> To Henry Hook
> With Mr. Basil H. Soulsby's best wishes for his promotion to this Uniform.
> Christmas 1895.
> British Museum. [33]

Soulsby, who was an Assistant in the Library, had only joined the staff in June 1892 and is not known to have been either a Volunteer or a member of the B.M. Rifle Association. The War Office letter is so final that it seems unlikely that Hook can have kept alive any hope of a "promotion" to St. James's. But perhaps he did; or perhaps his bid to become a Yeoman was still going the rounds of Museum gossip three years later?

NOTES

1. The quotation is from an item about Hook in *M.A.P.*, 10 February 1900.
2. Esdaile, *op. cit.*, p. 5.
3. "Richard Garnett" by Alfred W. Pollard, in *The Library*, July 1906.
4. *House List*, p. 13. In later years, a limited number of labourers were paid 26/- a week, the extra two shillings being for merit.
5. Ron Handley to G.D. Pillinger, 4 December 1986 (in Lummis File).
6. This discussion of the various grades is based largely on the papers in MRL.
7. G.W. Porter to Trustees, 5 October 1881; George Bullen to Edward A. Bond, 20 June 1881; John P. Anderson to Richard Garnett, 8 June 1890 (all in MRL).

8. Bullen to Bond, 3 January 1881 (in MRL).
9. Porter to Bond, 2 June 1881 (in MRL).
10. Porter to Trustees, 23 May 1883 (in MRL).
11. Miller, Edward, *That Noble Cabinet: A History of the British Museum* (London: André Deutsch, 1973), pp. 254-55 & 260: Barwick, G.F., *The Reading Room of the British Museum* (London: Ernest Benn Ltd., 1929), p. 122; Harris, *op. cit.*, pp. 313-15.
12. Anonymous article in *Rare Bits*, c. 1883 (in Furness Collection). See *R.D. & B.M.*, pp. 43-45, for a discussion of how the Dusters worked.
13. Porter to Trustees, 23 May 1883; Letter to Bullen, 6 March 1886, signed by 49 Attendants (both in MRL).
14. Binns, C.T., *The Last Zulu King: The Life and Death of Cetshwayo* (London: Longmans, 1963), p. 186.
15. *Illustrated London News*, 12 August 1882.
16. In Furness Collection.
17. Williams, Basil, *Record of the Cape Mounted Riflemen* (London: Sir Joseph Causton & Sons Ltd., 1909), pp. 17, 23 & 32. The force had earlier been called the Frontier Armed and Mounted Police.
18. Card in Furness Collection, dated 3/9/1881. He was told that: "If you will have the goodness to attend here [10, Blomfield St., E.C.] on Thursday the 27 day of October at 9.30 a.m., you will be examined by me [Wm. C. Burnet] and by the [Cape] Government Medical Officer. If approved you will have to sign Articles of Agreement and be prepared to sail from England on Friday the 28 day of October."
19. Unidentified cutting in the Furness Collection. Gregory W. Eccles was a Volunteer officer, and his relations which Hook are dealt with in the next chapter.
20. Item headed "Hook's grave", in the *Gloucester News* (date unknown), copy supplied by Norman Hook.
     There is no actual evidence that Hook ever worked in Gloucester in any capacity; but a cutting from a Gloucestershire newspaper in the Furness Collection (undated and unidentified) reports that he "is about to receive some appointment of trust in his native [*sic*] town of Gloucester." This item came from "a Military correspondent", who had it "*on dit*"; but whatever the prospect may have been, it came to nothing.
21. Original in Furness Collection. Wolseley had become a peer in 1882.
22. Christopher Teesdale (equerry to the Prince of Wales) to Edward A. Bond, 28 September 1884, forwarding a letter which the Prince had received. Teesdale's letter is endorsed in red ink: "Letter from H. Murray Lane, R. Coll: Arms, enclosed with reply—Sep. 30."; Francis Knollys (private secretary to the Prince) to "My dear Sir" [British Museum], 29 September 1884, forwarding the letter from Princess Christian. (Both of these letters are in Hook's envelope, B.M. Archives; but the enclosures were returned.)
     Henry Murray Lane was Chester Herald and also Registrar of the College of Arms. The College employed a porter, "almost certainly in uniform," the incumbent then being 67 years old. Although the College has no surviving correspondence on this question, a replacement for the porter may have been sought during 1884. (Letter from R.C. Yorke, College Archivist, to the present writer, 14 January 1999.)
23. This appears to be the case from official forms in the Furness Collection. The gap is very curious and it may be, of course, that some papers are missing. (Hook's service in the Volunteers is discussed in the next chapter.)
24. Unidentified cutting in the Furness Collection.
25. Paget, Julian, *The Yeomen of the Guard: Five Hundred Years of Service, 1485-1985* (Poole: Blandford Press, 1984), pp. 61 & 115.
26. *Ibid.*, p. 90.
27. Major Barker, D.A.A.G., to Hook, 11 July 1892 (in Furness Collection).
28. Original in Furness Collection.
29. Original in Furness Collection. There are also replies from Major-General Teesdale and Lord William Beresford (both V.C. winners); but these officers had no personal

knowledge of Hook's service.

30. R.D. Lane to the Officer Commanding, 24th Regimental District, Brecon, 25 July 1892 (copy in Furness Collection).
31. Draft of a letter dated "British Museum, July 14th. 1892" to "Lt General Sir G.B. Harman, G.C.B.", applying "for appointment to a vacancy in the Corps of Yeomen of the Guard" (in Furness Collection).
32. Paget, *op. cit.*, p. 109; Hennell, Sir Reginald, *The History of the King's Body Guard of the Yeomen of the Guard* (Westminster: Archibald Constable & Co. Ltd., 1904), pp. 253-54.
33. In Furness Collection.

Chapter X

MILITARY LIFE AT THE B.M.: TO 1904

1.

There had been a military tradition at the British Museum long before the present building existed. When Parliament brought the Museum into being in 1753, its Trustees had on their hands many thousands of books, manuscripts, rarities and curiosities, stored in three different places. So that these collections could be brought together and opened to the public, the Trustees purchased and renovated Montagu House, a fine seventeenth-century mansion "somewhat fallen into decay." The House stood exactly on the site of the present Museum but "is as clean gone as if it had never existed."

To visitors today, the Museum seems to be very close to the centre of London's enormous sprawl; but in the mid-eighteenth century Great Russell Street stood at the edge of the capital. Behind Montagu House were seven acres of formal gardens, and the ground at the back had become a convenient rendezvous for duellists. Beyond, to the north, farms and fields stretched away to Hampstead Heath. The collections were assembled in Montagu House seventy years before Peel created the metropolitan police force. "The eighteenth-century London mob could at times be a terrible threat both to property and persons"; but these irreplaceable collections were at first protected solely by the old system of watchmen and "constables of the division of Bloomsbury."[1]

The "London mob" reached its most terrible pitch during the so-called Gordon Riots, when "for almost a week during the early June of 1780 London was in the hands of a reckless, drunken and desperate mob." Part of the mob which burned Newgate Prison on the 6th of June afterwards marched to Bloomsbury Square, "shouting their intention of roasting alive Lord Mansfield [Lord Chief Justice] and the Archbishop of York." Montagu House was only a hundred yards west of the Square; and Lord Mansfield's house, at the northeast corner, would have been only too visible, from the upper windows of the Museum, as it was gutted by fire that night. The Lord Chief Justice escaped being "roasted", but his "precious library of rare books and manuscripts, legal reports and notebooks" was flung down into the Square and destroyed.[2]

No move was apparently made against Montagu House. Troops were "pouring into town at every avenue", and the York Militia arrived to garrison the Museum. This regiment stayed on for two months, the men camping on the lawns while the officers were put up in the House itself. One of the best-known pictures of the eighteenth-century Museum shows some civilian visitors at the tent encampment, one of the children marching alongside a soldier on sentry-go and mimicking his step. When the militiamen left, Montagu House was guarded by Regular troops, who were provided with five sentry-boxes outside the precincts and a guardhouse just behind, and at right angles to, the main building. The troops were not finally withdrawn until 1863, when they were replaced by the Metropolitan Police. This "sergeant's guard" comprised two N.C.O.s and twelve to fifteen privates, and was for many years "furnished almost exclusively by three regiments of Foot Guards—Grenadier, Scots or —Coldstream—from Knightsbridge, Portman Street or the Tower." Their guardhouse had an amazingly long life, surviving the departure of the troops by over a century and thus serving as a link between modern times and the days of Montagu House.[3]

The Trustees' sense of patriotism was stirred in 1803, at the height of the war with France. In that year, the Volunteer movement was flourishing as never before. The local corps was the Bloomsbury and St. Giles Association, and permission was given for this body to drill in the Museum courtyard. At the same time, the Association's band was allowed to practice in the gardens, "provided they did not damage the Egyptian antiquities" temporarily stacked there, "or harm the flower-beds." Unfortunately, Readers in the Library complained that their studies were "much disturbed and interrupted" by the band, so the martial music was stopped. During the next six years, the Volunteers insinuated themselves into various parts of the House and gardens. They "stored several barrels of gunpowder in the building which held the Museum fire engine"; and perhaps fearing that the national treasures would be destroyed without any assistance from Bonaparte, the Trustees ordered the gunpowder to be taken away. The corps was no doubt helping to defend London against the threat of invasion, but in going about their business they showed an understandable ignorance of the Museum statutes. Gradually, the Trustees' goodwill was eroded and in 1809 they told the Volunteers to leave.[4]

Montagu House was then "at peace" until March 1815, when the sergeant's guard was called into action. The Earl of Eldon—Lord Chancellor, and therefore a Principal Trustee—lived in Bedford Square, on the west side of the Museum gardens. London was again in turmoil and Eldon's house was attacked by a mob. The windows were smashed and iron railings torn up and used to break down the outer door. Lady Eldon and the children escaped into the Museum, while the Lord Chancellor brought a corporal and four privates through the gardens and into the back of the house. The corporal was a shrewd Scotsman and by leading his men in single file, and pretending that there was "no end" of soldiers behind him, he was able to drive out the rioters at bayonet point. Lord Eldon obviously admired the coolness of the "excellent corporal" and records sadly that he "was shot at Waterloo", three months later.[5]

In 1823, Parliament voted the first of many financial grants towards the piecemeal pulling down of Montagu House and its replacement by the present Museum. This proved to be an immensely long and complicated business. The sergeant's guard went daily about its duties amidst "the most horrible state of noise, dirt and dust."

"General Orders for Sentinels" were issued:

No. 1—They [sentinels] are not to quit their arms, nor to walk more than ten yards on each side of their Posts, unless in the execution of their duty, they are neither to converse, lounge, nor slope their arms upon their Posts, nor to remain in their Boxes in fair, or even in moderate weather, but are to walk about in a soldier-like manner, with their arms supported or carried. In standing at ease in front of their Boxes they are to maintain the same steadiness, as when in their Ranks, they are not to remain in that position more than ten minutes at a time.—Double Sentries are on no account to walk together. In paying Compliments they take the time from the right; on the appearance of an Officer they are to stand firm in any part of their Walk, with carried arms. They are to present arms to the Royal Family, the Colours of a Regiment, the Field Officer of the Brigade, to all armed parties of the Brigade commanded by an Officer and the Rounds.

Nos. 4, 5 and 10 read as follows:

No. 4—In the Gardens they are to prevent any damage being done to the pales, fences, trees, plantations, &c, &c, &c.
No. 5—They are to prevent the commission of depredations of all sorts; should they be attempted beyond the reach of their

Post, they must alarm the Guard.

No. 10—The men must not cut or make holes in their Sentry-boxes.—The Non-Commissioned Officers are desired to be particular in this point, and to report the offenders.

Several memoranda were added, including:

No. 2—The Serjeant is to be very particular in not allowing the men to put Ashes near any part of the Building, but to see that they are carried to the proper place amongst the shrubbery.[6]

By 1848—"the year of revolutions"—"most of the stout wall which had once protected the Museum along Great Russell Street had been taken down" and replaced by a "wooden hoarding." Behind this "frail barrier", the old House had almost gone and the new building was nearly complete. The Museum was thought to be very vulnerable to attack by Chartists who, on the 10th of April, were to meet nearby in Russell Square. The military guard was reinforced, so that two officers, fifty-seven men and twenty Chelsea Pensioners were at hand to stiffen the staff and the builders. Muskets, cutlasses and pikes were sent by the Board of Ordnance to arm the civilians. On the evening before the demonstration, an Engineer officer arrived "to advise on the construction of suitable barricades." Provisions for a three-day siege were brought in, and other precautions were taken, but all to no purpose. Chartists were far removed from "Gordon Rioters" and their day's demonstration in London fizzled out ingloriously. In fact, the direst threat to the new Museum came from the Chelsea Pensioners. They were put up for the night, "snugly arranged" in the Department of Manuscripts, and were found cheerfully smoking, "with their ammunition close beside them in open barrels, so that a spark might have blown them all up."[7]

How much of this history was still being retold when Hook joined the staff is impossible to say; but most of his colleagues spent their working lives at the Museum and there was a strong "oral tradition." At this point, organisations were created which he joined almost as soon as he came to the Museum.

2.

On the 22nd of January 1852, a member of staff had a letter published in *The Times* under the heading "A Rifle Corps":

SIR,—Having read letter after letter in the newspapers recommending the immediate adoption of means whereby our capabilities of self-defence may be increased, and having suffered daily disappointment in my expectation of an announcement that something had been done towards the formation of organized societies for rifle practice, I resolved to try what I could do by way of taking the *premier pas*, which, in this instance, seemed to me to be neither costly nor difficult. I am one of a large number of gentlemen employed in a public establishment of an eminently pacific character. I proposed that some of us and of our friends should combine for the purpose of learning, in the cheapest and quickest way, how to handle a rifle. The first 19 I spoke to instantly agreed to the proposal: the 20th refused, because he was already engaged as a member of a similar association. As most of us are not free till past 4 o'clock in the afternoon, we are to put up with lamplight practice in a London rifle gallery, until the spring evenings allow of our sallying forth a few miles, once or twice a week, into the country. A moderate weekly subscription will pay for the gallery and ammunition, and an entrance fee is to be imposed, for the purchase of a few good ordinary rifles—one to every five or six of us—and these, after serving our immediate purpose, are to be distributed among the members, as prizes for skilful shooting, at the end of a fixed period. Within a week from this time we shall be in full operation; and, from the eagerness with which the plan has been entered into by all to whom I have spoken, I have little doubt but that our example, if made known through your columns, will be followed by many thousands of the young men of London and the large provincial towns. Before Parliament has been open a week we shall certainly be able to present a numerously and most respectably signed petition for Government assistance and organization. C.K.P.

The writer was Coventry Kersey Dighton Patmore, an Assistant in the Library.[8] His job was to catalogue books for six hours a day (until he was "free" at four o'clock) but his true vocation was poetry. Although he told a fellow-poet that his "whole time is now absorbed in the business of a Rifle Club, which I have been mainly instrumental in getting up", he was, within a few years, to become popular as the poet of married love. Few people now read his "domestic epic", *The Angel in the House*, but its title gave his contemporaries a catch-phrase.

Patmore's letter was prompted by the second of the three "invasion panics" which disturbed early Victorian England. This one caused the government to revive the Militia, while "rifle clubs sprang into existence in London and all the chief provincial towns."[9] The body which Patmore helped to "get up" was the Metropolitan Rifle Club, and presumably his nineteen colleagues also joined the Metropolitan.[10]

185

Patmore has been credited with expanding his Club into "a proper volunteer Rifle Company", or with helping "to raise a Company of Volunteers from amongst members of the Museum staff", but neither claim seems tenable.[11] The "second panic" died down and the government refused to sanction the re-establishment of Volunteer corps.[12] "Attempts were made to form a Volunteer rifle corps in the Museum" during the "third panic" of 1859, and again in 1867 (after Patmore had retired), but both attempts failed.[13]

Patmore himself never seems to have been a *Volunteer*, and belonging to a rifle club was a totally different thing. What he may have helped to found is the British Museum Rifle Association. The early records of this club have disappeared, but there are indications that it was established between 1852 and 1859. In its original form, it survived until the First World War.[14] Hook would have been eligible to join as soon as he became a "Trustees' Man" at the end of 1881, and he was certainly present at the annual dinner of the following year. By that time—and no doubt long before—many members were referred to by military ranks; and this may have been the origin of a legend that the Association had links with the Rifle Volunteer movement. In one sense it did, as there was a considerable overlapping of members between the Association and several Rifle Volunteer Corps in London. Yet there was no *actual* link; and when the B.M. Rifle Association was revived between the Wars, military ranks were dropped.

These ranks are a very curious feature of the old Association. At first sight, they appear to be Volunteer titles but this theory is shaken when Hook's case is considered. In printed lists of prize winners for May and October 1889, he appears as "Private Hook, H. (V.C.)"; but he was then enrolled in the 17th (North) Middlesex Volunteer Rifles and had been appointed a lance-corporal in March 1887 and was a corporal by the time he took his discharge in November 1890.[15] Much more surprising is the fact that Rifle Association ranks bore no relation to Museum grades. John P. Anderson and James Baynes-Jago were Assistants in the Library and privates in the Association; but George Gatfield and John L. Miller were Attendants in the Library and sergeants in the Association.[16]

Even if the early records could be found, they would probably not explain a system which would have been well understood in its time but which is now inexplicable. Rifle clubs could develop into Volunteer corps; and there was one case in London—the 49th Middlesex (Post Office) R.V.C.—where staff formed a Volunteer corps whose designation included the name of their employer's organisation.[17] If the founders of the B.M. Rifle Association had expected that it would soon become a Volunteer corps, they may have instituted military ranks and then have allowed the system to

The Wood sisters, daughters of Henrietta and John P. Wood. (Left to right:) Florence Henrietta (later, Mrs. McPhail); Edith Agnes (later, as Mrs. Wills, Birmingham's first woman M.P.); Vara Gladys (later, Mrs. McCarthy). Photograph probably taken in Birmingham, before the First World War. (Courtesy, Mrs. Heather Warman-Johnston.)

*Raymond Hook as a gardener, in Abergavenny, c. 1933.
(Photograph taken by Mrs. Phyllis Davies, at "Blenheim", on
the Monmouth Road., where she was a "living-in" maid at the
time and got to know "Mr. Hook.")*

The house in Culver St., Newent (left-hand side), where Comfort Hook is believed to have lived while she was married to David Meyrick. (Photograph by Mr. Norman R. Hook, 2000.)

The Wood grave (left) in Newent municipal cemetery. In the centre background, the tree stump is at the site of Comfort Meyrick's unmarked grave. (Photograph by Mr. Norman R. Hook, 2000.)

continue long after it had ceased to have any real significance. Another peculiarity is that there seem to have been no *commissioned* ranks in this system, the highest rank apparently being Orderly Room (or Staff) Sergeant. The absence of officers was presumably due to the unofficial nature of the club: there was no authority which could have issued commissions to its members.

In the absence of other sources, two papers kept by Hook must be used to give an impression of club life in the eighteen-eighties. At the head of the Association was a President but this was no doubt a titular post. (In 1882, it was held by Dr. Samuel Birch, Keeper of Oriental Antiquities.) The actual administration was done by the Secretary. Since about 1859, this office had been filled by Hodgkinson Lowe, an Attendant in Printed Books. The club had its own funds—there must have been an annual subscription and probably an entrance fee—but "donors" also played an important part in its activities. They presented prizes for the shooting competitions, with service rifles, which were held each spring and autumn. Some cash prizes were awarded, ranging from £3 to 7/6; but the "donors" also gave, as more substantial prizes, such gifts as clocks, pipes and lamps.

In May 1889, the members shot for a Challenge Cup (and ten shillings) and this was won by Miller. There was also a "Handicap Series", with three prizes presented by a donor and "£12 added by the Association." Seven shots were allowed at 200, 500 and 600 yards; and Hook appears thirteenth out of the fifteen winners listed, scoring 73 points and winning ten shillings. (Miller was first with 89 points and won a clock.) At the October meeting that year, Private Anderson won both the Challenge Cup (with ten shillings) and the Challenge Badge (with £1), and also appears first amongst the eighteen winners of the "First Series of Money Prizes", gaining a further £3. (He was notable in another respect, having made the extremely difficult "leap" from Attendant to Assistant.[18]) Hook is shown as eighteenth in this competition, scoring 54 points (as against Anderson's 88) and again winning ten shillings.[19]

The Association held its annual dinners at Christmas-time, and they were evidently rather grand occasions. In 1882, the dinner took place on a Saturday at the Holborn Restaurant, which stood a few hundred yards from the Museum and near to the Holborn Underground Station. George Bullen (Keeper of Printed Books) presided in the absence of the President. It was Hook's first annual dinner and he preserved a lengthy newspaper report[20]—not surprisingly, as it includes the following paragraph:

Mr. Gregory Eccles [Assistant in Printed Books] drew the attention of the meeting to the fact that they had amongst them that evening one of the heroes of Rorke's Drift, viz., Private Hook, V.C., and proposed his health, which was most enthusiastically drunk.

The members and guests were kept busy drinking toasts and listening to the accompanying speeches: "Success to the Association"; "The Principal Librarian and Keepers of Departments"; "Visitors, &c." (responded to by Henry Stevens, the American bibliographer); "The Donors"; as well as "the usual loyal toasts." C.P. Colnaghi (Assistant in Printed Books), "the well-known amateur tenor, sang most delightfully."

More than half the report is devoted to "the Annual Topical Song of Mr. [Isaac H.] Jeayes, Manuscript Department . . . composed by him, touching upon in an extremely effective and amusing manner the salient points of Museum life during the past year." This is so much a period piece that a few of the twenty-eight verses should be given, to conjure up something of the atmosphere of an evening perhaps more distant in sentiment than in time.

Verses	*Commentary*
To the Member for Finsbury— he need have no fear That the *clôture* will e're be applied to him here.	McCullagh Torrens, who had proposed "Success to the Association."
There's a health, Volunteers, that you'll drink with delight. 'Tis the health of your colonel, who's with us to-night.	Col. Richards, 19th Middlesex R.V.C. (the "Bloomsbury Rifles").
We congratulate Eccles— a good marksman is he; A salad bowl's his, gift of Taylor, J.T.	Both Eccles brothers, Gregory and Dorset, were present. They were Assistants in Printed Books and Volunteer officers.
Mr. Taylor, we're always most happy to greet; There's a *tailor* we know we would rather not meet.	J.T.Taylor (B.M. Natural History, South Kensington) was a "donor."

And *Lowe* gets the lamp,   (
   and we all hope, I trow,   (
That the day is not near   (
   when his lamp shall get *low*.   (These verses refer to
                                   (the replacement of
Lowe's retired from the post   (Lowe by Miller,
   he so worthily filled,   (as Secretary of the
Here's to Miller's good health—   (Association.
   a successor well skilled;   (Miller had joined
                                   (the Museum staff in
He has won the first prize,   (1868.
   the much-coveted badge.   (
Don't forget when donations   (
   he cometh to cadge.   (

The clock goes to Layfield,   William M. Layfield was an
   and—a capital joke,   Attendant in Printed Books.
The meerschaum is Jago's—   Private Baynes-Jago had
   and Jago don't smoke.   responded to Torrens's toast.

3.

The toast to Colonel Richards leads naturally to Hook's life in the
Volunteers. In the romantic view, every citizen who ever undertook
to fight an invader, from Boadicea onwards, was showing the
"volunteer spirit"; but the ancient obligation of able-bodied men to
serve when called upon has already been mentioned in connection
with the Militia. Governments generally preferred the Militia to the
Volunteers because, as J.W. Fortescue says, they "could be compelled
to undergo training and to do what they were told." The more cynical
attitude towards Volunteers is well represented by Fortescue, who
was not himself a soldier but who writes from the standpoint of the
Regular Army: in this view, Volunteers never did and never could
amount to very much.[21]

As with the Militia, the Volunteers began to emerge in a distinct
form in the mid-seventeenth century. While the New Model Army
was engaged in the campaign which ended with the defeat of Charles
II at Worcester, "regiments of volunteers" were raised by Parliament
to garrison London and other towns. These volunteers were not to
expect pay unless they were on active service and, after Cromwell's
decisive victory, they were quickly disbanded with the thanks of the
Council of State.[22] Here was a basic tenet which was to endure for

two centuries: prompt disbandment at the end of an emergency. Two additional features emerged during the Jacobite rising of 1745 (when there was also a fear of French invasion): the word "Association" began to be used in such phrases as "Associations for Defence"; and it "was distinctly laid down by the Government" that these volunteer Associations "were to be subject to no other laws or regulations than those appointed by the corporations at whose instance and expense the bodies were raised."[23] The word "expense" is particularly important here.

At this stage, the essential differences between the Militia and the Volunteers were clear; but in an Act of 1758 "mention is first made of Volunteer additions to the Militia." This was carried further during the War of American Independence, when volunteers who were serving in a Militia regiment could "be formed into a *distinct* company." These volunteers were indistinguishable from militiamen except that they were serving with each other and not with "balloted" men; but there were also "independent corps of Volunteers" which had nothing to do with the Militia.[24]

The real flowering of the movement came with the French Revolutionary and Napoleonic Wars between 1793 and 1815, when "there sprang up an infinity of Volunteer corps." Much of the Regular Army was serving abroad and these corps were intended for local defence. Their members "were exempted from service in the Militia, upon producing a certificate that they had attended exercise punctually during six weeks previously to hearing of appeals against the Militia list." In other words, those who agreed to be properly trained as Volunteers could dodge the Militia.[25]

Unless their corps "elected to serve without pay," N.C.O.s and men "received two shillings weekly for two whole days' exercise of six hours each, or a number of hours in the week equivalent thereto." Only if a corps was "called out on actual service" would its members be entitled to full pay and then they would be subject to military discipline. These were the initial conditions, but they were varied over the years. Invidious and even farcical distinctions set in, notably during 1803. That June, Volunteers could be paid for eight five-days' exercises a year with a liability to serve in any part of their military district; but in August, the government decided that it could only afford twenty days' paid exercise a year, yet with a liability to serve in any part of Great Britain.[26]

One issue in particular perplexed the government: if "every Volunteer had the right to resign at his own will", how was discipline to be maintained? Each corps had its own rules and could fine members for neglect or insubordination, but these fines could only be *enforced* in a court of law. The War Office refused to intervene in disputes within corps, as this might be construed as an admission that Volunteers were "part of the statutory forces of the country." In Fortescue's view, Volunteers "were, therefore, practically under no control." By the "Levy en masse Act" of July 1803, the government at least tried to impose some discipline on *new* Volunteers by enforcing both attendance and good behaviour at training. Offenders were to be fined and, in default of payment, imprisoned for seven days: more significantly, *these* Volunteers were also "unable to resign their services at will." That October, the Law Officers of the Crown gave their opinion that *no* Volunteer could resign at will. After this ruling had "agitated the force all through the winter of 1803", the judges in the Court of King's Bench overturned the Law Officers' opinion. This was a decisive moment in the history of the Volunteer movement. In a subsequent Act, it was established that *any* Volunteer could give fourteen days' notice of his intention to resign—provided that his corps was not on active service—and this was still the position when Hook enrolled.[27]

Nevertheless, the government gradually addressed the question of discipline. "Inspecting Field Officers" were appointed "to super-intend the drill and field exercises" of Volunteers. This was a first step "towards connecting the Volunteers with the regular forces for purposes of discipline and training," and inspection by Regular officers became an enduring feature of Volunteer life. A second step was the organisation of Volunteers into brigades. The government was still concerned over "the election of officers" and "the control of corps by committees", so under an Act of 1804, "greater powers of discipline at large were granted to the Commanding Officers." A Volunteer could now be dismissed from his corps for misconduct and this inflicted on him an "instant liability" to serve in the Militia.[28]

Pitt the Younger—Colonel Commandant of the Cinque Port Volunteers, as well as Prime Minister—was the champion of the Volunteer movement, and his death in January 1806 marked the beginning of its decline. By the end of 1808, "the majority of the corps had transferred their services to the ranks of the newly created Local Militia." When Napoleon was exiled to Elba, the remaining corps were disbanded and, on the 6th of July 1814, all Volunteers received the Thanks of Parliament. Their services were not needed again until the early eighteen-thirties, when several corps were raised during disturbances related to the Reform Bill. The corps at Uxbridge, in Middlesex, survived until 1843—the last remnant of the "old" Volunteer movement.[29]

4.

When the third "invasion panic" broke out in 1859, there were plenty of precedents for the formation of new Volunteer corps. Yet the movement which was quickly revived—"despite considerable reservations on the part of both soldiers and politicians"—differed in three distinct ways from the movement which Pitt had encouraged.[30] It existed without interruption for nearly fifty years, until it was merged into Haldane's new Territorial Force in 1908; it had no connection, at any time, with the Militia; and, although the government soon became involved in the support and control of the new corps, there was never any question of these Volunteers being *paid* for training (but only for actual service).

Hook began—or perhaps recommenced—his long service in the Volunteers within a few weeks of joining the Museum staff. He enrolled in the 19th Middlesex (unofficially known as the "Bloomsbury Rifles") and was assigned to "H" Company. This unit was, in turn, informally called the "British Museum Company", as its headquarters were off Bedford Square, close to the Museum. The regiment had been formed in 1860 as the "37th Middlesex (St. Giles and St. George's, Bloomsbury)" and had been renumbered twenty years later.[31]

By the time of his company's annual dinner, in January 1885, Hook was a corporal. At the distribution of prizes that Saturday evening

A silver-headed drill-cane, presented to the non-commissioned officer making the highest aggregate of marks for attendance at drill, was won by Corporal Hook, V.C., with the highest possible score.[32]

The company commander told the members and friends at the dinner that they had 121 "efficients"—those who had attended a certain number of drills and musketry exercises during the year—and that

The average attendance [during 1884] at drills in plain clothes was 43, which was very good; in uniform 47, which was not so good. At the Brigade Drill the attendance was 54, and at the inspection 92—28 being absent on leave. They might do better than that.[33]

During 1885, Hook won a medal engraved as follows:-

XIX M*DX*
1st DRILL PRIZE
Corpl. HOOK, V.C.
H. CO[34]

Clearly, he was doing very well in the Bloomsbury Rifles; but some time after winning these awards, he wrote to Colonel Richards:

If there is a vacancy in the Staff of 19th. M.R.V. of any post in which I can be of *Service*—may I take the liberty of asking to be appointed to the Same as I find my Employment does not allow of me attending to the Company Drills as I should wish.[35]

This letter raises the question of employers' attitudes towards the Volunteers. The new movement had originally been strongly middle class, but "artisans . . . contributed the bulk of recruits after 1863." To an increasing extent, "the Force depended for its strength on a supply of working men in steady jobs." The employers of such men at first thought that their workers would be "improved" by the drill and the shooting but, long before Hook enrolled, they had become "conscious of the time off that the Volunteer in their employ demanded." By 1881, the *Volunteer Service Gazette* "considered that most employers were now opposed to the Movement," even though it then had a record strength of over 208,000 men.[36]

Like other employers, the Trustees of the Museum had at first taken a benevolent view of the movement. Twice in June 1860, Volunteers on the staff were given paid leave to attend their regiment's activities. The second occasion was the parade in Hyde Park, when 21,000 Volunteers were reviewed by the Queen. "London had arranged 'a general holiday' and the Trustees played their part by closing the Museum for the afternoon.[37] Quite soon, the Trustees either came to the conclusion that there was no longer a threat of French invasion, or—more likely—that they had been creating dangerous precedents. In 1864, a Committee Minute laid down the principle "that any absence on this account [Volunteer duty] must be part of the allowed vacation." In essence, they adhered to this principle for the rest of the century.[38]

5.

Hook was presumably not found a staff post and, on the 24th of January 1887, he resigned from the Bloomsbury Rifles. Two days later, he enrolled as a private in the 17th (North) Middlesex and was assigned to "B" Company. In March, he was appointed lance-corporal and eventually he regained his old rank of corporal.[39]

His new regiment had been formed in December 1859, when it had been numbered the 29th (North) Middlesex. It drew its support largely from the Marylebone and St. Pancras districts and, in its earliest days, had negotiated unsuccessfully with the Bloomsbury Rifles for a merger of the two corps. When Hook joined, the original uniform—"steel grey"—was still being worn, with a spiked helmet for full dress and a "glengarry" for undress. The Snider rifle had been replaced by the Martini-Henry and the firing range was at Child's Hill, near Hampstead Heath. The regiment seems to have drilled on Monday, Wednesday and Friday evenings and also on Saturdays. Drill and shooting practice were the staples of Volunteer routine but ambulance and signalling classes had been introduced in 1884.[40]

Discipline was still a problem in the Volunteers generally; but as the government supported the Force with "capitation grants"—based on the number of "efficients" in each regiment—it steadily increased its demands for closer control over this "citizen army." Regimental orders in 1880 had warned the men that they were forbidden "to smoke in the public streets while on duty"; and then they were reminded of "the necessity of . . . having their hair cut short and keeping it so," to avoid "the slovenly appearance long hair gave to men when in uniform." In the year before Hook's enrolment, the colonel "most reluctantly . . . had to resort to extreme measures . . . with certain members of the Corps who had failed to make themselves efficient for the past year." As military law could only be applied to Volunteers when they were "assembled for training and exercise with the Militia and Regular Forces", these backsliders in the 17th could only be taken before the local magistrates—who fined them thirty shillings each—and then be "dismissed the Regiment."[41] The fines would not have been welcome; but perhaps these men would have viewed with indifference "dismissal" from voluntary, unpaid duties which, if properly done, would have absorbed much of their spare time.

Apart from the weekly routine of drills, classes and shooting practice, the 17th had its yearly round of more public events. Each company gave an annual dinner; and the regiment held an "Annual Presentation of Prizes", and Regimental Ball, during January (in Hook's time, at the Holborn Town Hall). The Easter period was important for the whole Volunteer movement, when manoeuvres, and a review, were held on a large scale, at a town on the South Coast. At Whitsuntide, the 17th went under canvas for a few days at Acton, in West London; and, also in the late spring or early summer, there was a brigade drill at Hounslow, Middlesex. During the autumn, there might be a "march-out" or a shooting competition. Most years also brought such special events as the provision of a guard of honour, the lining of streets for a royal occasion, or (as in the Jubilee Year of 1887) a march past at Buckingham Palace.[42]

Hook's service in the Volunteers, and his membership of the Rifle Association, brought him into contact with nearly all grades of the Museum staff. A memento of two friendships with members of the Higher Staff survives in the shape of a copy of the *Historical Records of the 2nd Battalion, 24th Regiment, for the Campaign in South Africa, 1877-78-79.* This copy has been handsomely bound in green cloth, with gilt edges; and the fly-leaf is inscribed:-

G. W. Eccles

and

H.F. Birch Reynardson

had this book bound

for their friend

Henry Hook.

———————

British Museum

June 1887.[43]

Gregory Eccles had proposed Hook's health at the Association dinner in 1882. He was twelve years older than Hook and had been an Assistant in Printed Books since 1857. Like his brother, Dorset, he spent his entire working life in the Museum and was a Volunteer officer for many years. He retired in 1900 but, having been born in the year after Queen Victoria's accession, he survived until 1931. Herbert Birch Reynardson was six years younger than Hook and had joined Printed Books, as an Assistant, over a year after Hook's appointment. His career in the Museum was brief, by the standards of that time, as he resigned in 1889. Both Eccles and Reynardson had had classical educations and the latter had been to Eton and Christ Church, Oxford—about the best education that the country could provide. Their backgrounds and work were so entirely different from Hook's that they would probably never have been on speaking terms with him but for the fellowship of the Association and the Volunteers.[44]

Although he was "returned as an Efficient" four times in the 17th (North) Middlesex, Hook may not have been happy in the regiment.

He was by no means as outstanding there as he had been in the Bloomsbury Rifles, and was later to become in the Royal Fusiliers. The 17th had had a Crimean War V.C., Corporal Shields, who was a notable character in its early years; and in 1885, Sergeant Instructor Hall, who had served in the Zulu War, joined the permanent staff. For whatever reason, Hook made little mark in his new regiment and, on the 1st of November 1890, he took his discharge.[45] He remained out of the Volunteer Force for over five years.

6.

"Why should men join a military force which imposed on them obligations, but brought them no monetary reward?" This question was posed by the social historian of the movement, and he answered it rather disobligingly: "volunteering was primarily a recreation." He added that: "By the 1870s Volunteers were to complain that the counter-attractions of cricket and football were depriving them of potential recruits."[46] Patriotism had certainly been an important motive during the "invasion scare" of 1859, and was to be so again during the Boer War, but it seems to have been in abeyance for most of the time. One Volunteer colonel, giving evidence to a Royal Commission in 1904, remarked that " 'the bulk of my men join because they like the show, the dress, and they like the camp. I do not think they join from very high patriotic motives.' "[47] Earlier opinions suggest that rifle-shooting, rather than camp life, did most to encourage recruiting: in 1881, it was believed to give " 'as much sport to the men as pheasant and rabbit shooting does to those who can afford it.' " Perhaps most of all, men "found in the Volunteer Force something of the attraction of a club. They could meet their friends there, and enrolled in order to be able to do so."[48]

The attractions of shooting and social activities no doubt played their part in bringing Hook back to the Force; but his experience in having served in both the Regular Army and the Militia was very unusual at that time. In short, his enthusiasm for military life would have been exceptional amongst his fellow Volunteers. It was those considerations which also made him a natural choice as a Volunteer N.C.O., even though, generally speaking, "the world of the factory was reproduced on the parade ground"—that is, it was men in superior positions at work who most readily got stripes and commissions in the Volunteers.[49]

He enrolled again on the 20th of April 1896, in the 1st Volunteer Battalion of the Royal Fusiliers. This was to be his last regiment, in which he served to within two months of his death. He remained active until the end and was "returned as an Efficient" even in 1904, when his health was failing badly.[50]

His new regiment had a history as interesting as any in the Volunteer movement. It had its origins at the Working Men's College, in Great Ormond Street, Bloomsbury. In the autumn of 1859, "three strong companies" were recruited from amongst the students, with Thomas Hughes—author of *Tom Brown's Schooldays*—as Major-Commandant.

> By 1860 no less than half the total number of students were in the Corps. The little garden at the rear of the College was now fitted up with gas lighting; and the College resounded nightly to the clash of arms drill and the clump of heavy boots on the stairs. The notice boards became congested with drill orders and Corps notices, the coffee room became the forum for arguments about uniforms and marksmanship, and all energies were directed towards field days, reviews, and the Grand Rifle Ball.[51]

These student companies were incorporated into the original 19th Middlesex and Hughes resigned the command in favour of a professional soldier. The regiment was renumbered the 10th Middlesex in 1880 and, three years later, became the 1st Volunteer Battalion of the Royal Fusiliers. Scarlet had already replaced the original grey uniform, and the battalion adopted the Fusilier uniform and badge.[52]

In the Fusiliers, Hook achieved the rank of sergeant—by which he was usually known in the last years of his life—and became a musketry instructor. The photograph which epitomises this later period shows him in Fusilier uniform, with a peak cap, and an instructor's whistle attached by a chain to a white cross-belt. He must often have been at the headquarters of the battalion—33, Fitzroy Square—and it was probably there that he met his second wife.

Fitzroy Square is only ten minutes walk from the Museum and is unspoiled even today, with a railed garden in the centre and the unusual number of six plaques to former residents. The west side is the most "distinguished", with plaques to Lord Salisbury, the prime minister; and to George Bernard Shaw and Virginia Woolf. At the corner of the west and south sides stands No. 33, now part of the London Foot Hospital but hardly changed since Hook's day. The house has four storeys and a basement, and its impressive frontage on to the Square is dominated by a large window, with a column on each side, at the first-floor level (marking, presumably, the main room). At No. 33, the battalion had "a Club Room, Mess Rooms and a good Billiard Room" but the facilities for drill were not so good, and drills were held in the grounds of University College, Gower Street.[53]

The battalion had a rifle range out at Runnymede, near Egham, in Surrey. Return railway fares were a shilling or 1/3d but expenses of this kind were part of the cost of being a Volunteer. By 1895, either the Martini-Henry or the Lee-Metford could be issued and each rifle was inspected at least once a year. Company commanders recommended which of their men could be trusted to keep their rifles at home.[54]

As the century ended, the attitude of the Museum Trustees towards the Volunteer movement began to mellow, but even during the Boer War they were reluctant to give *paid* leave of absence. They did grant three Volunteers in the Library twelve days leave without pay "to attend camps of exercise"; but the War was over before more substantial concessions were made:

> The Trustees approved [14 June 1902] the allowance of special leave of absence on 16th June to Volunteers taking part in the military Review by His Majesty the King at Aldershot.

> [and]

> . . . the Trustees resolved [12 July 1902] that special leave of absence for six days be allowed to all Volunteers in their service who attend the annual camps for at least that number of days and who do not receive military pay.[55]

The Boer War made very little impact on the Museum staff, although one or two of the younger Attendants resigned so that they could enlist in the Army. It made much more of an impact on the Volunteer Force, as about twenty thousand of its men were accepted for active service in South Africa. Many other Volunteers who offered to go—at least 6,861 in 1900—"were rejected on medical grounds or because they failed to satisfy the efficiency standards."[56] Hook was in his fiftieth year at the outbreak of war and there could be no question of Volunteers of his generation going out on active service. They could only follow the news and welcome back their younger comrades.

Hook attended one such occasion in July 1902, when ten members of the Barking Company of Essex Volunteers were given a banquet in their honour. They had recently returned from South Africa and "were presented with silver watches, each bearing a suitable inscription, subscribed for by the townspeople." There were, of course, many toasts drunk that evening, including " 'The Visitors', for which Sergt. Pilkington [a correspondent with *Black and White* magazine] and Sergt. Hooke, V.C., replied, the latter coming in for a great ovation on rising to respond."[57]

NOTES

1. Miller, *op. cit.*, p. 62.
2. Hibbert, Christopher, *King Mob: The Story of Lord George Gordon and the Riots of 1780* (London: Longmans, Green & Co., 1958), pp. vii, 77-78.
3. *Ibid.*, p. 93; Miller, *op. cit.*, pp. 86-87 & 122; Harris, *op. cit.*, p. 59; *British Museum Great Court: Staff Newsletter*, No. 2, Spring 1998, with illustrations of the sentry-boxes; and also of the guardhouse as it appeared in 1845 and in 1970, a few years before its demolition.
4. Miller, *op. cit.*, pp. 120-21; Harris, *op. cit.*, p. 59.
5. Twiss, Horace, *The Public and Private Life of Lord Chancellor Eldon* (3 vols., London: John Murray, 1844), II, pp. 260-64.
6. "General Orders for Sentinels." (Handwritten copy, c. 1844, in B.M. Archives.)
7. Miller, *op. cit.*, pp. 167-72.
8. The text of the letter is taken from *Memoirs and Correspondence of Coventry Patmore* by Basil Champneys (2 vols., London: George Bell and Sons, 1900), I, p. 73.
9. Beckett, *op. cit.*, p. 164 (for the three "panics", the first of which was in 1846-48); Sebag-Montefiore, Cecil, *A History of the Volunteer Forces, from the Earliest Times to the Year 1860* (London: Archibald Constable and Co. Ltd., 1908), pp. 357-58.
10. Champneys, *op. cit.*, I, p. 74 & II, p. 176.
11. The "claims" come from Miller (*op. cit.*, pp. 284-85), who probably heard a Museum legend that there was a link between the B.M. Rifle Association and the Volunteers. No actual *evidence* of such a link has been found.
12. Sebag-Montefiore, *op. cit.*, p. 357.
13. Harris, *op. cit.*, pp. 297-98.
14. *The British Museum Rifle Association* (a mimeographed publication signed by G.D. Old [Director's Office] and dated 14 October 1980), p. 1, giving the date of establishment as 1852; unidentified newspaper cutting, dated 23 December 1882, report headed "British Museum Rifle Association" (in Furness Collection). This report describes the annual dinner of 1882, and notes "the retirement of Mr. Hodgkinson Lowe after 23 years' service as secretary." If this is accurate, Lowe had been secretary since 1859.
15. Printed pages headed "British Museum Rifle Association: Prizes" (pp. 34-35 from an unidentified publication, in Furness Collection); Rudd, Charles, *The Early History of the 17th (North) Middlesex Volunteer Rifles, 1859 to 1889* (London: R. and J. Widdicombe, 1895), p. 118.
16. These Association ranks are given in the two papers in the Furness Collection, cited in n. 14 & 15.
17. Beckett, Ian F.W., *Riflemen Form: A Study of the Rifle Volunteer Movement, 1859-1908* (Aldershot: The Ogilby Trusts, 1982), pp. 60 & 112. This is the most detailed work on the Volunteers as they existed during Hook's lifetime.
18. See *R.D. & B.M.*, pp. 43-46.
19. These details are given in the unidentified item cited at n. 15.
20. The cutting cited at n. 14.
21. For the "romantic" view, see *The Defenders: A History of the British Volunteer* by Geoffrey Cousins (London: Frederick Muller, 1968): and for the opposing view, Fortescue, the quotation being in *op. cit.*, VI, p. 183.
22. Cousins, *op. cit.*, pp. 52-53.
23. Sebag-Montefiore, *op. cit.*, pp. 194-95.
24. *Ibid.*, 48-52.

25. Fortescue, *op. cit.*, IV, pp. 217-18.
26. Sebag-Montefiore, *op. cit.*, pp. 173-74; Fortescue, *op. cit.*, V, pp. 203, 207 & 212.
27. Sebag-Montefiore, *op. cit.*, pp. 218-19, 310-15 & 328; Fortescue, *op. cit.*, V, pp. 199, 206 & 213-14.
28. Sebag-Montefiore, *op. cit.*, pp. 300, 325 & 328; Fortescue, *op. cit.*, V, pp. 219, 228 & 232.
29. Sebag-Montefiore, *op. cit.*, pp. 334 & 354-55.
30. Beckett, *Riflemen Form*, pp. 16 & 34.
31. He was enrolled on 20 February 1882, as No. 3980 (Certificate of Discharge, Army Form E. 551, in Furness Collection). Hook uses the term "British Museum Company" in the letter to Sir G.B. Harman, cited in Chapter IX, n. 31.
32. *Volunteer Service Gazette*, 7 February 1885. (This cane—24" long, and engraved: "Corpl. Hook, V.C. H. Co. Drill Lane, 1884. Bloomsbury Rifles"—is in the Furness Collection.)
33. *Ibid.*
34. The medal is engraved "1885" on the back; and is in the Furness Collection.
35. Undated copy in Furness Collection.
36. Beckett, *Riflemen Form*, pp. 93, 102 & 104; Cunningham, Hugh, *The Volunteer Force: A Social and Political History, 1859-1908* (London: Croom Helm, 1975), pp. 78 & 106.
37. Harris, *op. cit.*, p. 297; Cunningham, *op. cit.*, p. 1.
38. Standing Committee Minute of 13 April 1867, refusing Volunteers "the favour of a holiday on Easter Monday for the purpose of attending the review at Dover" and referring to an earlier Minute of 19 March 1864. But the Trustees made an exception in 1871, when they granted a week's leave, so that their Volunteer staff could attend the September manoeuvres. (Harris, *op. cit.*, p. 298.)
39. Certificates of Discharge from the 19th Middlesex and the 17th (North) Middlesex. His number in the latter regiment was 2629. Rudd (*op. cit.*, p. 118) mentions his appointment as a lance-corporal.
40. Rudd, *op. cit.*, pp. 3-103.
41. *Ibid.*, pp. 89 & 110; *Regulations for the Volunteer Force* (London: War Office, 1881), para. 924.
42. Rudd, *op. cit.*, pp. 113-27.
43. In Furness Collection.
44. There are Envelopes for Eccles and Reynardson in the series "Staff Applications & Testimonials, 1835-1935", B.M. Archives.
45. Rudd, *op. cit.*, pp. 22 & 107; Certificate of Discharge (in Furness Collection).
46. Cunningham, *op. cit.*, pp. 103-04 & 115.
47. *Ibid.*, pp. 108-09.
48. *Ibid.*, pp. 111 & 122.
49. *Ibid.*, p. 64.
50. "Discharge Certificate of an Enrolled Volunteer" (in Furness Collection). Hook's number was 6308.
51. Harrison, J.F.C., *A History of the Working Men's College, 1854-1954* (London: Routledge & Kegan Paul, 1954), pp. 82-83.
52. *Ibid.*, p. 85; Handley, Ronald E., *The First Londons* (Dover: Littledown Pub. Co., 1986), pp. 20-22.
    When a Volunteer regiment adopted scarlet for its uniform, dress regulations were enforced to avoid confusion between Volunteers and Regulars, *e.g.*, Volunteers were forbidden to wear gilded or brass buttons and badges.
53. Handley, *op. cit.*, p. 20.
54. *Ibid.*, pp. 40-42; Beckett, *Riflemen Form*, p. 137.
55. Standing Committee Minutes, 14 June and 12 July 1902.
56. Beckett, *Amateur Military Tradition*, p. 202.
57. *The Essex Times*, 12 July 1902.

Chapter XI

FAME AND THE READING ROOM: 1893-1903

1.

In June 1893, Lord Wolseley "came to the Museum to see some books for his *Life of the Duke of Marlborough*." Wolseley's considerable output as a writer had already provoked the comment that he wanted to be "our only littérateur" as well as "our only general"! The literary critic, Edmund Gosse, reckoned that the life of Marlborough was his friend's "principal contribution to literature"; and now the two volumes (all that were finished) were nearly ready for press. Before the studious general settled down to research, he was "conducted round the establishment" by Dr. Garnett, the Keeper of Printed Books. Then, according to *The Daily Chronicle*, Wolseley asked to see Hook "and greeted him in a most cordial manner." The report added that: "Mr. Hook is at present employed in the cloak-room of the reading-room."[1]

The general had evidently found Hook at his new work, doing "substitute" duty in the Umbrella Room (which adjoined the Gentlemen's Cloak Room and Lavatory). One of the other Dusters, George Joslin, had earlier been found full-time work in the Umbrella Room, and had escaped from dusting altogether. Another man, William G. Crosby, did "substitute" work at lunch times and in the evenings. The actual post of "Umbrella Caretaker" was held by Joseph Hibbs, an Attendant of nearly forty years service. His health was poor, which probably explains why he was doing work rather below his grade.

Any two of these three men took care of the Readers' sticks and umbrellas throughout the day, until six o'clock. The Reading Room stayed open until 8 p.m., so a roster for evening duty then came into force, with "extra pay" for everyone who worked the remaining two hours. As late as the summer of 1890, Hook had still been dusting all day; but during the next three years he had begun to do some "substitute" or evening work in the Umbrella Room. When, at the end of March 1894, Hibbs completed his forty years and retired, Hook was given his place, in preference to Crosby, the regular "substitute". This was the sort of arrangement much favoured by the Treasury: Hook was paid an extra two shillings, bringing him to 26/- a week, while Hibbs's salary had been equivalent to nearly £2 a week. (Neither Hook nor his fellow-Caretaker, Joslin, was ever given the grade of Attendant.)[2] Hibbs would have worn a frock-coat, but now it was decided to put the two Umbrella Caretakers into uniform. A journalist who observed the result was unimpressed by an outfit "something between that of a recruiting sergeant and an undertaker's mute." The reporter was being given his umbrella by "a short, broad-shouldered, kindly-looking man" and then noticed "one of the two medals shining on the breast of his dark uniform."[3] This, of course, was Hook's Victoria Cross; and despite the unflattering description, it seems probable that he was wearing the type of dark blue uniform worn by warders at the Museum until very recent times.

Hook was at last back in uniform. He comes first in an article headed "Where Our Heroes May Be Seen", which appeared in *The Success* in 1895. His post in the Umbrella Room was said to be shared sometimes "by another old soldier [unnamed], a veteran of the 11th Hussars." The account continues:

> Outside, at the great entrance gate [of the Museum], stands a stalwart, well-set-up warrior, whose "fine day, sorr," if he happens to know you, proclaims his nationality, and whose Egyptian medal was gained in the 2nd Life Guards, the silver trinket with a crimson ribbon alongside it telling of "long service and good conduct"; but while these [three] men have to some extent fallen on their feet, a striking contrast is not far to seek, for twenty yards away, at the corner of the opposite street [Museum St.], is one who has drawn blank in life's lottery since he left the army.
>
> Private Henry Pethers, after serving in the Middlesex Militia, the 46th Regiment, and the Marines for 22 years, 2 months and 15 days, during which time he marched some 1,500 odd miles in India, now occupies the exalted position of "licensed messenger", which enables him to stand in the east wind, holding horses outside the Museum Tavern and musing on the trenches before Sebastopol, where he was wounded, or the Ashantee War, in which he was twice hit! True, he has 1s. 3d. a day from the Admiralty, and the Crimean, Turkish and Ashantee ribbons— the medals went long ago—but he has also a cough, due to exposure and campaigning, . . .[4]

The Umbrella Room, where Hook now stood for the rest of his

working life, was on the right-hand side of the corridor which led from the Front Hall to the Round Reading Room. (Lady Readers had their own Cloak Room and Lavatory on the left-hand side of the Hall.) In the Round Room itself, George Knottesford Fortescue—who had befriended Hook in his earliest days at the Museum—now presided under the dome, wearing the top hat which had become the Superintendent's "badge of office." In its thirty-seven years of existence, it had become one of the best-known rooms in the world and certainly the best-known library room. In the last years of the century, the Room's historian saw a *galère* of notable people taking their seats:

> Lord Ribblesdale, very conspicuous by his fine, erect figure of some 6ft. 4ins.; the Countess of Lonsdale, a celebrated beauty; Lord Winchilsea; Baron Bunsen; Lord and Lady Colin Campbell; Lecky, the historian; Leone Levi, the economist; Leslie Stephen; Charles Bradlaugh; Hall Caine; Thomas Hardy; Rider Haggard; William Black, and occasionally W.E. Gladstone; while actors and actresses were well represented by Mr. & Mrs. Bancroft, Henry Irving, Charles Wyndham and Mary Anderson, who came to make a special study of the character of Lady Macbeth, and also to read up Veronese history when she took the part of Juliet. The pianist and composer, Edouard Silas, a quaint little figure, was always conspicuous in a Turkish cap.[5]

To this list deserves to be added "Erewhon" Butler, who came daily to the Reading Room and knew many members of the staff. He told a friend that: "I always give . . . [the umbrella men] 5/- at Christmas which no one else does, so they are very ready to do any little thing for me."[6]

As the fame of the Room increased, so did the number of its foreign Readers. During Hook's time, there was no more exotic group of Readers than the Russian *emigrés* who were conspiring to topple the Czar. They lived rather mysterious lives in London, convinced that Czarist agents were watching their every move and obsessive in their use of pseudonyms. Two of them had good reason to fear the Russian police: Stepniak (a pseudonym) had assassinated the head of the home secret service on the streets of St. Petersburg; while Vera Beldinsky (whose real name was Vera Ivanovna Zasulich) had wounded the Governor of St. Petersburg in his own office. Both were very striking personalities; but Miss Zasulich was also that most engaging of Reading Room figures, the eccentric intellectual. However blasé an Umbrella Caretaker may have become in watching the endless procession of Readers pass in front of him, he could hardly fail to notice Vera Zasulich, on her way in to resume her work on Rousseau:

She wore a shapeless grey dress made out of a piece of linen from the centre and sides of which she had cut holes for her head and arms. This piece of linen was thrown over her and held by a narrow belt while the edges hung loosely all around. On her head was something not quite resembling a hat, but rather a pie, made out of crumpled grey material, while on her feet she wore clumsy wide boots which she had made herself.[7]

Another *emigré* who came regularly to the Room was Vladimir Burtsev (pseudonym: N. Viktorov). He was a prolific writer on political and literary subjects and most ironically—in view of what happened to him—he published a long article entitled "The British Museum." In 1897, the Russian government made a complaint against him to the effect that he had "solicited, encouraged, persuaded, and endeavoured to persuade divers persons to murder his Imperial Majesty the Emperor Nicholas II of Russia." So at two o'clock on the afternoon of the 16th of December, Chief Inspector Melville, and several other detectives from Scotland Yard, came up to Burtsev's seat in the Reading Room. "Under some pretext" they persuaded him into the corridor where—in all probability, under Hook's gaze— a warrant was produced and Burtsev was taken off to Bow Street Police Station. In one of their favourite phrases, this seems to have been the only time when the police "apprehended" a Reader at his seat, even though Inspector Melville was tactful enough not to make the actual arrest under the great dome.[8]

Whether notables, *emigrés*, eccentrics or "Museum hacks" (copying or "devilling" for a pittance), the daily number of Readers never averaged less than six hundred during Hook's time as Umbrella Caretaker. As there were seats for only 458, these Readers were clearly not all there at the same time. In fact, the comings and goings of Readers during the day—and therefore the degree of busyness in the Umbrella Room—varied astonishingly:

Contrary to the ordinary experience of Public Libraries, which are usually comparatively empty in the morning and full in the later hours of the afternoon, the Reading Room is more crowded from 11 A.M. to 2 P.M. than at any later period: after 4 P.M. the number of persons present decreases with each hour from an average of over 350 at 4 P.M. to about 75 to 80 at 7.30 P.M. The number of persons entering the Room varies from over one hundred between 11 A.M. and noon to four, five or occasionally as many as ten between 7 and 8 P.M.[9]

A few years after *The Success* published "Where Our Heroes May Be Seen", *Answers* riposted with "What Becomes of V.C. Heroes." This magazine was consoled by the fact that "not a V.C. man is at present an inmate of any workhouse, although one or two *have been*"; but complained that these heroes were nevertheless "relegated to obscurity." The anonymous writer mentions Lord Roberts (hardly obscure!); and had found that "the Crimean veteran" was still "holding horses and running messages outside the British Museum gates." Hook is given a generous paragraph and he at least was never "relegated to obscurity"—the longer he worked inside the Museum, the more famous he became.[10]

The many newspaper and magazine items about him take several forms: there are brief items, pointing out that a Rorke's Drift hero is at the Umbrella Room (mild surprise sometimes being expressed at this "peaceful occupation"!); more extensive pieces dealing generally with his life; paragraphs (as in *Answers*) in which he appears with other V.C.-winners; and his several "full-dress" accounts of Rorke's Drift. The articles often bring out his courtesy and pleasant manner. One of the lengthier accounts describes him very precisely as he approached his forty-eighth birthday:

> He stands 5ft. 7in. in his socks, measures 42in. round the chest, and is a rather stout but hale and robust man, with a kindly expression of countenance, and a heavy fair moustache.[11]

At the turn of the century, he gained a new celebrity: as "General Buller's Double." Sir Redvers Buller had won his V.C. in the Zulu War and, during the twenty years which followed, he had risen steadily in rank until he was sent back to South Africa to command the British forces against the Boers. His reputation as a general was soon ruined but he was popular both with his troops and with the public at home, as this reports suggests:

> At the umbrella counter at the Reading Room of the British Museum, one will see a double of General Buller . . .
> In appearance Hook bears a strong resemblance to the now famous General. He has the same shaped head, the double chin, the close-set kindly eyes surmounted by the same shaggy eyebrows, and the prominent under lip shaded by the drooping grey moustache that has been made so familiar.
> What makes the illusion more complete is the military-looking peaked cap that Hook wears as a Museum attendant.
> On the occasion of the carnival organised in St. Pancras

for the Widows' and Orphans' Fund, Hook took part in the procession as General Buller, and even now there are people in St. Pancras who refuse to believe that the Hero of Colenso was not there in the flesh.[12]

Interviews with Hook seem to have been conducted at the Museum rather than at his home, and the mechanics of one such talk are exposed in the published text itself:

> . . . The conversation which the *Daily Graphic* representative had with him was punctuated by the silent exchange of umbrellas and tickets with incoming readers, though one or two of these had a word for the old V.C., and one reader had brought him a cutting from a newspaper relating to the survivors of the great day.[13]

It seems unlikely that Hook gained very much from all the interviews which he gave, except in terms of increasing celebrity. Contrary to what might be expected in the present "media age", there would have been no financial rewards for the telling and re-telling of his story, unless he was perhaps paid by *The Royal Magazine*. This particular article, the longest of his accounts, was "Gleaned and Edited by Walter Wood . . . from the Narrative of Sergeant Henry Hook, V.C." All his other interviews and accounts either appeared anonymously or were published under the names of the interviewing journalists. In these circumstances, the most that Hook could probably have expected was to be "treated" in the Museum's Refreshment Room.

This need not necessarily have been so. Edward D. McToy, a private in the 13th Regiment, acted as "military correspondent" for the Transvaal *Argus and Government Gazette* "through the Zulu campaigns", and his letters to the *Gazette* were then published as a small book. He must have been paid for his work as a correspondent and, in introducing his book, he says that "orders for some hundreds of copies" were at hand. McToy was unusual. In the Victorian Army, *officers* wrote for newspapers—Churchill is the best-known example—and McToy, as a private, did extraordinarily well to get such a post and to receive the "hearty thanks" of the *Gazette's* proprietors at the end of the War.[14] Most men in the ranks waited until their enlistments were over before going into print. William Green, of the Rifle Brigade, and Timothy Gowing, of the Royal Fusiliers, had accounts of their experiences printed and sold the copies to supplement their pensions. Sergeant-Major Gowing, whose book is now best known as *Voice from the Ranks*, claimed to have sold 24,500 copies of his first edition alone. More famous than these books are *The Recollections of Rifleman Harris*, which were written for him by Henry Curling, a half-pay officer. Curling may have paid Harris for his marvellous reminiscences of the Peninsular War, but this is uncertain and Harris died in a London workhouse. We might speculate that John Pindar did receive some payment for his *Autobiography of a Private Soldier*, which first appeared in the *Fife News*. Pindar, who enlisted in 1858, was extremely literate for a soldier of that era, and his recollections are well laced with literary flourishes and poetical quotations.[15] Harris and Hook shared the same handicap: they were good story-tellers but lacked the education to write about their own experiences.

At least nine of Hook's comrades gave an interview about the defence of Rorke's Drift—four in 1879, two in 1891, the others long afterwards[16]—but Hook was exceptional in being interviewed so many times. His progress as an interviewee is distinctly interesting. He gave his first interview less than a year after his discharge and what seems to have been his second about two years later. These are "raw" accounts. Hook was obviously not speaking very freely and consequently we seldom "hear" his own voice.[17] There was a marked change eight years on, when he was interviewed by *The Strand Magazine* for its series "Stories of the Victoria Cross: Told by Those who have Won it."[18] This is a first-person narrative: well-organised, detailed and presented in a good literary style. The number of interviews which he gave increased during the eighteen-nineties, that high point of Imperial enthusiasm. He once remarked to "the *Daily Graphic* representative": "Well, the truth is, I've told the story so often that I don't know that I've anything new to say about it now."[19] (But of course he did tell the story again!) By the time it came to his last interview, for *The Royal Magazine*, just before his retirement, he had polished and perfected the story. Even if he had lived longer, it is difficult to see how he could have had "anything new to say" about Rorke's Drift; but perhaps a more enterprising journalist would have got him to talk about his earlier experiences in South Africa and his views on Army life.

3.

Readers have always been demanding and, in those days, they were also much more class conscious and more inclined to stand on their dignity. Several incidents have survived to show that nerves sometimes became frayed at the Umbrella Room. In September 1895, A.C. Hall wrote to the authorities "complaining of injury to umbrella while given up at B.M." The outcome of this complaint is unknown, but the Umbrella men were presumably not held to be responsible for the damage.[20] A more general attack against "lower officials" was made in a letter to *The Daily Chronicle*:

> SIR,—I see someone has been complaining to you of the long waits for books which those who use the Reading-room at the British Museum have to submit to. I should like to add a little complaint of my own about matters there. The pens are shockingly bad; many of them frequently won't write at all.
>
> I have found also some of the lower officials in the room occasionally not too civil in their manner of addressing a reader. Quite recently I have had to complain of this to a chief British Museum authority. His way of dealing with the case I have not been satisfied with. One point has come out in connection with the correspondence that rather surprises me, and that calls, I think, for alteration. It is this, that when a reader wishes to complain of the conduct of any lower official, and asks this person for his name, he may refuse to give it, thus putting it out of the power of a reader to make it clear to a Museum authority who the alleged misdoer is. I consider that the Director of the Museum ought to request those who are under his rule to give their names to persons who desire to complain of their conduct.-
>
> I am, Sir, yours truly,
>
> BRITISH MUSEUM FREQUENTER.

This provoked two prompt letters of defence from other Readers, the first one bringing out an incident involving Hook:

> SIR,—Allow me to protest against the attack of a "Frequenter" on the courtesy of the attendants. Being a constant frequenter of over a quarter of a century entitles me to speak with an authority, based on experience. From the highest to the lowest, in common with many other habitual users, I have always found civility and courteous attention. The same lengthy experience also has brought to my knowledge many cases of most unreasonable conduct on the part of readers so trying to the temper, that an occasional growl is not only pardonable, but justifiable. Not many weeks ago I heard a "gentleman" in no gentle terms threaten to report one of the cloak-room attendants—an old soldier who wears the V.C.—for refusing to take charge of the "gentleman's" portmanteau and that of his wife for a week to save cloak-room charges at a railway station.—
>
> Yours, &c.,
>
> Aug. 7.   BOOKWORM.

SIR,—As a reader of more than twenty years' standing, and one who highly values the privilege of using the Reading-room, I would like to say that I have never once found the "lower officials", by which I presume "British Museum Frequenter" means the attendants, anything but civil and obliging—servility one neither desires nor expects. The attendants are a superior class of men; and I think the rule that they are not obliged to give their names to any individual who considers himself affronted a good one. Were it necessary—which, in my opinion, it never is—to report an attendant, it could be easily done without a pompous request for his name.

As regards the "long waits" for books, this depends entirely on the pressure of work at the time. I have frequently had books supplied in ten minutes. Finally, the pens are of very fair quality, and a new one can be had for the asking; and is always given with the utmost courtesy and dispatch.—

Yours faithfully,

Aug. 7. F.S. ROSS (B.A. Cantab.).

"Frequenter" replied the next day. Like the gentleman with the portmanteaus, he was obviously dissatisfied with the Umbrella Caretakers; but it seems unlikely that Hook, for his part, would have treated a Reader with "gross impertinence."

SIR,—I have read the letters of "Bookworm" and Mr. F.S. Ross which appear in your issue of to-day. These persons have used the British Museum Reading Room for upwards of twenty years; so have I. They tell us what they have observed there, as they have a perfect right to do. But their experience does not necessarily coincide with that of other readers. Mr. Ross makes one or two very odd remarks. In his opinion it is "never necessary to report an attendant." This represents the body to be quite an immaculate one. Surely it might be necessary sometimes.

Then if someone did wish to report an official, he could do it without asking for his name. So thinks Mr. Ross.

Now in the cloak-room there are two attendants. Suppose—as happened in my case the other day—one of these was grossly impertinent in his style of addressing me, how am I to complain of his conduct to the Director of the Museum, if he will not give me his name? I maintain that there ought to be a rule in a public institution like the British Museum, which would have enabled me to procure the official's name.

Of course, as civility is required from officials, so ought

members of the public to show it on their side, and if they signally fail they ought to be identified, and not allowed the use of the room in question. Though this note is anonymous, I am quite ready to give my name.—I am, Sir, yours truly,

Aug. 8.   BRITISH MUSEUM FREQUENTER.[21]

The later Victorian years were a time of pagaentry and of a burgeoning interest both in the Empire and in the Army which was then fighting the Colonial Wars. (Some newspaper cuttings which he preserved show that Hook was following the course of the Matabele War during the autumn of 1893. He must have been stirred by "Wilson's Last Stand", when the last few survivors are said to have sung "God Save the Queen" before they were assegaied.) He was almost certain of an invitation to any event commemorating Rorke's Drift, as this letter shows:-

Brecon,
South Wales.
7 Jan. 1898

Mr. H. Hook V.C.
    A Memorial Brass, recording the names of the N.C. Officers and Men of the 24 Regiment who fell at Isandlwana and Rorke's Drift in 1879, will be dedicated in the Priory Church here [the present Cathedral] on 23rd, January 1898.
    I would be glad if you could be present on the occasion.
    You could arrive here on Saturday and return on Monday, 24 January. Your expenses would be paid.
    Please inform me as early as possible whether you can attend.

E.S. Browne
Comnd: 24th. Regimental District.[22]

He of course accepted and presumably travelled down after duty on the Saturday, as there was then no Saturday half-holiday at the Museum. Everyone who had been serving with the regiment on the 22nd of January 1879 was invited and this included the five surviving Rorke's Drift V.C.s (Hitch, Hook, Robert Jones, William Jones and Williams) and also Private David Bell, who had won his V.C. for bravery at sea in 1867. They were accommodated at the Barracks in Brecon and, at midday on the Sunday, about sixty of these old comrades sat down to "a sumptuous dinner", provided by a local firm of caterers. The V.C. men sat at the head of the table; and when the troops formed up later, for the march to the Priory Church, they were placed immediately behind Colonel Browne, the parade commander, and the regimental band. They were followed by the other survivors from 1879; later members of the regiment; depot troops, militia, volunteers and cadets. This elaborate military *cortège* was matched by a civic procession from the Guild Hall. The memorial brass, which was dedicated during a lengthy service, is set in the wall of the south transept.

Afterwards, two separate suppers were served at the Barracks: "the Sergeants of the Depôt" entertained their fellow sergeants; while the "Soldiers of the 24th Regiment" (*i.e.*, corporals and privates, both serving and in civil life), ate together. Even on such a notable occasion, the very firm distinction between sergeants, and the rank and file, was thus maintained. Festivities continued on Monday. The regimental band played in the Market Hall; and the Depôt sergeants gave "their Annual Ball in celebration of the defence of Rorke's Drift." *Who* would have been invited to this ball is unclear; but as it began at 9 p.m., those like Hook, who had their livings to earn, would already have left Brecon.[23]

Colonel Chard had died less than three months before the ceremony at Brecon. When, in the autumn of 1897, it became known in Army circles that he was seriously ill, Hook wrote to his old commanding officer to express his sympathy. Chard's brother replied from the rectory near Taunton where the sick officer was being cared for: Chard himself was too ill to reply but was "proud to think that the gallant men of the 24th who stood by him at Rorke's Drift have not forgotten him." There was a P.S.: "Colonel Chard's condition I am sorry to say is hopeless."[24] So it proved, as Chard died on the 1st of November, not having quite reached the age of fifty.

As he was regarded as a Somerset hero, it was soon decided "to promote a memorial in the shape of a bronze bust to be placed in the Shire-hall and the endowment of a bed in the Taunton and Somerset Hospital for a soldier or a soldier's wife, widow or child." By that time, Lord Wolseley had become Commander-in-Chief of the Army—a great ambition fulfilled but a terrible disappointment in its reality. His opinion of Chard lay concealed from his contemporaries in his private journal, and the civic authorities of Taunton asked him to unveil the bust. No doubt it was his duty to accept, which he did; and he was then—as a sort of bonus—tendered the Freedom of the Borough.[25]

Hook received the following letter from the Town Clerk:-

Municipal Buildings,
Taunton
28" Oct. 1898.

Dear Sir,

    Ld Wolseley's Visit

I hope you may be able to be in Taunton on the 2nd. inst. I have pleasure in being able to send you (enclosed) a second class return ticket which will enable you to come here on Tuesday the 1st. inst. and return to London on Thursday or Friday.

    I have also to inform you that Colonel Cotton [commanding the 13th Regimental District] has instructions for you to be entertained at the Barracks during your stay here if you would like to be put up there.

    Kindly let me hear from you and return the ticket if you *cannot* come.

Yours truly
George H. Kite
Town Clerk

Sergeant Hook V.C.
British Museum
London.[26]

In Taunton, "arrangements had been made for a public holiday [on the Wednesday] but a south-westerly gale blew with tremendous force from the early hours of the morning, accompanied by a downpour of rain, which swept the streets and saturated military and sightseers alike." But the events of the day were largely indoors. It seems that Hook, John Williams, and Frank Bourne—who had become adjutant of the School of Musketry at Hythe—were in the Municipal Hall when Wolseley was presented with the Freedom of Taunton. They are certainly on the list of guests who attended luncheon at the Corn Exchange, immediately afterwards.[27] The menu gives some idea of what hearty Victorian appetites were tempted by:

Lobsters en Belle Vue

Foie Gras in Aspic	Galantine of Veal
Game Pies	Roast Pheasants
Chicken	Tongues
York Hams	Quarters of Lamb
Roast Beef	Dressed Beef

Veal and Ham Pies
Tomato Salad
Potato and other Salads

———

Apple Tarts		Stewed Pears
Charlotte Russe		Jellies
Genoa Cakes	Dessert	Parisian Pastry

After the usual toasts and speeches, the "brilliant company, numbering about two hundred" moved to the Shire Hall "in a procession of carriages . . . As the rain had now ceased all the carriages were thrown open, and the procession was therefore of a most picturesque character." At the Shire Hall, having listened to yet another speech, "Lord Wolseley, by pulling a cord, released the cover from the bronze, amid loud cheers." In his own address he managed to say nothing in praise of Chard which was not also bracketed with praise for the other members of the garrison. "He [Wolseley] remembered well going over the ruins of the buildings defended on that occasion, and wondering how Col. Chard and his comrades were able to maintain their position in the gallant manner they did. It was the pluck, perseverance and determination to which Lord Cork [the previous speaker] had referred which enabled them to do so, and the discipline of the men . . ."

As what Churchill called "the wonderful century . . . which secured to this small island so long and so resplendent a reign"[28] drew to its close, Hook's fame was acknowledged by an entry in *Who's Who*. Appearance in this worldly reference book is by invitation and the entrants supply their own details. The criteria for admission often include the attainment of a defined rank or position: thus, Black and Glyn (having reached general rank) were included; but not Chard or Bromhead (who only reached field rank); while the winning of the V.C. alone could not secure admission.

Hook's entry, which first appeared in 1899, reads:

HOOK, Henry, V.C.; *b.* Churcham, Gloucestershire. Served five years in Royal Monmouth Militia, afterwards in the 2nd-24th Regt., and took part in the Kaffir War at the Cape, 1877-78; and the Zulu Campaign in 1879, in which he was decorated by Sir Garnet Wolseley at the seat of war on 3 Aug. 1879; then served in Volunteers and is still Sergeant in 1st Vol. Batt. Royal Fusiliers. *Decorated* for the defence of the hospital at Rorke's Drift. *Address*: 33 Fitzroy Square, W.C.

Many entries in *Who's Who* are idiosyncratic but Hook's is notably so. He omits his date of birth; any reference to his parents or to his personal life in general; all his civilian occupations; and, as an address, he gives the headquarters of his Volunteer regiment as if it was his club (which it probably was, for social purposes). Once this singular entry had been included, it continued to appear each year until his death, and it was then printed in the first volume of *Who Was Who*. This was an extraordinary achievement for a working man, born without the slightest advantage in life.

NOTES

1. Garnett, Olive, *Tea and Anarchy!: The Bloomsbury Diary of . . . 1890-1893*, ed. by Barry C. Johnson (London: Bartletts Press, 1989), p. 204; Wolseley, *South African Journal*, pp. 330-31; Gosse, Edmund, "Some Recollections of Lord Wolseley," in *Aspects and Impressions* (London: Cassell & Co. Ltd., 1922). p. 279; *Daily Chronicle*, 30 June 1893.
2. G.K. Fortescue to E. Maunde Thompson, 30 October 1893. (This draft in the British Library Archives is printed in full in *R.D. & B.M..*, pp. 47-48); Standing Committee Minutes, 10 March 1894.
3. "How V.C.'s are Won: Private Hook at Rorke's Drift", in *V-C*, 5 November 1903. (Cutting in Furness Collection.)
4. *The Success*, Vol. I, No. 2, 10 August 1895. The unnamed Guardsman would have been a Gate Keeper, on about the same pay as Hook. Private Pethers would not have been on the Museum staff.
5. Barwick, *op. cit.*, p. 139.
6. Jones, Henry Festing, *Samuel Butler: A Memoir* (2 vols., London: Macmillan, 1920), I, pp. 399-400.
7. "Russian Political Emigrés and the British Museum Library" by Robert Henderson, in *Library History*, Vol. 9, Nos. 1 & 2, 1991, pp. 61-62.
8. *Ibid.*, pp. 64-66. William Melville was in charge of what later became the Special Branch. Burtsev was sent to prison for eighteen months, with hard labour and solitary confinement.
9. Fortescue to Trustees, 26 January 1903 (in MRL).
10. *Answers*, 22 January 1898.
11. "A Hero of Rorke's Drift" by Edward Vizetelly, in *The Sketch*, 20 April 1898 (with photograph).
12. Undated and unidentified cutting in Furness Collection. Colenso was one of the three British defeats during "Black Week" (December 1899); but this report may date from after Buller's return home in November 1900.
13. *Daily Graphic*, late 1897 (after Chard's death). (Cutting in Furness Collection.)
14. McToy, Edward D., *A Brief History of the 13th Regiment (P.A.L.I) in South Africa . . .* (Devonport: A.H. Swiss, 1880), pp. [iv] & 1.
15. Green, William, *A Brief Outline of the Travels and Adventures of . . .* (Coventry, 1857); reissued as: *Where Duty Calls Me*, ed. by John and Dorothea Teague (Petts Wood: Synjon Books, 1975), p. 53; Gowing, T., *A Soldier's Experience or A Voice from the Ranks* (Nottingham: Printed for the Author, 1897), p v; Folio Society version of Gowing's book, abridged under the title of *Voice from the Ranks*, ed. by Kenneth Fenwick (London, 1954), pp. vii & xiv; Harris, Benjamin, *A Dorset Rifleman* [a version of *The Recollections of Rifleman Harris*], ed. by Eileen Hathaway (Swanage: Shinglepicker Publications, 1996), pp. 11 & 173; Pindar, John, *Autobiography of a Private Soldier* (Fife, 1877).
16. These accounts are reprinted in Emery, *Red Soldier*, pp. 136-39; Holme, *Noble 24th*, pp. 279-93; and Lloyd, *op. cit.*, pp. 119-20.
17. The first two items cited in Chapter VI, n. 1.
18. Reprinted in Chapter VI.
19. "A Survivor of Rorke's Drift", *Daily Graphic*, late 1897 (in Furness Collection.)
    Of the various accounts of Rorke's Drift, attributed to Hook and published in his lifetime, the following are told in semi-fictional form:
    (i) "The Heroes of Rorke's Drift", in *The Funny Wonder*, October 1894;
    (ii) "Private Hook, V.C." by A.E. Bonser, in *Macmillan's Magazine*, October 1898.
    (iii) "The Hero of Rorke's Drift" in *The Home Magazine*, Vol. II, No. 29, 5 November 1898;
    (iv) "Our Short Story: At Rorke's Drift". (Unidentified cutting in Furness Collection.);

(v) "Victoria Cross Heroes. 1. Private Henry Hook. Rorke's Drift." (as iv.);
An account similar to these appeared in *The Scout*, 26 November 1910: "British Pluck at Rorke's Drift: A True Tale of the Zulu War" by C.L. McCluer Stevens.

20. Entry for 11 September 1895, in "Registers of In-Letters" (British Museum Archives). The original letter has not survived nor any further record of this matter.

21. Eight letters to *The Daily Chronicle*, dated between 7 & 8 August (but without a year), are preserved in the Furness Collection. The year would have been in the mid or late 1890s.

22. Original in Furness Collection. (Browne had won the V.C. at Hlobane Mountain, in the Zulu War.)

23. *The Brecon and Radnor Express*, 27 January 1898; *The County Times*, 28 January 1898; "Order of Service" at the Priory Church, Brecon; "Dedication of Memorial Brass", listing the events of 23 & 24 January 1898 (all in Furness Collection).

24. Charles E. Chard to Hook, 29 October 1897 (in Furness Collection). Chard died of cancer of the tongue.

25. *The Somerset County Gazette*, 5 November 1898.

26. In Furness Collection.

27. *The* [London] *Standard*, 3 November 1898; *The Somerset County Gazette*, 5 November 1898. Frederick Hitch was not in Taunton that day but was represented at the unveiling by "Private Hitch and Boy Hitch."

28. Churchill, Randolph S., *Winston S. Churchill*, Vol. II (London: Heinemann, 1967), p. 324.

Chapter XII

THE SECOND MRS. MEYRICK AND
THE SECOND MRS. HOOK: 1891-1904

1.

The Woods and the Preedys were old Newent families. They were craftsmen or people in a small way of business: carpenters, butchers, bakers. After Samuel George Wood married Emma Preedy in 1857, they had eight children, four boys and four girls.[1] The first two children—Mary, born in 1858; and John Philip, two years younger— are important in different respects. Mary "married well" and John became Hook's son-in-law.

There have long been legends of wealth in the Wood family, more particularly of a prosperous farm in Gloucestershire, and Mary's marriage offers the only sound evidence in support of these stories.[2] She became housekeeper to Walter Taylor, who owned the freehold of Wards Farm, near Lydney, in the Forest of Dean. Taylor had 134 acres and employed two other indoor servants and several farm labourers. He married Mary Wood in 1884 and she, and their only child, were the sole beneficiaries of his Will when he died in 1908. She sold the farm four years later. Nearby, was Perlieu Farm which, towards the end of the century, was leased or managed by Mary's two youngest brothers.[3] The "folk memory" of these farms seems to have become distorted and projected back in time, so that somehow they became part of the legend of Hook's marriage. But for the true connection between Hook and the Woods, we must turn to the life of Mary's eldest brother.

John Philip Wood was born in Church Street, Newent, on the 25th of August 1860. Church Street was one of the main thoroughfares of the market town and it has kept much of its old-time character. At that time, his father was a "master butcher", so it seems likely that the family lived over a rented shop. John, and the second of the four brothers, followed their Wood grandfather as carpenters and were "journeymen" all their lives.[4] Both brothers looked for employment outside the county and John was working at Hastings in 1881, where there was a good deal of private and public building going on. Their father had meanwhile become landlord of the King's Arms at Newent and the family later moved out to the Kilcot Inn.[5]

By this time, the Jones/Hook family had moved back to Kilcot. The Inn was their local hostelry and a meeting place for the country folk who lived between Newent and Gorsley. It stands back from the main Ross Road—a compact, two-storey building, with a bay window on each side of the front door. The Inn itself dates from the early nineteenth century but two of its outbuildings, a barn and a cider mill, are more ancient. It seems probable that this Inn had some part in Hook family history, and the story of a fight there has been handed down, presumably because it had some significance. One thing is certain: Samuel George Wood died in the Inn on the 4th of August 1889—from disease, not violence—and the tenancy then passed from the Woods.[6]

It seems quite possible that John P. Wood and Henrietta Hook met at the Kilcot Inn. Later recollections of her were that she was dark and always dressed smartly in black; she had "an air of authority" but was once seen dancing the "Cancan" with her sister. A young grandson who was taken for holidays abroad by his grandmother was "rather scared" of her; a grand-daughter's remembrance is that Henrietta was quiet and said little. These, of course, are impressions of the mature woman: none survive of the girl of seventeen who married in February 1891. The ceremony took place in the Whitefield Memorial Church, Gloucester, according to English Presbyterian rites. Henrietta had no occupation; but she had her father entered as a "Woodman" and gave his name as "Alfred Henry Hook."[7]

Her marriage marked the beginning of a break-up of the Jones/Hook household, which had held together for twenty years. A few weeks later, the Census enumerator found only five in the cottage at Kilcot, with the two remaining Hook children now at work. Raymond was a "Labourer" (presumably, on a farm) and Julia had become a "General Servant, Domestic." Their mother was still gloving. They were living in three rooms, so that Henrietta's departure would, in that sense, have been welcomed. She and John were nearby and their first child was born at Kilcot on the 21st of November 1891. This girl was christened Edith Agnes. Like her Hook grandfather, she emerged from the Gloucestershire countryside to become famous and, in her later years, she had very much his build and features. A second daughter, Vara Gladys, was born at Kilcot in 1893. During the next few years, the Woods moved nearer to Newent and settled along a stretch of the Ross Road which used to be called "The Squirrel." Their only son was born here in 1896 and christened Clement John.[8]

Although she had had to leave the Inn, Emma Wood continued to live in Kilcot. Her husband's business interests, which included farming land, brought her an income during her five years as a widow and, at her death, her children were given equal shares in the estate. By the time of his son's birth, this had brought John Wood at least £184 (or over £9,000 at present-day values). He may already have decided to leave rural Gloucestershire for the better prospects of a manufacturing town, and this inheritance would have made the move possible. Before the birth of their last child, Florence Henrietta, in January 1900, the Woods had settled in Birmingham.[9]

At much the same time, Julia met William Charles Matthews, a Herefordshire carpenter. He was the son of a "haulier"; about her own age; and turned out to be a "lady's man"; but nothing is known about their early relationship. By the late summer of 1898, she was pregnant and they, too, went to Birmingham, where they were known as a married couple. Their first child, Lilian Julia, was born in a "back-to-back" in the Jewellery Quarter on the 30th of May 1899— the first definite trace of Hook's descendants in the city. Quite soon, they moved out about half-a-mile and rented rooms on the edge of the Ladywood district. The Woods had a narrow terraced house in the Spring Hill area of Ladywood and the families were for a time living only a few hundred yards apart, separated by a main road. It must have been during this period that the two sisters went to Cottrell's Studio to be photographed in their late-Victorian finery.[10]

Before very long, both families left their fairly central situation for Aston Manor, outside the northern boundary of Birmingham. In Church Lane, not far from Aston Station, the Woods lived over a grocer's shop which Henrietta ran on her "own account." Samuel G.R. Wood (John's brother and fellow carpenter), his wife and small daughter, were only a few streets away. The Matthewses lived closer to the railway station, just off the busy Lichfield Road. Here—before reaching her fourth birthday—their daughter died of scarlet fever. Julia sometimes mentioned to her grandchildren, her sadness at this loss, when she was back at Kilcot and in old age. During her remaining few years in Aston, she had two sons who survived into adulthood. A few months before the birth of the first boy—who was given his father's Christian names in reverse order—his parents had the banns called at Aston Parish Church and were married there on the 10th of January 1904. The bride gave her father's name as "Alfred

Hook" and his occupation as "Woodman."[11]

Like his sisters, Raymond Hook also left home during the eighteen-nineties. He became a coachman and was working at Clay Cross Hall, Chesterfield, when he married Louisa Elizabeth Powell in September 1900. She had been born in the Herefordshire countryside, at Llangrove (between Ross and Monmouth), the daughter of a farm labourer who had had to "make his mark" when he registered her birth in 1874. She is remembered as "an exceptionally nice person and a very good cook", who always addressed her husband as "Hook."[12] Her father was dead by the time of the marriage and so—if we were to believe the marriage certificate—was the bridegroom's father, who appears as "Frederick Hook, deceased"; occupation "Woodman." This marvellously inaccurate entry at least establishes that all of Hook's children still regarded him, for official purposes at least, as a woodman!

In the early years of their marriage, they were employed at Pentre Court, a large house which lies well back from the main road between Abergavenny and Brecon. He was a "Coachman/Domestic." Their only child, Raymond Powell Hook, was born at Pentre Lodge, on the estate, in July 1904.[13]

By the summer of 1895, Comfort Hook had been a widow for eighteen years, in all but legal fact. Who can now say whether she really believed that her husband had been killed by the Zulus—the effect had been exactly the same, either way.[14] She had brought up her children and, while she may not have been dearly loved, she had done the best she could for them. Now they were beginning to leave home and her own parents—if they were still alive—would have been in old age. She was herself forty-five and may not have been that young in terms of health or appearance. The step which she took, on the 15th of June that year, was natural for those times and in her circumstances: she went in to Gloucester and was married in a civil ceremony.[15]

The bridegroom was David Meyrick, a Newent man who did various jobs during his life in the town and who was then working at a private house, as a groom. He was about ten years younger than Comfort and a widower of only seven months' standing.[16] The most striking thing about Meyrick (whose name is pronounced "Merrick") was that he married four times but apparently had no children. Comfort was the second Mrs. Meyrick. At the time of the marriage, he was living in the High Street, but he and Comfort later moved to the old part of Culvert Street, near the centre of the town. The row of antique, two-storey houses where they lived can be seen today: the back of the terrace on their side (the left-hand side from Broad Street) faces towards the Market Square.[17]

There is no reason to believe that Meyrick was not a good husband or that Comfort was not as happy with him as she was ever destined to be. The arrangement was nevertheless not a long one, as she died at home on the 11th of July 1900. The causes of her death are recorded as "Passive Congestion of Liver" and "Exhaustion." These terms give no clear idea of what was wrong but perhaps the word "Exhaustion" is most significant: she had had a hard life and may simply have been "worn out." She was buried with her predecessor, Sarah Jane Meyrick, in an unmarked grave in Newent municipal cemetery. A few yards away, in the shade of a glorious old tree, is the weather-stained but imposing headstone of the Wood grave.[18]

As for David Meyrick, he married again, six months later.[19]

2.

The Museum in Hook's day was not quite "monastic" but fewer than a dozen of his colleagues were women. These were the "Ladies [Cloakroom] Attendants", the "Housemaids" and, in later years, a "Charwoman": all roughly of his own grade and pay.[20] Most of his male colleagues were married, although there were some life-long bachelors. One of the most notable of these—an Assistant of great charm and polish—was R.A. Streatfeild, son of Commandant Streatfeild of the Fingo Levies. Streatfeild was a musicologist of literary tastes and had no connection with the Volunteers or the Rifle Club; but the two men must often have seen each other about the rooms and passages of the Library.

By the time that Hook became Umbrella Caretaker, it must have seemed to many at the Museum that he was settled into a single life. One of his daughters believed that "he lived alone for nearly seventeen years after his discharge from the Army."[21] He is said to have met his second wife at a smoking concert, and this may well have been one of the social events given by the Royal Fusiliers at 33, Fitzroy Square. Smoking concerts had been held there from at least the later eighteen-eighties.[22]

Ada Letitia Taylor was twelve years younger than Hook and her background was entirely different. Her grandfather, John Taylor, had been born in Gloucestershire but he became a Londoner in early life and, when he died in 1855, he was buried at Fulham. Ada's paternal grandmother, Letitia Jennings, was baptised in Rotherhithe—an area of South London now best known for the tunnel under the Thames—and when she died, three years before her husband, she was buried north of the River, in Hampstead. They were married in 1825, at Cripplegate Church, in the City of London.

John Taylor established himself as a silversmith, probably with a shop or business in the City, and he is believed to have prospered in the second quarter of the century.[23]

Their first child lived for only three months; but on the 5th of May 1829, a second child was born and was baptised at St. Giles in the Fields, Soho, and given the names William Frederick. Eight other children followed but William Frederick was ten years older than the next boy and he seems to have followed in his father's business. In the eighteen-fifties, he was living in Southampton Street, off the Caledonian Road and just to the north of King's Cross Station. He styled himself as a "jeweller" and there are several pieces of his work in the family, including a gold locket enclosing a tiny lock of his wife's hair.

Mary Gordon Young, who was three years younger than her future husband, came from Aberdeen and is remembered as a Gallic speaker. The details of how and where they met are now lost but the tradition is that the Youngs of Aberdeen disapproved of the marriage and would have nothing to do with the Taylors of King's Cross. Mary Young's father, William, had died before her marriage and his profession or standing in Aberdeen is obscure. There was nevertheless a very prominent family called Young in eighteenth and nineteenth-century Aberdeen. James Young, "Merchant Burgess", and "Rachel Cruickshank, his Spouse", together with their descendants, have a memoir devoted to them. Their eldest son, William, is known as "Provost Young", having held that office during 1778-79. Although there was evidently no direct connection between Provost Young (who died in 1814) and the father of Mary Gordon Young, it seems likely that there was some collateral link.[24]

One relative of Mary Young—probably a niece—who did keep in touch with her after her move to London was Catherine Stone Young. She was born in Dundee in 1852 and made an advantageous marriage, which later benefited both Hook's second wife (in her widowhood) and one of his daughters. Catherine Young married William D. Valentine, partner in an old-established printing and publishing firm. He travelled widely in its interests, so that the city's name was "often identified in remote corners of the globe by a casual reference to the productions of Valentine, Dundee." By the time of the Great War, the company's letterheading listed five international awards for "colour & photo printing." Valentine's series of picture post cards had become their most famous product, and these cards continued to be printed in Dundee until 1970.[25]

This was the background of Mary Gordon Young who, on the 14th of May 1854, at St. Pancras Church (near the railway station), married William Frederick Taylor. Their first child was born in

September of the following year, and another ten children arrived at fairly regular intervals until 1876. Ada Letitia (as someone noted in the family Bible) came into the world at "15 mins before 8 A.M." on the 30th of January 1863 and was baptised at All Saints, Islington. Her father is described on the birth certificate as a "Working Goldsmith." The family—which, with Ada's birth, now consisted of three girls and two boys—had moved a few hundred yards to Winchester Street, probably to a larger house.[26]

Winchester Street has not only been swept from the map (being renamed Killick Street) but all its Victorian property, except for a barrack-like school, has disappeared. Standing in the Caledonian Road, just around the corner from modern Killick Street, the observer can see a row of terraced houses in yellow brick, each of three storeys and a basement, two windows wide and with small iron balconies on the first floor. These houses, for comfortable artisans of the Victorian age, are no doubt very similar to No. 80, Winchester Street, which would have been very familiar to Hook in the early or mid-eighteen-nineties. The Taylors eventually had five daughters, and the youngest son, Frank, used to say that the house was noisy—the girls were very lively and went dancing a lot.[27] Apart from Ada, two of the family became particularly important in Hook's life. James, the second son, was later said to have been "Sergt. Hook's constant companion during his [last] illness."[28] The youngest sister, Eleanor, was close to Ada, even though there were eleven years between them. She married William John Heath, a professional soldier who served throughout the Boer War and also in the First World War. The two soldiers no doubt met at No. 80 and, when he was on leave in London, Heath used to call at the Museum to see his brother-in-law. Hook owned a polished, silver-mounted cane, nearly three feet long, of a type which by the eighteen-eighties had become "an essential part of the infantryman's walking out kit." The silver top is engraved with a leaf design and this, in turn, is mounted with a gold fox's head, which has ruby eyes. After her husband's death, Ada Hook presented the cane to her nephew, W.J.T. Heath, and it has been handed down in this branch of the family.[29]

While Hook was courting Ada Taylor, he was living about a mile away, in the Holloway area. His house —104, Hungerford Road— has gone but it was once part of a long terrace of three-storey villas, whose doors are at the top of high flights of steps. No. 104 stood at the Camden Town end of the road, two miles from the Museum, and he would presumably have rented only one or two rooms. It was probably during the same period that he joined the Loyal St. James's Lodge of Odd Fellows, in the "North London District" of the Manchester Unity. Although the St. James's has since closed, a Lodge has existed since the nineteen-thirties only a few minutes walk from Hungerford Road. It seems likely that Hook was living reasonably close to his Lodge and would have enjoyed both the ritual and the social life which the Odd Fellows provide. Almost certainly, he joined this Brotherhood mainly for its "provisions against sickness, old age and death." Security against sickness was a particularly anxious matter for working people before the National Health Service, and Hook must have become rather concerned about his own health during the eighteen-nineties. As he pondered engagement to Ada, it would have seemed prudent for him to have joined a friendly society such as the Odd Fellows.[30]

Their engagement presumably took place in the latter part of 1895 or early in 1896. They had heard that Comfort had gone to the Gloucester Register Office in June 1895 and a certified copy of the marriage certificate was obtained in the following February.[31] This gave Hook good grounds for divorce—by citing Meyrick as a co-respondent—which he could hardly have had by citing the allegation against Wedley. Yet even an uncontested divorce was then almost prohibitively expensive for working people—about £40 in legal costs—unless they could qualify for the "*in forma pauperis* provisions which allowed free legal service, tightly means tested, to petitioners without resources."[32] Hook was no doubt advised to see whether he came within these provisions and, in November 1896, he took his case to the Registrar of the High Court. The Registrar ordered that the "Applicant be at liberty to prosecute a suit for the Dissolution of his Marriage with Comfort Hook in forma pauperis."[33]

On the 25th of November, Hook signed a petition comprising four paragraphs and, on the same day, swore to these statements before a Commissioner for Oaths. The first two paragraphs relate to the facts of his marriage and his three children; the third describes the allegation against Wedley; and the fourth gives the details of Comfort's "ceremony of marriage" with Meyrick, after which she is alleged to have "lived and cohabited and habitually committed adultery with the said David Meyrick at High Street Newent." He swore that the statements in the first two paragraphs "are true" (which they plainly are); and that "the statements contained in paragraphs Nos. 3 and 4 of my said Petition I verily believe to be true." He further swore that "there is no collusion or connivance between me and my wife Comfort Hook in any way whatsoever"—which can readily be believed.[34]

The case came on before Sir John Gorell Barnes, at the Royal Courts of Justice in the Strand, on the 14th of January 1897. Neither the Respondent nor the Co-respondent appeared and the suit was left undefended. It seems that the Petitioner, and unnamed witnesses, gave "oral evidence" but there is no record of what was said: the case must have been decided largely on documentary evidence. The Judge found that the "Respondent has been guilty of Adultery with the Corespondent"; and pronounced that, for this reason, the Petitioner's marriage "be dissolved . . . unless sufficient cause be shown to the Court why this Decree should not be made absolute within Six Months from the making thereof."[35]

"Sufficient cause" was not shown; but either on advice, or for reasons now unknown, Hook proceeded with his second marriage after only three months. The banns were called at St. Andrew's, Islington, a large and grand church built for the residents around Thornhill Square, who were described at the time as "a well-to-do class, many keeping servants." The ceremony itself took place on the 10th of April 1897, with James and Eleanor Taylor as witnesses.[36]

The Hooks began married life a quarter-of-a-mile north of the "well-to-do" people, in the district which is called Barnsbury after the local railway station. Their home—4, Cumberland Street—stood close to the station and was probably a narrow, terraced house of three storeys, the upper storeys each having two windows; but they would certainly have shared the house with other people. Opposite the spot where Cumberland Street would have entered the present-day Roman Way, a small Victorian pub, "The Railway", still does business. North of the station, two public buildings brooded over the entire area: Pentonville Prison (which still flourishes) and the adjoining Caledonian Asylum (which has since disappeared). The roads around these grim institutions were "inhabited by many comfortable mechanics, railway men, clerks, and shopkeepers. A good number of labourers, cabmen and porters." Cumberland Street itself was reported to be "Fairly comfortable. Good ordinary earnings"; except for a small part at the eastern end, which was: "Mixed. Some comfortable, others poor."[37] At this stage, "fairly comfortable" was no doubt a reasonable description of the Hooks' circumstances.

In the following January, Hook's Uncle Joseph, who had enjoyed over thirty years as an Army pensioner, came to an extraordinary end. He was working as a gardener at Severn Bank Lodge, Minsterworth, and "was cutting branches from an apple tree, when the ladder broke, throwing . . . [him] to the ground and breaking his neck." Although he was seventy-one, he lingered for eighteen days in this state, and his death was described in the *Gloucester Journal.* He left £206—a good sum for a working man, in those days.[38]

The Hooks' first child was born on the 19th of February 1899 and christened Victoria Catherine. She was generally called "Queenie"; and her second Christian name almost certainly came from Mrs. Catherine Valentine, who became her god-daughter.[39] At some time during the next two years or so, the family moved about a quarter-of-a-mile to the northeast to 25, Lesly Street. They were still in the same kind of rented housing and amongst the same kind of "fairly comfortable" working people. When the Census was taken in 1901, the Hooks were sharing this house with two other families, each of five members. There were ten rooms in all, of which the Hooks had three.[40]

Hook's first family would have learned through the divorce proceedings that he was living in London and one of them eventually called at his house (probably during the Lesly Street period). The door was opened by a small child, who called Ada Hook. When the visitor asked to see her husband, Mrs. Hook promptly shut the door![41]

The Hooks' second and last child was born on the 11th of November 1902: she was given the old Taylor family name of Letitia and also Jean. This daughter became passionately devoted to her father's reputation but, as she was born, his health was already deteriorating.

NOTES

1. John Wood, father of Samuel George, married twice, his first wife having died in 1822. There were twelve children of his second marriage, Samuel George, born on 19 November 1834, being the seventh.

    Peter Preedy (1793-1861), father of Emma, also married twice and had twelve children by his second marriage. Emma, the eleventh child, was born on 2 December 1835.

    At the marriage of Samuel and Emma, at Gloucester on 19 July 1857, the occupation of John Wood was entered as "Carpenter" and of Peter Preedy as "Baker." Their children were: Mary, b. 1858; John Philip, b. 1860; Annie Elizabeth, b. 1862; Samuel George Robert, b. 1865; Agnes, b. 1866; Emma Jane, b. 1869; Charles Alfred, b. 1871; and Frederick William, b. 1873. There also appears to have been a girl, Emily, who died in 1863, aged 14 weeks.

    (Information from the marriage certificate; from certificates and Wills in Gloucester Record Office; and from the Preedy family, in a letter from Mrs. Esme Walker to Mrs. Heather Warman-Johnston, 7 September 2002, enclosing extracts from family records.)
2. There was apparently "a very wealthy man called Wood in Gloucester in the 18th century" and he, or another member of the family, is said to have owned "a large house" in Westgate St. (Letter quoted in n. 1.) William Wood of Newent owned Hill House Farm, a few miles east of the town and, in 1795, leased land for mining purposes; but it is unclear whether he was related to the John Wood whose son married Emma Preedy. See *The Mines of Newent and Ross* by David Bick (Newent: The Pound House, 1987), pp. 23-25.
3. Census return for 1881, showing the occupants and employees of Wards Farm; birth certificate of Agnes Mary Taylor, born at Lydney on 20 July 1882; marriage certificate of Walter Taylor and Mary Wood, Gloucester, 13 September 1884; Will of Walter Taylor (dated 16 March 1897), witnessed by Charles Alfred Wood (1871-1938) and Frederick William Wood (1873-1956), of Perlieu Farm, Lydney; "Particulars, Plan, and Conditions of Sale of . . . The Wards", to be sold by

auction on 22 June 1912 (Gloucester Record Office); Will of Agnes Mary Taylor, who died unmarried at Bristol on 24 July 1953. Some members of the Wood family benefited from her Will.

4. Details from J.P. Wood's birth certificate. The second brother was Samuel George Robert Wood (1865-1901). A "journeyman" was an employee (as opposed to a master).

5. Census returns for 1881 showing J.P. Wood as the "lodger" at 2, Trafalgar Cottages, Hastings; and five other members of the family at the King's Arms Inn, Newent.

6. Dept. of the Environment, *List of Buildings of Special Architectural or Historical Interest: District of Forest of Dean, Gloucestershire*, pp. 113-14. The Inn and its outbuildings are Grade II; information about the fight from Mrs. Evelyn Hudson, grand-daughter of J.P. Wood; S.G. Wood's death certificate.

7. Marriage certificate (18 February 1891). The recollections of Henrietta are those of Mrs. June Dutton; Mrs. Evelyn Hudson (interview, 20 September 2000); Mr. Denis A. McCarthy (telephone conversation, 1 October 2000); and Mrs L.R. James, of Newent (interview, 6 July 2000).

8. Birth certificates: Vara Gladys, 15 February 1893; Clement John, 25 May 1896.

9. Emma Wood died at Kilcot on 15 June 1894. Her personal effects were £63; but her husband's estate passed from her to their children. A detailed set of accounts has survived for the period June 1894—August 1895 showing that J.P. Wood received £96..8..4 and £88..10..0 during these years. (Copy supplied by Mrs. Esme Walker from the Preedy family records.)

   Florence Henrietta Wood was born at 39, Spring Hill Passage, Birmingham, on 26 January 1900.

10. Census return for 1901. It seems from the 1881 Census that W.C. Matthews was born in 1877 at Ashperton, about seven miles from Hereford. His father, Charles, was then an innkeeper at Ashperton and had been born in the village. His mother, Mary, came from Gloucestershire; and he had an elder brother, George.

    Lilian was born at "Back 22, Augusta Street" and, in registering the birth, the mother gave her name as "Julia Matthews formerly Hook." The family was at 9, Rosebery Ave., George St. West, at the time of the Census. Neither of these houses, nor the Woods' house, have survived the post-War "development" of Hockley and Ladywood.

11. Census return for 1901, showing the Woods at 149, Church Lane. (Aston Manor, which was then an urban district of Warwickshire, was incorporated into Birmingham in 1911.) S.G.R. Wood died of pneumonia at 19, Priory Rd. on 9 September 1901. His widow, Ellen, then married the youngest of the Wood brothers, Frederick. (Death certificate; information from Mrs. Esme Walker.)

    Lilian Matthews died on 16 December 1902 at 14, Poplar Grove, Sutherland St. (an address that no longer exists); and her parents then moved to the other side of Aston Station and were married from 8, Grosvenor Rd. They moved again to Cuckoo Rd., near Salford Park, for the birth of Charles William Matthews on 12 June 1904. (Information from official certificates and from Mrs. June Dutton.)

    The area of Aston in which the Woods and Matthewses lived has been changed beyond recognition. Only a few notable buildings—Aston Hall, the parish church and several large Victorian pubs—together with a few bits of terraced housing, remain from their day.

12. Birth certificate of Louisa Powell (26 April 1874); marriage certificate (22 September 1900), the ceremony being held at Monmouth Parish Church; interview with Mr. Cecil Berrington, at Abergavenny, 9 July 2001. Mr. Berrington is a brother of the late Edna Vera Hook, who married Raymond Hook's son in 1936.

13. Birth certificate, 30 July 1904.

14. *Colonnade*, pp. 15-16.

15. It has proved impossible to trace John and Anne Jones with certainty beyond the Census of 1891; but the marriage certificate suggests that he at least was still alive in 1895. The witnesses were John and Henrietta Wood.

16. Death certificate of Sarah Jane Meyrick, who died at Newent on 6 November 1894.
17. The road is now called Culver St.; and the house in which Comfort is believed to have lived and died is shown in the accompanying photograph.
18. Details from the death certificate and from the cemetery registers, kept at Watery Lane, Newent. Comfort Meyrick was buried on 14 July 1900 in a grave which had been purchased for or by Esther Hooper, a widow who died in 1880. Mrs. Hooper was presumably related either to David Meyrick or to his first wife.

    The Wood grave contains the remains of Samuel and Emma Wood; Mary Preedy, mother of Emma Wood, who died in November 1874, aged 84; and Emily Wood.
19. He married Mary Annie Trott, 40-year-old daughter of a farm bailiff, on 29 January 1901.
20. *House Lists* for 1882 and 1899.
21. *Colonnade*, p. 16.
22. Handley, *op. cit.*, p. 49.
23. Except where otherwise stated, the genealogical details of the Taylors are taken from a family Bible owned originally by Ada Taylor's father and now owned by Mrs. Elaine Bloomfield. It was shown to the present writer in September 1998 by Hook's great niece (by marriage), Mrs. Pat Kitto, who was also extremely helpful in discussing various points of the family's history.

    The entries in this Bible begin with John Taylor (b. 2 May 1796 and baptised near Newnham, Glos.) and Letitia Jennings (b. 4 February 1803). Their ten children are listed; then the eleven children of their second child, William Frederick, the father of Ada Letitia Taylor. When William Frederick married in 1854, his father's profession was given as "Silversmith."
24. According to the family Bible, Mary Gordon Young was born on 14 June 1832; but there is no record of her birth at the General Register Office for Scotland. Official registration was not compulsory in Scotland until 1855; and there is no reason to doubt the Bible entry.

    The family of Provost Young is described in: *A Short Memoir of James Young* by Alexander W.S. Johnston (privately printed, 1860); and in *Memorials of the Aldermen, Provosts, and Lord Provosts of Aberdeen, 1272-1895* by Alexander M. Munro (Aberdeen: Printed for the Subscribers, 1907), pp. 248-49. The Aberdeen Public Library kindly looked into the question of a connection between the Provost's family and the family of Mary Gordon Young, and supplied photocopies from the above books; but the Library gave no opinion about a possible link.
25. Unsigned typescript headed "Valentine and Sons, Ltd., Dundee", dated 23 October 1947, in the Lamb Collection, Dundee Central Library; Unidentified obituary from a Dundee newspaper on the death of William Dobson Valentine, 6 November 1907 (in Lamb Collection).

    Catherine Valentine died in 1912, after her son, Herbert J. Valentine, had succeeded her husband as head of the firm. Valentine & Sons Ltd. "ceased post card production in 1970 to concentrate on greeting cards and was taken over by Hallmark." In 1994, the company moved to Bath, although it is still styled "Valentines of Dundee." (Letter from the Dundee Central Library, 15 February 1999.)
26. The account given in *R.D. & B.M.* (p. 54) of how the Taylors and Hook both lived in Pimlico is unfortunately wrong. There are, in fact, two streets called Winchester and Cumberland close together in this district; and confusion arose because of a family tradition that Hook had at one time lived in Pimlico. (*Colonnade*, p. 16.) He may have lodged in Pimlico before moving north to Islington; but the Taylors always lived in the area around King's Cross and the Caledonian Road, as far back as it is possible to trace.
27. *Six* daughters were actually born but one (Emily: 1867-70) died in infancy. Frank Leonard Taylor (1876-1960) was the grandfather of Mrs. Pat Kitto.

28. *Gloucester Journal*, 25 March 1905. James Taylor was born in 1860.
29. William John Heath (1867-1957) was a Londoner and became a railway ticket collector after he left the Army. His son, William John Thomas Heath, was born in Hackney in 1900, where his mother was presumably living. Eleanor Ann Heath predeceased both her elder sister, Ada, and her husband, dying on the 1st of November 1928.

    Hook's cane was shown to the present writer by Mrs. Pat Kitto. It is no doubt more elegant and elaborate than most soldiers would have carried. Some typical canes of the period are shown in "Tommy Walks Out" by C.R. Coogan, in *Soldiers of the Queen*, June 1989, pp. 19-24, from which the quotation is taken.
30. *Gloucester Journal*, 18 March 1905; *Souvenir Brochure*, published by the Grand Master and Board of Directors on the occasion of the 175th Anniversary of the Society (Manchester, 1985), p. 9; Letter from H.W. Tatnall, District Secretary, to the present writer, 24 January 1986, saying that the St. James's Lodge had been closed and that it is doubtful whether any membership records now exist. (There are no papers relating to the Odd Fellows in the Furness Collection.)
31. "True Copy" of the Meyrick-Hook certificate, signed on 6 February 1896 (in J77/600, Public Record Office).
32. Hammerton, A. James, *Cruelty and Companionship: Conflict in nineteenth-century married life* (London: Routledge, 1992), p. 103.
33. The printed form, completed and signed by the Registrar on 19 November 1896, refers to "the Statement of Alfred Hook the Applicant, with the opinion of Counsel thereon, and Affidavit of said Applicant, sworn on the 12th day of November 1896." The last three papers are not in J77/600, which contains the surviving documents in Hook's divorce proceedings.
34. Papers in J77/600. Hook is described as a "Labourer"; but his place of work is not given nor is his V.C. mentioned. His residence is given at 104, Hungerford Rd.
35. "In the High Court of Justice . . . Hook against Hook & Meyrick", in J77/600. On the 27th of July 1897, the "Petitioner filed Notice & Affidavit (Decree Absolute)"; and on the 25th of August, a Vacation Judge "by his final Decree pronounced and declared the said Marriage to be dissolved."
36. Booth, Charles (ed.), *Life and Labour of the People in London* (4 vols., London: Macmillan & Co., 1892), II, Appendix, p. 20; Details from the marriage certificate. The bridegroom styled himself as "Alfred Henry Hook" and gave his occupation as "Attendant."
37. Booth, *op. cit.*, II, Appendix, p. 20; and accompanying "Descriptive Map of London Poverty 1889."

    The area around the Prison has been extensively developed and the street names changed. The description of the houses in what had been Cumberland Street is based on what little Victorian property remains in Roman Way, which runs roughly north and south, to the east of Caledonian Road, which it eventually joins.
38. *Gloucester Journal*, 5 February 1898; Death certificate; Probate of Will.
39. "Trust Settlement of Catherine S. Young or Valentine", subscribed at Dundee on 28 November 1907. (Scottish Record Office, Edinburgh.)
40. Booth, *op. cit.*, II, "Descriptive Map."
41. Interview with Mr. Cecil Berrington, 9 July 2001, who heard this anecdote in c. 1955/56, when he visited Julia Ann Matthews with his sister, Vera, and his brother-in-law, Raymond Powell Hook.

Chapter XIII

"A TRIUMPH": 1903-05

1.

In the autumn of 1903, a conversation took place of a type which had become very familiar to Hook. A writer who identified himself only as "J.H.K.-A." described how he

> Was coming out of the British Museum Reading Room when I met him first—a short, broad-shouldered, kindly-looking man in a uniform something between that of a recruiting sergeant and an undertaker's mute. He was handing me back my umbrella in return for a check, when one of the two medals shining on the breast of his dark uniform caught my eye.
>
> "Halloa!" I exclaimed, and my excitement and interest must have been very boyishly in evidence, for the old man smiled at me as I spoke. "Isn't that the Cross you're wearing?"
>
> "Yes, sir."
>
> "And the Zulu medal beside it—Why! you must be Sergeant Hook?"
>
> He smiled again—a pleasant, tired smile. "I'm all that's left of him, sir."
>
> What a difference! This man who handed me my umbrella and called me "sir" was the same who, with blazing rafters overhead and all Hell loose in front, stood fighting single-handed in defence of the wounded and dying on that long-ago day in the little hospital of Rorke's Drift.[1]

"*All that's left of him*"—this is the significant phrase. Hook's request to be given a dusting job, at the very beginning of his Museum career, was possibly an acknowledgement that he was no longer up to the rigours of outdoor work. The fatal consumption may already have been on him; but in the eighteen-nineties it seems to have been his head wound which gave him most trouble.

In May 1893, he was certified as having "Abscess on head", and in January 1898, as suffering from "Cephalalgia" (headache). Almost at the end of his life, he described how:

> All this time the Zulus were trying to get into the room. Their assegais kept whizzing towards us, and one struck me in front of the helmet. We were wearing the white tropical helmets then. But the helmet tilted back under the blow, and made the spear lose its power, so that I escaped with a scalp wound, which did not trouble me much then, although it has often caused me illness since.[2]

Late in January 1898, a few days after the dedication in Brecon Cathedral, a reporter from *The People* called at the Museum to interview Hook. He was sent on to Barnsbury, and found the old soldier "stretched on his bed, with an ice-water bandage round his forehead, and, literally, his martial cloak around him." Hook apparently said that his ordeal at Rorke's Drift had "left its traces in the form of an ague fever, which attacks him now and again"; but it was no doubt on this occasion that his doctor diagnosed "Cephalalgia." The reporter speculated that "the excitement of fighting his battles o'er again with his old messmates [at Brecon] had helped to knock him over."[3]

In May of 1904, he still felt well enough to be "anxious to view the Military Tournament at Islington"; but only three months later, his doctor was "recommending change in the country."[4] Sea or mountain air—for those who could afford it—or at least country air, was the Victorian doctor's staple remedy for consumption. London—with its smoke and fogs—and the Museum—with its dust—were about the last places for diseased and worn-out lungs. Country air was recommended, but how was it to be afforded? It was at this point that his grade became a handicap. The Attendants, and the Higher Staff, were in pensionable positions: they could face retirement with more assurance than the greater part of the working population. What the Treasury granted the labouring staff was a "gratuity"—a lump sum based on wages and length of service. When this sum was spent, Hook would have nothing to support his wife and two little daughters but his pension as a V.C.-holder. Beyond that lay only private charity, "outdoor relief" in a parish, or the workhouse.[5]

Hook's V.C. pension had remained unchanged since he had first drawn it in 1879. (During his lifetime, inflation was never the scourge which it later became; but while he was pondering retirement, a question was asked in the Commons about the "insufficiency" of this pension.[6]) There was provision for an increase to £50 a year on grounds of ill-health and, in October 1904, Hook applied to the Paymaster at Brecon for this increase. He was told to "attend at St. Georges Barracks [Orange St., near Trafalgar Square] to undergo a medical examination and forward the certificate of an Army doctor."[7] While the War Office was still considering his application in fairly leisurely style, Hook decided that he must leave the Museum.

When the Standing Committee of the Trustees met on the 10th of December,

> The Director submitted a letter, 26 November, from Henry Hook, V.C., Labourer, who had been in the Trustees' service since 1881, resigning his situation from 31st December on account of failure of health.[8]

After Hook had submitted a final certificate showing that he was "permanently disabled by ill-health from continuing his duties in the Trustees' service", the Treasury was "pleased to award to him a Gratuity of Forty pounds 6/11 which the Paymaster-General has received instructions to pay on or after the 1st January 1905."[9] He thus retired with a sum equivalent to about £2,000 by present-day standards; but, at about the same time, he learned that

> the Army Council have been pleased to increased your Victoria Cross pension to £50 a year, paid quarterly in arrear from 1st January 1905.[10]

His "ill-fortune" in having to leave work at least ten years before the usual retiring age was noticed in the outside world. *The Morning Post* carried a letter from "Colonial Loyalist", who remarked that Hook

> has a poor pittance of Service pension through the V.C., and generally appears to be in a bad way. Very little would go a long way with this distressed soldier, and no doubt a course of medical attention and some little provision to relieve him of his worries would keep him going. Mr. Leo Weinthal, the "African World", 34, Copthall-avenue, has consented to receive subscriptions for the benefit of Sergeant Hook.[11]

He was certainly at the B.M. as late as the 5th of December, and had the consolation of "a long chat" with Thomas E. Toomey, an old friend who was six years his senior. Toomey came from County Cork and had served for over twenty-three years in the 18th Regiment, half of the time in India. He had held non-commissioned rank more often than not and had won quite spectacular promotion during the Gordon Relief Expedition, rising from private to colour-sergeant in three weeks. Drinking—which had much earlier cost him his sergeant's stripes—ruined the end of his career, as he was reduced from colour-sergeant to corporal after the regiment's return from Egypt and less than three months before he left the Army. Yet he had studied in India for the Second Class Certificate of Education and turned to writing after his discharge, at the end of 1885. It must have been then that he got to know Hook. Although Toomey had not himself been decorated, he became an authority on the V.C. and was probably in the Reading Room quite often. In 1889, he published *Victoria Cross 1854-1899 And How Won,* a cloth-bound booklet consisting of a brief alphabetical entry for each of the winners. This was expanded, in 1895, into a substantial and well-illustrated volume entitled *Heroes of the Victoria Cross.*[12] After his friend's death, he sent his sympathies to Ada Hook, saying that "poor Harry" had been "the grandest sight" to be seen at the Museum![13]

Hook left the sad business of resigning from the Royal Fusiliers until almost the last moment, being discharged on the 23rd of January. On the following day, George F. Barwick, who had succeeded Fortescue as Superintendent of the Reading Room, wrote to him:

24 Jan 1905

Dear Hook,

I am very sorry to hear that your health has been so bad, but trust that the fresh air of the country will gradually restore you.

Enclosed I send you a cheque for £2 from myself, Mr. Liddell & another friend of mine, and I am glad to hear that the collection made by the African Paper is of such substantial benefit; I heard about it some time ago, but hardly expected that it would be so successful.

Yours faithfully,
G.F. Barwick.

Please acknowledge receipt in enclosed envelope.[14]

This is the last surviving record of Hook's connection with the Museum. He remains one of the best-remembered members of the staff and is still the only one to have won the V.C.

2.

Hook's doctor had advised him to return to Gloucester "to try what his native air would do for him."[15] The removal expenses were such a large consideration that he contracted with a Chelsea greengrocer, rather than with an ordinary removal firm, but, even so, nearly a third of his Treasury gratuity was swallowed up.[16] A house had been rented on the southern outskirts of Gloucester at an address (2, Osborn Villas) which no longer exists. These villas were connected to Rosebery Avenue, where some small, two-storey terraced houses can still be seen. It was no doubt at such a modest villa that the Hook family arrived, late in January 1905. Only one detail is known about the interior of their house: a large engraving of de Neuville's "The Defence of Rorke's Drift" hung over Hook's bed.[17]

His London Lodge of the Odd Fellows commended him to "the care of the brethren of the Phoenix Lodge, Gloucester . . . [as] he had no claim to a local medical man." The Phoenix Secretary wrote to Dr. Oscar W. Clark, who said that he would "look after Henry Hook with pleasure." Even though he was said to be "sinking rapidly," his condition made it desirable that he should "get out of doors as much as possible" and he was "taken for a drive as late as Friday", the 10th of March. The consumption had evidently been chronic for at least six months and it was now too late for either Dr. Clark or "his native air" to save him. He died early on Sunday morning, the 12th of March, four months short of his fifty-fifth birthday.[18]

Next day, Gloucester's evening paper, *The Citizen*, carried a lengthy tribute. On Tuesday morning, two London papers, *The Daily News* and *The Daily Graphic*, had generous obituaries. *The Monmouthshire Beacon* followed a few days later. "Mrs. Hook on Wednesday morning received touching letters from two of deceased's comrades, who were in 'The Drift' with him."[19] One of these letters was from John Williams, and should be given in full:

32 Pritchard Tce
Cwmbran
Nr Newport
14 Mch 05

Madam
    It is with Deep regret I learn from the mornings mail of the Death of my Comrade-in-Arms, your late Husband Henry Hook V.C. I tender to you my sincere Sympathy in this the hour of your bereavement and trust you will find some solace in the thought your late beloved Husbands memory will be cherished for his worth as a hero and a man so long has [*sic*] English History is read. again asking your acceptance of my Sincere Sympathy I remain Dear Madam

Yours very truly
John Williams V.C.

Mrs. Hook.[20]

The other letter mentioned by the *Journal* was probably from Frederick Hitch, V.C., but it seems to be lost. She of course received other letters, notably from the "English Correspondent" of the *Times of Natal*; from Lieutenant-Colonel Charles E. Curll, of the South Wales Borderers (who, for this occasion, signed himself "Comdg 2/ 24th Regt"); and from Major-General Irving Graham, Retd. Curll said that he had "started a subscription for the purpose of erecting a memorial to his [Hook's] memory, and I now hear that one has also been organised by the vicar of his parish [Churcham], and I think the two will be amalgamated and a handsome sum be raised." Graham, who had helped with the pension application, wrote that he had known Hook and "esteemed him greatly for 18 years." Realising that Ada Hook was likely to be in straitened circumstances, the kindly general added: "If I can do anything for you in the way of getting you a pension or a post as care taker etc I shall only be too pleased to do it." A less felicitous tone was struck by an acquaintance who promptly offered to buy Hook's medals![21]

The funeral was to have been held on the Friday but was "postponed until Saturday afternoon for the convenience of the military authorities, Oddfellows, and others."[22] The reason for this delay became apparent on the day, when the "striking and impressive spectacle" was on a scale which is now never accorded a citizen in private life.

By early afternoon, a gun carriage, drawn by four horses, was waiting at the house; and at 1.30, two companies of a Gloucestershire Volunteer battalion paraded outside. A firing party of twenty N.C.O.s and men presented arms as the coffin—draped with the Union Jack and bearing Hook's "head dress and side-arms"—was carried out and placed on the gun carriage. The procession was greatly augmented at St. Paul's Church on the way into Gloucester, and set off, in slow time, towards the city centre. The order was:

Police
Firing Party (with arms reversed)
Volunteer Artillery Band
Volunteer Drummers and Buglers

GUN CARRIAGE
(flanked by bearers from the South Wales Borderers and pall bearers from the 1st Volunteer Battalion, Royal Fusiliers)

Volunteer detachments (Rifles, Engineers & Artillery)
"Some 50 old soldiers and reservists" (including a Crimean veteran)
Carriages of the chief mourners, Odd Fellows, and others, including:

234

Ada Hook, as a widow, photographed at a studio in Northgate St., Gloucester. (Furness Collection.)

The late Sergt. Hook, V.C.   Funeral Proce

Hook's funeral procession
(Fu

...ing St. Paul's Church, March 18th, 1905

into the centre of Gloucester.
...ction.)

The funeral procession passing through Eastgate St., Gloucester, on the way out to Churcham.
(Furness Collection.)

Ada Hook and her daughters; Hook's mother, Eleanor, and two of his brothers, James and Henry Daniel; four Hook nephews, Frederick John, James Ambrose, Thomas Henry Merry, and Bernard Francis; a niece, Miss Edith Jane Hook; a brother-in-law and sister, William and Emily Wintle; Miss Gertrude Wintle; Hook's brother-in-law from London, James Taylor; and Frederick Hitch (who was unable to wear his V.C., which had been stolen).

"With the Oddfellows rode Mr. W.H. Hoare (who was one of the 24th Regiment, under Lord Chelmsford who arrived at Rorke's Drift on the morning after the terrible fight . . .)"

"Thousands of people lined the route through the city, along which many blinds were drawn and shops partially closed; whilst flags were to be seen flying at half-mast at the Guildhall and other places." On they went, past the cathedral, to the right, and over the Severn at Westgate Bridge. There, at the city limits, the pace was changed to quick time for the march out to Churcham, where Hook had wished to be buried. As the *cortège* neared the lane which for half-a-mile slopes steadily upwards to St. Andrew's Church, the pace reverted to slow time and the band played the Dead March in "Saul". "A large number of villagers" watched the procession move up to the church, where the vicar—a Volunteer chaplain—conducted a "fully choral" service. The Misses Lloyd Baker, of Hardwicke Court—the "big house" near the church—were not themselves present but sent a wreath of arum lilies, tied with white silk, as "A token of respect for a Gloucestershire hero."

Hook's grave had been dug in the corner of the small, walled churchyard which is farthest from the lane. (A contemporary photograph shows that this corner then had some large trees close by but which have since disappeared.) The grave itself had been "lined with laurel, bay and oak, the old symbols of victory and of valour in saving life." At the grave-side, the firing party fired the usual three volleys, with the band playing "incidental music" between the volleys. The buglers then sounded the "Last Post" and the band gave "an appropriate rendering of 'Jesu, lover of my soul.' "

With the service over, the firing party fixed bayonets and the *cortège* marched back to Gloucester to the strains of "Men of Harlech" and "All honour to the noble Twenty Fourth, of glorious renown"—an air which had been popular at the time of the Zulu War. As Lady Churchill was to remark after her husband's state funeral: it "wasn't a funeral—it was a Triumph."[23]

NOTES

1. "How V.C.s are Won: Private Hook at Rorke's Drift" by J.H.K.-A., in *V.C.*, 5 November 1903.
2. *Royal Magazine*, p. 344.
3. "Rorke's Drift: Recalled by a Gallant Defender of the Hospital", in *The People*, late January 1898 (cutting in Furness Collection).
4. Letter of introduction, dated 26 May 1904, from an officer "Formerly of the Royal Scots" (in Furness Collection).
   From 1890 until his retirement, the Museum received seventeen medical certificates in Hook's case, including the ones quoted above. None survive, and the only traces of them are in the "Registers of In-Letters" (B.M. Archives).
5. The reference at p. 57 of *R.D. & B.M.* to a gratuity being a "pension" is wrong. The original "old-age pension", provided by the state, was not introduced until 1908, and it was not available to people under seventy.
6. A slip of paper in the Furness Collection reads: "The M.P. for Aberdeen North (Capt. Pirie) has a question on the paper for today, about the insufficiency of the £10 annual payment." This slip was no doubt sent to Hook in the Museum.
7. "Station Paymaster, Brecon" to Hook, 18/10/1904 (in Furness Collection).
8. Standing Committee Minutes, 10 December 1904, p. 2021. Hook's letter has not survived.
9. "Treasury Letters," Vol. XI, 1903-06, CE29/11 (in B.M. Archives).
10. "Station Paymaster, Brecon" to Hook, 5/1/1905 (in Furness Collection). Under the heading "Bravery Rewarded" the news was reported in *The Monmouthshire Beacon* for 20 January 1905.
    By the system of payment in arrears, Hook received no benefit from the award.
11. "Sergeant Hook, V.C.: Local Hero's Ill-Fortune", in the *Gloucester Journal* for 7 January 1905 (copying an item in *The Morning Post*). "Colonial Loyalist" says that: "though employed for nearly a quarter of a century at the Museum he takes no allowance or pension, as he was not attached to the general staff." In fact, Hook *was* part of the "Establishment of the Museum" but had not reached a pensionable grade.
12. The first title was published by Alfred Boot of London, E.C.; and the second by George Newnes Ltd. Hook's entries are at pp. 31 and 224, respectively. These appear to be Toomey's only books; but he was the "compiler of the V.C. in Whitaker's Almanac, 1889."
    The details of Toomey's Army career are taken from his Record of Service (WO97/4037, Public Record Office).
13. Toomey to Mrs. Hook, 14 March 1905 (in Furness Collection).
14. In Furness Collection, which also contains an undated sheet of British Museum notepaper containing a list of fourteen names, headed by the Duke of Beaufort and including Lords Chelmsford and Wolseley. This list is almost certainly connected in some way with the raising of money for Hook, although the names are all of public figures rather than members of the Museum staff.
    The "Mr. Liddell" of Barwick's letter is probably Charles John Liddell, an Assistant in Printed Books between 1872-88.
15. *The Citizen* [Gloucester], 13 March 1905.
16. Invoice from W. Dale, Fruiterer and Greengrocer, of King's Rd., Chelsea, dated 27 January 1905 (in Furness Collection). The cost was £12..10..0.
17. *The Citizen*, 13 March 1905.
18. *Ibid.*; Death certificate, signed by Dr. Clark and giving the cause of death as "Pulmonary consumption 6 months."
19. *Gloucester Journal*, 18 March 1905.
20. In Furness Collection.

21. W.R. Bradbrook to Mrs. Hook, 14 March 1905; Curll to Mrs. Hook, 26 March 1905; Graham to Mrs. Hook, 13 March 1905; D. Hastings Irwin to Mrs. Hook, 15 March 1905 (in Furness Collection).
22. *Gloucester Journal*, 18 March 1905.
23. This description of the funeral is based on the article which appeared in the *Gloucester Journal* on the following Saturday (25 March). The *Cheltenham Chronicle and Gloucestershire Graphic*, for the same date, has a slightly different version of the article. The service at Churcham is described in more detail in the *Parish Magazine* for April 1905, p. 2.

    The undertaker's bill for £13..4..0 is in the Furness Collection.

Epilogue

Chapter 1

MEMORIALS

Ada Hook was forty-two when her husband died. She had no regular source of income to support herself and her daughters; and even when the Old Age Pension was introduced in 1908, she was far too young to qualify. She was a Londoner by birth and experience, while Gloucester held only the saddest of memories: the temptation must have been great to go straight back to Islington. Yet apart from the expense of moving back, it seems likely that the Taylors were in no better position to help her than her husband's family. Perhaps to save rent, or perhaps because Ada Hook preferred city life to the suburbs, Osborn Villas was given up and the little family moved to High Street and later to Westgate Street. In these two thoroughfares—in the centre of the city, within sight of the cathedral—she was to spend the rest of her life.[1]

At Brecon and Churcham, meanwhile, plans were being made to keep green her husband's memory. The South Wales Borderers had inherited the regimental number and battle honours of "the Noble 24th", and also the barracks at Brecon as a depot. At the other end of this market town, in the grey-stone cathedral, the regimental chapel has been established. The two rows of flags hanging from the walls, and the stained glass in the windows, make a bright display. In the corner facing the altar—actually in the south transept, rather than in the chapel—is a collection of large and ornate brass plates to officers and men of the 24th. These plates pre-date the creation of the chapel and all of them are dulled by age, though the duskiness of the corner is kind to their drabness. Perhaps few people now look closely at these old brasses: indeed, electric light is often needed to make the inscriptions easily readable. Yet in this retired corner, on the west wall, the visitor discovers a fascinating juxtaposition: Hook surrounded by general officers!

Major-General	Major-General Sir	
Henry J. Degacher	Wilsone Black	
(1835-1902)	(1837-1909)	Major-General Sir
		William Penn Symons
Henry Hook, V.C.	Lieut.-General	(1843-1899)
(1850-1905)	Richard T. Glyn	
	(1831-1900)	

Round the corner, at right angles to the chapel, is the plate to Major Bromhead, V.C., recording his death in 1891, at the age of forty-six.

Hook's plate—28" deep x 21" wide, with an oak-leaf border—has the following inscription topped by a crown and the regimental badge:

To the Glory of God

AND IN MEMORY OF

SERGT. H. HOOK, V.C.

24th REGT.

WHO DIED 12th MARCH 1905

THIS BRASS IS ERECTED BY OFFICERS

N.C.O.s AND MEN OF HIS REGIMENT

IN MEMORY OF HIS DISTINGUISHED

GALLANTRY AT THE DEFENCE OF

RORKE'S DRIFT   22nd JANRY. 1879

FOR WHICH HE WAS AWARDED THE

VICTORIA CROSS

A special service is held each year on the Sunday nearest to the 22nd of January, and the cathedral is reported to be "packed" on these occasions.[2]

Immediately after Hook's funeral, the Vicar of Churcham had written to the Gloucester newspapers that:

It would appear in accordance with the wishes of many that a permanent memorial of Sergt. Hook, V.C., should be placed in the Parish Church of Churcham, in which he was baptised. His widow and the other members of the family desire it, and I shall be very glad to receive and acknowledge subscriptions for this purpose. The exact form of the memorial must depend on the amount sent, but a grave-stone, a brass, a coloured window, and an organ have all been suggested and I shall be glad to learn the wishes of subscribers.[3]

The subscription raised £20..8..7 from Volunteer companies and private individuals. It was decided to place at the head of the grave a "white marble cross and die standing six feet high on a Forest stone base and kerb. The ornamentation . . . [to consist] of a large wreath of laurels suspended from a ring by ribbons in the centre of the cross, enclosing a reproduction, measuring some seven inches across, of [the Victoria Cross]." The lengthy inscription at the base of the cross was to conclude with a quotation from I. Maccabees, ix., 10, which had been used as the text for a sermon delivered in the parish church on the day after Hook's funeral:

If our time is come, let us die manfully for our brethren's sake, and not have a cause of reproach against our glory.

So eighteen months after the funeral, Churcham witnessed another military ceremony on a Saturday afternoon. Six Volunteer companies and three bands marched out from Gloucester Barracks, followed by Ada Hook and her daughters in a closed carriage. After a service at the grave-side, and a speech by the vicar, the memorial was unveiled by Colonel Curll. There were more speeches, a "dedicatory prayer", the sounding of the "Last Post", and finally the playing of the National Anthem by "the massed bands."[4]

On a more mundane level, word had got round that Hook's widow had been left badly off. Early in 1907, a fund was raised and the pounds and guineas which came in no doubt helped to keep her from actual destitution.[5] Yet this sort of private charity was not enough to support and educate her daughters, so she turned to the Royal Soldiers' Daughters' Home.

NOTES

1.   Mrs. Hook was living at 72, High Street in November 1908; at 193, High Street in May 1913; at 103, Westgate Street in November 1914; at 140, Westgate Street in August 1924; and at 178, Westgate Street at the time of her death in 1929. (Letters in the Furness Collection.)

2.   *Annual Report of the Friends of Brecon Cathedral for 1998*, p. 7.
        Hook's brass was certainly in place by September 1906, as it is mentioned in the *Gloucester Journal* for the 29th of that month.

3.   *Gloucester Journal*, 25 March 1905.

4.   *Ibid.*, 29 September 1906; and *Gloucester Chronicle*, same date.
        The phrase "Cpl. 2nd SWB" which appears in the inscription is both wrong and anachronistic. Hook never held non-commissioned rank in the Regular Army; and never served in the South Wales Borderers, which was not created until 1881.

5.   The Duke of Beaufort sent £1. (Letter in Furness Collection.)

Chapter 2

THE ROYAL SOLDIERS' DAUGHTERS' HOME

1.

The Crimean War is said to have marked the point at which "the private soldier became for the first time in his career an object of respect rather than of resentment."[1] It may also have marked the first time that true concern was aroused over the plight of his wife and family, while he was away on active service. Oddly enough, it was "A Naval Officer" who wrote to *The Times*, in February 1855, calling attention to "the destitution" of soldiers' families. The Editor—though "chary . . . of giving way to sentimental expression"—commended the "good feeling of the writer."[2]

It was an age of *laissez-faire*. In spite of the country's incomparable wealth, governments were extremely reluctant to spend money on welfare: this was the duty of conscientious citizens. In this case, the government's reliance on private charity was more than justified by a patriotic spirit brought on by the War. Within two day of *The Times* letter, a committee for the relief of destitution was formed at the National Club, followed quickly by two other committees at service clubs. At a public meeting on the 8th of March, it was proposed to set up a "Soldiers' Infant Home." Two months later, the Home had come into being and held its first meeting; and on the 4th of July, "the first infant girls were admitted into the 'home', the daughters of a soldier in the 10th Hussars, who was at that time in the Crimea."[3]

The Home's notepaper depicts Britannia guiding three girls towards an imposing building—girls only, as it had been decided that the purpose of the institution should be "For the Maintenance, Clothing and Education of the Daughters of Soldiers." ("Motherless *sons* of soldiers" could be sent to "Government Asylums" at Chelsea or Dublin; but it was to be ten years before the daughters of *officers* were provided with an equivalent of the Soldiers' Infant Home.[4])

The Home would be "open to the daughters of all soldiers in Her Majesty's and of the Hon. East India Company's armies; but that preference should be given—1. To entire orphans. 2. To motherless girls. 3. To girls whose mother may be living, but whose father is ordered on active service." As the number of girls who could be admitted depended on the amount of money which individuals or organisations donated or subscribed, the donors and subscribers were given the power to "elect" girls for admission. In the early days, for instance, an annual subscription of one guinea conferred "four votes at each election", while a donation of five guineas secured two votes for life, at each election. At an election held on the anniversary of the Battle of Inkerman (5 November 1855), ten girls were elected, the top candidate being given 3,986 votes and the tenth gaining 2,845. Any candidate below the last figure would have failed, though they could try again. The fathers of these ten successful candidates all came from different regiments of foot.[5]

Once elected:

> To train up these children in habits of industry is the earnest desire of the Committee of Management. Their education is not confined to school duties. Housework, cooking, washing and ironing, the charge of a dairy, and the care of young children occupy some hours of every day, and will contribute, as the Committee hope, under the Divine blessing, to fit these young girls to become industrious, intelligent, and honest women.
>
> It is also the intention of the Managers of the Soldiers' Infant Home to obtain situations for all the soldiers' daughters elected into the "Home" when they have arrived at a proper age, to inquire carefully into the peculiar abilities of each girl, and, if possible, to provide her with employment for which she has been previously trained. It is also part of the plan of the Institution afterwards to exercise a paternal supervision over those who have thus entered upon the active duties of life, and to afford a temporary home for those who, during the earlier years of their practical life may, from no moral fault, be unable to obtain a permanent home.[6]

The Committee of Management had taken "a large commodious house, in a most healthy position, on Hampstead-hill"; and here the girls were boarded and "trained up" for the first three years. (After two years, the institution's name was changed to "The Soldiers' Daughters' Home".) Rosslyn House stood behind what is now called Rosslyn Hill—the long slope which becomes Hampstead High Street and leads up to the Underground Station.[7] The average number of girls rose from thirty in the autumn of 1855 to over a hundred, so that larger and more permanent accommodation was soon needed.

The Home had received enough financial support to buy a freehold estate of about three-and-a-quarter acres, including "part of the house that had been built by Sir Harry Vane." Using Vane House as a nucleus, a "school house for 200 girls was built, together with a house for the schoolmistress and the pupil teachers."[8]

This estate was further up the Hill and fronting onto it. A plaque on an old piece of wall facing Rosslyn Hill marks the site of Vane House and of three successive buildings of the Soldiers' Daughters' Home (including the present one, which lies well back from the old wall). In June 1858, "this new asylum" was opened by the Prince Consort, who was "welcomed by a brilliant assemblage . . . planted a tree . . . and then inspected the buildings." The girls were nowhere to be seen—perhaps they would have been out place in "a brilliant assemblage"?—and there is regrettably no truth in the old Hampstead yarn that the Prince led them all up the Hill, from Rosslyn House to their new home in Vane House.[9]

Every girl had an admission number, which was entered in manuscript volumes entitled "Register of Girls." In the volumes which survive, the careers can be charted of those who entered from 1876 onwards: by the beginning of that year, there had been 661 admissions.[10] During the four years of Hook's service in the Army (1877-80), there were a total of 119 new admissions and no less than seventy-two of these girls went into domestic service at the end of their training. A further eight were appointed "pupil teachers" in the Home, and one girl went to a similar post in a church school: these appointments, of course, were signs of superior intelligence. Six died at the Home (only two causes were given: "consumption" and "congestion of the lungs") and another had to go into hospital. One failed to return from holiday; and, in two sad cases, the girls were sent back to their mothers "on account of mental deficiency." The remaining twenty-eight were "withdrawn" by their parents or guardians without recorded reasons. Those reasons were probably simple enough: the mother had remarried or was in easier circumstances; the girl was unhappy in institutional life; or the mother was unhappy without her daughter.

A different pattern emerges from four Edwardian years, 1905-07 and 1909, the period during which Hook died and his daughters were admitted. In those years, out of 121 new admissions, less than a third (37) went into domestic service. Nearly half (59) were withdrawn for various reasons or failed to return from holiday; and six more were found to be "too unintelligent for service", or were "not recommended for service." There was one pupil teacher but this system was evidently abandoned in about 1909. Thirteen were either expelled for misconduct or sent back "by order of the

Committee", which probably amounted to the same thing. (These seem to have been rare occurrences during the Victorian years.) Two died in hospital and one was sent to the workhouse. Two poor girls—apparently from the same family—were "refused re-admittance after holidays on account of the state of [their heads]": the midsummer holidays were not always beneficial. These differing patterns as between the Victorian and Edwardian years—more withdrawals, better health, worse behaviour—were no doubt due to changing social conditions.[11] In particular, while there was still a tremendous demand for domestic service—and most indoor servants were women—the circumstances of soldiers' families would, in many cases, have improved since mid-Victorian days.

Discipline at the Home was undoubtedly firm, so much so that a visiting inspector reported, in 1880, that "the discipline was so good as to lead him to suspect 'a deficiency of vivacity in the children.' " As late as 1916, the Army Inspector of Education "felt that a slight relaxation of discipline might prove advantageous to both pupils and teachers."[12] To balance this strictness, there was a scheme of "Rewards." Sums of money (usually £1 or £2) were given to girls whose employers reported well on their work, once they had left the Home. The outstanding "Reward-winner" seems to have been Florence Maud Stephens, who was at the Home between 1889 and 1897. She was given three Rewards (the usual limit) and then a "Special Reward" of £5. In response, she wrote a letter which is pasted into the Register and which gives a rare glimpse of one of the girls:

12th March 1920   "Leverton"
                                                        Argyle Rd
                                                  [London] N.12

Dear Sirs,
    The Cheque received this morning, & I feel it just for me to write & let you know how grateful I am for the kindness I have had bestowed on me. The reward I feel is the result of the care of my upbringing, & though may be an exception, in receiving the long service reward, there are I know many who appreciate what labour it must have involved, to bring so many of us up to the Standard, both Spiritually and physically, & much is due to those responsible, may many more girls
                                    follow the example, of
                                          Yours gratefully
                                                  F.M. Stephens

Victoria Catherine Hook (No. 1531) joined the Home on the 15th of January 1907, when she was nearly eight. She was one of two "Scholars" admitted that year, the term "Scholar" meaning a girl whose entire cost of maintenance was paid in advance by a person or fund. Her maintenance during her career at the Home was paid out of King Edward's "privy purse", though how she came to be chosen for this distinction is now unclear.[13] (Her father's V.C. and fame were presumably factors.)

Over 180 girls were then at the Home. It was on the same site but in buildings which date largely from the turn of the century. The brochure sent out to candidates for admission shows a confident, Edwardian "Front View" (facing the Hill); spacious, gas-lit rooms for the "Dining Hall", "Infirmary" and "Playroom"; and a large garden called "The Terrace." Behind the L-shaped "Main Building", the mid-Victorian schoolhouse remained (with extensions) and the two buildings were linked by a leafy cloister, dating from 1860. On the lawn in front of this cloister, a class could be taught in fine weather. The War Office had donated "some 16-pounder and 9-pounder guns for ornamental purposes to distinguish the military character of the Royal Home."[14]

The official *Brief History* mentions that "the whole running of the Home's affairs [until 1913] was in the hands of men." It is nevertheless clear from the *Annual Report* for 1906-07 that the *day-to-day* conduct of the Home was in the hands of women: Miss Anderson was the Superintendent; Miss Forrest, the Matron; and Miss Hassett, the Mistress.[15] The other teachers were also no doubt single women. Miss Hassett presided over both religious and secular subjects, as well as over "Physical Drill and Exercises." "Religious Subjects" were very important and the girls were examined annually by the Diocesan Inspector. They were examined separately in Arithmetic, Geography, History, Spelling, Composition and Recitation. In the examination held in May 1907, it seems that both mental and written arithmetic troubled most of the girls, but they did much better in other subjects. In the top class (Standard vi), the examiner found that the "Geography of Europe was well known, but the girls had not quite enough grasp of the significance of the early Hanoverian period as regards the expansion of the Empire in Canada and India."[16]

The girls were given three meals a day, with a supper added once they were eleven. They could have as much bread as they wanted and there was plenty of milk and some cocoa; but they could only drink tea on Sundays and there was no coffee at all. Butter or dripping was usually supplied, but not if there was treacle or jam with the bread. Midday dinner usually consisted of stew or "cooked meat", with "greens" and potatoes; but on Tuesdays and Thursdays there was no pudding. (The puddings were filling: "Suet Pudding and Treacle", "Sultana Pudding", and so on.) This diet no doubt "built up" the girls and was almost certainly more balanced and nutritious than they would have had at their own homes.[17]

They needed to be well nourished, as "the entire cleaning of the Home and School was done by the girls, who also worked in the laundry, bakery and kitchen."[18] This was to prepare them for their future situations as parlour maids, between maids, kitchen and scullery maids, housemaids and (in a few cases) nursemaids and waiting maids. As a relief from education and training, they were sometimes taken out for visits to such attractions as Madame Tussaud's and the Tower of London; or to sports days, drill displays and concerts. They also visited the Guards' Girls' Home and the Sailors' Orphan Girls' School and Home.[19]

Normally, candidates were not admitted under the age of six. As soon as her youngest daughter reached this age, Mrs. Hook wrote to the War Office to ask that she should be allowed to join her sister at the Home. Letitia Jean Hook (No. 1607) joined on the 27th of July 1909, one of twenty-eight admissions that year.[20] Like most entrants, of all years, she was "on the Foundation"—maintained from the General Funds of the Home. Conditions remained much the same, even after the outbreak of war in 1914. One parent withdrew her daughter in June 1915 "on account of the state of the country"; and, as the demand for factory workers increased, parents of older girls withdrew their daughters "to earn."[21] The outside visits took on a more patriotic air—for instance, a "Lantern Lecture on our Navy" and "an Entertainment in aid of the British Red Cross Society"—and there was the added excitement of Zeppelin raids on London. In March 1916, shortly before it was time for Victoria Hook to leave, Queen Mary visited the Home: "Her Majesty saw the girls in the dining hall, where they filed past."[22]

Rule IX provided that, when a girl reached the age of sixteen, "the Committee shall endeavour to procure a suitable situation for her, presenting her with an outfit, which shall always include a Bible and a Prayer-book." The Register shows that the Committee was not always successful in this endeavour: "[Returned] to her brother . . . as no place can be found for her"; or returned to her mother, "not having qualified for service in a Lady's house." Soon after the War, someone in authority summed-up the loss and gain:

The total number of Girls that have entered the Home since it was established in 1855 is 1714

Situations have been found for 783 Girls.[23]

The Committee had a very clear idea of what should be expected from an employer who offered "a suitable situation." Minimum wages and diet were laid down, and "Opportunities for self-improvement were to be given, the Sabbath was to be duly observed, and on no account was the girl to be allowed to sleep alone in a basement."[24]

Whether or not these admirable provisions survived a World War, Victoria Hook was found a "situation" which suited her well. She was "between maid" at 8, Wadham Gardens, a large, detached house in a secluded road near Primrose Hill. She had only to move about a mile from the Home. Fewer "Rewards" had been given since the turn of the century and she was the only girl admitted in 1907 who earned one: she was awarded £2 in July 1918.[25] Five years earlier, she had had a substantial "windfall." On the death of Mrs. Catherine Valentine, it was found that she had willed "to my god daughter [Victoria] Catherine Hook . . . the sum of One Hundred Pounds Sterling" (which would have been worth about £5,000 at present-day values).[26] Although this Will had been made in 1907, the younger sister, born in 1902, is ignored. Letitita Hook stayed on at the Home until the 8th of October 1919 and then became an "under-nurse" at "Eversleigh", a private house at Minehead.[27]

A last word must be said about the institution which served these sisters—and many other soldiers' daughters—so well. In 1944, its name was changed from "Home" to "School"; and it has since become "The Royal School, Hampstead." As late as 1965, all the fathers of the girls were soldiers or ex-soldiers, but this is by no means now the case.[28]

3.

Ada Hook's mother had died at the Islington Infirmary in February 1903. The family house in Winchester Street was still maintained, and her father stayed on there until shortly before his death in November 1905.[29]

Meanwhile, Hook's mother (Mrs. Eleanor Attwood) was still flourishing. By 1891, the Attwoods had moved to Gloucester, where they ran an "Eatinghouse" at 71, Westgate Street and lived over the premises. Eli Attwood died there in 1907; and his widow then lived with her youngest daughter, Emily, and later with her grand-daughter, Gertrude.[30] She died at home, of "Chronic Bronchitis", in the autumn of 1921. Her youngest son, Henry D. Hook, who was living at Monmouth, gave his mother's age as eighty-eight, but she was almost

The marriage of Vara Wood to Alfred Denis McCarthy, in the Nechells district of Birmingham, on 7 July 1918. The bridegroom is in naval uniform and the other sailor is probably "the best man" and also from H.M.S. Dido. Henrietta Wood is behind the bride; the bride's brother, Clement John Wood, is on the far right; his wife, Elsie (née Davis), is in front of him; his aunt, Julia Ann Matthews, is on his right; Florence Henrietta Wood is next to Elsie Wood. The boy on the left is believed to be Charles William Matthews, the eldest son of Julia Ann. (Courtesy, Mrs. June W. Dutton.)

Mrs. Louisa Elizabeth Hook, photographed on 28 September 1940, probably at Abergavenny. (Courtesy, Mr. Cecil Berrington.)

The grave of David Meyrick (Comfort Hook's second husband)
in Newent municipal cemetery.
(Photograph by Mr. Norman R. Hook, 2000.)

Julia Ann Matthews photographed at Kilcot, probably in "The Bungalow" and after the Second World War. The lady standing behind her is an old friend. (Courtesy, Mrs. June W. Dutton.)

certainly ninety.[31]

Ada Hook survived her mother-in-law by less than eight years. She was probably always struggling, financially; but for a few years at least she received £12 annually from Dundee, under "Mr. W.D. Valentine's Trust", and she also had the interest on the £100 which had been willed to her daughter, Victoria.[32] She would have been pleased to learn that her husband appeared in at least two cigarette card series featuring V.C.-winners, although there is nothing to show that she benefited in any material way. A few weeks after the outbreak of war in 1914, Player's issued a series of "small cards" under the title "Victoria Cross"; and "Private A.H. Hook at Rorke's Drift, 1879", is No. 18 out of twenty-five. (As 522 Crosses had been awarded by then, Hook's selection for this very limited series gives some idea of how his reputation stood in 1914.) He also has a card (No. 25) in a "famous group of sets" published by Taddy & Co., illustrating 125 winners from the inception of the medal until the end of the Great War. Both of Hook's cards depict the defence of the hospital, which he had come to personify.[33]

As far back as 1906, Colonel Curll, on behalf of the South Wales Borderers, had expressed an interest in her husband's V.C. and South Africa medal. She had naturally preferred to keep them for as long as possible; but in 1924, when she was evidently in need of money, she wrote to the regiment and was offered £50 for the Cross. This was accepted and Mrs. Hook also sent the campaign medal as part of the purchase. Both medals are now in the Regimental Museum.[34]

By 1925, both of Ada Hook's daughters had married. Letitia, who married first, used to tell how the registrar—hearing that her father was a V.C.-winner—had had a red carpet put out for the ceremony.[35] She lived in London for many years, where her husband, J.J.R. Bunting, was a civil servant. Her sister, Victoria, returned to Gloucester and after her marriage to Percival Smith, a shopkeeper, she lived in Westgate Street, near their mother.

The two brothers-in-law became concerned about Mrs. Hook who, despite the sale of the medals, was having "some rough luck." When she was apparently faced with being "turned out of her rooms", the Buntings suggested that they should put her up at their house in Brixton, but it was no doubt too late for her to return to London. Somehow or other, she survived her difficulties and stayed in Westgate Street until her last illness. (In her rooms were photographs of Lords Wolseley and Roberts, reminding her perhaps of the Victorian world which had already become deeply unfashionable.[36]) Ada Hook died of "cerebral haemorrhage", in Gloucester Royal Infirmary, on the 23rd of April 1929, aged sixty-

251

six. Her eldest daughter was "present at the death" and had her buried with her husband, at Churcham.[37]

Victoria Smith died in 1958 and Letitia Bunting followed in 1980; but their children—Mrs. Jean Furness and Mr. Henry Bunting—are still living in Gloucestershire.[38]

NOTES

1. Hibbert, Christopher, *The Destruction of Lord Raglan: A Tragedy of the Crimean War* (London: Longmans, 1961), p. 300.
2. *Brief History of The Royal Soldiers' Daughters' Home, Hampstead, 1855-1963.* [A booklet written by one of its governors.] Printed c. 1963 "for private circulation only" (cited hereafter as *Brief History*), p. 3.
3. *Ibid.*; Circular letter from the "friends and promoters" of the Home, dated 9 October 1855, asking for "generous support" in "alleviating a vast amount of heart rending misery"; Notice headed "Soldiers' Infant Home", in *The London Monthly Review Advertiser*, January 1857. (The last two items are in File H 362.73, Holborn Public Library.)
4. *Brief History*, p. 3; Osborne, Honor and Manisty, Peggy, *A History of the Royal School for Daughters of Officers of the Army, 1864-1965* (London: Hodder and Stoughton, 1966). This School was at Bath and admission was not free. There seems to have been no contact between the two institutions.
5. Notice in *The London Monthly Review Advertiser*, cited at n. 3. "This method of election remained in force until 1918", at least in its essentials. (*Brief History*, pp. 6-7.)
6. Notice in *The London Monthly Review Advertiser*, cited at n. 3.
7. Rosslyn House is described and illustrated in *Hampstead Past: A Visual History of Hampstead* by Christopher Wade (New Barnet: Historical Publications, 1989), pp. 43-45. It was demolished in 1896.
8. *Brief History*, p. 5. Wade (*op. cit.*, p. 44) has a contemporary drawing of these buildings.
9. *The Illustrated London News*, 19 & 26 June 1858.
10. There are three extant volumes: 1. From admission numbers 662-1949 (covering the years 1876 to 1925); 2. Nos. 1635-2552 (1910-51); 3. 1720-3201 (1916-70, when the system seems to have been dropped). The second vol. repeats information in the other vols. The Register of admissions Nos. 1-661 was apparently lost during the 1960s, when what is now called "the old building" (in which the Hook children lived) was demolished and replaced by the present structure. The extant vols., and the printed *Annual Reports*, are kept in the Bursar's office.
11. Seven Victorian years (between 1877-1900) and seven Edwardian years (between 1901-1907) were examined for voluntary withdrawals, expulsions and deaths. In the first period, out of 228 admissions, there were 78 withdrawals (20 of them in 1900), 4 expulsions (all in 1900) and 8 deaths. In the second period, out of 189 admissions, there were 76 withdrawals, 18 expulsions and 2 deaths.
12. *Brief History*, pp. 10-11.
13. *Annual Report, 1906-07*, p. 33.
14. *Ibid.*, p. 12. (The title "Royal" had been conferred in 1904.); copy of brochure, in red card wrappers, entitled *The Royal Soldiers' Daughters' Home, Hampstead* (n.p.,n.d.), in Furness Collection. This brochure has no text, other than captions. A framed photograph in the present building shows a class, at small desks, in front of the cloister.
15. *Brief History*, p. 14; *Annual Report, 1906-07*, pp. 12-13.
16. *Ibid.*, p. 11.
17. *Ibid.*, p. 14.

18. *Brief History*, pp. 10-11. "Outside help" was employed for the first time during the Great War.
19. *Annual Report, 1906-07*, p. 12.
20. War Office to Mrs. A.L. Hook, 19 November 1908, replying to her letter of the 14th (in Furness Collection). The date of admission is given wrongly in *R.D. & B.M..*, p. 62.
21. *Brief History*, p. 11.
22. *Annual Report, 1915-16*, pp. 9-12.
23. Note, dated 6 Jan. 1919, on the inside cover of the first vol. of the Register.
24. *Brief History*, p. 8. These conditions were drawn up in 1880.
25. Details from the first vol. of the Register. A "between maid" either helped two other servants, or combined the duties of two servants by doing, for example, the work of both a housemaid and a kitchenmaid.
26. Letters in Furness Collection; and "Trust Settlement", 8 November 1907, in National Archives of Scotland.
27. Details from the first vol. of the Register.
28. *Brief History*, p. 12; *Hampstead & Highgate Express & News*, 30 July 1965.
29. Mary Taylor died on 9 February 1903, aged 70; and William Frederick Taylor died in the Royal Free Hospital on 22 November 1905, aged 76.
30. The Gloucester City Directories show Eli Attwood as "Eatinghouse Keeper" at No. 71 between 1893 and 1908; Mrs. Attwood as Keeper in 1910; and Mrs. Ada Hook as Keeper in 1912. The Attwoods were living at No. 71 at the time of the 1891 Census.
    Attwood died of "Asthma" and "Heart Failure" on 20 November 1907.
31. Mrs. Attwood was living at 18, Windmill Passage, off Millhook St., where she died on 31 October 1921. (Details from the death certificate and from Mrs. Patricia Davis.)
32. Letters in the Furness Collection show that a £6 money order was sent twice yearly between May 1913 and July 1916 (but as W.D. Valentine had died in 1907, there may have been earlier, unrecorded payments); Letter from Mrs. Jean Furness to the present writer, 27 September 2000.
33. *The Cigarette Card Issues of John Player & Sons* (Cartophilic Society of Great Britain Ltd., 1950), p. 37. (A sample of Hook's card is in Lummis File.); "Cigarette Card Collecting and the British Militarist" by Cyril Mazansky, in *Soldiers of the Queen*, No. 55, February 1989, p. 4.
34. Curll to Mrs. Hook, 17 August [1906]; Adjutant, 1st Bn., S.W.B., to Mrs. Hook, 12 August [1924]; and letter from the regiment, 1 October 1924, enclosing a £50 cheque (all in Furness Collection).
35. She told this to the late Norman Holme.
36. Ron Bunting to Percy Smith, 27 October 1927; undated inventory of Mrs. Hook's rooms (both in Furness Collection).
37. Death certificate; bills relating to the funeral (Furness Collection).
38. Mrs. Bunting's ashes were interred in her father's grave.
    Henry and Nora Bunting, who have five children, celebrated their golden wedding anniversary in 2003. (*The Citizen*, 28 January 2003.)

Chapter 3

"CHAMPION OF BIRMINGHAM'S UNDERDOGS"

1.

Neither Raymond nor Raymond Powell Hook did any military service, though they both lived through the World Wars. Raymond was probably too old for the Great War and his son was evidently not "called up" for the Second World War. Memories of what had happened in the adjoining county kept them silent about their kinship to the V.C.-winner, but it still became known in Abergavenny.[1]

The elder Hooks left Pentre Court to run a small hotel on the road leading down from the railway station to the town centre. Close by, in a retired lane, is Hollywell Villa, where they lived for many years after giving up the hotel. Raymond Hook became a noted gardener, much in demand at the "big houses" between the Wars, and "very gentlemanly" in manner.[2] The younger Raymond spent his working life as a baker and confectioner in the town. He lived with his parents until he married Vera Berrington in 1936: she would have liked children but the marriage was childless. In this way, when Vera Hook died at Abergavenny in 1975, that branch of the Hook family came to a close.[3]

2.

Of all Hook's children, Julia Ann Matthews prospered the least. Most of her life was spent within a few miles of her birthplace and she remained, like her mother, a hard-working and plain-spoken country-woman. Her marriage also seems to have been rather unfortunate. She was kept busy during her last twenty years—from just before the Second World War—in bringing up four grandchildren: she used to say, "My job will be done when Colin's gone" (as he was the youngest of the four). In those days she was living at "The Bungalow", a small wooden building, creosoted black, on a hill slope behind the Kilcot Inn. A neighbour remembers her as short and stocky, always wearing an old-fashioned "double pinafore."[4]

One of the grandchildren was Mrs. June Dutton, and her childhood at "The Bungalow" is sharply etched on her memory:

> Gran Julia must have loved us in her own way but she was very strict with us, she kept a Mr. Tingle Tail (stick) on the mantelpiece. We never had the hugs and kisses that children should, most likely because she never had any from her very strict mother, Comfort Hook.
>
> It was nice when visitors came to stay at the bungalow, we had some good laughs with them. Gran Julia was also happier when Auntie Henrietta came, they both used to sit talking and giggling like children. I once caught them both doing the Cancan, kicking their legs up and swishing their skirts up and down, showing all their old-fashioned knee-length bloomers, which were all patched and darned. It was such a comical sight, they were red faced when they noticed me at the door.
>
> Uncle Raymond (Hook) used to visit Gran Julia but he was always very severe, we always had to go outside when he came. When Dad came to visit we always had a good time, walking over the fields picking mushrooms or hazelnuts. Auntie Henrietta sometimes came with her youngest daughter, Auntie Floss, and grand-daughter, Dorothy McPhail. Auntie Floss was always grumbling about something. She always seemed very sad, but she had a large goitre in her neck which may have been the reason.[5]

Her neighbour said of Julia Matthews: "The impression I want to leave you with is that she was a *good* woman."[6]

A final word should be said about David Meyrick, who survived his second wife, Comfort, by forty years. He became keeper of Newent municipal cemetery and lived in the lodge which now houses the cemetery records. His third wife died there in 1919 and an unmarried sister then kept house for him. His fourth wife, Dorothy, outlived him but is buried in the cemetery of which he was still custodian when they married in 1935. Very old residents of Newent can remember David and "Dolly" Meyrick driving about the town in a pony and trap, in the last days of the pre-War world.[7]

3.

In May 1922, work began on the Trinity Road stand at Villa Park, the home of Aston Villa Football Club. On its completion a year later, this "grand stand", with its advanced amenities and imposing facade, became the main entrance to the club's ground. The family tradition is that John Philip Wood was employed as a carpenter at Trinity Road, and this would have been a memorable culmination to his career. Later on, his health deteriorated badly and he died in 1932, in his seventy-second year.[8]

Three years after her husband's death, Henrietta lost her son in a strange accident. Clement John Wood was a press-tool maker at the well-known firm of Fisher & Ludlow; and this inquest report appeared in the Birmingham *Evening Despatch*:

> Dr. W.H. Davison (the Coroner) stated that on 19 December [1935] some metal sheets slid from a passing truck and struck Wood.
> Medical evidence showed that Wood was admitted to hospital suffering from laceration of the left heel and contusion of the heel bone. Death, which occurred four days after admission, was due to septicaemia following the laceration and contusion.
> The driver of the truck said he had a load of about two tons of metal sheets. He was only moving at a walking pace when the truck caught the corner of the office, in negotiating a bend, and the sheets, which were very greasy, slid off.[9]

In those years after the Great War, most of the Woods moved out from the Aston area to the suburbs of Erdington and Ward End. Henrietta's children had all married but, in that depressed era of small families, only Vara had more than one child. She married a sailor from H.M.S. "Dido", in the last summer of the War, and had two sons.[10] Florence McPhail opened an ironmongery shop in Erdington, but in 1946 she moved down to Hastings for the sea air.[11]

Edith, the eldest daughter, married in 1921 but never moved to the suburbs.[12] She had become a Socialist and spent her life in working-class areas, in and around the Nechells and Duddeston districts. By hard work and self-education, she rose steadily in the Co-operative and Labour movements, representing the Duddeston Ward on the City Council and becoming Member for Duddeston at the General Election of 1945. It was a "Labour gain from Conservative" and the first time that Birmingham had had a woman M.P. The *Sunday Mercury* claimed that Mrs. Wills was "the voice of the city's housewives and champion of Birmingham's underdogs."[13] When the Duddeston Division was abolished in time for the 1950 General Election, she returned to local government and was still doing public work, as far as her health allowed, up to her death in 1970. In another place, more will be said about her private and political life.

After the McPhails had left for Hastings, Henrietta Wood lived with the McCarthys at Capliano Road, Erdington, where she was pleasantly near to the city boundary and to Sutton Park. She died on the 11th of May 1951, survived by her sister and her two elder daughters. It is sad to say—though understandable enough—that she had never forgiven her father for what had happened, so long before, in the cottage at Mount Pleasant.[14]

NOTES

1. Interview with Mr Cecil Berrington, 9 July 2001; and letter dated 23 August 2001.
2. The hotel is now called the "Abergavenny." They had left there by 1924, when Raymond Hook's Will describes him as "Retired Licensed Victualler" of Hollywell Villa. Mrs. Phyllis Davies, who has lived in Abergavenny for most of her life, remembers him as a gardener in the 1930s. (Telephone conversation, 19 December 2000.)

   Louisa Hook died on 23 November 1948; and her husband on 24 May 1949, both at Hollywell Villa. He left about £2,000—a comfortable sum at that time.
3. Raymond Powell Hook worked at the "Welcome Café" and then at the "Trocadero Café", both in Frogmore St., in the town centre. His wife, Edna Vera Berrington, came from an Abergavenny family and was born in 1909. They were married in the parish church on 15 February 1936; living first near the two cafés and then at "The Chase", a largish house out of the centre. He died suddenly at home on 9 February 1971; and she died in hospital on 29 June 1975. (Marriage and death certificates; and information from Mr. Cecil Berrington, who was his sister's executor.)
4. Between the Wars, the Matthewses lived at the "Long House", Gorsley; but he left her for a time and then returned. W.C. Matthews is believed to have died in 1938; and both he and Julia are buried in Gorsley Cemetery but the headstones have been removed. (Information from Mrs. L.R. James; and from Mrs. June Dutton, the third of the four children of Charles W. Matthews, the eldest of Julia's two sons.)
5. Mrs. Dutton's account of her childhood, dated 26 August 2000.
6. Mrs. L.R. James to the present writer (interview, 6 July 2000).

   Mrs. Matthews died at "The Bungalow" on 14 March 1958, the only one of Hook's children to reach the age of 80. She left about £500.
7. Death certificate of Mary Ann Meyrick, who died on 2 July 1919; marriage certificate of David Meyrick and Dorothy Lodge, 7 November 1935 (Meyrick's sister, also called Mary Ann, having died in August).

   Meyrick died on 10 March 1940 and his grave is easily found on the far side of the cemetery from Comfort's unmarked grave. Dorothy Meyrick remarried but, on her death in 1976, she was interred with her first husband.
8. Inglis, Simon, *Villa Park—100 Years* (Warley: Sports Projects Ltd., 1997), pp. 112-17; information from Mr. Denis McCarthy and from Mrs. Esme Walker (the Preedy family had heard about J.P. Wood's work at Villa Park); Wood's death certificate. (He died on 9 March 1932, at Hallam Hospital, West Bromwich.)
9. *Evening Despatch*, 1 January 1936. In March 1918, Clement Wood had married Elsie Davis (1894-1987); and their daughter, Mrs. Evelyn Hudson, still lives in Birmingham.

10. Her husband was Alfred Denis McCarthy (1895-1965), who came from a large family in Hastings. Their eldest son, Mr. Denis McCarthy, told the present writer that his father was a professional sailor who had been in the Navy since he was a boy. He was discharged in the early 1930s but was then recalled for service during the Second World War. Vara McCarthy was a tailoress and did trade union work. She died in Birmingham in 1967.

11. Florence married Rankin Gourlay McPhail (1899-1971), from Kirkcaldy, in 1923; and their daughter, Dorothy, married in Hastings. Although the McPhails lived just behind the sea front, off Warrior Square, the change of air perhaps came too late; and Florence died at home in 1950, six days short of her fiftieth birthday. Her grand-daughter, Mrs. Heather Warman-Johnston, from an early age became very interested in her family's history.

12. Her husband was Frank Wills (1895-1979), a long-distance train driver. They had one son, Ronald, who died in 1999.

13. *Sunday Mercury*, 19 December 1948. Nechells and Duddeston are between Aston and the city centre. The Woods had lived in Nechells for some years after leaving Aston Manor.

14. She was buried in her son's grave at Witton Cemetery. There is now (2003) no trace of the grave, though the cemetery records show that its location is near the Ridgeway Gate. She left £700.

Chapter 4

A REPUTATION RESTORED

1.

Hook was famous amongst his contemporaries, who read about Rorke's Drift in their newspapers. The World Wars, the fall of empires and the reaction against the Victorian age epitomised by Strachey's *Eminent Victorians*, all tended to obscure his fame.

His grave was not much visited and eventually became difficult even to find. When Colonel Carne, of the Glosters, was awarded the V.C. during the Korean War, interest in the county's earlier V.C.-winner was revived and "there was talk of providing something more suitable in the future", in the way of a memorial to Hook.[1] Nothing was done until 1960, when the late Oscar Such, who had attended Hook's funeral as a boy, tried to find the grave. He had "almost given up when he found the stone, badly dilapidated but with the name still legible." Mr. Such approached the South Wales Borderers, whose regimental association took up the work of restoration and, that July, he was photographed at the graveside, in what appear to have been rather overgrown surroundings.[2] The grave has since been well maintained and has many visitors, despite the church's fairly isolated position.

A renewal of interest in Rorke's Drift came a few years later, with the film "Zulu" (1963) and Donald R. Morris's *The Washing of the Spears* (1965). In National Film Theatre *Programme notes*, "Zulu" is condemned as "exploitative pulp" for its neglect of "the Africans' point of view." Exactly the same phrase would apply to the film's "exploitation" of Hook's name in portraying a lying, thieving, hard-drinking Cockney who wins the V.C. more or less by accident. This grotesque distortion of Hook's character has perversely contributed to his fame, because so many people have seen "Zulu" and remember him as one of the most prominent members of its cast. The selection of Rorke's Drift as a war game, in 1978, had a similar effect. Hook, as a V.C.-winner, is represented by a separate counter, while nearly all of those who were not decorated have no individual identity in the game.[3] In more recent years, Hook has been given a page on the Rorke's Drift web site (rorkesdriftvc.com), together with his *Royal Magazine* account.

At a local level, fresh interest in Hook's life was stirred in 1980 by news of a forthcoming biography. This never appeared; but an exhibition was held that autumn, in the Gloucester Library, and a long article, speculating on his early life, appeared in the *Journal*. In 1988, Hook's great niece asked for help in solving the mystery of Hook's first wife; and features about "Gloucestershire's best known soldier" seem to have a perennial appeal.[4] In two of the more recent articles, new "facts" have appeared which can only add to the confusion which has, at a superficial level, always surrounded his life. It has been asserted that Mark Hook, the so-called "Safari Boy", is a descendant of the V.C.-winner, but there is no reason whatever to believe this story. Then it has been claimed that Hook "lived and worked at Newport"; and that "new evidence has revealed that he was in fact a teetotal lay minister." The "new evidence" is not provided and both of these statements are almost certainly wrong.[5]

On the 21st of January 1996, Vernon Harwood's documentary, "Henry Hook, V.C.: The Hero of Rorke's Drift", was broadcast on Radio Gloucestershire. This hour-long programme, made available as a B.B.C. tape, is in many ways the "antidote" to "Zulu." The contributors speak of Hook as a modest and exemplary hero: a *Boy's Own* hero of real life, much as his contemporaries saw him. However conscientiously the evidence of Hook's life is sifted, this basic premiss is confirmed; and his biography has been written in that spirit.

NOTES

1. Undated cutting from the *Stroud Journal*, headed "Zulu War Hero", in Furness Collection.
2. *Gloucester Journal*, 2 July 1960; *The* [Gloucester] *Citizen*, 9 July 1960 (with photograph).
3. Undated *Programme notes* for "Zulu" in a series of films shown at the National Film Theatre under the general title "Images of Empire"; "The Battle of Roark's [*sic*] Drift" (Historical Alternatives, 1978).
    It has recently been reported that "James Booth, who played Hook [in "Zulu"], says that the decision to play him as the rebellious barrack room lawyer was forced upon the production team by the backers in Hollywood who required a villain." (*The Assegai*, Newsletter of the 1879 Group, December 2002.)
4. "Alfred Hook, V.C." by George Webb, in the *Gloucester Journal*, 11 October 1980; "V.C.'s Mystery 'Wife' ", in *The* [Gloucester] *Citizen*, 22 June 1988. The items

which formed the exhibition are in the Local Studies Dept. of the Gloucester Library.

Other West-country items which have appeared in the last twenty years include: "Gloucester's V.C." by John Southgate, in the *Gloucester News*, 10 December 1987; "Hook: Hero or villain?" by Ross Hayman, in the *Western Daily Press*, 23 January 1993; and a sequel to Hayman's article, entitled "The magnificent seven of the 24th Foot", which also appeared in the *Press*. This sequel discusses the well-known rumour that the Producers of "Zulu" originally intended to make Frederick Hitch, V.C., the "malingerer" but decided, instead, to use Hook's name. See also "Riddle of the VC hero: Flowers left on grave 116 years after battle" in the *Sunday Express*, 3 December 1995.

5.   *Daily Mail*, 26 November 2001; *The* [Gloucester] *Citizen*, 29 November 2001; *South Wales Argus*, 7 December 2002.

261

Appendices

A: THE HOOKS AND AGINCOURT

Two brothers, John and Phillip Hook, are supposed to have gone out from Taynton to serve Henry V in France. At Agincourt

> during the Melee the King's Armour and Shield were glistening in the sunshine. The brothers Hook realised the danger to the King's life and immediately covered his armour by tearing up some of their uniform thus sheltering him from the sun.
>
> After the Battle the King called the brothers to his presence and told them that by their prompt action they had saved his life and that he wished to reward them by making them Knights of Armour at Court. The brothers who were farmers explained that they were anxious to return to their home and so the King rewarded them instead by giving the Eldest money whilst the other was given the Crooke's Estate at Kilcot [three miles northwest of Taynton]. Nourse says that thereby hangs the saying "by Hook or by Crook." This estate still belongs to the Hooks as also does a 6-foot sword which Phillip used at Agincourt.[1]

This sword appears in another version of the legend. In this story, the King is "Supposed to be H. VIII" and the battle took place on a Sunday. (Agincourt was fought on a Friday.)

> ... it happen'd quickly thatt the King, and those that he was talking with, was hemed in by Sum that was sent out in order for Scouring—Mr. Hook, one Hundman, who lived at Tiberton, and another man of Glorshire, and a few more, got the King safe from the Enemy; when they found themselves enclosed, they was much a frighted, by reason ye King was amongst them; but Mr. Hook, a valent man, said to the King, "Here, Harry, hold the rag" [the ensign] they did whatever they could, that the King might not be known; Mr. Hook, Hundman, and the other, with their broad swoards, cutt away through the throung. The King followed them, and got safe off, leaving the rest a fighting and killing one another: for this good office these men had done, the King asked what he should give them ... Mr. Hook and the

other . . . [said] they would accept of what his Majesty would be pleased to give: his pleasure was, first, to make them gentlemen bearing a coat of arms; the sword to be kept to show their vallar, and likewise a good estate was given ym and their heirs forever, viz. Crook's estate, ancestor of the Hooks.[2]

In Monmouthshire—where Henry V is a "great national hero"—the King's life is said to have been saved by ancestors of a prominent county family:

> . . . the never-to-be-forgotten battle of Agincourt on 25 October 1415 was the occasion when ancestors of the Vaughan family, Roger Vaughan and his father-in-law David Gam, seeing the King's life in peril, placed themselves between him and the attacking foe thereby saving his life with the loss of their own. In gratitude Henry conferred the honour of knighthood on these brave men as they lay dying on the battlefield.[3]

Perhaps none of these tales of valour and chivalry should be taken literally; but Crookes Park, near Kilcot, still survives and the estate is undoubtedly of ancient origin. The real question is whether there is any connection between the Hookes of Crookes Park and the line of Hooks which includes the V.C.-winner. None has so far been found, so a link between Agincourt and Rorke's Drift remains only a stirring thought.[4]

NOTES

1. The quotation is taken from a typescript, headed "The Hook Family", prepared by the late John J.R. Bunting, Hook's son-in-law, now in the File entitled "Private Henry Hook, V.C." at the Regimental Museum, Brecon. Mr. Bunting became interested in the family's history and his correspondence with the Museum Curator is in the File.

    The "Nourse" referred to is no doubt Timothy Nourse (d. 1699), who was born and died at Newent and who would have been familiar with local history. He was an Oxford graduate and his entry in the *Dictionary of National Biography* describes him as a "miscellaneous writer."

    The modern biographer of Henry V gives a reconstruction of Agincourt which has no such incident as the covering-up of the king's armour. To the contrary, Henry wore that day "a splendid basinet upon which had been fixed a rich golden crown." He "was not afraid to draw attention to himself through the use of banners and the wearing of a crown. It is likely indeed that Henry . . . deliberately acted in this way to draw the enemy towards him, aware that the vital work of his archers in the wings would be facilitated if this could be done."—*Henry V* by Christopher Allmand (London: Methuen, 1992), pp. 88-89.

2. Fosbrooke, Thomas Dudley, *Abstracts of Records and Manuscripts respecting the County of Gloucester . . .* (2 vols., Gloucester: printed by Jos. Harris, 1807), Vol. 2, p. 211. Fosbrooke gives his source as "MSS. Nourse."

In the entry "Hooke of Crookes Park" (Burke's *The Landed Gentry*, 1952 ed., p. 1277), Thomas Hooke is identified as the man who is said to have been given "the estate of Crookes Park" for "saving the life of Henry V at Agincourt"; and the lineage is dated from this event. His "great sword" is still with the family and is illustrated in *The Citizen* [Gloucester], 12 July 1983.

3. Vaughan, Mary, *Courtfield and the Vaughans: An English Catholic Inheritance* (London: Quiller Press, 1989), p. 5.
4. Patricia M. Davis to the present writer, 5 September 1997; and Commander Michael Hooke to the present writer, 17 November 1998.

B: THE RIDDLE OF HOOK'S DATE OF BIRTH

Hook first seems to have given his date of birth, for official purposes, when he enrolled in the Militia on 7 May 1869. He gave his age as 18 years and 9 months: if we accept this, he was born in February 1850.[1] When he enlisted in the Army on 13 March 1877, he gave his age as 23 years and 8 months: if we accept *that*, he was born in August 1853.[2] His "Final Description" at discharge on 25 June 1880 states: "Age 27 years"; and his entry for the Census of April 1881 reads: "Age last birthday 27." When called on to give his date of birth to the British Museum authorities, he wrote in his own hand: "July 29 1853"; and the age given to the Census enumerator in 1901 was 47.[3]

It seems from these last five statements that Hook had established his year of birth as 1853; but a draft letter, dated 14 July 1892, gives his age as 38.[4] If we accept this, he was born in 1854; and this date is supported by a marriage certificate, which gives his age as 43 on 10 April 1897. He also gave his age to several reporters: 29 July 1851 (to a Gloucester newspaper in 1895); "only 43 now" (to a newspaper in late 1897); "forty-five years of age" (*The Sketch*, 20 April 1897).[5]

After his death, on 12 March 1905, the confusion continued. The death certificate gives his age as 53, as did the inscription on his coffin plate; but this would put his date of birth in 1852. When he was buried at Churcham, six days later, the entry in the Parish Record of Burials also recorded his age as 53; but underneath these figures a correction has been written: "54 See Baptismal Register 1850." When the *Parish Magazine* published Hook's obituary, it confirmed this correction, saying that he was "born in the Parish in 1850."[6]

What can be the explanation of this extraordinary muddle? It seems probable that Hook knew that he had been born in 1850, and that this was also known in his home parish. His "change of mind" apparently came when he enlisted and deducted three-and-a-half years from the age which he had given to the Militia authorities. In the autumn of 1881, when applying for appointment to the British Museum staff, he must have been in a quandary. If he had given his date of birth as 1850, and his certificate of discharge had then been called for (or if the War Office had been asked for details of his service), the inconsistency would have been exposed and he might have lost the appointment. A note on his Museum papers shows that, in fact, he gave his age as 28, which coincides with his having been discharged from the Army at 27.[7] Assuming that he deliberately changed his age when enlisting, this no doubt had something to do with the processes of enlistment, and is discussed in Chapter IV. Yet this by no means explains why, after 1881, so many different dates were given for his birth; and, almost certainly, this problem is now beyond solving.

NOTES

1. "Enrolment Accounts and Training Pay Lists of the Royal Monmouth Militia" (WO 13/1534 & 13/1535, Public Record Office).
2. "Parchment Certificate of Discharge" (in Furness Collection).
3. The "Final Description" forms part of the "Parchment Certificate"; Paper dated "Oct. 13—84" in Hook's envelope in the series of "Staff Applications & Testimonials 1835-1935" (B.M. Archives).
4. Draft of letter to "Lt General Sir G.B. Harman, G.C.B.", dated at the British Museum, July 14th, 1892 (in Furness Collection).
5. Cuttings in Furness Collection.
6. Inscription recorded in *Gloucester Journal*, 25 March 1905; book of "Burials in the Parish of Churcham", which has a long entry under Hook's name, perhaps reflecting the fact that the vicar was a Volunteer chaplain: "Alfred Henry Hook, V.C. Sgt. [*sic*] 24th Regt. (Rorke's Drift)."; *Parish Magazine*, April 1905, p. 2.
7. Pencil note "28 years of age" on a letter from E.A. Bond (Principal Librarian) to his Office, dated 28 Nov. 81 (in Hook's envelope, cited at n. 3).

C: HOOK'S FIRST KNOWN INTERVIEW

HOW HE WON HIS VICTORIA CROSS.—As our Monmouth correspondent states, it is a well-known fact that it is always with great difficulty that a soldier who has very active service, and especially if he has so signally distinguished himself as the hero of this notice, can ever be cajoled into talking of an engagement. But after many futile attempts, our correspondent managed to elicit the following interesting facts from Mr. William [*sic*] Hook, V.C., late of the 2-24th Regiment. The reader is particularly requested to understand that Mr. Hook had the statement given below drawn from him in answer to numerous questions, all of which were given reluctantly, and totally without any idea of boasting. Instead of giving the answers as received, we prefer to give them in the form of a narrative; "I was in the army three years and a hundred and sixty-three days, and I only had nine months training in England before I was sent out to Zululand [*i.e.*, South Africa] on active service; but I should say that I was in the Royal Monmouth Militia for five years previously, being now not quite twenty-six years of age. After I had been "out" three months I joined the Good Templars at Pieter Maritzburgh, and kept that pledge as long as I remained in that country. As you are aware "(we saw his letters)" in all my letters home I made no allusions to any serious hardships, nor attempted to credit myself with any deeds of bravery, it being my desire not to alarm my parents. One man who was not within eighty miles of Rorke's Drift sent home a fictitious account of the battle; his letter got into the papers, and the colonel saw it; the man, who was a corporal, was tried and reduced for the offence. I was on guard at the hospital at Rorke's Drift, when the attack upon it was made, and there were nine others with me. Almost the first thing I knew was that I was fighting "over the soles of my boots in blood." The hospital was fired by the blacks. How did poor Macksfield [*sic*] of Monmouth die do you ask? Well "(and here a suspicious watery appearance came into the speaker's eyes)" I think I only know; he was a sergeant, and was a very smart young fellow when he was last at home, but when

270

he got out there the climate did not agree with him, and he was attacked by dysentery, and a kind of rheumatic fever, which made him quite mad. Poor fellow, in his delirium he tried to get at the enemy, but I tried all I could to keep him back, having one or two narrow shaves of being killed myself in the attempt; however, all I could do was useless, he got among the crowd of savages, and soon fell wounded, being killed soon after,—not burnt to death as some suppose. I was able to identify him after because I knew where he fell and he had a blue check shirt on; there wasn't much left to identify—only a small piece of his shirt as large as a lady's handkerchief, and a small part of his body, all the rest was burnt. But "(with a fiery flash of the eye)" the man who killed him was killed and fell in the fire. But I don't like talking of these things— Yes, in the smoke I did manage to carry seven out of the nine who were with me to a place of safety—the other two were killed. I got off very lucky, only getting a scar on the head, which looks now more than it was even when it was done. Many of us were over two years without knowing what it was to sleep in a bed, and often had to rabble away the mud and water from the ground before we could lie down upon it, using a stone covered with our helmets for a pillow. No, we had no waterproof sheets, or top-coats [after Rorke's Drift]— I had a mealy sack, with holes cut in it for my arms and head to go through for a top-coat, and I have seen officers with no other. A lot of our young men could not stand it, and were invalided in the first twelve months; they were too young. Yes, I got the Victoria Cross, and a day or two ago the Zulu War [*i.e.*, South Africa] medal. The cross was presented to me not much more than 600 yards from the spot where the hospital stood. I was sorely tempted to break the pledge the day I got the cross,—even the officers offered me drink, but I firmly refused; I had not even been in the habit of drinking my allowance of rum; I gave that away. I was very ill when I came home and that is why I left the army."—Mr. Hook, V.C., is now living in Monmouth, his native town [*sic*].

[From an unidentified West-country newspaper, 21 May 1881. Furness Collection.]

D: A NOTE ON THE BRITISH MUSEUM LIBRARY

Between 1973 and 1998, considerable confusion was caused by the co-existence of the British Museum and the British Library in the same building in Bloomsbury. This was the result of an Act of Parliament, which had transferred three of the Museum departments (collectively and informally known as the British Museum Library) to a newly-created body, The British Library.

While the British Library thus came into being as recently as 1973, the British Museum had been founded two hundred years earlier and its first reading room had opened in 1759. The famous Round Reading Room, with its surrounding "Iron Library", had been in use since 1857 and remained basically unchanged during Hook's lifetime. He was fortunate in serving during a long period of stability, during which whatever changes were made were as nothing compared with earlier and later upheavals. The Iron Library was reconstructed during the 1930s, leaving only a "period piece" of the old structure in the Southwest Quadrant. The Round Reading Room—which had passed into the hands of the British Library in 1973—was closed down on 25 October 1997; and the surrounding book stacks were then demolished.

Later in the autumn of 1997, the new British Library building at St. Pancras began to be used by Readers; and the process of closing the other library rooms in the Museum was completed late in the following year. Due to this separation of the national library from the national museum, the official records relating to Hook's career have also been separated. Those interested in his life will find most of the papers they need in the British Museum Archives; but there are some mentions of him in the British Library Archives at St. Pancras, together with some valuable reports on the pay and conditions of men of his grade.

Glossary

Contemporary spelling or usage	*Modern usage*
Buffalo River	Mzinyathi River
Caffre, Kafir, Kaffir	Xhosa
Cetewayo, Chetewayo	Cetshwayo
Fingo	Mfengu
Gaika	Ngqika
Galeka	Gcaleka
Helpmakaar, Helpmakair	Helpmekaar
Isandhlwana, Isandlana, Isandwhlana	Isandlwana
Kaffir Wars	Cape Frontier Wars
Kreli	Sarhili
Quintana	Centane
Sandilli	Sandile

BIBLIOGRAPHY

Manuscript Collections

British Library Archives.
British Museum Archives.
Furness Collection (private).
Gloucester Public Library, Local Studies Dept.
Gloucester Record Office.
Holborn Public Library, Local Studies Dept.
National Army Museum, Chelsea.
Newent Municipal Cemetery.
Public Record Office, Kew.
Regimental Museum, Brecon.
Regimental Museum, Monmouth.
Royal School, Hampstead (records of the Royal Soldiers' Daughters' Home).

Main Contemporary Articles relating to Hook

1881: "How he Won his Victoria Cross", 21 May (reprinted as Appendix C).

1883?: "The Victoria Cross: How, Where, and by Whom Won", *Rare Bits*.

1891: "Stories of the Victoria Cross: Told by Those who have Won it", *The Strand Magazine*, Vol. I, May (reprinted in Chapter VI).

1895: "Where our Heroes may be Seen", *The Success*, 10 August.

1897: "Rorke's Drift Heroes", *The Westminster Gazette*, 3 November.
"The Victoria Cross . . . From Rorke's Drift to the British Museum", *The* [London] *Morning Leader*, 11 November.
"A Survivor of Rorke's Drift", *Daily Graphic*, late 1897.

1898: "What Becomes of V.C. Heroes", *Answers*, 22 January.
"Rorke's Drift: Recalled by a Gallant Defender of the Hospital", *The People*, late January.
"A Hero of Rorke's Drift", *The Sketch*, 20 April.

1900: "The V.C. at the Museum", *M.A.P.*, 10 February.

1903: "How V.C.s are Won: Private Hook at Rorke's Drift", *V-C*, 5 November.

1905: "How They Held Rorke's Drift", *The Royal Magazine*, February.

Books, Pamphlets, etc.

[Acland-Troyte, J.E.], *Through the Ranks to a Commission* (London: Macmillan & Co., 1881).

Adams, Jack, *The South Wales Borderers* (London: Hamish Hamilton, 1968).

Allmand, Christopher, *Henry V* (London: Methuen, 1992).

Barnett, Correlli, *Britain and Her Army, 1509-1970* (Harmondsworth: Penguin Books, 1974).

Barrett, C.R.B. (ed.), *The 85th King's Light Infantry* (London: Spottiswoode & Co. Ltd., 1913).

Barwick, G.F., *The Reading Room of the British Museum* (London: Ernest Benn Ltd., 1929).

Beckett, Ian F.W., *The Amateur Military Tradition: 1558-1945* (Manchester: Manchester University Press, 1991).

—— —— ——, *Riflemen Form: A Study of the Rifle Volunteer Movement, 1859-1908* (Aldershot: The Ogilby Trusts, 1982).

Bellairs, William, *The Military Career* (London: W.H. Allen & Co., 1889).

Bennett, Ian H.W., *Eyewitness in Zululand* (London: Greenhill, 1989).

Bick, David, *The Mines of Newent and Ross* (Newent: The Pound House, 1987).

Binns, C.T., *The Last Zulu King: The Life and Death of Cetshwayo* (London: Longmans, 1963).

Blake, Robert, *Disraeli* (London: Eyre & Spottiswoode, 1966).

Blatchford, Robert, *My Life in the Army* ([London:] The Amalgamated Press Ltd., [1910]).

Blood, Bindon, *Four Score Years and Ten* (London: G. Bell & Sons Ltd., 1933).

Blythe, Ronald, *Akenfield: Portrait of an English Village* (London: Allen Lane, The Penguin Press, 1969).

Booth, Charles (ed.), *Life and Labour of the People in London* (London: Macmillan & Co., 1892).

Bourne, George, *Change in the Village* (London: Gerald Duckworth & Co., 1955).

Brief History of the Royal Soldiers' Daughters' Home, Hampstead, 1855-1963 (privately printed, c. 1963).

Brookes, Edgar H. and Webb, Colin de B., *A History of Natal* (Pietermaritzburg: University of Natal Press, 1965).

Burnett, John (ed.), *Useful Toil: Autobiographies of Working People from the 1820s to the 1920s* (London: Routledge, 1994).

Butler, William, *An Autobiography* (London: Constable & Co., 1911).

Caird, James, *English Agriculture in 1850-51* (London: Longman, Brown, Green and Longman, 1852).

Champneys, Basil, *Memoirs and Correspondence of Coventry Patmore* (London: George Bell and Sons, 1900).

Churchill, Randolph S., *Winston S. Churchill*, Vol. II (London: Heinemann, 1967).

Churchill, Winston S., *The Boer War. . .* (London: Leo Cooper, 1989).

—— —— ——, *The Story of the Malakand Field Force* (London: Leo Cooper, 1989).

Cigarette Card Issues of John Player & Sons, The (Cartophilic Society of Great Britain Ltd., 1950).

Clarke, Sonia, *Invasion of Zululand, 1879* (Johannesburg: The Brenthurst Press, 1979).

—— —— ——, *Zululand at War, 1879* (Johannesburg: The Brenthurst Press, 1984).

Coghill, Patrick, *Whom the Gods Love. . .* (Halesowen: privately printed, 1968).

Colenso, Frances E., and Durnford, Edward, *History of the Zulu War and its Origin* (London: Chapman and Hall, 1880).

Correspondence Respecting the Affairs of South Africa (H.M.S.O.: Command Papers, 1878-79).

Coupland, Reginald, *Zulu Battle Piece: Isandhlwana* (London: Collins, 1948).

Cousins, Geoffrey, *The Defenders: A History of the British Volunteer* (London: Frederick Muller, 1968).

Crealock, John, *The Frontier War Journal of Major John Crealock, 1878*, ed. by Chris. Hummel (Cape Town: Van Riebeeck Society, 1989).

Cunningham, Hugh, *The Volunteer Force: A Social and Political History* (London: Croom Helm, 1975).

Davies, E.T., *Monmouth V.C.s* (Monmouth: The Regt. Museum, c. 1991).

Disraeli, Benjamin, *Letters to Lady Bradford and Lady Chesterfield*, ed. by the Marquis of Zetland (London: Ernest Benn Ltd., 1929).

Elrington, C.R. and Herbert, N.M. (eds.), *A History of the County of Gloucester* (Oxford University Press for the Institute of Historical Research, 1972).

Emery, Frank, *Marching Over Africa: Letters from Victorian Soldiers* (London: Hodder & Stoughton, 1986).

—— —— ——, *The Red Soldier: Letters from the Zulu War, 1879* (London: Hoddder & Stoughton, 1977).

Esdaile, Arundell, *The British Museum Library* (London: George Allen & Unwin Ltd., 1946).

Farwell, Byron, *Queen Victoria's Little Wars* (London: Allen Lane, 1973).

Follow the Drum (London: National Army Museum, 1988).

Fortescue, J.W., *A History of the British Army* (London: Macmillan & Co. Ltd., 1899-1930).

Fosbrooke, Thomas Dudley, *Abstracts of Records and Manuscripts respecting the County of Gloucester* (Gloucester, 1807).

Fraser, John, *Sixty Years in Uniform* (London: Stanley Paul & Co. Ltd., 1939).

French, Gerald, *Lord Chelmsford and the Zulu War* (London: John Lane, The Bodley Head, 1939).

Garnett, Olive, *Tea and Anarchy!: The Bloomsbury Diary of . . . 1890-1893*, ed. by Barry C. Johnson (London: Bartletts Press, 1989).

Gon, Philip, *The Road to Isandlwana: The Years of an Imperial Battalion* (Johannesburg: Ad Donker, 1979).

Goodfellow, Clement Francis, *Great Britain and South African Confederation, 1870-1881*, (Cape Town: Oxford University Press, 1966).

Gowing, T., *A Soldier's Experience or A Voice from the Ranks* (Nottingham: privately printed, 1897).

Green, William, *Where Duty Calls Me*, ed. by John and Dorothea Teague (Petts Wood: Synjon Books, 1975).

Grey, Edwin, *Cottage Life in a Hertfordshire Village* (Harpenden: Harpenden and District Local History Society, 1977).

Hamilton-Browne, G., *A Lost Legionary in South Africa* (London: T. Werner Laurie, 1912).

Hammerton, A. James, *Cruelty and Companionship: Conflict in nineteenth-century married life* (London: Routledge, 1992).

Handley, Ronald E., *The First Londons* (Dover: Littledown Publishing Co., 1986).

Harford, Henry, *Zulu War Journal*, ed. by Daphne Child (Pietermaritzburg: Shuter & Shooter, 1978).

Harries-Jenkins, Gwyn, *The Army in Victorian Society* (London: Routledge & Kegan Paul, 1977).

Harris, Benjamin, *The Recollections of Rifleman Harris*, ed. by Eileen Hathaway under the title *A Dorset Rifleman* (Swanage: Shinglepicker Publications, 1996).

Harris, P.R., *A History of the British Museum Library, 1753-1973* (London: The British Library, 1998).

Harrison, Brian, *Drink and the Victorians* (London: Faber & Faber, 1971).

Harrison, J.F.C., *Early Victorian Britain, 1832-51* (London: Fontana, 1988).

—— —— —— , *A History of the Working Men's College, 1854-1954* (London: Routledge & Kegan Paul, 1954).

Hattersley, Alan R., *Pietermaritzburg Panorama* (Pietermaritzburg: Shuter and Shooter, 1938).

Hay, George Jackson, *An Epitomized History of the Militia* (London: "United Service Gazette" Offices, 1905).

Hennell, Reginald, *The History of the King's Body Guard of the Yeomen of the Guard* (Westminster: Archibald Constable & Co. Ltd., 1904).

Hibbert, Christopher, *The Destruction of Lord Raglan: A Tragedy of the Crimean War* (London: Longmans, 1961).

—— —— ——, *King Mob: The Story of Lord George Gordon and the Riots of 1780* (London: Longman, Green & Co., 1958).

Historical Records of the 2nd Battalion, 24th Regiment . . . Embracing the Kaffir & Zulu Wars (Secunderabad: privately printed, 1882).

Historical Records of the 2nd Battalion, 24th Regiment for the Kaffir War of 1877-8 (Pietermaritzburg: privately printed, 1878).

Hobsbawm E.J., and Rude, George, *Captain Swing* (London: Lawrence and Wishart, 1969).

Holme, Norman, *The Noble 24th* (London: Savannah, 1999).

—— —— ——, *The Silver Wreath: Being the 24th Regiment at Isandhlwana and Rorke's Drift, 1879* (London: Samson Books, 1979).

Horn, Pamela, *Joseph Arch, 1826-1919* (Kineton: The Roundwood Press, 1971).

—— —— ——, *Labouring Life in the Victorian Countryside* (Stroud: Alan Sutton, 1987).

—— —— ——, *The Rise and Fall of the Victorian Servant* (Stroud: Alan Sutton, 1990).

—— —— ——, *The Victorian and Edwardian Schoolchild* (Gloucester: Alan Sutton, 1989).

—— —— ——, *The Victorian Country Child* (Kineton: The Roundwood Press, 1974).

Hughes, M. Vivian, *A London Family: 1870-1900* (London: Oxford University Press, 1946).

Hungry Forties, The . . . (London: T. Fisher Unwin, 1904).

Inglis, Simon, *Villa Park—100 Years* (Warley: Sports Projects Ltd., 1997).

Jackson, F.W.D., *Hill of the Sphinx: The Battle of Isandlwana* (London: Westerners Publications Ltd., 2002).

James, Henry, *Letters*, ed. by Leon Edel (London: Macmillan,1976).

Jefferies, Richard, *The Toilers of the Field* (London: Macdonald, 1981).

Johnson, Barry C., *Rorke's Drift and the British Museum: The Life of Henry Hook, V.C.* (London: The Johnson-Taunton Military Press, 1988).

Johnston, Alexander W.S., *A Short Memoir of James Young* (privately printed, 1860).

Jones, Henry Festing, *Samuel Butler: A Memoir* (London: Macmillan, 1920).

Kenworthy, J.C. (compiler), . . . *Lieutenant John Rouse Merriott Chard* . . . (Combe St. Nicholas, 1994).

Kingsford, P.W., *Builders and Building Workers* (London: Edward Arnold, 1973).

Kissack, Keith, *Life in the Militia . . . 1778-1810* (Monmouth: Regt. Museum, n.d.).

—— —— —— , *Victorian Monmouth* (Monmouth: The Monmouth Historical and Educational Trust, [1988]).

—— —— —— , *A Walk Around Monmouth* (Monmouth: The Monmouth Historical and Educational Trust, 1992).

Knight, Ian, *Nothing Remains but to Fight: The Defence of Rorke's Drift, 1879* (London: BCA, 1993).

Laband, John P.C. (ed.), *Lord Chelmsford's Zululand Campaign, 1878-1879* (Stroud: Alan Sutton Publishing Ltd., 1994).

—— —— —— , *The Rise and Fall of the Zulu Nation* (London: Arms and Armour Press, 1997).

—— —— —— , Thompson, P.S. and Henderson, Sheila, *The Buffalo Border, 1879* (Durban: University of Natal History Dept., 1983).

Lawrence, T.E., *The Mint* (Harmondsworth: Penguin Books, 1978).

Lehmann, Joseph H., *All Sir Garnet: A Life of Field Marshal Lord Wolseley* (London: Jonathan Cape, 1964).

—— —— —— , *Remember You Are an Englishman: A Biography of Sir Harry Smith* (London: Jonathan Cape, 1977).

Leyland, N.L. and Troughton, J.E., *Glovemaking in West Oxfordshire* (Oxford City and County Museum, 1974).

Lloyd, W.G., *John Williams, V.C.: A Biography* (Bridgend: privately printed, 1993).

Lummis, William M., *Padre George Smith of Rorke's Drift* (Norwich: Wensum Books Ltd., 1978).

Lyttelton, Neville, *Eighty Years: Soldiering, Politics, Games* (London: Hodder & Stoughton, [1927]).

Martineau, John, *The Life and Correspondence of the Right Hon. Sir Bartle Frere* (London: John Murray, 1895).

McCalmont, Hugh, *Memoirs*, ed. by C.E. Callwell (London: Hutchinson & Co., 1924).

McToy, Edward D., *A Brief History of the 13th Regiment (P.A.L.I.) in South Africa* (Devonport: A.H. Swiss, 1880).

Miller, Edward, *That Noble Cabinet: A History of the British Museum* (London: André Deutsch, 1973).

Milton, John, *The Edges of War* (Cape Town: Juta & Co. Ltd., 1983).

Mingay, G.E. (ed.) *The Victorian Countryside* (London: Routledge & Kegan Paul, 1981).

Molyneux, W.C.F., *Campaigning in South Africa and Egypt* (London: Macmillan & Co. Ltd., 1896).

Montague, W.E., *Campaigning in South Africa* (Edinburgh: William Blackwood & Sons, 1880).

Morris, Donald R., *The Washing of the Spears* (London: Jonathan Cape, 1966).

Munro, Alexander M., *Memorials of the Aldermen, Provosts, and Lord Provosts of Aberdeen 1272-1895* (Aberdeen: privately printed, 1907).

Napier, Gerald, *The Sapper VCs: The Story of Valour in the Royal Engineers and its Associated Corps* (London: The Stationery Office, 1998).

Noel, W.F.N., *Some Records of the Royal Monmouthshire Militia* (Monmouth: printed at the "Beacon" Office, 1886).

Norris-Newman, Charles L., *In Zululand with the British Throughout the War of 1879* (London: W.H. Allen, 1880).

Old, G.D., *The British Museum Rifle Association* (1980).

O'Neil, Robert, *Cardinal Herbert Vaughan* (Tunbridge Wells: Burns & Oates, 1995).

Owen, Bryn, *Welsh Militia and Volunteer Corps. 2: The Glamorgan Regiments of Militia* (Caernarfon: Palace Books, 1990).

Paget, Julian, *The Yeomen of the Guard* (Poole: Blandford Press, 1984).

Parr, Henry Hallam, *Major-General Sir Henry Hallam Parr*... ed. by C.F. Brickdale (London: T. Fisher Unwin Ltd., 1917).

—— —— ——, *A Sketch of the Kafir and Zulu Wars* (London: C. Kegan Paul & C., 1880).

Paton, George; Glennie, Farquhar; and Penn Symons, William, *Historical Records of the 24th Regiment* (London: Simpkin, Marshall, Hamilton, Kent & Co., 1892).

Pindar, John, *Autobiography of a Private Soldier* (Fife, 1877).

Platts, A. and Hainton, G.H., *Education in Gloucestershire: A Short History* (Gloucester: Gloucestershire County Council, 1954).

Price, Victor J., *Aston Remembered* (Studley: Brewin Books, 1989).

Red Book, The [a reprinting of contemporary reports in Natal newspapers. Pinetown, Natal: 2000].

Red Earth: The Royal Engineers and the Zulu War, 1879 (Gillingham: Royal Engineers Museum, [1996]).

Regulations for Field Forces in South Africa (1878).

Regulations for the Volunteer Force (London: War Office, 1881).

Repington, Charles Á Court, *Vestigia* (London: Constable & Co. Ltd., 1919).

Richards, Frank, *Old-Soldier Sahib* (London: Faber & Faber Ltd., 1965).

Robertson, William, *From Private to Field-Marshal* (London: Constable & Co. Ltd., 1921).

Rogers, H.C.B., *Troopships and their History* (London: Seeley Service Ltd., 1963).

Rudd, Charles, *The Early History of the 17th (North) Middlesex Volunteer Rifles, 1859 to 1889* (London: R. and J. Widdicombe, 1895).

Sargeaunt, B.E., *The Royal Monmouthshire Militia* (London: The Royal United Service Institution, 1910).

Sebag-Montefiore, Cecil, *A History of the Volunteer Forces from the Earliest Times to the Year 1860* (London: Archibald Constable and Co. Ltd., 1908).

Skelley, Alan Ramsay, *The Victorian Army at Home* (London: Croom Helm, 1977).

Smith-Dorrien, Horace, *Memories of Forty-Eight Years' Service* (London: John Murray, 1925).

Spiers, Edward M., *The Army and Society, 1815-1914* (London: Longman, 1980).

―― ―― ――, *The late Victorian army, 1868-1902* (Manchester: Manchester University Press, 1992).

Stevenson, Lee, *The Rorke's Drift Doctor: James Henry Reynolds, V.C.* (Brighton: Lee Stevenson Publishing, 2001).

Streatfeild, Frank N., *Kafirland: A Ten Months' Campaign* (London: Sampson Low, Marston, Searle & Rivington, 1879).

Symons, Julian, *Buller's Campaign* (London: Cresset Press, 1963).

Thompson, Flora, *A Country Calendar* (Oxford: Oxford University Press, 1979).

Thompson, Leonard, *A History of South Africa* (New Haven: Yale University Press, 1995).

Told from the Ranks, collected by E. Milton Small (London: Andrew Melrose, 1898).

Tomlinson, K.M. (ed.), *The Church of St. Mary the Virgin, Newent* (Newent: Perpetua Press, 2000).

Toomey, Thomas E., *Heroes of the Victoria Cross* (London: George Newnes Ltd., 1895).

―― ―― ――, *Victoria Cross 1854-1889 and How Won* (London: Alfred Boot, 1889).

Trollope, Anthony, *South Africa* (Gloucester: Alan Sutton Publishing Ltd., 1987).

Trustram, Myra, *Women of the regiment: Marriage and the Victorian army* (Cambridge: Cambridge University Press, 1984).

Twiss, Horace, *The Public and Private Life of Lord Chancellor Eldon* (London: John Murray, 1844).

[Vaughan, J.F.], *The Soldier in War and Peace* . . . (London: Burns & Lambert, 1855).

Vaughan, Mary, *Courtfield and the Vaughans* (London: Quiller Press, 1989).

Wade, Christopher, *Hampstead Past: A Visual History of Hampstead* (New Barnet: Historical Publications, 1989).

Watson, Graham, *Militiamen and Sappers* (Monmouth: Published at the Castle, 1996).

Watson, Margaret, *The History of Aston Ingham* (Ross-on-Wye: Chimes Publishing Inc., 1991).

Wavell, Earl, *Soldiers and Soldiering* (London: Jonathan Cape, 1953).

White, A.C.T., *The Story of Army Education, 1643-1963* (London: George Harrap & Co. Ltd., 1963).

Wilkinson-Latham, Christopher, *Uniforms & Weapons of the Zulu War* (London: B.T. Batsford, 1978).

Williams, Basil, *Record of the Cape Mounted Riflemen* (London: Sir Joseph Causton & Sons Ltd., 1909).

Wilson, Monica and Thompson, Leonard (eds.), *A History of South Africa to 1870* (London: Croom Helm, 1982).

Wolseley, Garnet J., *Cyprus 1878 . . . Journal*, ed. by Anne Cavendish (Nicosia: Cyprus Popular Bank Cultural Centre, 1991).

—— —— ——, *The Soldier's Pocket-Book for Field Service* (London: Macmillan, 1882).

—— —— ——, *South African Journal, 1879-1880*, ed. by Adrian Preston (Cape Town: A.A. Balkema, 1973).

Wood, Evelyn, *From Midshipman to Field Marshal* (London: Methuen & Co., 1906).

Worsfold, Basil, *Sir Bartle Frere* (London: Thornton Butterworth, 1923).

Wyndham, Horace, *The Queen's Service* (London: William Heinemann, 1899).

Yorke, Edmund J., *Rorke's Drift, 1879* (Stroud: Tempus, 2001).

Articles and Papers

Benson, Stephen, "Colour Sergeant Frank Bourne of Rorke's Drift", *Soldiers of the Queen*, No. 19, November 1979.

Bond, Brian, "The Effect of the Cardwell Reforms in Army Organization, 1874-1904", *Journal of the Royal United Service Institution*, Vol. CV, No. 620, November 1960.

Bravendar, John, "Farming in Gloucestershire", *Journal of the Royal Agricultural Society of England*, Vol. XI, 1850.

Bunting, Henry, "Alfred Henry Hook, 1850-1905: Gloucestershire's first V.C.", *Local History Bulletin*, No. 45, Spring 1982.

Butterfield, P.H., "Observations on the Zulu War, 1879", *Africana Notes and News*, Vol. 26, No. 1, March 1984.

Dunne, W.A., "Reminiscences of Campaigning in South Africa, 1977-81", *Army Service Corps Journal*, February 1892.

Emery, Frank, "Soldiers' Letters", *Soldiers of the Queen*, Vol. IV, No. 15.

Fox, A. Wilson, "Agricultural Wages in England and Wales during the Last Fifty Years", reprinted in *Essays in Agrarian History* (1968).

Gosse, Edmund, "Some Recollections of Lord Wolseley", *Aspects and Impressions* (1922).

Gawler, Colonel, "British Troops and Savage Warfare", *Journal of the Royal United Service Institution*, Vol. XVII, No. LXXV, 1873.

Guest, Bill, "The War, Natal and Confederation", *The Anglo-Zulu War: New Perspectives* (1981).

Hanham, H.J., "Religion and Nationality in the Mid-Victorian Army", *War and Society* (1973).

Henderson, George, "Henry Hook V.C.—Hero of Rorke's Drift", *Gloucestershire: the County Magazine*, March 1987.

Henderson, Robert, "Russian Political Emigrés and the British Museum Library", *Library History*, Vol. 9, Nos. 1 & 2, 1991.

James, Henry, "London" and "London at Midsummer", *English Hours* (1981).

——— ——— ———, "The Suburbs of London", *London Stories and Other Writings* (1989).

Jenner, Henry, "George Knottesford Fortescue: A Memory", *The Library*, January 1913.

Johnson, Barry C., "Henry Hook, V.C.", *Colonnade*, No. 13, November 1967.

283

Knight, Ian, " 'Cruel Slaughter and Bloodshed': Some Reflections on the Battle of Rorke's Drift", *Journal of the Anglo Zulu War Historical Society*, June 1998.

——— ——— ———, "The Dalton V.C.", *Soldiers of the Queen*, No. 45, June 1986.

Mazansky, Cyril, "Cigarette Card Collecting and the British Militarist", *Soldiers of the Queen*, No. 55, February 1989.

Murray, David, " 'Scum of the Earth' ", *Soldiers of the Queen*, No. 85, June 1996.

Shorland, Madge, "A brief history of the parish of Churcham, Bulley and Birdwood", *Forest of Dean Mercury*, 31 May 1968.

Staff-Sergeant, A, "How to Make the Army Popular", *Saint Paul's Magazine*, Vol. VII, January 1871.

——— ——— ———, "Why the Army is Unpopular", *Saint Paul's Magazine*, Vol. VII, December 1870.

Webb, George, "Alfred Hook V.C.", *Gloucester Journal*, 11 October 1980.

Newspapers

Citizen (Gloucester), 1905, 1960, 1983, 1988, 2001, 2003.
County Times (Brecon), 1898.
Brecon and Radnor Express, 1898.
Daily Chronicle, 1893.
Daily Mail, 2001.
Essex Times, 1902.
Evening Despatch (Birmingham), 1936.
Gloucester Chronicle, 1906.
Gloucester Journal, 1870, 1873, 1898, 1905, 1906, 1960, 1980.
Illustrated London News, 1858, 1882.
London Monthly Review Advertiser, 1857.
Monmouthshire Beacon, 1870, 1872, 1873, 1879, 1898, 1905, 1964.
Somerset County Gazette, 1898.
South Wales Argus, 2002.
Sunday Express, 1995.
Sunday Mercury (Birmingham), 1948.
Standard (London), 1898.
Times of Natal, 1879.
Volunteer Service Gazette, 1885.
Western Daily Press, 1993.

INDEX

287

290

ISBN 0-9517115-5-5 (Clothbound ed.)
ISBN 0-9517115-6-3 (Paperbound ed.)

Copyright 2004